Anthropology of Contemporary Issues

A SERIES EDITED BY

ROGER SANJEK

From Working Daughters to Working Mothers

IMMIGRANT WOMEN IN A NEW
ENGLAND INDUSTRIAL COMMUNITY

Louise Lamphere

Cornell University Press

Ithaca and London

First published 1987 by Cornell University Press.

International Standard Book Number 0-8014-1945-X (cloth)
International Standard Book Number 0-8014-9441-9 (paper)
Library of Congress Catalog Card Number 86-32952
Printed in the United States of America
Librarians: Library of Congress cataloging information
appears on the last page of the book.

The paper in this book is acid-free and meets the guidelines for
permanence and durability of the Committee on Production Guidelines
for Book Longevity of the Council on Library Resources.

For Peter and Peter Bret

Contents

Contents

Illustrations and Tables

[ix]

Photographs

Preface

Since World War II, more and more wives and mothers have been employed outside the home, a fact that represents perhaps one of the most important social transformations that has occurred in the United States during the past forty years. As historians have pointed out, however, "women have always worked" (Kessler-Harris 1980); they are not newcomers either to productive work or to paid employment. In the eighteenth and nineteenth centuries, women living on family farms produced goods for household consumption or for sale, and as the industrial revolution transformed the American economy, young women were among the first textile-mill workers. More important, women have always labored in the home doing chores that we label as housework and child care. In this era when paid employment seems so important, we often forget that housework and child care are "work" and that they are vitally important for the survival and reproduction of families as well as society. This book provides an analysis of both kinds of women's work—that which is in the home and that which is paid and outside the home. It brings together these two separate spheres (family and work) and shows how they have been interconnected in the lives of women in a New England industrial community—Central Falls, Rhode Island.

The title *From Working Daughters to Working Mothers* emphasizes the major change in women's paid labor during the past seventy years, highlighting the family connections of women employees. In 1915 most employed women were young and unmarried; they lived at home and their wages helped to support working-class families. In Central Falls they came from a variety of ethnic backgrounds (French-Canadian, Irish, English, and Polish), and they worked in textile mills. In 1977, the year of our research project, most employed women were married, and many were mothers of young children. Women still identified themselves as French-Canadian, Irish, or Polish, and there were new immigrants as well: Portuguese-speaking women from the Azores and Portugal and Spanish-speaking women from Colombia. Some worked in textile mills, but others were employed in apparel, jewelry, toy, and other light manufacturing firms. Thus in Central Falls, as in New England as a whole, the transformation of the female labor force from one of working daughters to one dominated by working mothers involves the history of immigration and the formation of ethnic communities. It entails the intersection of class, ethnicity, and gender.

To provide an understanding of the dynamics of this transformation, I have integrated contemporary data gathered from participant-observation and lengthy interviews (an "anthropological" approach) with data from state census records, newspapers, and oral histories (a "historical" approach). I have set women's work in the context of the changing political economy of Central Falls, from Samuel Slater's first textile mill in nearby Pawtucket in 1790 to the manufacturing economy of the 1970s, when small firms were housed in old textile mills. The expansion of the textile economy in the late nineteenth and early twentieth centuries was largely responsible for the recruitment of two waves of immigrant families to Central Falls. Irish, French-Canadian, English, and Scottish families arrived in the nineteenth century, whereas Polish, Syrian, and Portuguese immigrants came after 1900. Family strategies for bettering their economic situation through immigration and for adjusting to the industrial economy contrasted among ethnic groups. The sex segregation of textile jobs, with its attendant wage hierarchy, set the stage for the recruitment of working daughters into mill jobs as spinners, twisters, and winders. Yet the place of these working daughters within their own families and the domestic role of their mothers varied from ethnic group to ethnic group, depending both on the wages of family males and on the time of the ethnic group's migration. The decline of the industry during the 1920s and 1930s was largely responsible for a new set of family strategies, and labor shortages during the 1960s brought the recruitment and employment of a third wave of immigrants: the Portuguese and Colombians. In this historical period wives, not daughters, were recruited to wage employment. This in turn brought about a rearrangement of housework and child care not present in earlier periods.

This brief overview glosses over some of the important continuities and changes in women's work, which will become apparent as the story of Central Falls working women unfolds. It also only alludes to some of the important differences among ethnic groups, which, I argue, are largely a product of a group's location in a particular niche within the local economy rather than a reflection of different values. Finally, there are important variations within each ethnic group, a theme that will become important as I discuss the strategies at home and at work of contemporary immigrants, using extensive interview data and my own observations in an apparel factory.

Overall, in this book I hope to give a dynamic picture of working-class women, one that sees them not as passive victims but as active agents who forge a range of tactics and behaviors both to deal with their wage jobs and to help their families to cope with the industrial order. Three examples (the names are fictitious) illustrate the different strategies that emerge at different historical periods covered in this book. Rose Forcier, a French-Canadian daughter, went to work in 1907 at Coats and Clark after her father became ill, but she continued to help her mother with ironing at night. Stella Szymanski lost her textile-mill job during the Depression and sewed clothes at home to support her unemployed husband and two young children. Consuelo Sánchez worked a third shift in a textile mill in 1977 and then returned home to care for her five-year-old and to see her two older children off to school while her husband worked the first shift. Each woman's strategies grew out of a different relationship to the local economy and to her family, but each illustrates the active way in which women have coped with their families' needs both in the workplace and in the home. The argument presented in this book shows how these strategies emerged at each historical period and how they were connected to each other through the changing political economy of a particular community.

The contributions of a long list of individuals have made this book possible. Most important were members of the National Institute of Mental Health Project, including Carol Rodman, Ann Bookman,

Deborah Rubin, and Ewa Hauser, who conducted ethnographic research. Ricardo Anzaldua, Aida Redondo, Rebecca Matthews, Carlos Pato, Filomena Silva, and John Sousa conducted interviews with Colombian and Portuguese couples; their interviews and translated transcriptions were particularly important in providing material on working mothers and their families. Special thanks are due to those who worked on the historical data, including the tedious tabulation of the Rhode Island census data: Deborah Rubin, Sonja Michel, Christina Simmons, Kate Dunnigan, and Susan Benson. The historical perspective that I learned from housemates Susan Benson, Christina Simmons, and Kate Dunnigan, as well as from my association with Judith Smith and Mari Jo Buhle, gives this book an added dimension that I could not have provided from my anthropological training.

The Central Falls Free Public Library was generous in allowing project members to quote from the two oral-history collections in their possession: the Central Falls French-Canadian Oral History Project, with interviews conducted by Marcel Dufresne, and the Central Falls Spanish Oral History Project, with interviews conducted by Mercedes Messier. The University Library, Special Collections, at the University of Rhode Island also gave permission to use the interviews in the University of Rhode Island Oral History Project, Mill Life Series, 1970–76. Finally, Ewa Hauser provided me with copies of her oral-history interviews, conducted during her dissertation research. These materials gave me important insights into the Polish community in Central Falls.

I am also indebted to several agencies that supported this project and the writing of this book. They include the Center for the Study of Metropolitan Studies, which funded the initial project during 1977; the Ford Foundation, which awarded me a Faculty Research Fellowship on the Role of Women in Society (1975–76); Brown University, which granted me a sabbatical during 1979–80; Wellesley College Center for Research on Women, which awarded me a fellowship as part of its Faculty Development Program (1981); and the Pembroke Center for Research and Training on Women, which awarded me a Faculty Fellowship during 1984–85.

During the drafting and editing of the manuscript I was helped by Joan Scott, former director of the Pembroke Center, who graciously read the first draft of the manuscript and suggested ways to make it into a coherent book. I also thank manuscript readers Karen Sacks and Carol Stack for helpful comments and Lois Gonzales for checking my tables and helping me trim the manuscript. I am grateful to the *American Ethnologist* for giving permission to use material published in my 1986 article (Lamphere 1986a) in chapter 1. Rowman and Allanheld have given permission to incorporate data from a previously published article (Lamphere 1986b) in chapter 6; parts of chapter 6 have also appeared before in my article in Linda Cordell and Stephen Beckerman, eds., *The Versatility of Kinship*, copyright © 1980 by Academic Press, Inc. Monthly Review Press and *Feminist Studies* have permitted me to use material from my published articles (Lamphere 1979, 1985) in chapter 7, and portions of chapter 7 use information from my article in Karen Brodkin Sacks and Dorothy Remy, eds., *My Troubles Are Going to Have Trouble with Me*, copyright © 1984 by Rutgers, The State University.

I am indebted to Roger Sanjek, series editor, whose careful copy editing made the book much more readable; to Mary De Vries, whose copy editing caught my many errors; and to Marilyn Sale and Peter Agree of Cornell University Press for overseeing the publication process. Many individuals helped me to obtain pictures, including Denise Bastien at the Rhode Island Historical Society, Priscilla Brewer at the Slater Mill Historic Site, and Ellen Spilka at the Pawtucket Public Library. Scott Molloy generously gave me permission to use many of the historical photos he collected while documenting Rhode Island textile strikes and women's activism. Christine Corrigan provided some wonderful contemporary photos of Central Falls residents, as did Stephen Cabral and Margaret Randall. Bronwen Zwirner gave me photos of women working in an apparel factory, which help to illustrate what sewing in an industrial setting is really like. I also thank Margaet Randall for printing two photos for the book and Matt Schmader for drawing the figures and one of the maps.

I thank my housemates over the years, including Edward and Susan Benson, Kate Dunnigan, Barbara Melosh, Christina Simmons, and Bruce Tucker, as well as John Miller and Wallace Sillampoa, since a collective-living environment eased the burden of housework and cooking and made it possible for me to live in Central Falls during my fieldwork. Peter Evans was a constant source of support during the field research and throughout the years of writing, especially in sharing the care and raising of our son Peter Bret. I also acknowledge the assistance of the Central Falls residents we interviewed; they gave us precious time and shared their family histories and daily lives with us. Finally, my coworkers in the apparel factory were helpful in training me as a sewer and in sharing their perspective on work with me. Their help and cooperation have enriched my understanding of the lives of contemporary working mothers.

LOUISE LAMPHERE

Albuquerque, New Mexico

**From Working Daughters
to Working Mothers**

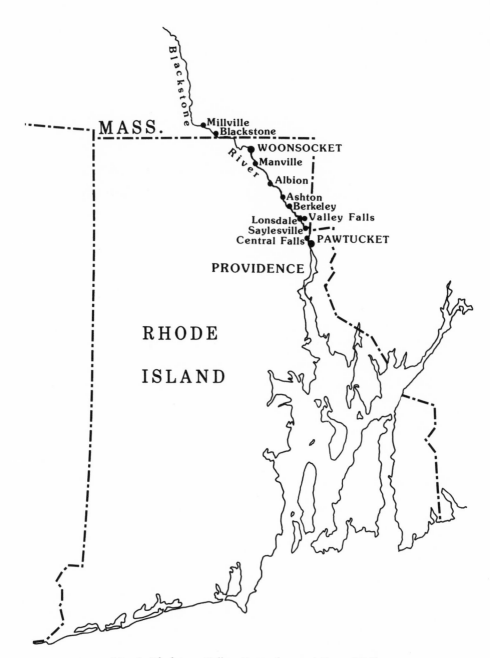

Map 1. Blackstone Valley, Pawtucket, and Central Falls

The Field Research

This book began as a study of contemporary immigrant families in which the wife worked outside the home. As the research evolved, it became a much more complex study of working-class women, which combined history and anthropology and which focused on a number of ethnic groups in an urban industrial setting. From a study of women's strategies for coping with work and family, it evolved into an analysis of the historical interconnections between class, ethnicity, and gender.

In 1975 I applied for research funds to the National Institute of Mental Health (NIMH) Center for the Study of Metropolitan Problems to study working-class families in which the wife was employed, that is, "dual-worker" families. I had spent a year in London in 1971–72 working with Robert and Rhona Rapoport, who had studied professional or dual-career families (Rapoport and Rapoport, with Bumstead, 1978; Rapoport and Rapoport 1971). Using their lengthy interview method, I had interviewed London dual-worker families. I wanted to pursue this issue in the United States, examining the ways which ordinary working-class families deal with young children when the mother is working full time. However, I wanted to select a community in Rhode Island that would enable me to focus on recent Portuguese immigrants, thus examining issues of ethnicity as well as class and gender. My problem was to isolate the strategies that dual-worker families used both at home and in the workplace to cope with the daily chores and responsibilities in a family with two working parents and young children.

As an anthropologist I had been trained to use participant-observation as my primary method for understanding social behavior and the cultural conceptions of how family life worked. During my fieldwork in the mid-1960s I had lived with a number of families in a Navajo community, participating in their everyday activities and gathering case material on who herded sheep, cared for planted fields, and participated in Navajo ceremonies (Lamphere 1977). This methodology works well in rural areas, but it needed to be adapted to urban research on families, as I discovered in London. Although it is possible (and fruitful) to do participant-observation in workplaces, churches, and other community institutions, it is difficult to "hang around" families who live in closed-off apartments or homes and in which much of the day is spent in a workplace equally walled off from the outside observer. The Rapoport methodology, which involved lengthy interviews conducted separately with both husbands and wives by same-sex interviewers, seemed to be a reasonable substitute for living with a family. Two to four hours of taped interview could give rich data on the details of work and a family's daily schedule and how housework, child care, and finances were handled. Having both the husband's and the wife's views could at least get at the complexity of family life, although one might never know who "really" did the vacuuming and the dishes. Thus I planned to interview fifteen Portuguese dual-worker couples and fifteen non-Portuguese couples from second- and third-generation ethnic groups. In addition, I planned to work in a factory, using participant-observation to understand the details of women's work outside the home. I was hoping through this two-pronged strategy (the interviews and the factory employment) to be able to connect work and family life, which had been treated separately in the social science literature.

Once I received the NIMH grant I set out to select a study community. The selection of the community, as well as the way in which the project developed, was the outcome of a number of intellectual influences: the growing attention being paid to women's wage work through the influence of the women's movement, the original research being conducted by social historians on women's employment and family life, and the increasing attention being given to the issue of ethnicity within anthropology. I was attracted to Central Falls, Rhode

Island, for several reasons. First, it was relatively small and compact. With a population of about twenty thousand, it seemed "manageable" for an anthropologist who was used to handling a community of about one thousand. Second, I knew that Portuguese were settling there, along with recent Colombian immigrants, a combination that might prove interesting. Third, there were plenty of industrial firms operating out of old textile mills, so it seemed likely that I would find a place to work. I could have chosen East Providence, Pawtucket, Bristol, West Warwick, or other communities with large Portuguese populations; however, these towns were larger and more sprawling, and industry was combined with other economic activities (commerce, fishing, services).

At the time I was also beginning to be influenced by research being done by women historians in Rhode Island. Judith Smith, then a Ph.D. candidate at Brown, was conducting a study of Jewish and Italian families using the Rhode Island State Census data as well as birth, marriage, and death records (Smith 1985). I had seen the census books for 1915 and 1925 and knew they were a potentially rich source of data on neighborhoods, since the census was collected on a house-to-house basis and the handwritten entries contained data for 1915 on country of origin and occupation as well as relationship to the head of household. The 1936 census was coded on holograph cards filed by name, which meant one had to reconstruct a neighborhood using a city directory to find the names that went with each address. However, the 1936 census had valuable data on unemployment as well as occupation and place of work. Choosing a small town like Central Falls meant that working with these census materials would be easier than working with them in a larger political unit of forty thousand to sixty thousand. All of these factors led to the selection of Central Falls, a community that became more and more fascinating as I learned about it.

When I began the research project, I was part of an increasing number of feminist anthropologists and social historians who were interested in the study of women's work. As middle-class intellectuals and as women influenced by the women's movement and particularly socialist feminism, we thought it was important to study and document the lives of ordinary women, primarily working-class women, as a counter to the middle-class bias both of the women's movement of the time and in the social science literature. Many of us were conducting or planning to conduct "shop-floor" studies of the labor process,

[3]

women's activities on the job, and informal relationships. Ann Bookman had worked in an electronics plant near Boston, examining the role of gender and ethnicity in a union drive (Bookman 1977). Nina Shapiro-Perl was engaged in a dissertation on Rhode Island jewelry workers that included her own experiences working for a jewelry firm (Shapiro-Perl 1983). Helen Safa and her students (Lynn Bolles, María Patricia Fernández-Kelly, and Charity Goodman) had conducted a study of an apparel plant in New Jersey (Safa 1983), and Heidi Hartmann and Dorothy Remy were about to embark on a study of women and Blacks in a meat-packing plant in Maryland (Remy and Sawers 1984). Sociologists were also becoming concerned with the employment of women in "ordinary jobs," exemplified most clearly in the research of Roslyn Feldberg and Evelyn Glenn on Boston clerical workers (Glenn and Feldberg 1979). These contemporary studies by social scientists were complemented by the work of several historians. Susan Benson had begun her dissertation research on department-store workers (Benson 1986), and Barbara Melosh was conducting a historical study of nursing (Melosh 1982). Judith Smith's study of Italian and Jewish families also contained rich material about women's paid employment (Smith 1985).

Some of us met for a weekend in the Connecticut woods during the summer of 1977, in the middle of my research project, giving me the sense that others were very much at work on the same issues—how ordinary women's work was shaped by the structure of a particular economy, industry, or institutional setting and how women's work and family lives were connected. This meeting was both the outgrowth of a network of relationships and a stimulus to continue to expand the network. The interaction between anthropologists and historians has been particularly fruitful since analyses of women's resistance strategies and of women's informal work culture have emerged from this interchange.

Finally, during 1974–75 and during a semester at the Bunting Institute funded by a Ford Foundation fellowship, I had begun to read widely in the literature on ethnicity, looking for material about women in different ethnic groups. Reading this literature, some written by historians, some written by sociologists and anthropologists, I was struck by the isolated nature of each "ethnic literature." The extensive literature on Italian-Americans seemed completely divorced from the literature on Poles, Jews, Irish, or Portuguese. There were some important exceptions, but even Nathan Glazer and Patrick Moynihan's classic study (1963) seemed more concerned with the issue of assimilation and the ranking of ethnic groups in terms of "success or failure." Relatively few books were genuinely comparative, and almost none focused on women. It seemed important, therefore, in a study of Central Falls, to look at women of different ethnic backgrounds and to make some careful and specific comparisons about work and family.

The Central Falls research, as it developed, became a genuine team project. While I was teaching at the University of New Mexico during the fall of 1976, I hired Carol Rodman, a Brown anthropology graduate student, as a research assistant. She volunteered in one of the local health centers and supervised Rebecca Matthews and Carlos Pato, who began interviewing recent Portuguese immigrants. We selected families through contacts with Portuguese counselors in the public schools, since we wanted to interview recent immigrants who had at least one child under six years of age. Aida Redondo, a Brown student from Colombia who already knew some of the Central Falls Colombian families, began interviewing Colombian women with small children. Given Aida's contacts in the Colombian community, it made sense to focus on both the Portuguese and the Colombians as examples of recent immigrants.

Late in the fall of 1976, Ann Bookman made a survey of the industrial firms in the Central Falls and Pawtucket area. She also began a clipping file from the local Pawtucket newspaper. This survey was invaluable in giving us an overview of the kinds of industries still operating in Central Falls and the number, gender, and ethnic background of their workers. By the time I began working on the project full time in January 1977, we were beginning to see how complex and interesting the community was. There were two French-Canadian parishes; two Polish churches (one Catholic and one Polish National church); two Syrian churches; an Irish parish, where the Spanish-language mass was held for the Colombian community on Sunday; and an Episcopal church. There were a host of ethnically connected voluntary associations and gathering places—a Portuguese club, two Colombian groceries, and a Colombian restaurant; a Polish club and a local grocery that specialized in kielbasa; and a shop that sold French-Canadian pork pies. Ethnicity seemed to be everywhere in this working-class community. I was beginning to learn that for most of working-class Rhode Island, ethnic communities were still alive and well, although certainly changed from those of the early twentieth century. There seemed to be a rich history of ethnicity as well as a complex contemporary set of relationships between new immigrant groups and older ethnic neighborhoods.

In February 1977 I took a job in a local factory and continued to direct the project in the evenings and weekends (when I was trying to write field notes as well). I was laid off for two and a half months between April 1 and June 15, but I worked again during July and August, quitting before Labor Day to devote myself to the project full time.

During the summer of 1977 Deborah Rubin, a Brown graduate who was enrolled in the anthropology Ph.D. program at Johns Hopkins, was hired to interview contemporary French-Canadian dual-worker families so that we would begin to understand the French-Canadian community. By and large these families were not employed in the local factories and mills but nevertheless were all of working-class background. One couple ran a small news store; one wife, a teacher, was married to a man who worked on the assembly line in an automobile plant in Massachusetts; and another was a nurse married to a truck driver. In my view, they were at the more comfortable upper sector of the working class whereas the Portuguese and Colombian couples we were interviewing were less well off, making between $3.35 and $4.50 an hour in textile, jewelry, apparel, and wire-processing jobs. At the same time, Marcel Dufresne was completing interviews for the Central Falls French-Canadian Oral History Project. These tapes, available at the Central Falls library, gave us an important glimpse into French-Canadian immigration to Central Falls and into the development of the French community during the late nineteenth and early twentieth centuries.

Ewa Hauser, a graduate student in anthropology at Johns Hopkins, also joined the project during the summer of 1977. A native of Poland, she interviewed a number of Polish-American dual-worker families. Some were older second-generation Polish women who were still working in Central Falls factories, and several were recent Polish immigrants employed in either textile or apparel factories. Later, Ewa returned to Central Falls to conduct a historical study of the Polish community, interviewing many of the older men and women about their immigration and early work experiences. I have used a great deal of the material she collected for her dissertation, "Ethnicity and Class Consciousness in a Polish-American Community" (Hauser 1981). Thus the data on the Poles in Central Falls are much richer and more detailed than for the French-Canadians or the English and Irish.

Throughout 1977 we continued to interview Portuguese and Colombian couples. Ricardo Anzaldua, then a Brown undergraduate, interviewed Colombian husbands while Aida completed interviews with fifteen Colombian wives. Ricardo was also able to take notes on the Spanish Oral History Project in the Central Falls library. These interviews, conducted by Mercedes Messier, traced the history of the Colombian community in Central Falls and were invaluable in documenting the story of their immigration. Filomena Silva, a bilingual teacher, and John Sousa, a high school teacher, conducted interviews with a number of Azorean couples. Finally, Carlos and Rebecca were able to interview four Continental Portuguese families, inasmuch as we had discovered that a number of Continentals lived in Central Falls, an extension of the Continental community in nearby Cumberland.[1]

Simultaneously, in addition to undertaking the interviewing and participant-observation, we were beginning to explore the history of Central Falls through the Rhode Island census data. We chose three neighborhoods to study in detail. Although drawing boundaries around neighborhoods is sometimes a difficult and arbitrary task, two of these neighborhoods (French-Canadian and Polish) had two very clear "centers"—a business district and parish church (or churches in

---

1. Continental Portuguese, whether rural or urban, often consider themselves superior to Portuguese from the islands—the Azores, Madeira, and Cape Verde. Azoreans and Madeirans are predominantly rural, are less educated, and have regional accents that are often denigrated by Continental Portuguese speakers. All of these populations are racially white, and Cape Verdeans are of mixed African and European racial heritage. They speak Crioulo as a first language, although most also speak standard Portuguese. In the United States they are often considered "Black," but Cape Verdeans themselves identify as Portuguese (Meintel 1984). In the 1915 census, Portuguese immigrants were listed as either citizens of Portugal or of the Azores. It is likely that most came from the Azores, but because of the ambiguity, I have used the more general term *Portuguese* to refer to early immigrants. From parish histories it is clear that the Pawtucket community is dominantly Azorean and that the Continental Portuguese settled in Valley Falls, north of Central Falls. In 1977 we interviewed both Azoreans and Continentals living in Central Falls, and I have distinguished between the two groups in the text and in tables because there are some differences. I did not include Cape Verdeans in the study because in the 1970s there were few in Central Falls. Since that time, the Pawtucket population of Cape Verdeans has increased, and they have established a Cape Verdean parish in the old Jewish synagogue on the southern border of the Polish neighborhood near Pawtucket.

the Polish case). We chose a third neighborhood near the Coats and Clark Mills, which in 1915 had a mix of English, Irish, and Scottish residents. We could have selected a more "Irish" neighborhood near the Irish parish but believed that it was more important to examine a neighborhood that was not focused on ethnic institutions or a commercial center, since some portions of Central Falls did seem less ethnically defined.

Deborah Rubin worked on 1915, 1925, and 1935 Rhode Island census data for the French-Canadian neighborhood as part of her study. Her paper "French-Canadian Working Families: Labor Participation in a New England Textile Center" (Rubin 1978) was the first analysis of the French-Canadian historical data, drawing on the census data and Dufresne's interviews as well as her own. Christina Simmons tackled the Polish neighborhood, spending hours in the record center with the census books and then constructing charts of household composition, occupational structure, female labor-force participation, and patterns of boarding. She also worked on the English-Irish neighborhood, a task that was completed by Sonja Michel, who constructed most of the charts.

In each neighborhood, we drew a sample of every fifth house. Since many houses are multifamily or "three-decker" houses, there were often several families at an address. We then made census sheets for each household at the address using the 1915 and 1925 census books. The data from the 1936 census were more difficult to compile. We had to reconstruct households from holograph cards on each individual that were filed by last name, not address. We were usually able to locate a husband, wife, and children but rarely found boarders (who would have had different last names). To add to our problems, street numbers had changed in the Polish and English-Irish neighborhoods between 1915 and 1936. We had to walk the streets with city directories to make sure we chose 1936 addresses that identified the same buildings we had selected for 1915 and 1925.

Other historical data came from two sources. Kate Dunnigan took notes on oral-history interviews with Central Falls residents, which had been collected in a study of mill workers by historians at the University of Rhode Island. They included some material on women's work, family organization, and community institutions for Irish, English, and French-Canadians. Susan Benson conducted a study of industrial homework in Rhode Island, using the raw data collected by the Women's Bureau of the Department of Labor. Some of her sample included women from Central Falls, particularly Polish and Lithuanian women who were "tag stringers" during the Depression.

I returned to my job at the University of New Mexico during 1977 but spent the summer of 1978 working with others to complete tape transcription and charts from the census data. By this time it was clear that we had rich, complex historical material (from census and oral histories) for the French-Canadian and Polish neighborhoods between 1915 and 1935. We knew less about the English and Irish, but with some of the oral histories available at the University of Rhode Island, we could piece together a picture. Then we had good interview data on contemporary Colombian and Portuguese immigrants, along with my observations in a contemporary workplace where Portuguese women worked alongside women from French-Canadian, Polish, Italian, Irish, and other backgrounds. At first it seemed easiest to treat each kind of data separately in article form, as illustrated by my articles on women's strategies in an apparel factory (Lamphere 1979), on Portuguese families (Lamphere 1980a), and on a comparison of the French-Canadian and Polish women immigrants (Lamphere 1980b).

Would it be possible to put all of this material into a book, one that would be both historical and anthropological and that would examine women's roles as they changed during the twentieth century? Was it possible to combine an interest in gender, class, and ethnicity into a coherent framework? I believed it was possible, but it meant that the gap between 1935 and 1976 had to be filled in terms of what had happened to the Central Falls economy. A framework was needed to encompases both the historical and the contemporary data.

During the next three years, I worked on a book manuscript, adding historical depth to the data we had already collected by researching the beginnings of the textile industry and piecing together immigration histories of the French-Canadian, Irish, English, and Polish communities through secondary sources. A Mellon Fellowship at the Wellesley College Center for Research on Women during the spring 1981 allowed me to work on the gap between 1935 and 1976 by researching the history of the decline of the textile industry and the history of women's roles in labor conflict. I found this research to be particularly difficult since there is no good historical source on the Rhode Island textile industry in the twentieth century and no statewide enumeration of strikes after 1915. I struggled to make sense of each rash of mill closings, and for most strikes, I had to rely on newspaper accounts. Fortunately, there is an excellent analysis of the

1922 textile strike by a Brown undergraduate (Jaffee 1974), two taped interviews with women organizers, and some research done by local historians (Buhle, Molloy, and Sansbury 1983; *Radical History Review* 1978).

By the end of 1981, I had a detailed draft of a book manuscript, but I was forced to delay further work on the book because I was awarded a National Science Foundation grant to study dual-worker families in Albuquerque, New Mexico (a Sunbelt counterpart to the Frostbelt study in Rhode Island). Finally, in the summer of 1984 I was able to return to the manuscript. A Pembroke Center Faculty Fellowship allowed me to concentrate full time on the book in the fall, with comments from Joan Scott, Pembroke Center director, to guide me in rethinking the manuscript.

I had used the notion of coping strategies in discussing family life and the notion of women's strategies of resistance in analyzing women's work on the shop floor. Yet these constructs, although I wanted to retain them, failed to bring together the historical and contemporary material and to provide a framework for connecting the home and work lives of immigrant women. I turned to the Marxist literature on production and reproduction as providing a set of conceptual tools that could integrate diverse data on what I now saw as the central historical trend—the transition from a labor force composed of working daughters to one of working mothers. I began to see strategies in the context of the allocation of productive and reproductive labor and to be able to account for variation in strategies within and between ethnic groups through changes in a developing political economy. Here the history of immigration and family life cycle interacted with the economy to place women in very different situations at different historical periods and within and between different ethnic populations.

Although I am not trained as a historian, I have come to take history seriously and not just as a backdrop or single chapter in what is basically a contemporary account. I often felt frustrated using historical sources, since as an anthropologist I was used to asking what happened, rather than having to piece bits of information together to guess at a sequence of events. I was particularly frustrated that various sources never seemed to fit together. For example, I found wage data for 1915, but they were from a mill in Pawtucket, so it was a "leap of faith" to assume that the ethnic and gender hierarchy replicated the experience of those living in our three sample neighborhoods in Central Falls. In a second case, the Univerisity of Rhode Island Oral History Project gave us some material on Irish, English, and French-Canadian women, but the interviews were often full of gaps, and the interviewees were often not from our sample neighborhoods. When Ewa Hauser was able to combine her own oral-history interviewing with the Rhode Island census data, I felt more confident about the picture we obtained. Finally, I had to rely on newspaper accounts of strikes, despite their bias, since we did not have time to conduct oral-history interviews, and our one attempt was a failure. Ewa Hauser asked Polish men and women about strikes and religious schisms but was given only flat denials or cursory comments. (See Hauser's 1981 dissertation for a full analysis of the contradictions between written and oral histories within the Polish community). I am sure that a historian would have treated the materials I have used differently, perhaps constructing more of a narrative or relying less on an abstract theoretical framework. However, from my perspective as an anthropologist, historical data have enriched and deepened my view of Central Falls, giving it a multidimensional aspect that a purely contemporary study would have lacked.

In writing the first draft of this book, I changed the name of the community as well as that of individuals to provide anonymity for living people. This practice made the book less useful to historians and possibly to the city as well. In the end, I decided not to alter the name of the city, but to change only the names of all individuals, both those cited in twentieth-century censuses and in interviews whether collected by project members or others. I have retained the names of early mills and their owners (which have long since gone out of business) but have not used the names of contemporary firms or the factory where I worked. I have also changed the names of my coworkers. I hope that this compromise between the standards of accuracy used by historians and the anthropologist's ethical commitment to protect their consultants and informants is workable.

Central Falls has always had the reputation of being a working-class "bedroom community" or even ghetto—a small enclave with a shady reputation and more bars per square mile, it is said, than any other Rhode Island community. In contrast, I have tried to present historical and contemporary material to show how it is a microcosm for many of the social processes that have characterized Rhode Island and the industrial Northeast. The development of industrial capitalism, the incorporation of immigrant workers into an industrial labor force, the creation of ethnic neighborhhoods, and the importance of female labor both at home and in the workplace are all interconnected in Central Falls as in other communities in the Northeast. In this book, I have been able to examine the interplay of class, gender, and ethnicity as they are interrelated through a changing political economy. Feminists in the 1980s believe that we need a more complex and varied notion of womanhood, one that takes into account the rich variety of women's experiences and that accounts for differences rather than focuses on "essential" timeless similarities. I have tried to present such an analysis in this book, one that embeds women in the context of the family and workplace but also one that treats them as actors rather than passive recipients. Thus what began as a rather simple study of Portuguese immigrant dual-worker families has turned into a more complex analysis of women in working-class families from a variety of different ethnic backgrounds. The evolution of this book has been long, but I hope it will contribute to our understanding of women's roles both in the past and the present.

PART I

Theoretical Framework

[1]

From Working Daughters
to Working Mothers

The noise was such that I cannot describe it for you. You couldn't imagine it, if you don't go to hear it. It is such a crash that nobody can communicate with others, perhaps only to look and read lips or by sign language.

> Polish woman describing her first textile
> job as a single immigrant, 1916

I only work because of the money. Do you know what it is to have to work eight hours there? There is nothing that I like about my job. Nobody likes to work [there] and this work was made for a donkey to do.

> Colombian immigrant mother describing
> her job in a toy factory, 1977

The most difficult thing for a working mother is to have to come home from work and have duties. That weighs you down.

> Colombian mother who works as a weaver, 1977

The increase in women entering the paid labor force has been one of the most important changes in the United States economy in the post–World War II period. The participation of women in wage labor, however, has a long history in the United States. It began in the early years of the industrial revolution, in the late eighteenth and early nineteenth centuries, when young girls were employed in the first textile mills in Rhode Island and Massachusetts. The most recent element of change is not only the increase in the proportion of women workers but also the fact that women have been wives and working mothers rather than employed daughters.

This historical transition—from working daughters to working wives—can best be seen in the lives of immigrant women: women who have just arrived in the United States and who have taken paid jobs to support themselves and their families. In Rhode Island, an industrial state and a center of the textile industry, immigrant women have long been employed for wages. In 1900, 78 percent of the foreign-born white female population between the ages of sixteen and twenty were employed outside the home.[1] In 1980 immigrant women in Rhode Island were still working for wages, but a large proportion of them were wives and mothers. For example, 78 percent of Portuguese immigrant wives and mothers were employed outside the home as were 67 percent of Latin American immigrant mothers.[2] The evidence is clear. At the turn of the century, two-thirds of immigrant daughters worked for wages, and in the 1980s, two-thirds of immigrant wives and mothers are so employed.[3]

The focus of this book is an analysis of this transformation, one that characterizes the United States as a whole. The process can be particularly well documented in an industrial state like Rhode Island, where there is a long history of working women. I analyze the reasons for the increasing incorporation of women into wage labor and for the transition of the typical female worker from "working daughter" to "working mother." I also examine the impact of this change on the workplace and on the family. My task has been to identify the similarities and differences between the experiences of the Polish woman quoted above, first employed as a weaver when she came as a young, single

1. For categories with larger proportions of married women, the labor-force participation was smaller. In 1900, 58 percent of women between the ages of twenty-one and twenty-four were employed whereas only 31 percent of women between the ages of twenty-five and thirty-four years were working for wages. Compared to immigrants, labor-force-participation rates were somewhat lower for young, sixteen- to twenty-year-old females of foreign parentage, that is, 67 percent, and much lower for sixteen- to twenty-year-old native-born females of native parentage, that is, 41 percent.

2. In 1980, in the state as a whole, 68 percent of the wives with children between ages six and seventeen (husband present) and 47 percent of wives with children under age six were employed. If single mothers are added in, the proportion of working women with children between ages six and seventeen is still 68 percent, and the proportion of women with children under six slightly less at 45 percent.

3. Young daughters, especially in a working-class state like Rhode Island, are still likely to be employed. In 1980 the labor-force-participation rate of 48 percent for sixteen to nineteen year olds indicates that many women are still in school, but among women between the ages of twenty and twenty-four, 66 percent are working for wages.

woman to New England in 1915, and those of Colombian wives and mothers who migrated to the same community during the 1960s and 1970s and who found employment in textile mills and other light industries.

We have come a long way in the past fifteen years in our understanding of women's work outside the home. Yet a review of recent research shows an explainable, but no longer necessary, separation of data collection and analysis. Anthropologists and sociologists have focused primarily on contemporary employment, and historians have examined paid labor in the nineteenth and early twentieth centuries. Few studies have tried to integrate an analysis of women's work in both the past and the present. Both anthropologists and historians have tended to study the workplace, without complementary attention to the role of women workers in their families. Although many researchers have written about working-class women or women of one ethnic background, little has been done to compare women of different ethnic backgrounds within a single community, work situation, or historical period. This book is a step in the direction of integrating these three themes: women's paid employment in the past and present, women's work for wages and its relationship to women's family roles, and the variation in women's paid work as seen through the contrasting experiences of women from different ethnic groups.

Using an analytic framework that will integrate these concerns, I focus on the growth and decline of the local economy of Central Falls, a textile-mill town of twenty thousand in Rhode Island. In the context of this local example of capitalist expansion and change, I examine women's labor in terms of the concepts of "production" and "reproduction." By using a framework that incorporates both the productive and reproductive aspects of women's labor, I go beyond the more static concepts of work and family, or the notion of two "spheres" (one at work and the other at home). As I make clear in the following discussion it is important not to think of the terms *production* and *reproduction* as glosses for the terms *workplace* and *family*. As I use them, they are analytic concepts that point to important relationships and changes that may occur in either "place."

For Marx, and for recent Marxist feminists who have used the notion of reproduction, this concept is more broadly defined than as simply "having babies" or as the bare "facts" of fertility and demography that characterize a population. For Marxists, production entails reproduction, and there are elements of both productive labor and reproductive labor in the factory and in the household. When women are tending spinning frames or looms, they are producing a product (cloth), but their labor is set in a system of social relations in which they sell their labor for a wage and work for someone who owns the machinery and the factory they work in. As Marxists would interpret this situation, they are working for capitalists who own the means of production and extract surplus labor, which appears in the form of profits. Yet there are also elements of reproduction in the factory or textile mill. The means of production must be reproduced or replaced, that is, the machinery needs to be repaired, the buildings refurbished, and new machinery incorporating the latest technology purchased. Furthermore, the social relations of production, the divisions between owners, managers, and workers, need to be reproduced through the continuous replacement of individuals in these categories and through the socialization of workers and managers to their jobs, including an acceptance of the system as legitimate.

The major link between the workplace and the household or family is that the family is where labor is reproduced. Workers are fed and clothed, and young children are socialized to become the next generation of workers. Thus much of the work done by women (either wives or daughters) in the home is reproductive labor—from the processing of food, to the washing of clothes, to the care and feeding of young infants. In the early stages of capitalism, when many families were farm families or artisans, much of the work in the household was also productive. Women grew crops in a garden, made their own cloth, or churned their own butter. Many of these products were for family consumption. Thus women produced "use-values" rather than goods for exchange. Whether women's work at home in the contemporary period still produces "use-values" or whether it is productive or non-productive labor has been a continuing source of debate among Marxists. However, there is a sense in which women's labor produces use-values for the family as well as reproducing the labor of family members.

There are also ways in which "production" finds its way into the home, even though most productive work does not take place there under either industrial or monopoly capitalism. First, the organization and scheduling of work impinge on and determine the family's schedule for eating, sleeping, and leisure time. Second, the wages paid to adult male workers determine whether other members of the family will work for wages in order to provide subsistence for the household.

Third, and most important, depending on the family status of working household members, their participation in the labor force may necessitate the reallocation of reproductive labor within the home.

On the other side of the coin, the organization of production is limited by the organization of reproductive labor in the home. Clearly, there are limits on the hours and scheduling of work, because employers have left reproductive tasks like cooking, cleaning, and sleeping to be done in the home. Similarly, wages must be high enough, at least, to reproduce the work force. In addition, production may be influenced by the way in which family and kin ties are utilized by either employers or workers. Both employers and workers have used kin networks to recruit workers. Owners of capital have consolidated their ties with others through marriage and hired and trained their sons and sons-in-laws to succeed them. Family, kin, and community ties sometimes formed the basis of worker resistance but at other times fostered conservatism. In these latter instances husbands and fathers submitted to low wages and poor working conditions because they had families to support. Some working daughters may have been docile employees because of socialization in the family and their subordinate position in relationship to their parents (Tentler 1979). Finally, as I argue in the last chapter of this book, women often bring their family roles to work, using their common identities as women, wives, and mothers as a way of bridging age and ethnic differences. Activities that stress these family identities may fit either into a women's work culture of resistance or into a firm's attempt to build a loyal work force and nonresistant work culture.

The organization of productive and reproductive labor (whether in the workplace or home) does not make for a seamless, nonconflicting set of relationships under capitalism. Women and men are actors and actively engage in relations of resistance, accommodation, or coping in each setting. In examining the organization of productive work, I have also focused on women's strategies for dealing with the nature of that work and the social relations on the job. Since under capitalism owners attempt to obtain as much labor from workers as possible (Marx's "extraction of surplus labor"), many strategies on the job concern the resistance to this extraction, including owners' control over work conditions. But there are also strategies for accommodation and coping. Resistance strategies can range from strikes and walkouts to more informal methods of undermining management's policy or preserving one's autonomy on the job. Coping strategies may help to minimize the effects of management policy or adjust to a measured system of pay.

Within the family, there are also strategies for dealing with the allocation of productive and reproductive labor. Sometimes provoking conflict, these strategies concern the ways families cope with the demands and limits placed on them by wages, the need for several wage workers in the family, and the kinds of reproductive tasks that must be done.

This account of the relationship between the allocation of productive and reproductive labor has thus far been uncontextualized and ahistorical. My purpose in this book is to show how the organization of production and reproduction interact and change. As capitalism has expanded, more and more women have been incorporated into the wage labor force, but the jobs that they have filled and the wages that they have received have been profoundly influenced by the reproductive roles they have held in the family. Daughters were initially recruited to wage jobs, since their labor within the home could be dispensed with, and since their subordinate role within the family could also justify low wages and semiskilled work. In the initial stages of capitalist development, then, the allocation of productive labor was influenced by the organization of reproductive labor. More recently, the converse has been true. As more working mothers have been recruited to productive work outside the home, reallocation of reproductive labor within the family has followed.

Recent Research on Women, Work, and Family

Within sociology and anthropology in the 1960s and early 1970s, many of the studies that focused on working women dealt with contemporary middle- and upper middle-class women: women as doctors, lawyers, and academics, with some attention to the female professions of teaching, nursing, and social work. In England, a study called "Women in Top Jobs" focused on architects, managers, civil servants, and BBC professionals (Fogarty, Allen, Allen, and Walters 1971; Fogarty, Rapoport, and Rapoport 1971; Rapoport and Rapoport 1971). In the United States, collections on women in science and other professions (Theodore 1971; Mattfeld and Van Aken 1965) were followed by more specific studies of women in particular occupations (Stromberg and Harkess 1978; Kanter 1977; Ashley 1976; Rossi and

Calderwood 1973; Epstein 1970; Lopate 1968). There have also been additional studies of two-career, middle-class families (Aldous 1982; Rapoport and Rapoport, with Bumstead, 1978; Safilios-Rothschild 1976; Rossi and Calderwood 1973; Kim, Roderick, and Shea 1972).

The study of women in professional and managerial careers, while leading to an important examination of the impact of female labor-force participation on the dual-career family, focuses on only 20 percent of the female work force. It leaves out the very different experiences of women in ordinary clerical, factory, and service jobs. These latter women, most likely to be married to blue-collar, service, or white-collar nonprofessional husbands constitute dual-worker families. Their experiences at work and the strategies for coping at home are much different from those of more highly paid professionals.

Earlier research on working-class families in the United States and England often portrayed women as wives and mothers with little experience in work outside the home (Komarovsky 1964; Rainwater, Coleman, and Handel 1959; Young and Willmott 1957). Although 15 to 17 percent of sampled families contained working wives, men's jobs received much more attention than those of the women. These studies evaluated working-class family life from a middle-class perspective, commenting on the restrictive nature of the blue-collar work or on the liabilities of family patterns for upward mobility or community organizing (Gans 1962:266). Lee Rainwater and his colleagues took this analysis the furthest by depicting working-class wives as passive receptors of the world around them (Rainwater, Coleman, and Handel 1959:44).

More recently, writers and researchers on working-class women have begun to focus attention on women's experiences at work, particularly in factory employment, clerical jobs, and service occupations. Several studies in the early 1970s (Tepperman 1976; Braverman 1974; Garson 1972; Langer 1972) offset the growing literature on professions and showed how various kinds of women's clerical and white-collar work were becoming more routinized and more like factory work. At the same time, a number of anthropologists, including myself, studied women in industrial jobs. Some have focused on "runaway shops" and the internationalization of labor (Fernández-Kelly 1983; Nash and Fernández-Kelly 1983), and others have analyzed the "shop-floor" experiences of United States women in blue-collar jobs in textiles, apparel, canning, jewelry, and electronics (Zavella 1987; Shapiro-Perl 1977, 1983; Lamphere 1979; Bookman 1977). A collection edited by

Karen Brodkin Sacks and Dorothy Remy (1984) summarized much of the research of the late 1970s and early 1980s, examining changes in women's clerical, sales, and factory jobs as well as women's resistance strategies.

Anthropologists' and sociologists' recent interest in women's ordinary work has been paralleled by an expanding literature by historians. New research has redocumented the extent of paid female labor in the past and showed that rather than being passive, working-class women have participated in labor struggles, union drives, and women's protests. (This literature is extensive but is well summarized in several texts and collections on the social history of women's work and family roles, for example: Kessler-Harris 1982; Kessler-Harris 1980; Cott and Pleck 1979; Cantor and Laurie 1977; Baxandall, Gordon, and Reverby 1976.) There have also been a number of historical case studies of women's occupations that have focused, as have some of the anthropological studies, on women's work culture (Benson 1986; Cooper 1986; Melosh 1982).

Although much of this newer research has emphasized women in the workplace itself, the research of other historians has focused on the intricate connections between women, work, and family. Louise Tilly and Joan Scott's book *Women, Work, and Family* (1978) was perhaps one of the most important in drawing our attention to the relationship between family organization and women's work outside the home as it developed and changed in nineteenth- and twentieth-century England and France. Thus one outcome of the recent attention paid to women's labor-force participation has been an attempt to bridge the dichotomy between work and home that has plagued the sociological and anthropological literature. With few exceptions, research usually works from one side of the dichotomy, looking for the impact of the other side. Some studies emphasize the conservative impact of the family on women who work, whereas others see family ties and values as important ingredients in resistance.

Leslie Tentler (1979), to use a historical example, argued that workroom socializing (e.g., the exchange of confidences about boyfriends or the sharing of oranges and chocolates among work friends) underwrote a romanticized dream that women would marry and leave the paid labor force: "The typical women's work community, then, was a youthful, sex-segregated social world where important conservative values about femininity were reaffirmed by women themselves. Among their peers, young working women were encouraged to seek future security and mobility through marriage rather than employment. They learned to accept a work world that defined women as dependent and marginal employees" (Tentler 1979:80).

Sallie Westwood (1984) made a slightly different point in her study of a contemporary apparel plant in England. She also examined women's informal socializing and described the rituals surrounding weddings and engagements, which take place at work or among work friends after hours. After detailing shop-floor relationships in a British garment factory, she described vividly the bride's ritual and the hens' party. These two activities, surrounding engagement and marriage, show acceptance of male definitions of women; although full of jokes and ribaldry, they support accepted notions of femininity: "Shopfloor culture offers to women at work a version of woman and they take upon themselves elements of this in ways which tie them more firmly to a 'feminine' destiny and the culture of femininity. However, it is a deeply contradictory culture which the women fashion: it reveals a resistant and creative attempt to overcome the stultifying aspects of the capitalist labour process—only to find that this creativity has bound itself securely to an oppressive version of womanhood" (Westwood 1984:6).

On the other hand, Sacks has argued that it is precisely the values and social connections forged in the working-class family that made it possible for a group of female Black hospital workers to stage an effective walkout and begin a union drive in a southern city. Clerical workers used skills and values that were part of their family life (settling conflicts, emphasizing responsibility, and demanding autonomy as adults) in the workplace. They helped socialize doctors and others to be members of a team rather than bosses in a hierarchy. Their ability to take initiative and build networks resulted in women's becoming "center people" in the mobilization of workers against management: "Center people, then, exemplify more general working class values and are important parts of a more general process by which workers bring family members to the workplace, turn relatives into co-workers and friends, and makes friends like sisters or godparents. From this vantage point, I see a continuity between family and work—in how work, both wage and non-wage, is defined—which is absent from a management perspective and which underwrites workers' militance" (Sacks 1984:299).

The seventh chapter of this book returns to the theme of women's work culture. It explores, much as Sacks did, the connections between family and work that are part of women's work culture and that may feed into a culture of resistance on the job. Although I examine, as other studies have, the connections between family and work by focusing on the workplace, this task is part of a larger analysis that also examines the family and work connections in the context of the home. Both workplace and family need to be seen within a single framework of development and change. Thus my chapter on women's work culture comes at the end of a lengthy analysis of the organization of productive and reproductive labor in a Rhode Island industrial community as it developed between 1820 and 1970.

Production and Reproduction: Toward an Integrative Framework

A number of feminist theorists (Vogel 1983; Barrett 1980; Edholm, Harris, and Young 1977; O'Laughlin 1974, 1975) have utilized Marx's notion of reproduction in analyzing women's status in both capitalist and precapitalist societies. Rather than recapitulate their analyses, I have taken from their work what is useful in building a framework for my analysis of working daughters and working wives in industrial Rhode Island.

As Marx pointed out, production and reproduction are two sides of the same coin. Humans have the capacity to use their mental and physical capabilities to create "use-values" or useful things that satisfy human needs of some sort (Vogel 1983:138). Labor power is thus a human capacity that is put to work in the labor process. But labor power gets consumed as it also produces something; it is used up and must be replenished or reproduced. In Marx's own words, "A society can no more cease to produce than it can cease to consume. When viewed, therefore, as a connected whole, and as flowing on with incessant renewal, every social process of production is, at the same time, a process of reproduction" (Marx, *Capital*, 1:531, quoted in Vogel 1983:138–39).

Although linked, production and reproduction are not the same thing. Reproduction is a condition of production, since it involves the replacing of labor power and the social relations in which labor power is embedded in a particular mode of production. It is not, in itself, a form of production, because it does not involve raw materials and tools that are combined with labor power that is organized in a system of social relationships and that results in a product (Vogel 1983:139).

[24]

In thinking about the reproduction of labor power in a capitalist mode of production (and leaving aside the reproduction of tools, machinery, and the social relations of production), several issues arise. First, the labor power of the direct producers—the wage laborers— must be reproduced. They need to eat, sleep, have their clothes washed and repaired, and live in some sort of housing that is also maintained. Second, other members of the working class who are not employed for wages must be maintained, whether they are elderly parents, a wife, or a sick relative. Third, a new generation of wage workers needs to be cared for and raised to adulthood. Labor expended in aspects of reproducing labor power is what Marx called "necessary labor," although not all entail a direct relationship to wages.

Wages do provide a proportion of the means of subsistence. Workers bring home wages, which permit the purchase of commodities on the open market; however, a certain amount of supplementary labor is usually necessary to consume these commodities. Firewood has to be chopped, meals cooked, clothes made from cloth, or new kitchen cupboards constructed. Also, a great deal of supplementary labor is expended just in refurbishing the commodities that workers and those they live with use in daily life. Dishes need to be washed, beds made, floors swept, and laundry done. Both kinds of supplementary labor may be expended to maintain those working for wages and those who are not (the elderly, the sick, or a wife). Finally, these two kinds of supplementary labor, and a host of other tasks, must be performed in the bearing and raising of children who will be the wage workers of the next generation (see Vogel 1983:143–44). The supplementary labor involved in the first two sets of tasks is usually thought of as housework, and the third kind of supplementary labor is thought of as child care.

Most Marxist feminists thus argue that only the last, the generational replacement of labor through childbearing, involves a necessary division of labor by gender. Women carry and deliver children and thus must be maintained during this period and also, in many historical situations, during the period the child nurses. Although women, as childbearers, need to be maintained for only a finite amount of time, Vogel argued, families historically have become the site for the maintenance and the generational replacement of labor power, and women historically have been associated with the necessary labor of transforming commodities for consumption, refurbishing other commodities, and feeding, bathing, and tending to children. Men histor-

[25]

ically have been involved more fully in wage labor, which includes both necessary labor (what is actualized in the wage to purchase commodities) and surplus labor (what is taken by capitalists in the form of profits) (Vogel 1983:146).

Women, however, have also worked for wages, and their position within capitalism as wage workers is of central concern to any analysis of production and reproduction. Marx's insights into the nature and development of production under capitalism thus have general relevance for women workers as well as for men. The organization of production under capitalism, based, as it is, on the extraction of surplus labor in the form of profits, leads capitalists, the owners of the means of production, to expand continually.

Several aspects of the capitalist drive to expansion concern us here. First, as capitalism expands it draws more and more individuals into the wage labor force. As capital grows, it demands progressively more labor. However, this tendency is opposed to the drive for surplus value, which forces capitalists constantly to augment productivity, chiefly through the introduction of machinery (Vogel 1983:67). The introduction of machinery often throws workers out of jobs and creates a surplus labor force, a population of potential workers who are ready to be employed and drawn into the labor force at periods when the system is expanding. But the introduction of more complex machinery also creates what Marx called more "constant capital" (as opposed to variable capital, or labor), the expended labor embodied in machinery that has replaced human labor power. In the long run this has meant that an industry can produce the same quantity of goods with much less labor.

Both the drawing in of more laborers and the continual replacement of labor with machinery takes place within a process of concentration and monopolization. Marx's analysis of the logic of capitalism and the creation of crises in a business cycle indicates that at each downturn in the cycle some firms go out of business and other firms survive and expand. Finally, the drawing in of more laborers and the use of more complex machinery has also been accompanied by a more complex division of labor in the production process. Here Harry Braverman's work, building on Marx, shows the historical impact of scientific management in the United States and documents the process of deskilling and continually dividing jobs as work is mechanized (Braverman 1974).

These four processes—the progressive expansion of the work force,

[26]

increased replacement of labor with machinery, increased concentration, and increased deskilling—have occurred in the historical development of capitalism in the United States. All have affected women in the labor force. Women increasingly have been incorporated into productive labor as wage laborers, their work has been transformed and eliminated by new technology, they have come to work in larger and larger firms, and their work has become increasingly deskilled, in a more and more complex division of work tasks.

To analyze who gets drawn into a growing labor force and into what jobs in a historically specific situation is one objective of this book. I examine the organization of productive and reproductive labor and how this changes over time in a local economy within developing capitalism. We will see how women of different ages, marital status, and ethnic backgrounds become incorporated as wage laborers and how this incorporation relates to the structure of their families. Because women and their families are not passively brought into the industrial system, an examination of a particular case through time can also be used to isolate the strategies used by families to allocate labor to productive and reproductive activities. In regard to the workplace, I also look at the ways that wage workers, both male and female, respond to and resist the continued effort of employers to extract surplus value by making workers work harder and produce more for the same wages.

In this book, then, I examine the development of industrial capitalism in one Rhode Island community of twenty thousand: Central Falls and the surrounding area of Pawtucket and the Blackstone Valley. This is a setting in which we can see the beginnings of the recruitment of women into a textile-mill labor force and its continued expansion for more than 120 years. We will see that the system expanded and changed from small mills to large, family-owned concerns and then to a collapsing and declining textile economy. This was eventually replaced in the post–World War II period by a more mixed industrial economy with, once again, small, family-owned firms, although now interspersed with a few branch plants of multinational corporations, still recruiting an immigrant labor force.

Whether men or women were incorporated into this growing industry, and which jobs they entered, depended a great deal on the relations of production and reproduction in the previous mode of production. As one mode of production was transformed into another, the former mode's organization of production and reproduction set the stage for the way these activities became structured. Thus in Paw-tucket, Samuel Slater's recruitment of children to run his machinery in 1790 (mainly seven- to twelve-year-old boys but including two girls) "made sense" in the context of the artisanal community in which he built the first textile mill. Later, recruitment of young daughters as weavers also "made sense" and grew out of the organization of families in the nonindustrial local economy. Their recruitment "fit" with the sexual division of labor, proper women's and men's jobs, and the actual work that various categories of men and women were already doing. By this time children were no longer appropriate to run the newer, more complex machines, but wives and mothers were oc-cupied with domestic and child-care tasks, older artisan males were too expensive, and young men were occupied in apprenticeships. Daughters were the most expendable members of local families, both those of artisans and of impoverished farmers. They were the cheapest to hire because of their subordinate place in the organization of pro-duction and reproduction embodied in family life at the time.

However, as the textile economy continued to expand in the late nineteenth and early twentieth centuries, the ways in which women were drawn into an industrial economy was not the same for all wom-en. In dealing with these differences it is important to examine the allocation of productive and reproductive labor within the family and to view women and other family members as forging strategies to deal with their situation. First, structural factors such as the age, marital status, and family position of a woman were important in shaping her own or her family's allocation of her labor. Second, the developmental cycle of a family itself influenced the kinds of strategies families and women followed. The position of young married couples with small children differed from older couples with teenage sons or daughters in terms of the reproductive tasks (e.g., child rearing) that needed to be taken care of and the possibilities of allocating the labor of sons and daughters to productive wage labor outside the home.

As the recruitment of labor through migration became important in the United States, and as the textile-mill economy changed and ex-panded between 1840 and 1920, family strategies again varied, both between ethnic groups or for each ethnic group over time. Popula-tions of different national backgrounds were incorporated into the United States economy and into the local Central Falls economy at different historical periods. Where male and female family workers would fit within the industrial economy very much depended on who was there before them and whether the system was expanding or contracting. The development of ethnic neighborhoods and ethnic institutions was also conditioned by patterns of urban growth, which was in turn related to the expansion or contraction of the local industrial economy. For these immigrant workers, it seems appropriate to talk about "economic niches," which members of ethnic populations come to fill in a local economy, and to look at women's productive and reproductive roles in relation to the allocation of the labor of males in their families. As the local economy was transformed, so was the place that members of an ethnic group held within it, and so was women's relationship to productive and reproductive labor.

Women as Strategists

My framework for the analysis of productive and reproductive labor emphasizes women's strategies. I argue that women must be viewed as active strategists, weighing possibilities and devising means to realize goals, and not as passive acceptors of their situations. This treatment of women as strategists derives from the more general work of political anthropologists (Swartz, Tuden, and Turner 1966; Barth 1959, 1966; Leach 1954). I follow Jane Collier (1974), who argued that the family could be defined as a "political arena" in which women, as well as men, actively strive to attain goals, often manipulating their relationships to other family members to achieve these ends. Others have followed Collier's lead by analyzing women's strategies in relation to marriage (Bledsoe 1980), to their position within domestic groups (Lewin and Browner 1976), and to their culturally defined roles in religious sects (Borker 1976; Rake 1976). Applying a strategy model to the analysis of women's situations helps to examine processes, to deal with variation and change, and to account for shifts in overall structural alignments.

There are difficulties with the strategy approach since the model makes utilitarian, maximizing assumptions about human behavior and often claims "psychological reality" for strategies (Silverman 1976). Although I accept the assumptions of rationality and goal-oriented, maximizing behavior, I carefully place strategies within an analysis of a local economy that often constrains choices. I do not assume that choices are wholly "free." To deny the strategy approach and its assumptions, I argue, is to "buy into" the stereotype of passive work-

[29]

ing-class women that was prevalent in the social science literature of the 1950s. However, unlike research on natural decision making, much of the data I use in this book (from census books, newspaper reports, interviews, and participant-observation) does not lend itself to fine-grained analysis of individual decisions and choices. Thus I cannot claim psychological reality for the strategies I uncover. Rather, I have adopted an observer's definition of strategies: patterns that the analyst is able to abstract from interviews, observed behavior, commentary on everyday events, or census schedules. In this approach, analysis of the local economy at different historical periods helps us to understand the patterns in what individuals do or tell us, patterns that might not be apparent to women or their families. My analysis thus focuses not on the psychological reality of women's and families' strategies but on the relationship between patterned activities and social and economic constraints.

It is also helpful to distinguish between strategies of resistance and those of coping or accommodation. Many family strategies for the allocation of productive and reproductive labor can be thought of as ways of coping with the exigencies of the labor market at a particular time; their goal is to support the whole family. Many strategies in the workplace are ones of adjustment and consent as well. Early studies of the shop floor tended to focus on resistance, that is, the tactics and actions, along with shared beliefs and concepts, that workers use to undermine their employer's control of the workplace. But as Nina Shapiro-Perl has eloquently argued in her study of Rhode Island women jewelry workers (1983), if we saw all women's actions as resistance, we would expect more unionized shops, more walkouts, and much more labor turmoil than has occurred in the past and even today. In other words, an analysis of women workers needs to assess the balance between strategies of accommodation and strategies of resistance, as well as management's tactics, if the dynamics of the workplace are to be understood.

The use of a strategy approach, coupled with an analysis of transformations in productive and reproductive labor, is particularly helpful in comparing women of different ethnic backgrounds. One of the major liabilities of the literature on women and ethnicity is that most studies are not comparative. They focus on one ethnic group and, with regard to women's level of participation in the labor force, resort to cultural values as the major explanatory variable. For example, Polish women are said not to have worked outside the home (Lopata 1976: 99); Italian family values are said to account for women's participation in those food-processing and canning factories near Buffalo where they could be chaperoned by male relatives (Yans-McLaughlin 1979). These studies rarely try to pinpoint variation within a local ethnic population or examine the impact of a local economy on women's behavior. Polish women may not have worked in mining communities or in Midwestern industrial cities, not because of Polish family values but because these economies used male labor to a much greater extent than female labor. Similarly, for Italian women in Buffalo, where male industrial jobs prevailed, women's work opportunities may have been as restricted by the local labor market as by family values. In New York with a contrasting labor-market situation, Italian women were employed unchaperoned in the garment industry, in small shops, and in industrial homework.

In Rhode Island, the local economy based on textiles and jewelry has pulled many women into semiskilled wage jobs. Women's labor-force participation in Rhode Island has been shaped less by cultural values than by the nature and growth of the textile industry. Women's labor-force participation varies from one ethnic group to another but is best understood by looking first at the timing of a group's entrance into the local economy and then at women's strategies for the allocation of productive and reproductive labor in the context of the family developmental cycle.

In sum, this book examines the transformation of women's roles in productive labor from that of a wage-earning daughter to that of a wage-earning wife. The book also explores how these two stages of the incorporation of women into an industrial economy have affected their position in the family and their strategies of resistance at work.

Working Daughters and Economic Expansion

The next three chapters of this book tell the story of wage-earning daughters in Central Falls' past. This is not to say that there were no employed wives, mothers, or widows, but the overwhelming proportion of women employed in the textile-mill economy were young, single women. On the whole, wives, mothers, and widows were contributing to the reproduction of the labor force, and daughters, like fathers and sons, were contributing wages to families and households. These wages allowed for the purchase of commodities (individual consumption), but they were also crucial for the reproduction of labor.

These three chapters span the period between 1790 and 1940 and interweave a number of themes: the expansion and decline of the textile industry, the growth and elaboration of a division of labor in the textile mill, and the incorporation of different ethnic populations into the mill social structure and the growing urban community of Central Falls. These three processes shaped the experience of immigrant daughters and the way in which their labor was utilized for both productive and reproductive activities in the textile mill and in the home.

As we will see, there were important variations on the theme of the daughter involved in direct capitalist production and the mother involved in reproductive activities. Some wives and mothers were able to use their reproductive skills (cooking, doing laundry, cleaning) to support boarders or wage-earning relatives who contributed their wages to the household. Here activities that maintained and reproduced wage laborers were extended to include those outside the nuclear family, putting additional cash in the hands of the housewife. Some single women did not live with their fathers and mothers. They were boarders themselves and turned a portion of their wages over to the housewives who acted as "hostesses." In extended families, wives often helped to maintain a mother-in-law or aunt who was not a wage worker; these women in many cases also contributed some reproductive labor to the household themselves. Other relatives in extended families, both male and female, contributed wages. Finally, in several instances, wives and mothers produced at home. They took in industrial homework. They became wage laborers but in a context apart from the hierarchical division of labor in the mill or factory, yet controlled by the factory owners through low wages and the unsteady nature of the work.

In chapter 2, I discuss the expansion of the textile economy between 1790 and 1915 and the creation of a class structure composed of mill owners, on the one hand, and workers, on the other hand. Workers, however, were recruited from populations of immigrants of different nationalities creating a divided working class. During its formative period (1790–1865) in Central Falls, the textile industry was at first characterized by small, family-owned mills and an unstable but growing working class. The use of female wage labor in both spinning and

weaving began when mill owners hired daughters of artisan and farming families to work in the mills. In the period just before the American Civil War, immigrant Irish families were pulled into the textile-
labor-force system, in the years following the potato-famine exodus.
Irish daughters joined their Yankee counterparts in the mills but at a
time when work conditions and pay were deteriorating and the labor
force as a whole was becoming increasingly proletarianized.

In the period of expansion in Central Falls (1865–1900), the textile
industry continued to grow, and a well-defined and stable upper class
of mill owners developed. Workers, now from several different ethnic
backgrounds (French, English, and Scottish), were incorporated into
this expanding industrial capitalist economy. Finally, in the period of
stabilization (1900–1920), populations of "new immigrants" (Polish,
Portuguese, and Syrian) came to Central Falls and nearby Pawtucket.
During both periods, there was an expansion of the division of labor in
the mills such that jobs were arranged in an elaborate wage hierarchy
and women and men were incorporated differentially. Thus gender
and ethnicity were used in complex ways to divide workers. By 1915
the privileged jobs in the mills were held by English, Scottish, Irish,
and French-Canadian men (usually fathers), while women (usually
daughters) were employed in "middle-range" jobs, such as spinning,
twisting, creeling, and warp tending. Young men and women (sons
and daughters) were employed in low-paying, entry-level jobs (such as
doffing or sweeping). Only a few women were able to gain entrance to
the higher paying jobs in weaving and drawing-in in the weave room.
Some rooms, such as spinning rooms, were largely female. Here
daughters of the well-established ethnic groups such as the English,
Irish, and French worked. Other rooms included a mix of recent-
immigrant male workers and female labor drawn from more well-
established groups. Gender, age, and ethnicity interacted in complex
ways, but the overall system was one in which men as members of the
earliest ethnic groups were concentrated in the higher paid jobs,
women of all ethnic backgrounds in the middle-range jobs, and men
and women of the "new-immigrant" groups in the lowest paid jobs.

In chapter 3, I examine the lives of working daughters. The expansion of the textile economy and the logic of Central Falls' growth as an
urban area created separate ethnic communities, each with its own set
of institutions. These institutions were formed to deal with the hardships of industrial life, but they also created a sense of community
identity, often in opposition to other ethnic populations. Women's

[33]

social identities were thus defined ethnically as they took part in the neighborhood social institutions that were important to the social reproduction of the Central Falls working class.

If we look at women and their families during these years we can see that incorporation into the mill economy varied from one ethnic group to another. The differential incorporation of immigrants within an expanding economy meant that families of each of the different ethnic groups came to occupy different "economic niches" within Central Falls and Pawtucket. As a result, family strategies for allocating productive and reproductive labor thus varied along ethnic lines as well.

This variation is shown from an analysis of 1915 census data, taken from three ethnic neighborhoods. Originally settled between 1870 and 1890, the French-Canadian neighborhood in Central Falls, by 1915, was a "mature ethnic community." Most parents were foreign born, and many had young teenage sons and daughters. Fathers and sons occupied jobs in the textile and machine-tool industries and even more commonly in the building trades. Most wives and mothers did reproductive work in the home to maintain wage-working household members and to care for young children. A few took in boarders. Most French-Canadian families sent older children, both daughters and sons, into the mills to earn wages. Thus there were two distinct phases of work for women: women as daughters worked for wages in jobs with "intermediate pay" (as spinners, twisters, and winders), while wives and mothers worked inside the home. This pattern of wage-earning daughters and mothers who worked at home in activities that maintained and reproduced labor was common in 1915 among families of Irish and English-Scottish descent in our second neighborhood.

In the third Central Falls neighborhood in 1915, a different set of family strategies marked the newly arrived Polish population. Here the division was between wage-earning single and married women who were boarders and the wives and mothers who acted as "hostesses" and provided the reproductive labor that maintained wage workers. The Polish population was very young in 1915; virtually no one in the neighborhood was over forty-five years of age. Men in our sample (husbands, single men, and the few teenage sons) held the lesser skilled, low-wage jobs in the mills, while women (along with some men) could more readily obtain the more skilled jobs as silk weavers. Women thus supplemented the wages of men in several

[34]

ways. Wives could expand their reproductive work to support other wage earners who paid for room and board. Young women could remain employed after marriage if the couple continued boarding, with much of the reproductive labor that would have been expected of them as a wife done by the "hostess." These couples and the single female boarders supported the reproductive work of the "hostess" through cash payments in return for food and lodging.

In chapter 4 I turn to the last phase in the story of working daughters in Central Falls, examining women at work and in their families during the initial decline of the textile industry (1920–40). Here I analyze women's strategies in a period when mill owners and agents were attempting to extract more labor from workers in the context of the Depression.

At work we see women involved in more and more resistance to employer strategies to deal with the textile-industry crisis. Early in the 1920s, these strategies involved both a reduction of wages and an increase in working hours. Later, mill owners' strategies included tighter organization and coordination through associations, the use of scientific management techniques that led to speedup (working at a faster pace) and stretch-out (tending more machines), and the merger of separate firms. Although women from ethnic communities had been involved in strikes and walkouts before the 1920s and 1930s, this period included a number of large strikes involving women of different ethnic backgrounds in Central Falls and Pawtucket. I focus on the general strike of 1922, the silk strike of 1931 in Central Falls and Pawtucket, and the general strike of 1934.

As we shall see, there was widespread strike participation by women during these years, with evidence of militancy on the part of women from the "newer" ethnic groups, the Portuguese and the Poles. Women from ethnic communities mobilized in support of strikes, but there was also conflict among families of the same ethnic population over this support. The strikes may have provoked periods of "class mobilization" (to use Ewa Hauser's term; see Hauser 1981) rather than ethnic mobilization, but unfortunately we do not know enough about the informal mechanisms that might have created solidarity among women across ethnic lines. All three of these strikes failed to unionize Central Falls textile mills permanently. It was not until the 1937 Textile Workers Organizing Committee drive that mills were unionized. Then, in response to a successful union contract and a protracted strike, two of the largest silk mills in Central Falls were

[35]

liquidated. Small family-run mills that survived this period were able to avoid unionization. The late 1930s and the closing of the big silk mills, however, ended the dominant role of the textile industry in the Central Falls economy.

The economic decline and the closing of mills had an enormous impact on the strategies that families and women used in allocating productive and reproductive labor. By 1935 the new immigrant communities of 1915 had matured and had begun to look more like the French-Canadian, English, and Irish populations. In the Polish neighborhood, for example, boarding declined, and many families were at the stage in the developmental cycle when daughters and sons would have been wage earners. However, in the midst of the Depression, the family strategy of sending daughters into the paid labor force was no longer viable. With a third of the mill labor force unemployed and a third working part time, the youngest and oldest workers were the hardest hit. The Polish neighborhood perhaps suffered the most. In some cases, wives and mothers were able to find work when their husbands, sons, and daughters were unable to do so, although English women were the most successful in getting jobs. Some daughters (primarily English) were staying in school, others were at home, and still others were trying to find work. Nationally, it was not until World War II that many married women began to work in the paid labor force. However, the increasing number of working wives and mothers during the late Depression foreshadowed a trend that developed fully in the 1960s and 1970s.

The incorporation of more working daughters into the labor force in the period between 1870 and 1920 had little impact on the sexual division of labor in the family. Fathers were still the primary breadwinners, especially among young families. Even in families in which sons and daughters were employed and their paychecks added to family income (and the reproduction of their labor), wives and mothers were the ones who continued to do most of the work that transformed purchased commodities into use-values and raised the children. Wage-earning daughters helped with ironing, cooking, and other chores, but the male-female division of labor at home was left largely untouched.

At work, working daughters joined men in labor militancy, but the weakness of textile organizing efforts meant that mills remained unorganized until the late 1930s. Issues that might have challenged the mill wage hierarchy were left untouched as were issues that concerned women workers per se. Tentler (1979) and others have argued that women's position in the family as daughters and the potential of marriage and escape from factory life dampened women's ability to challenge their work situation. I see things differently. The potential for militancy was there, but the unions were unable to convert this into a permanently organized work force for several reasons: the trade union rather than industrial organizing strategy of the United Textile Workers, the mill owners' success in keeping workers divided through the existing pay hierarchy, and the weakness of government efforts like the National Recovery Act (NRA) in failing to provide a climate of support for trade union organization. Although ethnic communities became divided during strikes, many women were indeed willing to walk off their jobs to protest a wage cut, a stretch-out, or a speedup or to demand fairer hours and pay.

Working Mothers

In chapters 5, 6, and 7, I focus on the contemporary period—the era when more and more wives and mothers have joined the labor force in Central Falls. The analysis of the position of Portuguese and Colombian immigrant women in the Central Falls economy in the 1960s and 1970s reveals a number of parallels with the early history of Central Falls. First, there is the continuing theme of the incorporation of immigrant families into different sectors of the economy. Colombians were recruited to the textile industry, while Portuguese migrants were more dispersed over several industries. Thus each group occupied a different "economic niche" within Central Falls. However, since the timing of their migration in relation to the domestic group cycle was the same, with relatively young families with children arriving in the late 1960s and early 1970s, family strategies were similar. The differences were slight, more like those between French-Canadian and English families in 1915 than the sharp contrast that existed between the French-Canadians and Poles at the same period.

A second continuity is the continued importance of the multiworker family. As in the nineteenth and early twentieth centuries, male wages remained low enough that most households needed more than one wage worker to provide for the family's subsistence. Whereas daughters and sons filled this role in the earlier period, wives (and teenage children when present) filled this role in the 1970s. The third

[37]

similarity with the past is that women were still being incorporated as wage workers through their employment in semiskilled, low-wage jobs. This continues a historical pattern of gender division in the textile mill and within industry in general that began, as we have seen, in the early nineteenth century.

The fourth theme of continuity is that immigration in the contemporary period, as in the past, is part of a family strategy to improve the immigrant's economic circumstances. Immigration histories of both Portuguese and Colombian families emphasize this theme, although there are closer parallels between the Portuguese and the rural migrants of the past (Irish, French-Canadians, and Poles). Colombian families are similar to British immigrants in that they came from urban areas. Many Colombian males were skilled textile workers in their own country before immigration. Nevertheless, for both Colombians and Portuguese, continued links to the homeland recalls the immigration histories of earlier populations. Women as wives, mothers, and sisters are often important links in aiding the migration of other family members and in using their kin and neighborhood ties to find housing, jobs, and child care in the United States.

Despite these continuities, there also have been a number of changes in work and family life. One of the most important has been the incorporation of working mothers into the labor force. This transformation needs to be examined in the context of those changes in the Central Falls economy between 1940 and 1965, which set the stage for recruiting new immigrants and for the increasing participation of married women in wage jobs. Chapter 5 deals with these changes, and chapter 6 examines changes in the allocation of productive and reproductive labor in Colombian and Portuguese families as a result of the wife's labor-force participation. Finally, chapter 7 focuses on the organization of productive labor on the shop floor and examines women's strategies in a multiethnic work force in one Central Falls workplace.

In chapter 5, I trace the changes in the Central Falls economy. The Depression brought economic decline to the textile industry and a number of the major silk mills closed in the late 1930s. However, textile mills persisted, and Central Falls and the surrounding Blackstone Valley continue to be the area where the remaining textile industry in Rhode Island is concentrated. Other light industries (apparel, toys, jewelry, and jewelry cases) have moved into the old textile mills, providing wage work for women and some men, while wire-processing plants offer employment to males.

The organization of ownership has also changed. There are no longer large family-run plants. Instead, the remaining large firms have been bought out by multinational corporations or have closed. The majority of factories today are small family-run businesses. Some of them are textile mills that have survived since the decline began, often owned by male members of Central Falls ethnic groups. There are also recently established jewelry firms that are small and family run. In the 1980s Central Falls remains an industrial, working-class community.

In the Vietnam-era upsurge of the economy, textile-mill owners needed skilled workers and recruited them from urban Colombia, primarily from Medellín and Barranquilla. The Protuguese came on their own to Central Falls through chain migration, as part of a wider migration from the Azores to New England. As a result, they are dispersed through various industries. Thus these two ethnic groups occupy different economic "niches" within the local economy, determined by the labor needs of particular industries and the historical period at which they were recruited. Unlike previous ethnic groups who concentrated in specific neighborhoods in Central Falls because their immigration either coincided with the expansion of the community or with the abandonment of neighborhoods by the elite, Portuguese and Colombian families in 1977 had not been able to concentrate in any particular neighborhood but were residentially scattered. However, like their predecessors, both populations formed ethnic associations and attempted to preserve and construct an ethnic identity. For the immigrant Portuguese, this meant amalgamating with second generation Portuguese-Americans and participating in their parishes and associations as well as founding some of their own clubs. For the Colombians, this has meant "starting from scratch" and putting together their own associations, some of which bridge the division within the community between immigrants from Barranquilla and those from Medellín.

Chapter 6 examines how Portuguese and Colombian families reallocated productive labor within the family when wives entered the labor force as well as husbands. This does not mean that daughters are not in the paid labor force. Many Portuguese daughters leave school at age sixteen to work in factories to help support families. But in the families we studied, those with young children, relatively few of the older children had reached school-leaving age. Portuguese and Colombian women arrived in a historically constituted situation where married women of other ethnic groups had been increasing their labor-force participation since the 1940s. The reforms of the 1930s— such as raising the school-leaving age—kept teenage labor out of the job market and helped produce a more educated labor force in the long run. These reforms are not extraneous to growth and change in capitalism. They are part of the processes of incorporating more individuals into wage labor, including more wives, and of upgrading the skills of the labor force to meet the needs of monopoly capitalism for increasing numbers of clerical workers.

The strategy of recent Portuguese and Colombian families in allocating productive work to both husbands and wives thus makes sense in this historical situation. They entered a context in which this was rapidly becoming the norm and where other strategies used in the past (taking in boarders, housing other working relatives) were less viable. Also, the stage of the domestic cycle in which these new immigrant families found themselves meant that few daughters were available for productive work outside the home. But there is also an interaction between productive and reproductive labor here. The nature of reproductive labor, that is, the daily maintenance work that can be labeled housework, has also changed, making cooking, cleaning, washing, and shopping less labor intensive. This has made wives and mothers more available for productive work, even if they continue to do most of the reproductive labor within the home.

Chapter 6 also explores the implications of the wife's labor-force participation for changes in the allocation of reproductive labor within the family and for changes in its balance of power. The interviews with Colombian and Portuguese dual-worker couples indicate two trends. First, female wage earners are adults and have more leverage on family decisions than younger daughters once had. Their absence from home for forty to forty-five hours a week means that someone must fill their place. Hence there have been some transformations in the gender division of labor of housework and child care. Second, in some families there continues to be an emphasis on male authority within the family. The father is still seen as the breadwinner, and family values emphasize the wife's respect for the husband and the children's respect for their father. There are interesting and subtle differences between the Colombian and Portuguese families in the working out of these family values and notions about gender. There is also a good deal of variation within each set of couples both in terms of adherence to a family ideology that emphasizes male authority and in terms of the actual division of labor in the household regarding child care and housework. Males participate in some tasks now that they did not undertake before immigration, yet preserve an ideology of male authority. In general, men's behavior has changed more than have their notions about authority and respect.

Chapter 7 examines women's productive labor in the Central Falls apparel factory where I was employed. I focus primarily on resistance strategies, the ways in which women resist management's attempt to extract more labor from them in a wage-work system. These strategies involve both behavioral and cultural aspects. They include tactics and actions and shared notions and beliefs about work that run counter to those of management. Resistance strategies comprise an important part of women's work culture. As Susan P. Benson and Barbara Melosh put it, work culture includes:

> the ideology and practice with which workers stake out a relatively autonomous sphere of action on the job. . . . A realm of informal, customary values and rules, [work culture] mediates the formal authority structure of the workplace and distances workers from its impact. Work culture is created as workers confront the limitations and exploit the possibilities of their jobs; it is transmitted and enforced by oral tradition and social sanctions within the work group. Generated partly in response to specific working conditions, work culture includes both adaptation and resistance to these structural constraints. (Benson 1986:228)

Another aspect of the strategies I outline is the ways in which they forge links across ethnic boundaries. Whether a work culture primarily becomes one "in resistance" to management or becomes coopted by management depends on the nature of management strategies and the state of a particular industry within the overall economy. As I have argued elsewhere (Lamphere 1985), both management strategies and larger economic and political forces beyond the shop floor in a particular firm or industry may either strengthen or weaken women's initiatives on the shop floor.

During the 1920s and 1930s women's strategies of resistance were best exemplified in numerous strikes and walkouts. These were strategies resulting from management's attempts to cut pay and enforce the stretch-out or from government's persistence in siding with management during the NRA period. From the sources I had available I was able to learn very little about the informal aspects of women's work culture on the shop floor. However, through participant-observation in a contemporary apparel plant, I was able to examine daily the more informal kinds of strategies. In chapter 7, I analyze four of them: (1) socializing new workers in the context of the training program; (2) creating ties among workers in the face of ethnic conflict through "humanizing" and "familizing" the work context; (3) socializing new workers to informal work rules within a department; (4) outguessing new management policy with regard to the organization of production and worker layoffs.

In all four sets of strategies, women's use of cultural notions and their behavioral tactics cut across ethnic lines. We might hypothesize that such strategies (or similar ones) took place in the textile mills of Central Falls in the 1915–40 period, building a foundation for massive resistance as seen in the strikes. Or we might hypothesize that such strategies work better now that many workers are assimilated and English speaking and are able to bring new immigrant workers into a more homogeneous working-class shop-floor culture.

In general, I would argue that characteristics of the present period—the transformation to monopoly capitalism with the increased incorporation of women into the paid labor force—has had greater implications for change in the allocation of productive and reproductive labor in the home than it has had for women's position in the workplace. In the workplace, if anything, women's strategies of resistance are tenuous and have not resulted in a major transformation. This tenuousness, I would argue, is not related to women's family position or cultural values. It arises, rather, from the development of the productive system itself. The key factors are the internal job stratification within industries and between sectors of the economy, the impact of the new international division of labor on women in industrial jobs, and the difficulties of unions, both in the past and present, in combating management's control over wages and the conditions of work.

A focus on production and reproduction elucidates the complex interaction between work and family over a long historical period. The differential incorporation of immigrant populations into a stratified labor hierarchy set the stage for the creation of ethnic communities but also allowed for the possibility of variation in family strategies for dealing with the industrial system, particularly in terms of their allocation of productive and reproductive labor. The historical thrust of industrial growth and decline in Central Falls has meant that the productive system as constituted in the workplace has shaped the family more than issues of reproduction have shaped the workplace. However, the nature of reproductive labor and its allocation in the family has, in some periods, been important. For example, the initial incorporation of young daughters into industrial work was grounded in their "expendability" in the family economy since mothers could absorb the reproductive labor they lost through a daughter's wage job. In the recent period, the changing nature of reproductive labor in the home has supported the incorporation of wives and mothers into the paid labor force.

Within the two overall trends of increasing female labor-force participation and the transformation of the female labor force from working daughters to working mothers, it is important to emphasize variation. The experiences of working women, particularly immigrant women, are shaped by a local economy, the timing of their entrance into it, and the stage of family life cycle in which women find themselves. Cultural values and family ideology may also vary as women use these things to interpret their experiences. The emphasis on strategies, both of women and of the family as a unit, reminds us that immigrant women have not responded to change in a passive way but have actively forged a range of tactics and behaviors to cope with their relationship to the productive system. They have rearranged their family lives at home and resisted management's efforts to control the conditions of their labor in the workplace.

PART II

Working Daughters and Economic Expansion, 1790–1940

[2]

Early Working Daughters:
Pulling Immigrant Families
into the Textile-Mill Economy

Young girls were among the twelve children hired by Samuel Slater during the first year he operated America's first spinning mill in Pawtucket between 1790 and 1791. These early wage-earning daughters, who tended carding machines and dressing and spinning frames, were replaced by young adult women when the textile industry matured during the 1820s. The second-generation women workers were spinners, who tended the more complex spinning frames, and weavers, who operated the new power looms in the small mills that began to dot the streams in Rhode Island (Kulik 1980). They were primarily daughters of impoverished Yankee farm families. Some came to mill towns and boarded with friends or local families. Others migrated with entire families who came to work in the emerging mill system. The fathers were hired as skilled workers, the mothers labored at home, and the children, including teenage unmarried daughters, tended the machines in the mill. As the textile industry in Rhode Island expanded during the post–Civil War period (1865–95) native-born working women were replaced by daughters of immigrant families. In Central Falls the immigrants were Irish, French-Canadian, and English families. In the third period of stabilization (1890–1920) they were followed by families of Polish, Portuguese, and Syrian origin. By 1915 working daughters of different ethnic origin worked beside each other in the textile mills, but they experienced their family, neighborhood, and community relationships in the context of ethnicity.

The incorporation of immigrants into the textile-mill economy coincided with the differentiation of the class structure into a mill-owning capitalist class and a wage-earning working class. During the nineteenth century, the working class became increasingly divided as each new stream of immigrants was incorporated. Working daughters, especially those of Yankee, Irish, and British background, were part of the mill protests and strikes that constituted the more militant responses to mill owners' attempts to cut wages or worsen work conditions.

With the exception of English daughters, wage-earning immigrant women came from rural areas. These French-Canadian, Irish, Polish, and Portuguese women and their parents had been part of a productive family economy—either tenant farmers or rural small-scale producers. The family was a context in which women engaged in both productive and reproductive tasks. The sexual division of labor assigned most of the agricultural tasks to men, and legal systems often supported their dominance within the family in terms of inheritance, property rights, the ability to obtain credit, and ties to the nondomestic world. Wives and daughters produced goods at home for family use or for sale on the market. In other words, they were engaged in productive labor. In addition, they performed reproductive labor that transformed some of the products they grew or purchased into consumable items (cooked meals or made new clothes) or that involved the cleaning and household chores necessary to refurbish those items. This work helped to reproduce their own and their male kin's labor, but women were also engaged in the child-care tasks important in reproducing the next generation. Men were also engaged in reproductive labor since many male tasks in a rural setting (house construction, repair, wood chopping) helped to maintain the family farm and reproduce the family's daily subsistence.

Immigration to Central Falls thus meant a transformation of the family economy from commodity production to a family wage economy in which productive and reproductive labor were increasingly segregated. Productive labor became wage labor and was associated with a workplace. Reproductive labor was associated with the home and family, although most of the wage was spent on commodities to reproduce the labor of both the wage workers and nonwage workers. The labor of wives at home became increasingly confined to reproductive activities, and daughters were increasingly drawn into productive

[48]

work in the mills, though retaining some reproductive responsibilities at home.

As the descendants of immigrants remembered the experience of their parents and grandparents, they described the incorporation of families into a wage economy but also imparted a sense of the strategies families used during this process of incorporation to obtain jobs, to find a place to live, and to create supportive community institutions. Daughters and wives often immigrated as dependents, and some oral accounts emphasized the activities of men, rather than those of their wives and daughters. Overall, family migration strategies seem very similar. Oral histories stressed financial need but also emphasized continued ties to the rural farm and attempts to retain the possibility of return migration. The demographic structure of migration varied from immigrant population to immigrant population; for example, it was predominantly single males and families for French-Canadians and both single males and females as well as young families for the Poles.

In all groups, however, the migration process created a chain of links between kin, with some family members migrating first and providing housing, jobs, and contacts for those who followed. Women tended to migrate as wives and daughters, although some widows and unmarried daughters came independently. Women, once settled in Central Falls, also provided important links for their nieces, cousins, and sisters, as well as for brothers, nephews, and other male kin and their families. The important contrast between women of different ethnic backgrounds was a matter of life-cycle timing, access to housing within an expanding urban environment, and the position of various family members in the local economy. Each population group entered the expanding Central Falls textile economy at a different time and located in a different neighborhood. These dynamics are explored in chapter 3, and the growth of the textile industry and its ability to recruit wage-earning women from differing cultural backgrounds is detailed in this chapter.

Early Wage-Earning Daughters and the Formation of the Textile Industry, 1789–1865

Pawtucket, Rhode Island, next door to Central Falls, was the birthplace of the cotton-textile industry in the United States. Elements of this new productive process were drawn from individuals and groups located throughout the class structure of mercantile capitalism. Capital came largely from merchants, some of whom had already invested in other industries; technical knowledge, from skilled artisans and iron workers; and workers, from the small artisan class and the large rural farm population. Mill-working daughters were recruited from some artisan families but increasingly from the rural farming population.

Moses Brown, a Quaker and member of the prominent Brown family of Providence, financed the first textile mill. The Brown family were not only wealthy merchants, but they owned two important industrial enterprises, a candle works and an iron furnace that manufactured cannon during the American Revolution. In 1789 Moses Brown, with his son-in-law William Almy and his cousin Smith Brown, began to invest in the textile business, buying up the best existing machinery and hiring workers, many of whom were soon employed in hand techniques when it became apparent that the spinning frames would not work. In December 1790 Moses Brown received a letter from Samual Slater, a young English mechanic who had worked thirteen years for Arkwright's firm in England, offering to manage a spinning mill using machinery based on Arkwright's water-powered spinning frames. Slater came to Pawtucket in January 1791. With the aid of a carpenter (Sylvanus Brown) and a skilled iron worker (Oziel Wilkinson), he was able to use his working knowledge of water-powered spinning to construct a working spinning frame within three weeks. On the basis of this first success, Slater agreed to construct additional machinery for a mill. He was offered one-half of the profits and agreed to bear half of the costs as well. Despite technological difficulties, Slater and the skilled artisans he employed were able to build the carding machines, drawing and roving frames, and additional spinning frames and place them in a producing mill by the end of December 1791.[1]

Slater's success was partially due to his own skill but also to the heterogenous nature of Pawtucket's local economy in which mechanics, carpenters, and iron workers were crucial sources of knowledge in building and running the first mill. Also important was the financial backing of Brown and Almy, the firm that for more than a generation had been combining an interest in overseas trade with industrial pro-

---

1. A more detailed and complex account is given in Kulik 1980, chap. 2, and I have relied heavily on Kulik's research for the material in this section.

duction and that increasingly turned family profits away from mercantile activities into industrial development.

The Embargo Act of 1807 and the disruption of overseas trade throughout the War of 1812 provided further impetus to the domestic textile industry. In 1809 Nicholas Brown, a brother of Moses Brown, and Thomas Ives, his son-in-law, because of the decline in their trading business, helped to capitalize one of the largest cotton-spinning companies yet organized in Rhode Island. This venture, the first of several organized by Brown and Ives, eventually made them one of the most powerful textile-manufacturing families in northern Rhode Island. Daughters from the mercantile upper class, as well as from the more modest ranks of mechanics and iron founders who became mill owners, married, and these unions served as important links between men. Business ties between father and son-in-law were common. For example, Moses Brown first established the firm of Brown and Almy in 1789 because of the impending marriage of his daughter Sarah and his desire to have Almy settled "in some satisfactory way" (Kulik 1980:122). This example, like the father and son-in-law link that established the Brown and Ives firm, indicates that a judicious marriage created important kin ties for these men. The same was true for men of more modest means like Samuel Slater, who married the daughter of Oziel Wilkinson.

In contrast, it was before marriage that daughters of artisans and farmers came to play an important role outside of their families—that of workers for the early mills. The early Rhode Island mills actually performed only part of the production of cloth. Until the 1820s bales of cotton were opened and "picked" (to loosen the fibers and remove the dirt) at home by children (Ware 1966:23). In the mill, the cotton was carded, made into "roving" or ropelike spun cotton, and finally spun into thread. The cotton yarn was then bleached, dyed, and distributed to be woven in homes by women or by master male weavers. Thus in this very early period, female children were engaged as outworkers for mills, while older women (both unmarried and married) continued to produce cloth at home.

Slater and others who created the first spinning mills in Rhode Island initially employed children (both boys and girls), since operating the carding machines, roving machines, and spinning frames required relatively unskilled labor. Kulik's careful account of Slater's first efforts to employ children indicates that nine of the workers he hired during his first year of operation were boys and three were girls;

[51]

Girls and women tending carding machines in a nineteenth-century mill. *Progress of Cotton Series* by J. R. Barfoot. Slater Mill Historic Site, Pawtucket, R.I.

several came from artisan families and others from families whose primary source of support seemed to be the labor of children. The young girls (between seven and twelve years of age), like Eunice and Ann Arnold and Ann Jenks, tended carding machines, drawing frames, and spinning frames in Slater's first mill. The boys did similar work, but several seemed to accept work in the mill as a sort of apprenticeship. The monotony and low skill required was a disappointment both to them and their fathers (Kulik 1980:194–201).

There were several conflicts over the children's wages during this initial period of operation, partially since Almy and Brown were late in paying their workers. Fathers tended to be the major partisans in these disputes, rather than the children, but because of their financial needs, they were often unable to succeed either in withdrawing their children's labor or in winning a demand for better pay. Kulik's data show, moreover, that child workers often owed more for rent or for

Men supervised women who tended the drawing frames that transformed a "sliver" of cotton into roving. Progress of Cotton Series by J. R. Barfoot. Slater Mill Historic Site, Pawtucket, R.I.

goods purchased at the local store than could be covered by their meager wages.

The first three working daughters and their male counterparts were from local Pawtucket families, but increasingly, Slater, Almy, and Brown turned to the poor and to rural families outside of Pawtucket for workers. The turnover of children was high during the initial years of the industry, with many working only a few months. Artisans and even local farmers began to see little advantage in the factory labor of their children, since for the boys it did not provide a skilled trade and even for girls the wages were so low that their labor hardly paid the cost of its reproduction. However, among the early workers were some women who clearly had few alternatives to mill work. For example, Rebecca Cole and her four daughters came to Pawtucket in 1795 from a rural area, and she and three daughters were employed in Slater's mill. After a year Mother Cole began operating Slater's "beaching meadow," and Hannah, one of the daughters, eventually became a mule spinner. These two women clearly crossed the divide between female and male jobs, an unusual occurrence but something that was possible in the early years of the industry (Kulik 1980;205–8).

As the local labor pool of children was diminished, mills advertised for families with many children so that the fathers could be hired as skilled workers or find other wage jobs in the community while the children tended the machines (Ware 1966:29; Kulik 1980:204–5). Gary Kulik gave several convincing examples of how difficult it was for families to subsist on the wages of the children and argued that within ten years the mills had created a class of families who, as Almy and Brown described them, "were dependent on daily labor for their support" (quoted in Kulik 1980:210). This system was generally called the "family system" of labor recruitment. For example, in one of Slater's mills in 1816, there were:

> 1 family with 8 members working
> 1 family with 7 members working
> 2 families with 5 members working
> 4 families with 4 members working
> 5 families with 3 members working
> 8 single men
> 4 single women

> (Ware 1966:199)

This system is often contrasted with the boardinghouse, or Waltham, system established in the large, highly capitalized mills in Waltham, Lowell, Lawrence, and other Massachusetts towns. The first of these mills were financed by the Boston Manufacturing Company under the direction of Francis C. Lowell, a wealthy Boston merchant (Ware 1966:60–61). These larger mills used more complex machinery, integrated both spinning and weaving under one roof, and drew for their labor force on a population of young farm women. An older labor force was needed to work the more complex machinery of these larger mills, and the Boston Associates established boardinghouses under the direction of matrons to attract the daughters of Yankee farmers to a system that would be consonant with rural morality. Girls were strictly supervised, church attendance was mandatory, and there was an evening curfew (Foner 1977:xvii). These Massachusetts mill girls left behind a rich written legacy, and the ties created in the boardinghouses and later protests over working conditions have received a great deal of attention by researchers (Dublin 1979, 1982; Eisler 1977; Foner 1977).

Both the boardinghouse system and the family system used the labor of young females but organized the reproduction of their labor power in different ways. In Lowell the company employed women to provide for the food and upkeep of the young workers who paid for their room and board by the week. In Rhode Island unpaid female family members did the cooking, laundry, and housekeeping for young working daughters, who presumably still provided some household labor to help their sisters and mother. Daughters who boarded with families may have aided the females in their host families, washed their own clothes, and cleaned the room where they slept.

The dichotomy between the family system and the boardinghouse system is overdrawn, Kulik has argued (1980:249). There were many similarities in the recruitment of labor and the administration of the mills in Rhode Island and the more northerly mills of Massachusetts and New Hampshire. Differences in technology, mill size, and the type of labor recruitment were much more related to the availability of capital and the sources of local water power than to some overarching commitment to hiring families or recruiting a predominantly female labor force. In addition, Rhode Island was not as conservative and backward in introducing the power loom and other innovations of the early nineteenth century as some writers have argued, perhaps overemphasizing the importance of the Lowell mills in the history of American business and technology. With the rise of the boardinghouse system, the center of the textile industry moved to Massachusetts, and Rhode Island mills, still focusing on yarn production, suffered from the competition.

After 1817 and the invention of a second kind of American-made power loom, more Rhode Island mills brought weaving under the same roof as spinning. Technological changes in the roving and spinning machinery, as well as in the introduction of the power loom, meant that children could no longer be hired to run the fast-paced, newer machines. For example, in Pawtucket child labor decreased from 70 percent of the work force in 1820 to 40 percent in 1831, while the proportion of women increased from 16 to 30 percent and the proportion of men increased from 15 to about 25 percent (Kulik 1978:14). Young women also began to be employed as weavers, but they were recruited within the context of the family system or as

[55]

daughters of men who were artisans and farmers in the industries and farms surrounding the mills. Some daughters lived with their families while employed in the mills; others came from rural areas and board-ed with friends or local families. The experience of working daughters in Rhode Island was certainly very different from that of daughters who boarded and worked in Lowell. The percentage of female weavers who worked alone, without kin in the same mill, was nearly 60 percent in two mills in Providence and Pawtucket. At the Black-stone Mill across the border in Massachusetts, fewer than 10 percent of the weavers were without family in their workplace.

Reasons for the recruitment of unmarried daughters to tend the new power looms and to work as spinners in the textile mills of the 1820s relate to the daughter's position with respect to the allocation of productive and reproductive labor on the rural farm. As the farm economy eroded, the household needed cash to purchase items it no longer produced. The home labor of daughters was less necessary, and their wage employment became more advantageous.

At the same time that young unmarried women (ages fourteen to twenty-four) were being pulled into the mill labor force, women's work at home was being altered by the production of spun-cotton yarn and later cloth. Alice Kessler-Harris noted that "a woman who in 1790 could expect to produce all her own yarn and weave her own cloth found that by 1830 it was hardly worth her while to sit at the loom" (1982:26). In 1825 in New York State women produced nine yards of finished textile goods per person but only four yards by 1835 and only a quarter of a yard by 1855 (Kessler-Harris 1982:26). The result was that the farm family needed female home labor much less and cash much more. Even though the birth rate began to decline, farm fami-lies found it worthwhile to send their daughters into mill work, either to the Massachusetts boardinghouses or to a mill village near their own farm in Rhode Island and Connecticut.

Mill owners sought the cheapest form of labor to run their ma-chines, especially in the early years with the unpredictability of both the machinery and the market. Although mills that used the boar-dinghouse system and the family system were organized along differ-ent principles, sex and age were the primary determinants of the labor hierarchy that developed. The technical requirements of many jobs (at first carding, roving, and spinning and later weaving) made it possible to hire less skilled labor. As Heidi Hartmann pointed out in her historical analysis of the development of occupational segregation,

Drawing-in was one of the highly skilled and best-paid jobs for women in early cotton mills. Progress of Cotton Series by J. R. Barfoot. Slater Mill Historic Site, Pawtucket, R.I.

young women and children could be defined as "cheap labor" because of their position as secondary producers in both the rural farm and urban artisan family. They were individuals who held a less-valued place both in terms of cultural ideology and in the economic rewards that their labor could reap (Hartmann 1976:152–53).

This would certainly have been true for teenage and young adult daughters who came from poor rural families into jobs that had been occupied by children (both boys and girls) such as tending roving, spinning, and carding machines. But the low value of female labor was of special advantage in recruiting females to tend the new power looms. Daughters would work for much less, as much as half the wages a male would demand. This followed from the difference between women as subordinates in rural households versus the position of males as heads or potential heads of households. In addition, male hand weavers had already attained a skill they were unwilling to degrade through the acceptance of lower wages. Daughters, on the

[57]

other hand, had no experience as apprentices or wage laborers; this meant that they had no articulate standards of customary pay and no clear sense of a fair day's work (Kulik 1980:344). They were willing to work at the wages mill owners offered, given the lack of other good alternatives.

A wage hierarchy developed early in the mills, where men were hired for the very few skilled jobs (as second hands, overseers, and mule spinners), while daughters and children were hired to tend most of the other machines. Thus in Lowell in the 1830s wage-earning daughters made $1.90 a week plus board, which amounted to another dollar a week, while men made an average of $0.80 a day or $4.80 for a six-day week. Family mills, more typical in Rhode Island, paid in credit and often held back pay for weeks at a time, so neither males nor females may have reached the wage levels paid in Lowell. The male-female differentiation was present, however, with women earning half as much as men (Kessler-Harris 1982:37). Thus the pattern was set for paying female labor at a lower rate, a pattern that continued throughout the history of textiles in New England even when immigrant daughters replaced Yankee mill girls.

There seems to be a complex relationship between the working daughter's rural background and her potential for resistance. Kulik has argued that their work experience in the paternalistic and kin-centered rural economy gave an objective reality to mill owners' attitudes that young women without industrial or artisan experience were much more easily managed than men. As one preacher put it, "Women are much more ready to follow good regulations and are not captious, and do not clan as the men do against their overseers" (quoted in Kulik 1980:343). But this is not the full picture. Rural values of independence fostered a resistance to wage cuts or policies that threatened that independence.

The Emerging Class Structure and Female Protest

Wage-earning daughters in Rhode Island were part of families that were experiencing proletarianization and the emergence of a class structure that opposed mill owners and their employees. In the pre–Civil War period this class structure was not rigid. There was a great deal of turnover in mill ownership, with many men loosing their positions as they were caught in the series of economic crises that

[58]

became part of the business cycle. In addition, many men were able to remain as farmers or artisans, relatively independent of the mill economy, and most children and teenage daughters worked at home rather than in the mills.

The mill-owning class emerged from several different segments of the late eighteenth-century class structure. Mill owners did not gain cultural hegemony over working-classss communities in the pre–Civil War period (see Kulik 1980; Kulik and Bonham 1979). An examination of the beginnings of what became the largest mills in the Blackstone Valley surrounding Central Falls shows a variety of patterns of ownership and growth. The two branches of the Brown family were important in financing Slater's mill and the Blackstone Company, but members of farming and commercial families, as well as upwardly mobile mechanics and self-taught engineers, also became part of the growing network of mill owners. Almost all were from old New England families of Quaker, Baptist, or Congregational background. Some had family histories that dated from the period of the Mayflower or to Roger Williams's settlement in Rhode Island. Kin connections were also important. Sons of men who established mills were trained in their father's, brother's, or other relative's mills and went on to establish mills of their own. Men who were born in the 1820s and 1830s and who established mills in the 1850s and 1860s often had some formal education and may have had experience in a commercial house rather than in skilled mechanical jobs. Those men whose fathers had established themselves in business were able to step into or start new firms with the help of family expertise and capital. By the 1850s and 1860s mills that were surviving the cycle of crisis and growth were the basis of wealth that supported a distinct and stable upper class.

Mill owners reacted to the business cycle (a decline in the price of cotton, which led to an overproduction of yarn and cloth; a glutting of the market; and a depression in the industry) by cutting wages or increasing the speed of the machines. During the period 1820–60 the price of cotton cloth dropped, and profits for mill owners fell. At the same time, there were tremendous changes in technology with the invention of several new machines. As mill owners pressed workers to work faster and increase output, work conditions deteriorated, and there was relatively little compensation in the form of raised wages (Ware 1966).

One of the first reactions on the part of workers to deteriorating conditions was the 1824 Pawtucket strike led by wage-earning daugh-

[59]

ters. Women's strategy here was to withdraw their labor. Mill owners, in reaction to losses from the declining price of cotton and two summers of drought, decided to cut the piece rates of the women weavers and to increase their hours. "On the morning of the strike, over one hundred female weavers met, selected a leader, and vowed not to return to the mills until the old rates were restored" (Kulik 1983:4). They were joined by their families, other workers, artisans, and villagers who paraded through the streets and kept the mills shut for a week. During this period a fire broke out in one of the mills. The mill was saved, but the mill owners drafted a public statement calling for a solution to the strike. Three days later, a compromise had been reached, and workers were back in the mills. Although the nature of the compromise remains unknown, we may guess that the women's actions were successful.

Kulik has argued that their success was related to support from their families and the local working-class community. Pawtucket was a heterogeneous community of artisans, mill workers, and farmers whose daughters were often mill workers. They had developed an "oppositional culture" and had not acquiesed to the docility required of the mill owners' churches or Sunday schools. When work in the mills became oppressive for young female workers, their resistance gained the support rather than the rejection of their fathers, brothers, and unrelated male coworkers. "Unlike the young mill women of Lowell, who developed strong and cohesive ties to each other, but had none to the local community (and who consequently lost their strikes of the early 1830s), the weavers of Pawtucket not only drew strength from each other, but from the community as well" (Kulik 1978:19). In other mill villages in Rhode Island, protest was less likely since mill owners controlled a greater share of the local job market and often mill housing and the company store as well.

Central Falls, 1790–1860: From Chocolate Mills to Textile Mills

While wage-earning daughters in Pawtucket were part of a situation more clearly demarcated by a developing industrial elite and an opposing working class, the mill girls in Central Falls, adjacent to Pawtucket, were still part of the small-scale development that characterized the surrounding industrializing areas. In 1820 Central Falls was still a small settlement, situated on a falls in the river where a

View of Falls from Cross. St. Bridge, Central Falls, R. I.

The "central" falls of the Blackstone River, which provided water power for the industrializing nineteenth-century village of Central Falls. Courtesy of the Rhode Island Historical Society.

cluster of mills and houses were located. The river's water power had first been used for a snuff mill. After a dam had been constructed in 1780, a local tool manufacturer had been able to start a forge, part of which had been used to make chocolate. This gave the name "Choco-lateville" or "Chocolate Mills" to the settlement (Kennedy 1978:7).

In 1823, because of repeated disputes over water rights, the Mill Owners Association was formed, and six "privileges" were set up with access to the water from the river. During the 1820s these six water-power privileges were occupied by spinning and weaving operations. "Chocolate Mills" had become a series of textile mills. The emerging mill-owning class, typical of the region, came from Protestant farming and small-business backgrounds, although none of these families was as well off as those in Pawtucket.

The Jenks family, which traced its ancestry in New England to 1645, acquired what later became Privilege 1 in 1807. Here they built a machine shop and later, at Privilege 6, a cloth mill. In the next generation, the son and son-in-law founded a textile machinery firm (Fales and Jenks), which eventually moved to the west side of Central Falls and became one of the largest machinery firms in the area (Kulik 1978; Grieve 1897:20). Members of another branch of the Jenks family built a textile mill on Privilege 2 in 1824. Later in 1839 one of their brothers, with the help of his son-in-law and the son-in-law's brother, began operating a mill on Privilege 5.

The Wilkinsons, who helped Slater start his first spinning opera-tion, in 1822 established a mill near Valley Falls, just up the river from the mills at Chocolate Mills. They closed the mill after being ruined in the depression of 1829. The area remained underdeveloped until the Chace brothers from Pawtucket bought the property in 1849 (Ken-nedy 1978:8). Men from two other families became mill owners in the 1850s. Benjamin Greene, a descendent of a famous Rhode Island general, Nathanael Greene, worked as a second hand in one of the Central Falls mills beginning in 1824. Eventually, he became an over-seer and then started manufacturing thread in mills where others invested the capital. In 1855 he went into partnership with a book-keeper, Horace Daniels, and leased the mill on Privilege 6 to man-ufacture thread. In 1866 they moved across the river, building a new mill. It became one of the largest employers in Central Falls and the adjoining portion of Pawtucket during the end of the nineteenth century.

These early mill owners were all men from old New England families. They had work experience in mills before beginning businesses that survived and expanded. Kin ties between fathers and sons or sons-in-law, or between brothers and brother-in-law, were important in putting together the capital and expertise to begin their new enterprises. It was the marriage potential of daughters from these families, rather than their labor power, that was crucial to class formation. Women were important links between men. Family ties also became business ties.

Less is known about the Central Falls working class and the role of wage-earning daughters. As in Pawtucket, young women, children, and even older men who were heads of families were probably recruited from impoverished farm families throughout the state as they found it more and more difficult to survive. Just before the Civil War, the size of mills and the number of workers increased. "It is estimated that in 1832 about 500 people were employed in manufacturing; by 1850 there were 800 and over 1000 in 1860. Many of the workers were women and children who were paid lower wages than men. In 1850, for example, the Chace family employed 210 workers—90 men and 120 women; Benedict and Wood employed 13 men (whose wages averaged $13 a month) and 27 women (who earned an average of $11). Most employees in the textile industry worked a six-day week, twelve to fourteen hours a day" (Kennedy 1978:13).

It is difficult to tell if working families developed an "oppositional culture" that set them apart from the mill-owning class. There is no evidence of strikes like the Pawtucket strike of 1824, although young females employed as weavers and spinners were no doubt feeling the continued deterioration of working conditions without an increase in wages. Central Falls was more heterogeneous than smaller mill villages in the Blackstone Valley to the north. There, one mill owner often controlled housing, a store, and the local church and thereby wielded a greater degree of hegemony and power over his employees than did the Central Falls privilege holders.

Some Central Falls mill owners, however, did own nearby housing, which was rented to working families, and they also built their own Baptist and Congregational churches in the developing commercial area. Nevertheless, the mill owners did not seem to have acted in concert in lowering wages or speeding up work and hence did not provoke a communitywide reaction among young women workers. It is also possible that the male artisan and worker tradition was weaker in Central Falls than in Pawtucket, producing no strong group of male

[63]

workers threatened by the mill owners' power and willing to support young women workers or organize a protest themselves. In addition, Central Falls' more proletarianized and poorer farm families may have felt more vulnerable and less able to resist the actions of a particular mill owner.

The Coming of the Irish and the Beginnings of a Divided Working Class

The great influx of Irish immigrants into New England and Central Falls in the 1840s and 1850s had a major impact on the labor force employed in the mills. It created a more permanent working class but one that was divided between Yankee and immigrant. Yankee families had experienced the process of incorporation into a wage economy through sending their children and young daughters into the mills or perhaps being incorporated as an entire family. The experience was often temporary, with the possibility of leaving mill life still open. This was especially true for the Lowell girls before 1840; they were able to enter the mills to broaden their own experiences and save for marriages or future education (Dublin 1979:30–40). Escaping mill employment was less likely under the family system in Rhode Island in which daughters' wages supplemented the income of families of impoverished farmers or those who had already been pushed off their land into mill villages. Anthony Wallace (1978:65) has argued that mill-worker families in Pennsylvania through the 1840s were often able to save money and leave mill life to buy farms in the Midwest. This may also have happened in New England, as well, especially during the agricultural depression of 1837–40, which forced families out of farming and also out of the region (Ware 1966).

For Irish immigrants, and for the French-Canadians, Poles, and Portuguese who followed them decades later, the story was different. Their historical trajectory was one of proletarianization and incorporation into a wage economy. Becoming a family dependent on wages coincided with entering an alien country where they were marked as different in religion, speech, and cultural heritage. For the Irish the transformation from rural, semi-independent producers to dependent wage workers in an urbanizing environment was irreversible. It also placed them at the bottom of the wage hierarchy and gave them limited access to housing.

[64]

Although more than one million men and women left Ireland before 1845, the flow of immigrants to England and the United States increased fourfold in the potato-famine years that followed (Groneman 1978:257; Lees and Modell 1977:401). Prefamine migrants tended to be males or families, but in the postfamine years an increasing number of single young women joined the migration and located primarily in New York City (Groneman 1978:260–62). There were Irish immigrants in New England during the 1830s, but it was not until after 1840 that they began to take jobs as mill workers.

In Central Falls, Irish males first worked in railroad and canal construction. As they settled in the community, they eventually found work in the mills and stores. By 1860 the Irish were a significant part of the town's labor force. Most Irish immigrants were from rural areas. Many of the women had worked on their families' small plots of land or as hired agricultural laborers when farm income declined (Groneman 1978:259).

Sources on the Rhode Island Irish are few. Thomas Dublin's study of Lowell suggests a number of trends that may have taken place in Rhode Island as well. The presence of an Irish labor force that would accept jobs for lower pay meant that (1) men began to replace women in mill jobs, particularly weaving; (2) the distinction between men's and women's jobs began to blur; (3) wages of the lowest-paid men and the highest-paid women overlapped; and (4) Irish women were placed in the low-paying carding and spinning jobs while Yankee women received preference for the weaving and dressing jobs. As the proportion of Yankees declined in the mills, new improvements in machinery allowed owners to run machines at a faster pace and to deskill the jobs of those who remained. All of these developments contributed to the "proletarianization" of the female labor force (Dublin 1979:160). Irish daughters, in greater numbers than daughters of Rhode Island farm families, brought home wages to supplement those of their unskilled laborer and low-paid mill-worker fathers.

In Rhode Island, as in Lowell, the presence of the Irish added ethnicity to the age and sex hierarchy in the mills. This created conflict among wage-earning daughters. "Native-born and immigrant alike were exploited by the changing conditions in the mills, but the fact that the native-born were likely to blame the newcomers for their plight made the prospect of united protest unlikely" (Dublin 1979: 162).

Beyond the mills, there is ample evidence of class, not ethnic, conflict on the political level, with Yankee and Irish working-class men united against landowners. The Dorr War, for example, an unsuccessful uprising in 1842 led by Thomas Dorr, would have given voting rights to working men by eliminating the property qualification for voting. The movement included many Irish supporters, but this unity between the newcomers and Yankee workers did not seem to reverberate in the workplace. Nor is there good evidence for either conflict or unity among Irish and Yankee working daughters.

Irish wage-earning daughters, however, did participate on their own in workplace protest in Rhode Island. On March 24, 1859, eight Irish women led by a worker called "Black Bridget" struck for higher wages at the Georgiaville Mill in southern Rhode Island, one of a series of strikes in 1858–59 that followed the Panic of 1857 and its many mill closings. Workers realized that mill owners were profiting from the improved conditions of 1858 while wages remained low and company stores continued to overcharge. Zachariah Allen, the overseer, ended the strike by firing the female Irish speeder tenders and hiring new workers. Commenting on the Irish militancy, Allen wrote in his diary that Black Bridget and her sister were "so passionate . . . in attacking abusively all those who do not comply with their wishes that they seem to be deranged at times" (Hoffman and Hoffman 1983:14). Black Bridget and her sister had to leave the area since all housing was owned by the mill, the single source of employment. Their militant actions also made it unlikely they would find employment at nearby mills. The harshness of employer sanctions gives a clue as to why no Irish-led protests or strikes occurred in Central Falls in the same period.

By the advent of the Civil War, the textile industry had come to dominate the Central Falls economy. Mills grew from an average of 85 workers in 1850 to 106 in 1860 as more steps in the production of cloth became industrialized. The conversion from water to steam power and the construction of the railroad meant that mills could relocate away from the river, thus opening new areas for residential and commercial expansion. The outlines of a class structure separating mill owners from mill operatives, with ethnic (Yankee versus Irish) divisions within the working class as well, had developed by the time of the Civil War. These changes set the stage for further industrial expansion and the incorporation of additional ethnic groups in the post–Civil War period.

[66]

Central Falls during the Age of Expansion

The period between 1865 and 1895 was characterized by the tremendous expansion of the textile industry. The Civil War itself provided enormous profits. At first Rhode Island financial interests supported the South, but once war was declared, mill owners enthusiastically churned out cloth for Union uniforms and other war-related items (McLaughlin 1978:146). The companies owned by Brown and Ives, for example, profited enormously; the boom continued, and during 1871 family members made profits amounting to 65 percent of their capitalization (Hedges 1968:259). With such returns the Brown family was able to build a number of new brick mills along the Blackstone River Valley.

This expansion had two consequences. First, the Central Falls and Pawtucket families who controlled the most important textile mills of the Blackstone Valley consolidated into a wealthy and powerful upper class. They built sumptuous houses and financed the building of churches, libraries, and even university lecture halls. Second, the building of new mills and the expansion of old ones meant the need for more workers, both male and female. This labor was provided through the continued immigration of Irish families and by a new influx of French-Canadian and English families into Central Falls and the mill towns of the Blackstone Valley. This multiethnic labor force did not mingle and blend into a unified working class. The reasons for this are complex. Among them were the patterns of urban growth, the contrast between the Protestant English and the Catholic Irish and French-Canadians, and the tensions that developed between French and Irish over Irish domination of Catholic institutions. Despite the proletarianization of all workers and the continued deterioration of working conditions and wages, the organization of labor in the textile mills themselves—with the domination of the English and Scottish in the higher paying male jobs and the use of age, gender, and ethnicity to divide the labor force—operated to prevent bonds from developing.

In Central Falls the local upper class was less affluent and owned smaller mills than did the upper class in Pawtucket. Nevertheless, it came to dominate the political and cultural life of the town, leaving its mark on the architectural quality of the city. In 1863 the machine company owned by Fales and Jenks was moved to a new three-story brick mill adjacent to the railroad. As the march of industry away from

The Central Falls Woolen Mill (1870) and the Stafford Mill (1824, 1860s) created an impressive industrial river front, along with a new dam and power trenches rebuilt by Rufus Stafford. Pawtucket Public Library.

the river continued, they soon moved a second time to an even larger site near the new Conant Thread Mill on the west side of Central Falls. Their landholdings near the railroad were taken over by the Sprague family, one of the most prominent in Rhode Island. Between 1865 and 1873 they hired numerous French-Canadian immigrants since their mills were near the developing French neighborhood. When the Panic of 1873 brought about their financial ruin, the Sprague family was forced to sell the mill. Although the Spragues' presence in Central Falls was brief, their financial interests touched on and even controlled the lives of working-class residents in the city.

New mills continued to be built along the river during the 1860s. Rufus Stafford built a dam over the river, organized the Stafford Manufacturing Company, and acquired the mill at Privileges 1 and 2. A woolen company took over the old Fales and Jenks mill at Privilege 4, and a newly formed "hair cloth" company built a three-story brick mill in 1866 in Privilege 6 (Kennedy 1978:20). Greene and Daniels moved their thread mill across the river to a new five-story building.

These same families also built substantial houses in the southern part of the city. Stafford built an impressive house near the Congregational Church, not far from the house built by David Fales. Other houses, like the Benjamin Greene mansion, Horace Daniels' house, and the home of Hezekiah Conant, were built farther away from the business and commercial center. The Daniels house was later inhabited by D. G. Littlefield, who helped form the American Hair Cloth Company and who later became lieutenant governor of Rhode Island.

With the expansion of the mills came a parallel growth in the labor force. "It is estimated that in 1860, 1059 people worked in the industries of Central Falls and by 1870 that number had almost doubled to 2253. Eight years later, the figure was 2641—an indication of the slackened pace of growth [due to the depression period of the 1870s]" (Kennedy 1978:20).

The town's population increased to 9,052 in 1870 and 15,828 in 1895 (Community Focus 1976:6). The influx of workers brought a building boom, and many "three-decker" houses were built for mill-working families. The French-Canadians and the English made up most of the new immigrants. Both groups, one rural and one urban, were pushed from their native homelands to the United States because of local economic conditions exacerbated during the period 1870–90.

The French-Canadian Migration and Family Strategies

There are important similarities between the migration of French-Canadian women and that of Irish women several decades earlier. Wives and daughters came as part of family groups (although a substantial proportion of Irish immigrants were single women and many of the early French-Canadians were men). Both populations were from rural Roman Catholic backgrounds marked by severe overpopulation and land fragmentation. Immigration brought families into urbanizing areas dominated by the textile-mill economy. Daughters were recruited to the mill labor force, as were their brothers and fathers, although French-Canadian men also worked in the building trades, just as some Irish men had been employed as laborers in building canals and railroads. Wives and mothers were needed at home to carry the burden of housework and child care, helped by older children and mill-working daughters in the evenings and on Sundays.

Historical sources make clear the basis for migration as part of a family strategy for bettering their economic situation. French-Canadian oral-history accounts reveal the way in which migrating families constructed their family's migration as a balance between financial need and the desire to retain a connection with rural Canada. Wage labor was viewed as an alternative to rural poverty, but family members often came as part of a Canadian-Rhode Island "chain." They often used kin ties in locating jobs and housing, and members of a kin network relocated in small towns throughout northern New England with others following at a later date. Women were important actors in forging these links, as were male kin.

French-Canadian immigration to the United States was fueled by French policies, which gradually led to an impoverished rural population too large for its land base. In the seventeenth century, most rural "habitants" were peasant farmers who had semifeudal relationships with the "seigneurs" who had been granted large tracts of land by the Crown. Under this system, less rigid than in Europe, many peasants acquired land rights during the eighteenth century. At the same time, the Crown encouraged population growth and expansion into uncolonized areas by offering "bounties" to those who married early and by importing young girls to marry available males (Miner 1939:4–5).

After French-speaking Canada came under British rule, the population could no longer expand into new areas. Within a hundred years agricultural lands became fragmented and overpopulated (Conley and Smith 1976:135). With English domination, French villages not only fought for economic survival but for cultural "survivance," the preservation of their religion, language, and culture. "'La foi et la langue' became the twin pillars supporting French Canadian cultural persistence. The bond between language and faith became inseparable" (Conley and Smith 1976:134).

Although the first French-Canadian immigrants to New England were political refugees from the failed 1837 Quebec insurrection, many more arrived during the Civil War when mill owners needed to replace the men called away to war (Lawrence 1931:216). Mill owners actively recruited French workers by sending bilingual employees to Canada, hiring French-Canadian agents, advertising in Canadian newspapers, and using railroad agents as recruiters (Hareven and Langenbach 1978:19; Ducharme 1943:36, 38–39).

At first French-Canadians migrated to the northern parts of New England. Only later did they gradually move to Massachusetts and Rhode Island. The migration slowed after the Panic of 1873 but picked up again in the 1880s and peaked in the 1890s (Wessel 1931:193, 188, figure 5). French-Canadian men were willing to work for low wages at the dirtiest, noisiest, and most difficult jobs in the textile mills (Conley and Smith 1976:135). They won a reputation as "the Chinese of the East," often being used as strikebreakers. Initial recruitment was of male labor, but when men brought their wives and young children, daughters as well as sons went to work in the mills upon reaching fourteen years of age.

Even until the 1880s and 1890s, much French-Canadian migration may have been seasonal. There were two patterns. Some families came in late fall, seeking winter work in the factories, and returned to their Quebec farms in the spring and summer. Alternatively, young unmarried men remained on the family farms in the winter and then traveled to New England in the spring and summer to cut wood, do construction work, or work in brickmaking. They would save their earnings to help pay their own or their families' debts on the farm (Bonier 1920). Repeated seasonal migration brought migrants to several employment centers before their final settlement in Rhode Island.

Oral-history interviews conducted by Marcel Dufresne with Central Falls French-Canadians give us their reconstruction of the immigration of their grandparents. Grandfathers and fathers of these interviewees—individuals from small business or trade background as well as several cultural leaders (priests, nuns, schoolteachers, and credit-union employees)—may have had a better start in the United States than the average mill worker or carpenter. These accounts of immigration, however, reveal patterns common to the French population. On the one hand, these interviews emphasize the French-Canadian need for cash and a willingness to become incorporated into the wage economy in response to deteriorating conditions on the farm. On the other hand, they stress family efforts to retain land in Canada, either through seasonal migration or through sending only a few family members to the United States. This dual allegiance to both a Quebec farm and wage labor in the United States meant that members of a sibling group or larger kin network were spread from a home village in Canada to several locations in New England. Men seemed to be the major actors in migration stories, either coming as young individuals or as heads of families, but women as sisters, aunts, and wives often served as important links for new families who would arrive to find work and establish themselves in a community like Central Falls. The major exception was nuns who migrated as part of their order. They served as teachers in the early French New England communities and provided links to New England for members of their families who later migrated.

Several men and women spoke of the financial necessity of immigration and of the importance of wage labor in the mill economy as an alternative to rural poverty. Immigration was part of a family strategy of survival and even betterment. As one interviewee stated: "Grandfather immigrated here because he was a farmer. There, farmers were having a tough time, especially in getting very little for their work. I mean meat, wool . . . they were selling pork at the time. . . . I think all they were getting for that was three cents a pound."

Another man, whose family immigrated to Massachusetts, returned to Canada, and later came to Rhode Island, concurred: "The reason we came was lack of money. We were on a farm and there was no money, so I suppose my folks decided to come here like a lot of others that were their sisters and brothers . . . and friends. It was an immigration."[2]

Even small tradesmen were in financial difficulties, as the son of a man who made butter and cheese recounted: "And through some bad deals, through inspectors, there was a lot of competition in that field . . . so we lost most of our money. And I had an uncle who lived in Central Falls and also an aunt. So being a big family, we decided to come to Central Falls because there were a lot of mills. And they [his brothers and sisters] got to the age of working at fourteen. . . . One at a time, they were ordered to start supporting the family."

These accounts show the importance of kin, both male and female, in providing the connections needed for a family to immigrate. They also illustrate the way in which daughters and sons were pulled into the mill economy as they reached working age. Other interviews stress not only economic need but a continued allegiance to the farm. "The reason they [French-Canadians] came here in the winter time

2. These and other quotes in this section are taken from the Central Falls French-Canadian Oral History Project. Interviews were conducted by Marcel Dufresne and are available at the Central Falls library. I have omitted names or given pseudonyms to individuals to be consistent with my policy of not using the real names of living people in this book.

[was] so that they could go work in the mills and make a little money and sublet their farms in the winter to someone who stayed there. Or one of the family would stay. They'd come here and make a little money. In the spring they'd go back to their farming."

Actual histories of family migration show how families became dispersed, and how one sibling might become the nucleus of a reconstituted household after arriving in Central Falls. The Tessier family left Canada in the 1880s and traveled to a Massachusetts town to work in the mills. The father, mother, two sons, and newborn daughter "didn't stay long because it was mostly an Irish town." A third son remained and became a carpenter and draftsman, but the rest of the family moved to Valley Falls, just north of Central Falls. The second son married and moved to two other towns in the area before finally settling in Central Falls with his mother, wife, and five young children.

In another family, the youngest son became a hat maker. He left Quebec in the 1870s and with two other siblings traveled to a Massachusetts hat-making center. He arrived there during a hat-maker's strike and soon decided to continue to Central Falls where relatives were already established. He eventually found work in a lumberyard in a town near Central Falls. Three of his siblings remained in Canada: the eldest brother who inherited the farm, a sister who married there, and a sister who entered a convent.

In most cases, individual men or male heads of families took the lead in immigration. In others, however, women, especially widows, migrated with their children. For example, a widow lived with her three children in a New England paper-mill town where her recently deceased husband had run a small store with his father and brother-in-law. With no way of earning a living, she asked a traveling salesman if he knew of a "good French community" where she could relocate and open a small store herself. His answer brought her to Central Falls where she set up a small business. Here a woman made an active choice to immigrate within New England, relying on ties of ethnicity rather than of kinship.

In another case of French-Canadian ethnic rather than kin linkage, a woman provided the possibility for a stranger to remain in Central Falls. Again this indicates how similarities in cultural heritage made possible bonds within the working class, although this in turn divided one segment, the French, from others, the Irish or English. "[There is] one incident about someone [my grandparents] knew. . . . [A man]

[73]

came down along without his family and he said to [my grandmother], 'If you want to feed me, I'll be willing to sleep in the cellar at night and have my meals with you.' She agreed even though she didn't know the man really well except that he came to her and asked, could she do that. She said yes, and when he found work and everything, he paid her back for the meals she had fed him and all."

Since kinship and ethnicity were such important factors in helping to place French-Canadian families in the Central Falls mill economy, it is not surprising that these ties would be important in finding housing, building institutions, and creating a well-defined French community within Central Falls.

The English-Scottish Immigration

At the same time that increasing numbers of French-Canadians were joining Irish workers in Central Falls, another group of very different background were also becoming part of the textile labor force: English and Scottish workers. Unlike the French-Canadians and Irish, the English and Scottish immigrants came from urban areas and had previous industrial work experience (Erickson 1972:30–31). Since many English and Scottish workers began to move out of industrial occupations or to place their children in clerical, teaching, and other white-collar occupations by 1900 or 1910, it has been harder to learn much about the experiences of English working daughters in Central Falls. The institutional centers of English life—the churches, clubs, and taverns—were largely clustered in towns and mill villages bordering on Central Falls, and British labor militancy was evident in Blackstone Valley mill villages rather then in Central Falls itself. By 1935 there were few English and Scottish families in our neighborhood samples. All of these factors make it difficult to reconstruct the English presence in Central Falls.

Like the French-Canadians, the English migration seemed to be a family one, although a number of single men came to the United States in the 1870s and 1890s. The proportion of families declined in the 1890s owing to an economic slump on both sides of the Atlantic but picked up again during the prosperous years after 1900 (Thomas 1973:58–68). In New England, English and Scottish migration primarily meant incorporation into the textile industry. Most of the men had previous experience as mill workers. Among English male textile operatives, 70 percent had worked in textiles before immigration and among the Scottish, 39 percent held such jobs (Berthoff 1953:23). At first, the United States attracted both skilled and unskilled male workers in similar proportions (Thomas 1973:59), but after 1895 the unskilled share declined as southern and eastern European migrants crowded out unskilled British migrants. The skilled British immigrants continued to dominate the skill hierarchy in the Rhode Island mills.

As early as the 1870s British men filled a substantial number of the skilled positions in Blackstone Valley mill towns such as Ashton and Lonsdale, north of Central Falls. These male workers, like those in Fall River and New Bedford, found conditions in American mills harsher than those to which they had been accustomed. Mule spinners had only one assistant rather than two, and weavers had to tend eight looms rather than four. Machines were run at a faster pace, and in the mule-spinning room, men were pushed to outproduce one another as each spinner's productivity record was posted visibly on a chalk slate (Berthoff 1953:35). One Fall River spinner commented, "I always thought they were tyrants at home. . . . We could always make a complaint of any grievance there. But here . . . we are told that if we don't like it, we can get out" (Berthoff 1953:35).

Resentment against the superintendents and overseers mounted in the Blackstone Valley mill towns (Buhle 1977:47). In 1876 a one-third cut in wages provoked a strike among Lonsdale workers, many of them British. Women weavers walked out and led a march from mill to mill, spreading the strike. Other strikes followed in the next few years, as did an attempt to form a national organization of cotton and wool operatives (Buhle 1977:47). Working daughters were as active in these protests and organizing efforts as were their fathers and brothers. The industrial background of the older male British workers may have led to their participation in these strikes, but working daughters must have been activated by the deteriorating conditions in the mills as well as by prounion sentiment in their families.

British workers actively participated in the Knights of Labor in the 1880s. They established local "assemblies" including a heavily supported one in Central Falls. The Knights engaged in many community activities and had the support of both Irish and British clubs and associations. Their newspaper reported the activities of local British immigrants in foot races, marching drills, and organized cricket clubs and featured a feminist columnist as well (Buhle 1977:57). The Knights also organized a mothers' group and started a day-care center in a working-class neighborhood in Providence. The Knights' candidates met defeat in 1886 elections because many workers were still disenfranchised by the Rhode Island property requirement, and nationally, the Knights were blamed for the Haymarket riots of that year. They also lost several important strikes in Rhode Island because of well-organized counterefforts by manufacturers who, among other things, blacklisted Knights members. However, the Knights represented a significant attempt to consolidate ethnic institutions and clubs into a wider, multiethnic working-class culture. Their failure was a setback to the possibility of a united working class.

Little is known about the British in Central Falls in this period, beyond their numbers and distribution. By 1895 there were 3,580 French-Canadian, 2,022 English and Scottish, and 1,504 Irish residents.

> These three early ethnic groups, French-Canadians, English, and Irish, retained their numerical superiority over the next twenty-five years. Many of these immigrants and their children lived near their countrymen in ethnically cohesive neighborhoods where family, language, and customs were maintained. The central portion of Central Falls, for example, was the home of much of the Irish population, the French-Canadians tended to settle in the eastern and western sections of the city; the English were concentrated in the south. (Kennedy 1978:40)

In 1895 Central Falls became politically independent from the neighboring, largely rural town of Lincoln. This was not through its own doing. The rural landowners and those who controlled the small mill villages voted overwhelmingly to set Central Falls free. Thus Central Falls became incorporated as an independent city, home to a working-class, largely Catholic, foreign-born population from the British Isles, Ireland, and French Canada.

The Period of Stabilization and the New Immigrants

Between 1895 and 1915 the textile industry began to stabilize. The large firms maintained their preeminence, controlled by a small millowning elite. Two major technical innovations, the advent of the high-speed loom in 1895 and the replacement of mule spinning by ring spinning, made it possible to increase production and enlarge the size of existing mills. More workers were hired, especially during the boom years of 1900 to 1904 and in 1915, as the impact of World War I began to be felt.

During this period the demand for new workers was filled by immigrants from southern and eastern Europe. Between 1895 and 1915 the population of Central Falls increased from 15,838 to 23,708 and became still more diversified ethnically. In nearby Pawtucket, the new mill workers were Italian or Greek; in Central Falls, they were Polish and Syrian. Also in Pawtucket, the Portuguese first entered service and laboring jobs and then began to be incorporated into mill jobs as they arrived in the city from other areas of New England settlement. Members of the upper class began to move out of the neighborhood they had occupied in Central Falls, near the early commercial and industrial area adjacent to the river. Their place was taken by Poles, mainly from the Austrian portion of partitioned Poland. A number of Jewish and Armenian families entered the same neighborhood, and Syrians settled in the central part of the city. In 1895 there were seven Austrian Poles in the community, but by 1905 there were 849. By 1915, 1,658 foreign-born Poles and a total Polish population of 2,514, including American-born children, resided in Central Falls.

The Polish Immigration

The Poles, like the Irish and the French-Canadians, came to Central Falls from rural peasant backgrounds and had a strong Catholic religious heritage. Galicia, the area within Austria-Hungary that provided the majority of immigrants to Central Falls, was characterized by a rural economy similar to that of Ireland and French Canada in the midnineteenth century. Land was severely fragmented and overpopulated. Polish landlords ruled Galicia with some autonomy, and the Austrian government did not repress Polish religion or customs. There was little nationalistic sentiment uniting rural peasants and other groups as in British-dominated French Canada. In addition, class divisions in Galicia were much sharper than in other parts of partitioned Poland or in French Canada. The serfs had been emancipated only in 1846, and landlords still controlled 37 percent of the land even at the end of the nineteenth century.

Galician landlords had not commercialized agriculture and did not attempt to introduce cash crops or improve agricultural techniques.

Peasant holdings were small and continued to grow smaller throughout the end of the nineteenth century. Although the minimum
amount of land needed for subsistence was ten "morgi," or about
thirteen acres, more than 80 percent of the farms were under this size,
and by 1896 the average peasant holding had dropped to about four
morgi, or less than six acres (Fox 1922:39). Holdings were scattered
(Kieniewicz 1969:84); population growth and the division of land
among family members exacerbated the situation (Zubrzycki 1953:
255).

Rather than being absorbed into industry as was occurring in other
parts of Poland, Galician peasants had only the choice of immigrating
seasonally to Germany or abroad. Most immigration was abroad,
mainly to the United States, with remittances and return migration
having a great impact on villages. Galician emigration totaled one
million persons between 1871 and 1914. Between 1892 and 1913 more
than 17 percent of the entire population left Galicia.

Ewa Hauser, who interviewed Polish immigrants to Central Falls,
argued that emigration was a class movement: "Emigration was a
collective action, not the sort of individualistic behavior more typical
of competitive capitalist systems. It was an attempt to subsist without
maintaining the traditional feudal and personal dependencies that
were now measured by the economic dependence of the rural pro-
letariat on the landlord. Whether temporary or permanent in effect,
overseas migration was undertaken with the idea of improving the
immediate economic position of the migrants' family at home" (Hauser 1981:43).

Between 1890 and 1910 the net immigration ratio was about 60
percent, meaning that almost half of the immigrants returned to Poland. Others sent money back to their families. Vicenty Witos pointed
to the impact on the economy of his native village near Tarnow in
Galicia, identifying fifty-six of the sixty-two households in one sector
of the village that were involved in emigration. "In that time a steady
stream of dollars was pouring into Galicia from the States. The later
well-being of the village ought to be attributed mainly to emigration.
With the 'American' money, not only were farms saved from financial
ruin, not only were agricultural machines purchased and new homes
built, but also a substantial amount of the manorial land was bought by
the peasants who thus enlarged their existing small farms or created
new ones" (Witos 1964:190; translation by Ewa Hauser).

Oral-history interviews with Central Falls immigrants, although fil-

[78]

tered through their own experience in the United States, include accounts of serfdom, the peasant rebellion of 1848, and exploitation of the peasants by both landlords and priests (see Hauser 1981:255–77). Polish gentry opposed emigration and took steps to suppress it. Many peasants who left Galicia nonetheless returned, hoping to better their position within the class system. For those who remained in the United States, the Polish oral histories have striking similarities to those of Central Falls' French-Canadians.

Many Polish immigrants to Central Falls between 1895 and 1920 stressed the financial necessity of immigration, since they lived on farms too small to yield subsistence. Mrs. Nicynski, for example, came from a farm in a little village near Tarnow where she lived with her parents, four siblings, and maternal grandparents. Her father was the first to immigrate to the United States. She recounted his rationale: "My father then thought, 'I earn little, but I will bring my children here,' because he had only nine morgi of land, and when the children grow and want to get married, how could he divide it and on what would he stay? So my father thought, 'I will give them the whole of America and so they will have it and live here.' See, and he was right in doing this because we had a better life here, because we worked in factories and live really well."[3]

Mr. Walowski, who came from a family of eight children and lived on a farm of eight morgi, reiterated the same difficulty: "There wasn't anything to divide. I thought that if I stayed in Poland, I would have liked to become a carpenter. That's what I would have liked to become. But when I came to America, I still wanted to go back, but then I got married, [and] my wife didn't want to hear anything about going back to Poland."

Dr. Roczera, an American-born Pole, said that his father had been in much the same situation, coming from a large family of eleven children: "So, all right, the boys would get the land, [but] what would the girls get? Dowry was never land. They would get money and puff comforters, because in a big family like that, well they would divide the land between the five boys. And already they had little land to speak of. So anybody that could get away went to America. My father and his two brothers came to America. There were six boys and five

3. The quotes in this section are from oral-history interviews conducted by Ewa Hauser as part of her dissertation research during 1977 and 1978. Copies of the interviews are in the author's possession.

girls. . . . So they divided the land with the fellows [three sons] that were left."

As Roczera pointed out, daughters in this system did not inherit land and faced marrying a son from an equally poor family. Many daughters immigrated independently, often with an aunt or other relative, but against their parents' wishes. Mrs. Polofsky, whose family had a large farm but seven sons who would inherit it, said: "Why should we all be working on farms? When we were little it was all right, but when we started to grow up, father would have divided the farm into little pieces and we would have been very poor. I wanted to go with other girls [emigrate with other female relatives?], and my mother didn't want to let me go because I was the only girl [in her nuclear family], but I left."

Even those better off in the class system emigrated to improve their economic situation. Mr. Mankovich, whose father was an overseer on an estate, made this point: "He wanted even better work. He had a nice job for the landlord, but you see, they didn't pay too much at the estates. He made more money when he came to America."

Several interviews stressed that migrants expected to return. As in the French-Canadian situation, migration was seen as a way to hold on to one's farm and rural traditions. Mrs. Nicynski's daughter said, "People were coming here to make money. If they made enough, they were going back to Poland, and if they didn't, well they would bring others to America so they could stay here, and then later they would be better off." Mr. Walowski clearly enunciated his desire to return, but like many others, he was prevented from doing so by the outbreak of World War I. "I came here to earn money. I was very concerned to earn money and pay back my brothers. I had three brothers here. I wanted to go back to Poland and work on my father's farm, but unfortunately the World War began."

Like the French-Canadians, many Poles immigrated in nuclear families. Most French-Canadian families, however, were in the middle phase of their developmental cycle as a domestic group, that is, with young children. The Polish position was different. Polish immigration included many single males and females who formed their families after coming to the United States. Unmarried daughters often came separately from their parents, perhaps with a sibling, aunt, or even covillager. They therefore played a more independent role in migration than did French-Canadian daughters. Polish wives either came with their husbands or were sent for later. Some remained in

Poland and never migrated. Once established, Polish wives, like French-Canadian wives, provided links for later immigrant relatives. Ties with covillagers were also important in directing immigrants to a particular urban area and in helping them to obtain jobs and housing.

Mr. Mankovich's father immigrated first, and then he sent for his wife and children. "He came on a ship with people who were from the same place where he was born. They were going to Chicopee [in Massachusetts] and Central Falls, and he was going to Webster [also in Massachusetts]. Then he came to Central Falls with his neighbors from Wola Wadowska." The father changed his destination during the journey partially because local village connections could provide him with contacts in the United States. Later the father sent the fare for Mr. Mankovich's mother, brothers, and sister, but Mr. Mankovich did not join them until he was seventeen.

Mrs. Nicynski's father also immigrated first, coming to the United States around 1890. The result of the family's American sojourn was to reestablish most of the family back in Poland. The father returned to Poland and brought his wife back to the United States on the second trip, leaving four children with their maternal grandparents. Each child was sent for separately. The oldest brother arrived in 1900, at age fourteen, and Mrs. Nicynski came in 1902 when she was ten years old. Another brother was born in the United States but became sick. The parents had Mrs. Nicynski take her baby brother back to Poland to recuperate, but after eight months she returned to Central Falls with a younger sister. The next year, 1907, the parents returned to Poland, but Mrs. Nicynski remained and married in the United States. The mother reimmigrated once more, staying with her daughter a year, but died before she could return to Poland. The father remarried and had additional children in Poland.

As young children, daughters were sent for by their parents and often traveled with relatives. Young teenagers were more independent, sometimes negotiating the migration by themselves. Mrs. Szymanski had a brother and sister in the United States before she came. Her father had died, but her mother and younger sister remained on their small farm. Mrs. Szymanski immigrated first to Chicopee, Massachusetts, where her brother and sister-in-law lived. "They took care of me and asked at the factory. Then, it was customary that somebody got it [a job] for others . . . spoke for them."

Mrs. Nowicki, who had lost both parents as a child, immigrated with her aunt. Her godmother, with whom she stayed when she arrived in Central Falls, sent the ship tickets. Mrs. Bielecki's mother, another orphan, was chosen from among her siblings to be the first to immigrate. "Someone from America sent her money to come here. The older girl [of five children] said that she had the responsbility to stay on the farm that used to be her parents'. She was eighteen or twenty. The second child was my uncle—well, they didn't want to let the only man out of the farm because there was too much work. So they didn't let him go. The third child was my mother and she was fourteen then, and they let her come. She came first to her uncle [her mother's brother]."

As in the Irish and French-Canadian cases, hardships in the Polish economy created the conditions for the immigration of Polish wives and daughters to Central Falls. Migration was very much a family strategy, although daughters and sons or even young wives and children migrated separately to join relatives already in the United States. In some families, fathers came first and sent for their wives and children at a later date. In others, couples immigrated, leaving their children in Poland with relatives for a time. Young women and men were allowed to immigrate with relatives or godparents or to go to siblings already established in the United States. Emigration was also a solution for some daughters in families where one or both parents had died. Kin ties within both the nuclear family and the extended family provided important links in establishing new immigrants in Central Falls. The proportion of young families and single adults in the Polish migration created a different population mix than that of the French-Canadian population already settled in Central Falls. French families were older, and single immigrants were male and represented in relatively small numbers. Arriving during the period of stabilization of the textile industry, the young Polish population was recruited to jobs not yet monopolized by members of the groups that preceded them. Their late arrival in the local economy meant that Polish wives and daughters filled very different productive and reproductive roles than did the French-Canadian women in 1915.

Other New Immigrant Women: The Syrians and the Portuguese

Syrian and Portuguese wives and daughters also arrived in Central Falls at the time of the Polish migration. By 1915 there were 768 persons born in Syria and 153 of Syrian descent in Pawtucket, as well as 22 Syrians who were part of our French-Canadian neighborhood sample in Central Falls. By 1920 the Central Falls Portuguese population numbered 152 with 1,102 more in the neighboring town of Pawtucket.[4] There were already 5,207 Syrians in Rhode Island in 1915 and a much larger Portuguese population of 18,013, including both foreign-born members and those with foreign-born fathers.

Syrian migrants came from what is now Lebanon. Most were Christian, either from the Maronite or Melchite sects or from Greek Orthodox backgrounds. Although Syria during the nineteenth century was an underdeveloped, poor, agricultural country, and economic reasons played a part in early immigration, the rationale for leaving was primarily political. Syrian Christians were particularly oppressed by Turkish rule, and most of the migration to the United States occurred during a period (1890–1914) when about one-fourth of the Lebanese population left the country to avoid the invasion of Turkish troops and the ensuing disease and poverty that caused many deaths (Kayal and Kayal 1975:65). Between 1900 and 1915 approximately 84,000 Syrians came to the United States. Nearly 18,000 arrived during the two peak years, 1913 and 1914, when Turkish hostility was at its most intense. In the early years of immigration very few women came. Even after wives and children began to join their husbands in the years just before World War I, female immigration was only about one-third of the total (Kayal and Kayal 1975:69–71).

At first Syrians settled in New York City, in a neighborhood near Wall Street, becoming involved in peddling and trade and then in other commercial enterprises. Syrians who settled in Lawrence, Massachusetts; Paterson, New Jersey; and Central Falls became workers in the textile mills. In Central Falls, many became silk weavers as the silk mills began to expand just before and after World War I. By 1900 there were enough Syrians in Central Falls to establish their own church (Kayal and Kayal 1975:83). Two churches were eventually created, a Greek Catholic or Melchite church and a Syrian Orthodox church. Syrians settled mainly along one street at the edge of the French neighborhood, many men boarding with families. There was also a large concentration of Syrian families in nearby Pawtucket.

In 1915, as shown in a study of sixty-five Syrian households in

4. In 1915 there were only 7 Portugal-born individuals and 8 individuals of Portuguese descent in Central Falls and 225 Portuguese-born and 254 of Portuguese descent in Pawtucket. The Portuguese population thus experienced its greatest increase in these two towns between 1915 and 1925.

Pawtucket, approximately one-third of the households were extended families and one-seventh contained boarders. Most of these households were young couples with small children, but many Syrian wives took in boarders or relatives, often brothers or brothers-in-law, doing reproductive work that added to family income. Many Syrian husbands and single men were silk weavers. The labor-force-participation rate of single daughters was relatively low, only 44 percent, but those who did work were employed in the textile mills, many as weavers (Schneider 1981:19–20, 37–38).[5] This pattern also fits the cluster of Syrian families who were part of our French-Canadian neighborhood sample in Central Falls. In these six households, the men were primarily weavers, and wives took in boarders; there were no daughters old enough to work, but one adult sister was employed in a knitting mill.

The Portuguese were an impoverished, rural population much like the Irish, French-Canadians, and Poles. There have been, however, two waves of immigration, one between 1890 and 1924 coinciding with the immigration of the Poles and Syrians and a more recent post-1965 wave of migration, which has brought thousands of Portuguese to New England. Portuguese-speaking immigrants have come from four areas: rural Continental Portugal, Madeira, the Cape Verde Islands, and the Azores. Although a number of Madeirans and Continentals settled in Valley Falls, north of Central Falls, during the 1920s, the Portuguese in Pawtucket in 1915 were from the Azores.

The push for emigration from the Azores stemmed from the impoverished status of rural agriculturalists on most islands. Land was largely in the hands of a few wealthy proprietors. Peasant families were forced into a position of renting land for their cows, working as agricultural laborers for the landowners, and tending vegetable gardens on their own small home plots of land. Men did most of the herding and agricultural labor, although women cultivated home gardens and tended chickens or pigs. The Azorean economy suffered a decline between 1890 and 1924, and many young men left to avoid military service. The Azorean economy was traditionally exploited by continental Portugal, since agricultural goods were heavily taxed as were imports from the mainland. Taxes and the unequal division of land made life difficult for rural villagers.

---

5. Of the twenty-three women who were employed in the sample, fifteen were single; twenty women worked in textiles and seven of them were weavers.

Between 1899 and 1919, 144,000 Portuguese settled in the United States with most arriving between 1907 and 1917. Although some immigrated to Hawaii and California, the largest number came to Massachusetts and Rhode Island (Taft 1923:125). Immigrants came as young families, although many men came as single individuals. In general, the Portuguese men became unskilled laborers, with their specific work shaped by the particular local economy (Taft 1923:102). In Providence Portuguese men, including the Cape Verdeans, worked as longshoremen and dockhands, coal and brick workers, hand operators in oyster and screw companies, and pork packers in meat houses. Most of the dock and coal workers were single men, particularly Cape Verdeans who lived in lodging houses (Ferst 1971:22). Portuguese daughters worked mainly in lace factories, laundries, and cotton mills.

In Pawtucket the Portuguese population was much smaller in 1915 than it was in Providence. Most were young families where wives worked at home caring for young children. Husbands had wage jobs as laborers in butcher shops, coal yards, vegetable markets, and on farms. Daughters over fourteen years of age worked primarily in textile and lace mills. As more and more Portuguese entered the Pawtucket area, and as sons and daughters reached working age, a larger proportion entered the textile mills. However, they did so in the unskilled jobs—as combers, speeder tenders, spinners, and doffers. The more skilled jobs were already occupied by men and women from immigrant groups that had arrived earlier. Statistics on male employment in Providence in 1915 indicate that the Portuguese, along with the Syrians and Italians, were at the bottom of the wage scale (Rhode Island 1921:224).

The Portuguese in Providence formed a tight, ethnically defined neighborhood where Cape Verdeans, Continentals, and Azoreans all resided. In contrast, the Pawtucket Portuguese were much more scattered, indicating that new immigrant groups could not always concentrate in the same neighborhood when others were there before them. The establishment of a Portuguese parish church took place in Providence in 1885, but it was not until the 1920s that a Portuguese parish was established in Pawtucket.

The recent immigrant groups—Poles, Syrians, and Portuguese—found themselves entering a textile economy at a period of stabilization. Their recruitment to the mill labor force was at the bottom with little chance for advancement. This was more true for male workers than for women, who were more likely to be placed in women's jobs along with French, Irish, and English females and paid at the same level as these older immigrants.

Women's Place in the Social Relations of Production

The development of the textile industry created a two-class system that became increasingly differentiated as production became more complex and as new kinds of workers were recruited to fill jobs in the expanding mills. The labor process as implemented by mill owners created a skill hierarchy, using age and gender as ways of allocating individuals to different tasks. The precedent for hiring daughters and female children from rural families was set by the early Rhode Island mill owners. Families were recruited as units to work in the mills. The wage structure established by mill owners insured that men would be the most highly paid members of the family but that their wages could not support an entire family (Lahne 1944). Sons and daughters were needed as additional wage laborers, and the labor of the wife was necessary both to feed and clothe the family and to provide supplementary cash, through taking in boarders, housing relatives, or engaging in industrial homework. These wage differences and the differential recruitment of fathers, sons, and daughters were based on assumptions deriving from the sexual division of labor and the allocation of productive and reproductive tasks found in past economic and social structures.

In the rural farming families of mercantile capitalist New England, as well as in the semifeudal systems that prevailed in nineteenth-century Ireland, French Canada, Poland, and Portugal, men as husbands and fathers controlled most of the important productive agricultural tasks. Women were engaged in productive tasks as well, often working in the fields, tending gardens. or raising small animals. Women produced many agricultural and handcrafted items for family use or for sale on the market. When used by the family, these products (whether cooked food, soap and candles, or woven cloth) helped reproduce the family labor force. When exchanged in the market, the cash was used to purchase products, which in turn were used in reproducing the family. Children participated in this sexual division of labor, and their help was extremely important in maintaining the family productive economy.

With the transition to a family wage economy under industrial capitalism, Yankee husbands and fathers were pulled into the labor force, and they sold their labor for wages, at wage rates befitting their status within the rural household. They continued to do productive labor but under a different set of relationships. They probably engaged in less reproductive labor in the home. Wives and mothers continued to work at home but spent less time producing products for family use and for the market and more time on cooking, cleaning, household maintenance, and child care—all tasks that contained fewer elements of processing or production and more elements of maintenance and reproduction. Daughters and sons were released from productive and reproductive work in the home and recruited to the industrial economy as wage laborers. Irish, French-Canadian, Polish, and Portuguese rural families experienced the transition to a family wage economy through immigration. They, too, were incorporated into this system, which assumed that men were household heads and that their labor was more valuable than that of women, teenage sons, and daughters.

Creating a Labor Hierarchy and the Role of Age, Gender, and Ethnicity

In an industrial capitalist system each worker is hired and fired on an individual basis for his or her labor power, not on the basis of kin connections or membership in a group. The 1915 pay books from one mill indicate that there were minute differences in pay among workers, even among those doing the same job. These pay differences may have been based on seniority, skill, productivity on a piece-rate system, or other factors. However, the net result was that each worker was divided from her or his coworkers, even in the same room where many workers were doing the same job. Furthermore, other markers such as gender or ethnic background could potentially divide workers from one another within the same job category. Finally, the job categories were hierarchically arranged by pay. Men and members of older ethnic groups were more concentrated in the higher paying jobs, women in the middle-range jobs, and men and women of newer ethnic groups in the lowest jobs. Data from the Lorraine Mill, part of the Sayles family enterprises, show how the gender and ethnic hierarchy in 1915 worked in practice, and oral-history data give a sense of what women's jobs were like. These data on wages, the production process, and the gender and ethnic hierarchy are presented in appendix A.

Counterposed to these sources of division were other sources of connection and solidarity. Relatives often "spoke for" other kin to persuade an overseer to hire them, a practice common in the type of "simple control" practiced in nineteenth-century mills. Also, many workers came from the same neighborhoods and belonged to the same parishes or voluntary associations off the job. However, it is important not to underestimate the atomizing and individualizing nature of the wage contract under capitalism and the fact that informal groups and social solidarity on the job had to be created usually out of a collection of strangers or acquaintances with only a smattering of kin and friends. The skill and job divisions, the hierarchical wage system, and the gender and ethnic diversity within the mill were thus potentenial sources of division that had to be overcome.

In 1915 in Central Falls, English, French-Canadian, and Scottish men held the skilled jobs of overseer, second hand, loomfixer, and weaver. Some French-Canadian and Polish women were weavers along with Syrian men. These last two groups had made a niche for themselves in the expanding silk mills. Young French, English, and Irish women worked in the semiskilled jobs as spinners, twisters, winders, and spoolers. Young boys of the same ethnic groups held the lower paying male jobs of doffer, sweeper, back boy, and spinner. Polish men were more likely to be in the lower paying jobs in the picking and carding rooms, and many Polish and Portuguese men were laborers in machine shops, warehouses, and coal yards, earning less than the English and French-Canadian women who worked in the cotton-textile mills.

This hierarchy was not exact, and in some rooms within the mill men and women worked at the same jobs. Some of this overlapping is related to technological changes in cotton production during the nineteenth and early twentieth centuries. Machines were improved so that they could do more processing without human intervention, deskilling the worker's job and turning him or her into a mere machine tender. The speed of certain machines was also improved, and devices for stopping machines automatically were installed so that fewer workers were needed to produce the same output. This meant that employers could hire the same number of workers to tend more machines, thereby "stretching out the work" and making employees work at a faster pace to keep up with machines that were more complex and producing more. Both of these changes meant that young women and men could still be hired to run some machines, but since the work took less skill, they could be paid lower wages. In other cases, particularly in roving and weaving, the machinery had become heavier and was run at a high speed, calling for more male labor. Thus a male weaver could take care of more plain looms than any woman, and on the high-speed Northrup loom male weavers were preferred (Copeland 1917:113–14).

In 1915 entry jobs for young (fourteen- to sixteen-year-old) males, like those of doffer, sweeper, can boy, or lap carrier, always hovered around $5.00 to $8.00 a week. Slightly older women of Irish, French, and English background worked for $9.00 to $12.00 a week in jobs tending machines in the middle stages of the process. The Polish, Italian, and Portuguese men who worked as pickers, carders, and speeder tenders earned about the same wages, $10.00 to $12.00 a week. The weave room offered the best jobs for women of English and French-Canadian background as well as for the more recently arrived Polish women. Although it took over a year to learn the job well, weavers could earn between $15.00 and $18.00 a week, although men tended to earn more than women. The privileged jobs in the mills— those of the loomfixers (who earned $16.00 to $20.00 a week), the second hands ($13.50 a week), and overseers or foreman ($27.00 a week)—were largely monopolized by English, Scottish, and occasionally Irish and French-Canadian men. Compared to the many weavers, the numbers of loomfixers, second hands, and overseers in a mill were small, so that English, Scottish, and French-Canadian men were clearly at the top of the "pecking order."

Between 1870 and 1910 the absolute number of women in textile mills increased, but the relative proportion declined from 51 percent in 1870 to 38 percent in 1910. The proportion of men increased from 32 to 51 percent during these forty years and the percentage of children declined from 17 to 11 percent (Copeland 1917:112). Thus with the expansion of the industry, men obtained a larger share of the work in some departments, and in New England the increased supply of adult male labor came from the stream of immigrants who were willing to work for comparatively low wages (Copeland 1917:118–22). Men did not completely replace women in most jobs; instead, their increasing proportion meant that some rooms within the mill showed more of a gender mix, while others remained relatively gender segregated. But even when women worked at the same job as men, their wages were usually less, possibly because they could not produce as much as the men or possibly because of differential time on the job or differential pay rates.

Conclusions

As the textile-mill economy in Central Falls expanded between 1815 and 1915, the increasing need for labor was filled by immigrant families who were pulled in from productive family economies in Ireland, French Canada, Portugal, and Austrian-occupied Poland. An exceptional immigrant group, the British and Scottish skilled male laborers, had previous experience in textiles and thus were able to hold a privileged position within the mills after immigration.

Immigrant families did not partake passively in the transformation of their lives from peasants to workers. They actively forged strategies that varied with the local economies of origin and helped them deal with their new place in the textile-mill economy. Families migrated seasonally or in segments, hoping to use cash from the industrial economy to hold on to declining farms (as in the French-Canadian and Polish cases). Family ties, first among members of the nuclear family and then among kin within an extended family network, were crucial in the process of immigration. "Chain migration," the sending by kin networks of some family members before others, was used in finding a city of destination, housing, and jobs in the new industrial situation.

How kinship was used and who came first varied considerably within and between ethnic populations. The French and Portuguese tended to migrate as families, but both populations contained many single male migrants. Among the Irish and later the Poles, numerous young single women came to the United States, some bringing other family members at a later date, others marrying and establishing their own households within a decade after immigration. Some Poles arrived as family units, other men sent for their wives and children over a period of years, and still others stayed only for a few years, eventually returning to Poland but perhaps leaving a married son or daughter in the United States. French families sent daughters and sons tentatively to explore work in the mills, or family segments migrated seasonally before choosing to settle permanently in the United States. All of these patterns reflect both the difficult economic circumstances in which rural families found themselves during the late nineteenth and early twentieth centuries and the uncertainty of industrial work where periodic recessions brought layoffs and unemployment as well as wage cuts and a deterioration of working conditions.

The same system that pulled immigrant families into wage work also distributed them into a hierarchically arranged labor process. Capitalist wage labor inherently treats human labor in an individualistic and atomizing manner, hiring each on the basis of production needs and paying each on an individual basis. The "simple" or paternalistic control excercised by overseers and the complex method of calculating wages only emphasized this, despite the importance of kin ties and even ethnic backgrounds in hiring decisions. On the whole, gender, age, and ethnicity interacted in a complex way, uniting and dividing workers at the same time.

Working daughters were sometimes in situations in which gender, pay, and work conditions united them but in which there were differences in ethnicity to overcome. Thus they tended roving, spinning, and winding machines in rooms where French-Canadian, English, and Irish girls worked together. In other situations, as in the weave room, where both males and females were weavers, there was a gender as well as an ethnic mix. In all of these contexts, minute differences in pay divided women as did differences in religion, language, and culture. The work experience might have been able to override these differences, if the overall hierarchy had not made it clear that the English and Scottish men held the supervisory and skilled positions, while Irish and French-Canadian men held the lesser skilled jobs. There may have been some preference for English-speaking girls in the higher paid jobs, but since young women were paid much less then men regardless of ethnicity, the male skill hierarchy probably defined the ethnic pecking order. As we shall see next, the creation of separate ethnic neighborhoods functioned to continue and strengthen ethnic differences, so working daughters experienced a culturally distinct and homeogenous family and community life steeped in traditions very different from their coworkers.

[3]

Working Daughters, Ethnic Neighborhoods, and Family Strategies

It was from nuclear families and kin networks that wives and daughters were pulled into the textile-mill economy in Central Falls during the periods of expansion and stabilization. Under industrial capitalism, in contrast to the rural economies from which families came, productive work took place in the mill under a wage contract. Reproductive labor remained in the household, usually composed of a nuclear family but often including boarders or other relatives. Since these families were recruited from different cultural and national populations, similarities in language, religion, and customs became the basis for creating a community among urban strangers. Central Falls became a working-class town, ethnically defined populations emerged in particular neighborhoods, and new groups were pushed into available areas not yet dominated by older groups.

Reproductive activities necessary to the functioning of industrial capitalism took place in the context of common language and customs. The families and individuals from French Canada, Ireland, England, and Galicia did not come to Central Falls as collective units or ethnic groups. They identified themselves with villages or regions. Thus the formation of an ethnic group by members of an ethnic category had the potential of uniting portions of the working class.[1] During the first

1. An "ethnic category" includes those who share a common heritage including a distinctive language, set of customs, religion, or other cultural symbols. An "ethnic group" results from the process by which members of an ethnic category become members of an interest group who share economic and political interests and stand together in continuous competition for power with other groups (Cohen 1969).

twenty years after immigration members of each ethnic category formed parishes, schools, benevolent societies, and other institutions based on a common ethnic identity. Although most groups—the French-Canadians, Poles, Portuguese, Syrians, and unskilled English and Scottish—remained shut out of the formal political arena for a generation, they did coalesce into interest groups, formed around a set of ethnic institutions that protected them from the harshness of industrial life. As Stanley Aronowitz said of semiskilled and unskilled workers:

> They did not remain "unorganized" in the social meaning of the term, even if they could not affiliate themselves with traditional working class institutions. Instead, they formed thousands of social and fraternal groups for the purpose of mutual aid and protection against the vicissitudes of urban and industrial life. Nationwide organizations such as the Sons of Italy, the Polish National Home, the Workmen's Circle, and the German Workmen's Benefit Fund served a two-fold purpose, providing a place where persons who spoke the same language and shared the same woes could congregate as well as important services such as health benefits, burial sites, pensions, and college scholarships. (Aronowitz 1974:151–52)

The formation of ethnic neighborhoods and the creation of ethnic institutions was a process repeated over and over again in industrial urban settings between 1870 and World War I. These institutions created ethnic groups, the first stage of organizing members of an ethnic category outside the workplace. Such organizing occurred during a time when formal union structures were dominated by northern Europeans and textile unions organized on a craft basis were very weak. Ethnic institutions, particularly those dominated by the Catholic church, often had a conservative function. Although the church "provided the opportunity for working class families who felt stranded in large cities to overcome the isolation of urban living," it also encouraged an ideology that the worker "should be satisfied with his station in life and not attempt to reach beyond his class" (Aronowitz 1974:167, 169).

For wage-earning women, most of them daughters, the creation of ethnic neighborhoods and ethnic institutions meant that their nonwork experience was confined to ethnic settings. Neighborhood, church, and leisure activities created networks of families bound together through a common identity as French-Canadian, English, or Polish. This tended to solidify ethnic ties at work, rather than to

[93]

encourage the building of ties across ethnic lines. Oral-history material from French-Canadian and Polish women indicates that, in retrospect at least, women defined their nonwork life around ethnic institutions. It is difficult, however, to assess historically the full impact of ethnic institutions on divisions within the working class. Data from contemporary shop-floor situations, as we shall see in chapter 7, indicate that ethnic divisions persist but that they can be overcome in the work setting under particular situations.

The Family in Relation to the Mill Economy: Three Neighborhoods Contrasted

Three neighborhoods in Central Falls were selected in order to understand the importance of ethnic institutions and to examine the family's relationship to the mill economy. In 1915 virtually all working-class families in these three neighborhoods sent their daughters and sons over fourteen years of age out to work. But beyond this, families from different ethnic groups varied in the strategies they used in allocating the labor of their members.

The French-Canadian neighborhood in 1915 represented a well-developed commercial and residential area (see Map 2). This neighborhood was adjacent to one of the oldest French-Canadian Catholic parishes in Rhode Island and included a commercial street that housed a number of French-Canadian voluntary associations and small businesses. The Polish neighborhood in 1915 was similar to the French one in that it was the center of two Polish parishes, a thriving commercial district, and a residential area with a distinct ethnic population. The Poles, however, were a newly arrived population compared with the French population, whose roots in the city went back thirty-five to forty-five years. The third neighborhood, one containing predominantly English, Scottish, and Irish families in 1915, was an example of an urban area that was not clearly identified with one ethnic group but where several working-class ethnic populations resided. Located next to the Coats and Clark Mill, it was primarily a residential neighborhood and not the center of religious, educational, or commercial activities. By 1935 when the Rhode Island census was taken, many Polish and French-Canadian families had moved in, making the neighborhood even more "mixed" in its ethnic composition. The French and Polish neighborhoods, however, were still dominated by these ethnic groups and continued to be even after World War II.

[94]

The Creation of a French Neighborhood and Parish

French-Canadian families whose men worked in the mills or the building trades congregated in an area of Central Falls that in the 1870s, the period of the initial immigration, was largely undeveloped. In 1870 the Fales and Jenks families, prominent manufacturers, controlled large tracts of the neighborhood's land, and the Sprague Mill, located on the railroad, was the largest manufacturing firm. There was only a scattering of houses, and they were occupied by English-surnamed families. By 1915 the neighborhood was entirely built up. The amount of industry bordering on the neighborhood had increased. The Sprague Mill was operating under different ownership as the U.S. Cotton Company. The Waypoyset Mill, which produced silk and cotton mixed goods, had been built, and a glass works had been located along the growing commercial street. A small stocking mill and two other small silk mills were also located in the neighborhood. Most of the streets in the neighborhood were lined with three-decker houses occupied by worker families. Broad Street had developed into a commercial area, and a complex of parish buildings had been built on land purchased from the Jenks family.

French-Canadian women and men conceptualize this neighborhood in oral-history interviews as a French village, not an industrial working-class neighborhood. They emphasize its ethnic qualities and contrast it to the neighboring Irish community. As one woman recalled: "Broad Street was a little French community, a beautiful little village. There was a village on Dexter Street, also. . . . Beginning at Fales Street and going as far as Lincoln Avenue. . . . From Lincoln Avenue down, there wasn't as many [French families]."[2]

The neighborhood was established by cutting several streets through a rock formation that originally separated the French population from the Irish neighborhood formed during the same period. The theme of ethnic opposition is apparent in the following description.

> The barrier that existed due to that rock formation on the West side of Broad Street kind of separated the Broad Street area from the westerly section that developed later. Like Fletcher Street . . . that was built up by mostly French contractors. And they finally moved westerly. . . . The first street that could go through was Cowden Street. . . . The

2. In writing this section I have quoted from the oral-history interviews with older French-Canadians that were conducted by Marcel Dufresne in 1977 and deposited at the Central Falls Free Public Library.

Map 2. Central Falls with three sample neighborhoods

BLACKSTONE RIVER

Moshassuck
Cemetery

French-Canadian
church (second parish)

Irish parish church

COWDEN STREET

LONSDALE AVENUE

English/Irish

DEXTER STREET

Coats and
Clark Mills

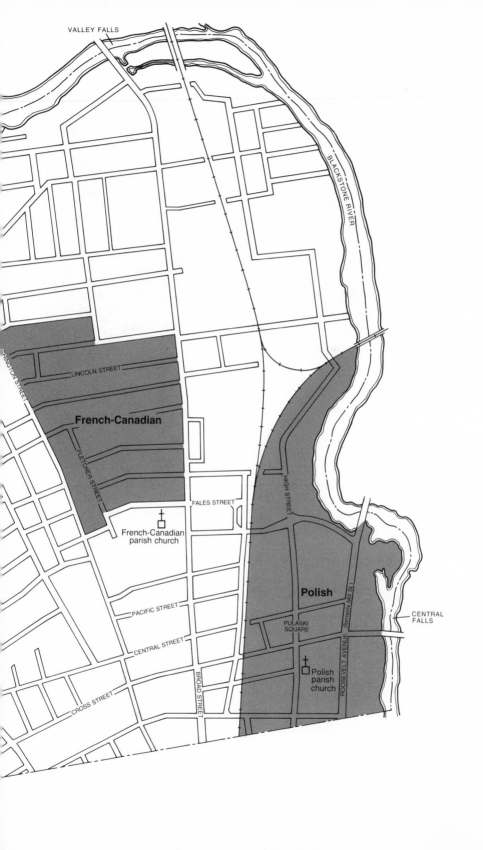

VALLEY FALLS

BLACKSTONE RIVER

LINCOLN STREET

French-Canadian

FLETCHER STREET

FALES STREET

HIGH STREET

French-Canadian
parish church

PACIFIC STREET

Polish

CENTRAL STREET

PULASKI
SQUARE

CENTRAL
FALLS

ROOSEVELT AVENUE (formerly Mill St.)

Polish
parish
church

BROAD STREET

CROSS STREET

RINGTON STREET

Broad Street, the heart of one of the two French-Canadian neighborhoods in Central Falls, around 1915. "A beautiful French village" recalled one resident. Courtesy of the Rhode Island Historical Society.

French started in that area. Then they started to go down Cowden Street. And then on Lincoln next to the college [the Sacred Heart Academy, which was housed in the old Sprague store]. But as you went down the hill, you met more resistance. It was then Irish. It was sort of a dividing line. . . . Washington Street was about the dividing line between the French village and that of the Irish village that was formed over [by] Holy Trinity.

The majority of immigrants to this neighborhood became mill workers or skilled workers in the building trades, an economic niche opened up by the town's growth. The enormous increase in productivity of the textile industry between 1870 and 1915 fueled the expansion of Central Falls and of other urban areas in the region. The building of the neighborhood and its ethnic institutions involved French-Canadian contractors, small businessmen, priests and nuns, and medical personnel, all of whom became the community elite that emerged in the first two decades of the twentieth century.

Among the French contractors who played a substantial role in the building of the neighborhood and parish during the early part of the century was a company that employed as many as 120 men as painters, tinsmiths, plumbers, and carpenters. In some years the owner and his men built as many as thirty-five houses. This was primarily a French-Canadian work force, although the plumbers tended to be Irish. The firm also was engaged in construction projects for the local parish.

Along the main commercial street, Broad Street, several imposing three- and four-story buildings were built, all with French names, which housed a number of French-owned businesses including a furniture store and hardware store, as well as several French voluntary associations. The street was also the location of the two largest grocery stores, which sold preserves, pickles, mustard, breads, and cakes, all made on the premises. Their horse teams delivered foodstuffs to neighborhood families, indicating the substantial size of the trade. The owners, important members of the French-Canadian elite, became influential in local politics and were able to place French-Canadians in good jobs and positions in local government. Of the seven other grocery stores in the area, four were owned by French-Canadians. Three of the four bakeries and confectionaries were owned by French families, as were the three variety stores and four of the six liquor stores and pool halls. Four barbers, a bootblack, several dressmakers, a milliner, a watchmaker, and a harnessmaker were also French-Canadian. Only in the area of dry goods and clothing did another ethnic group predominate. Jewish entrepreneurs held five of the seven businesses, and French-Canadians owned two.

Clerks in the largest Broad Street store often served as middlemen or "brokers" between the English-speaking population and the new immigrants in the 1870s and 1880s. Their position often gave these men connections to start their own business, buy land, build a house, or provide for the education of their children. From his position first as a salesman and then as head bookkeeper at the Broad Street store, Edna Frechette's father was able to buy a piece of land, build a house on it, and become an alderman, all while still a young man. His two sons attended college. His daughter Edna was able to attend a year of business school before becoming a teacher in the parish school and then working as a bookkeeper in several local stores—all rare accomplishments for a mill-town woman during the 1920s and 1930s.

Emily LaVallee's maternal grandfather owned a small store and served as a "broker" for new immigrants. He would send train tickets to immigrants and after they arrived would find them apartments, jobs, food, and clothing. "He wasn't very rich, but he shared," his

granddaughter said. Emily's father took over the business and expanded it greatly during World War I. His daughters worked in the
mills, but the son studied for the priesthood and later became a
doctor.

In addition to the increasing number of small businessmen, priests
and nuns were part of the elite of this expanding French community.
As one woman said, "It was the priests really who brought people
here. . . . They usually went to the clergy, first thing. They were
really going for the Bible" (meaning following the advice of the
priests). The cluster of parish buildings, closely identified with the
neighborhood, included the church, a rectory, a grade school, a gymnasium, a convent, and an academy for boys.

The beginnings of the parish stemmed from a visit from Father
Charles Dauray to the area in 1872. He came to Rhode Island from
Canada because of ill health but was urged by the pastor of one of the
few Roman Catholic churches in the area to celebrate Mass for
French-speaking parishioners. They walked miles to attend services at
the English-speaking (Irish) parish.

As a result of Father Dauray's visit, several families petitioned the
bishop to start a French-speaking parish. The bishop urged Father
Dauray to remain in the United States, stating, "Father Dauray, they
need you more here than in Canada" (Kennedy 1978:52). Father
Dauray temporarily held services in a local armory and raised two
hundred dollars from mill-working parishioners to purchase property
in Central Falls on which to build a church. The parish was incorporated in 1874 as the first French-speaking parish in Rhode Island, and
by 1875 a frame church was completed (Notre Dame Church 1974:5).

In 1875 Father Dauray was transferred to Woonsocket to start another French-speaking parish there. The Central Falls parish was
served by a succession of other priests, including Father Joseph
Beland who was responsible for much of its expansion and growth in
the early twentieth century. Father Beland purchased a house for a
rectory, built a gymnasium for community activities, and oversaw the
building of a new grade school, which opened to twelve hundred
students in 1910. The Sisters of Saint Anne, who had been teaching in
the community since 1891, took over responsibility for the new
school, while their old school, in the converted Sprague's store, became the new academy for boys administered by the Brothers of the
Sacred Heart.

Oral histories cite the church as the center of community activities, especially on Sunday. Mass was conducted in the morning, and the children would attend catechism in the afternoon. The adults attended vespers at 3 P.M., and plays and other entertainment were organized in the parish gym during the afternoon as well. Sunday was also a day of family gatherings, and older French-Canadians remember gathering at a grandparent's home for a supper of typical French dishes (soups, beans, meat stews) or a French specialty like molasses pie (*pâté à fourloche*), molasses taffy (*la tirée mélasse*), and headcheese (made with suet, onion, and pepper).

In addition to the church, a number of associations were formed to provide for the health and material needs of French working-class families. Three of them were insurance associations that had their own meeting halls for social functions as well. They were L'Union St. Jean Baptiste, the Association Franco-American, and the Cercle Jacques Cartier. The first of them was founded in the 1890s and provided protection for burial expenses. It consisted of male members, but there was an auxiliary branch for women. Among its social activities were picnics in the pine woods at the north end of town, where members and their wives would sell clamcakes, sandwiches, and chowder. Another association, Le Foyer Club, was dedicated to the preservation of the French language and culture. It was organized into five groups that corresponded to the five French parishes in Central Falls and Pawtucket; it provided more purely social functions than did the church.

A crucial institution was the credit union, L'Union de Credit de Central Falls, which was established in 1915. It was promoted by the local priest but had a lay board of directors. Patterned after a local French institution in Canada called "La Caisse Populaire," it helped French-Canadians get small loans unavailable from commercial banks and give sympathetic treatment to new French-speaking immigrants.

French-Canadians not only had difficulty getting loans but also faced discrimination in medical care. Doctors who had immigrated from Canada to set up practice had difficulty being admitted to the Irish-controlled Catholic hospitals. At the encouragement of the local priest, one of the local doctors started a hospital in Pawtucket that was moved to a new building in Central Falls proper in 1925. The hospital had a lay board of directors, many of whom also served on the board of the Credit Union.

The creation of these institutions—the parish, the schools, the insurance societies, and the hospital—was a response both to the needs

of a population of working-class immigrants and to their position relative to previous groups, primarily the Irish. In the spheres of religion
and education, the French met considerable resistance from the Irish,
who through creating their own institutions had come to dominate the
Catholic church in America. Some of the conflict stemmed from different traditions in the French and Irish versions of Catholicism. One
member of our project described this difference: "In Quebec, the
parish was the focus of religious and social activity with the *curé*
largely responsible for decision-making, usually in coordination with
three laymen who formed the parish council. The Irish-Americans, on
the other hand, had established a more centralized authority system
in which the parish priests were largely overshadowed by the bishop"
(Rubin 1977:7).

These organizational differences became magnified in what became
a struggle over limited resources. Irish and French struggled for control over institutions that immigrants had created outside the system
of production rather than over the control of work and the economy
itself, which would have pitted both groups more directly against mill
owners. In Rhode Island the conflict between the Irish-controlled
church and the French-Canadians came to a head in the Sentinentelle
Affair during the 1920s. In opposition to the Irish bishop, two parishes
in Woonsocket and Central Falls attempted to retain control of parish
funds and maintain the teaching of the French language in parish
schools.

Even in the mill economy, however, French-Canadians were
placed in competition with the Irish, since mill owners used French-
Canadians as strikebreakers and thus set one group against the other.
Competition between workers within the mill thus became phrased as
ethnic conflict rather than as rivalry generated by the wage and skill
hierarchy. As one French-Canadian said: "The Irish migrated after
the potato famine. They came from New York [City]. The French in
the 1860s were put in the textile mills and were used to fourteen hour
days and the owners preferred them. They were called 'the French
Coolies.' The animosity started then and has not quite yet died out."

Given Irish-French structural opposition within the mill employment structure and within the Catholic church, it is not surprising
that French-Canadians conceptualized their relationships with the
Irish in terms of conflict and discrimination. One French-Canadian
described the situation in his own family: "My grandfather used to go to

St. Patrick's in Valley Falls where they were not too readily received by the then, of course, dominating Irish parish. You perhaps know of the animosity that developed between the two racial groups. . . . [It was] due to the fact that the Irish came in to Central Falls immediately following the potato famine, in the Holy Trinity area and Dexter Street, which was then predominantly English and also Irish."

Oral histories indicate that the French were often assaulted on the way to Mass. Conflict arose on the boundaries between the territory already staked out by the Irish and the area where the French-Canadian population was settling. As one man viewed the conflict, "During my father's time, they [the French-Canadians] couldn't cross that bridge into Valley Falls. They'd get their clothes ripped off and battle with bricks and what the hell not."

By the turn of the century this animosity had quieted down, although some recalled being laughed at because of their accents or being called "Canada Bucks." Others remembered sporadic fights among young boys of Irish, English, and French backgrounds, but some French-Canadians recalled having Irish friends as children.

The French parish and its related institutions not only were the center of a neighborhood but were the focus of "survivance," the French-Canadian concept that summarized the importance of retaining the French faith, language, and cultural heritage in a largely alien land. Survivance embodied a kind of amalgam of nationalistic and religious commitment that had its roots in the eighteenth- and nineteenth-century Canadian experience, whereby French citizens felt themselves both politically and religiously discriminated against by the English Protestant majority. Gerstle wrote that

> this sense grew in opposition to conquering English armies at a time when most French-Canadians lived in a rural, semi-feudal society in Quebec. As a consequence, it managed to reject many of the ideals usually associated with the Enlightenment and the English industrial revolution . . . democracy, individual rights, and material progress. It reaffirmed the primacy of the community over the individual, and the preservation of the community of French Canadians in an Anglo-Saxon land became the major religious and secular concern. (1978:163)

Two centuries later survivance was still the key symbol that legitimized and provided a rationale for the building and maintenance of two French neighborhoods in Central Falls. The French-Canadian community was characterized by a unique set of religious and voluntary institutions and was set apart from other ethnic groups and from the upper class mill owners who dominated the local economy.

The creation of French institutions entailed the recruitment and creation of a professional and small business elite who took the leadership roles in them. Women from mill-worker families did not participate in the direct running of these associations, although they certainly were an integral part of church activities and association gatherings where women undoubtedly prepared the food and refreshments. French wives shopped in French-owned stores, sent their children to the parish grade school to be taught by the nuns, and attended Mass regularly. Wage-earning daughters in 1915 thus grew up in a neighborhood in which most of their primary associations were French and where they learned to identify themselves as French-Canadian girls rather than as "working girls." It is difficult to know what implications this might have had for interethnic relations among wage-earning daughters in the mills, but certainly the strength of ethnic identity would have meant that ethnic boundaries were something to be overcome in the work setting, rather than a source of solidarity among working women who shared the same places in the production process.

The Irish Community

The French community in Central Falls was formed partially in opposition to the Irish parish in the adjoining town of Valley Falls where a church had been established in 1857 following the arrival of many Irish. In 1870 there was a cluster of Irish families living in Central Falls itself on the streets northwest of what became the French neighborhood. Not until 1889 were there enough Irish families in Central Falls to petition for their own parish.

Irish families first used the Temperance Hall on High Street for church services, the same building used twenty years later by the incoming Polish immigrant community. Later they were able to purchase several lots, take out a loan for the church building, and erect a church that was completed in 1892. That year the parish began holding its annual boat trip and shore dinner. On the first excursion 2,000 men, women, and children participated, suggesting that the parish contained about 400 families (Holy Trinity Parish 1972:25). A convent and school were completed and opened for 487 pupils in 1906.

A number of social activities were centered in the parish, creating an atmosphere that bound family, church, and ethnic group together. In the 1890s a number of social groups that included women and children were established within the parish, including the Children of Mary Sodality and the Holy Name Society. A parish club was founded in 1910 for young men between the ages of eighteen and thirty-five; it sponsored an annual minstrel show, as well as lectures, dramas, and dances. After 1915 club membership declined because movies and the automobile offered alternate forms of entertainment, but another club was started in the 1920s to raise funds for the community center, which was built in 1925. Katherine O'Brien recalled some of these events: "They had a great many [activities]. We used to have an excursion. We used to go out on a little boat they called the Pontiac. . . . [They] used to have minstrel shows and go up on Sunday afternoons and dance and practice, you know, and then they'd have different shows. . . . They'd have a St. Patrick's Day show, and they'd have maybe a Christmas play, and the children would always have them . . . and there was quite a lot of activity."[3]

Oral-history interviews indicate that most children of Irish descent attended the parish school. Others attended public school and were confirmed in the parish church. As in the neighboring French parish, Irish women attended Mass, catechism, and vesper services on Sunday. Women were also part of gatherings held in family homes, which sometimes included musical entertainment. Katherine O'Brien recalled her own family's amusements: "My sister Margaret . . . was a violin player, and Grace and Mary [two other sisters] played the piano. Oh, we used to have a wonderful time. . . . Kids used to go out, we had nice times growin' up. Everybody, the ones that played musical instruments, they'd all come up, drums and everything. They'd practice for all the minstrel shows and everything."

Other women remembered attending the movies, frequenting the dance halls, or having parties with young people. These activities indicate a growing youth culture that was working class in character

3. This and the following quotations concerning the Irish and British communities were taken from the University of Rhode Island Oral History Project, Mill Life Series. Interviews were conducted in 1975 and 1976 and are available in the Special Collections of the University of Rhode Island library.

Pacific Street, Central Falls, around 1915. A few blocks south of the French-Canadian neighborhood, this street was filled with comfortable working-class multifamily homes. Courtesy of the Rhode Island Historical Society.

but possibly unconnected with ethnic group solidarity, much as described by Katherine Peiss in New York City (Peiss 1985). One Irish woman, a winder at Coats and Clark, described her leisure time as follows: "[We used to go to] dance halls, all the time. . . . I guess I was about eighteen when I started going with this young fella and . . . we used to go dancing every Thursday and every Saturday night. . . . On Tuesday I would go to the pictures."

The Irish parish bordered on a commercial area where a number of small businesses were located. In 1915 they were operated by French, Jewish, English, and Irish proprietors with no one group predominating. The Irish-owned businesses included a bakery, drug store, variety store, grocery and coal company, dry-goods store, and barber shop. Also living in the neighborhood was an Irish liquor dealer, an Irish blacksmith, an Irish painter, and another Irish grocery-store owner.

Although formed later than the French community institutions, the Irish parish by 1915 continued to flourish and serve the Irish population, which was partially concentrated near the church and school complex and partially scattered through the west and south sides of the city. The 284 individuals in 63 households who were part of our sample from the Coats and Clark Mills neighborhood probably constituted about 10 percent of the parish. Irish working daughters, too, were part of an ethnic community that shaped their identities and marked them as different from the French-Canadian girls with whom they worked.

The British and Scottish Community

Published sources reveal relatively little about the community institutions that might have formed a basis for leisure and family activities for the British and Scottish daughters employed in the Central Falls mills. Although, after the French, the British were the second largest immigrant group in Central Falls, they were not as residentially cohesive as the French. Like the Irish, the British and Scottish families were scattered throughout the southern and western portions' of the city.

On a national level, many British institutions fought what British immigrants perceived as Irish attempts to dominate political life. The British-American Association, which had eleven branches in Rhode Island, was established to counteract Irish slurs on the British Crown and Irish resistance to the celebration of Queen Victoria's jubilee. The association also opposed growing Irish political power, especially in the Democratic party, and Irish attempts to establish parochial schools. Two weekly papers, *The British-American* and *Western British America* published in New York and Chicago, printed the views and activities of the association.

Although there was no predominantly British neighborhood in Central Falls, several churches serving congregations of British and Scottish descent were established in the nineteenth century. In 1865 an Episcopal congregation was organized and its church erected in 1872. The original members could have been mainly overseers, mill superintendents, and their families, but by the end of the nineteenth century, the church was no doubt attracting the growing population of working-class immigrants. A Methodist church was built in 1868, and a Presbyterian church, which served Scottish immigrants, was erected in 1895.

Published sources indicate that many English and Scottish immigrants were not regular churchgoers. For example, one English immigrant said of his mother: "And she didn't go to church Sunday. That was a busy day. She had to cook dinners Sundays, you know. Sundays are always a big dinner day. And so she was busy around the house." British and Scottish children in Central Falls most likely attended the public school built near the Coats and Clark Mill in 1877 or the school erected in 1888 in the southern part of the city near the Presbyterian and Methodist churches.

British and Scottish immigrants were easily identifiable in census records from 1915 and had established a number of religious and recreational organizations. However, whereas French-Canadian and Polish populations remained concentrated in ethnic neighborhoods and were attached to ethnic organizations well into the 1930s and 1940s, British and Scottish immigrants were more upwardly mobile and easily assimilated to American culture. As Rowland Berthoff analyzed this assimilation:

> What, then, was the nature of the British immigrants' experience in industrial America? In two major respects it differed from that of most other foreigners. While Irish, Italian, or Polish peasants endured years of poorly paid rough labor, and while Germans or Scandinavians were more apt to go into farming, many of the British, trained in the mines and factories of the foremost industrial nation, moved directly into the best-paid American jobs. With the exception of the Welsh- and Gaelic-speakers, they were also more at home in American society and culture than were any other immigrants. Both the economic and social adjustments were relatively so easy that they could enter into American affairs as equals of natives of the country. (Berthoff 1953:211)

Assimilation was made possible not only by the cultural similarities between the British immigrants and their Yankee counterparts but also by the expansion of the textile economy, which allowed British men to dominate the most skilled occupations. As the textile economy declined in the 1920s and 1930s, these immigrants were undoubtedly in a better position to shift into white-collar, sales, and other jobs that took them away from industrial work and into the more middle-class sector of the economy.

The Polish Community

Polish women who came to Central Falls settled in the original heart of the city, the neighborhood adjacent to the textile mills on the river. By the time the Poles arrived, between 1895 and 1910, the upper class mill owners and middle-level overseers were moving away to more surburban locations. The area had long included worker housing, often owned by mill owners, but additional three-story housing was built to fill in vacant lots and eventually provide housing for new immigrants.

A number of mills still lined the river and provided employment for the new Polish immigrants. Although in the period between 1890 and 1915 two cotton mills had been closed and the hair cloth mill had cut its labor force drastically, the lace mill employed 321 workers in 1915 and about 200 workers for the remainder of World War I.[4] Oral-history data indicate that a number of these workers were Polish.

A small silk mill employed 125 workers, including some Poles, while the Greene and Daniels Thread Mill, across the river, employed 227 men and 204 women, a number of whom were recent immigrants. Most important, however, was the Royal Weaving Silk Mill, which by 1915 employed 422 men and 472 women. Some Poles worked at this company's facilities in the old hair cloth mill and in a new weave shed on the river, but many Polish women walked the mile or so from their neighborhood to the new Royal Weaving Mill in Pawtucket where they worked as silk weavers and winders. Polish men were also employed at two local wire companies, and a neighborhood printing company, a paper-box factory, and a company that made windshield wipers may also have employed the new immigrants.

The neighborhood contained a number of small businesses, mainly in a block square just west of the river—an area that was later called Pulaski Square. Most of these businesses were owned by non-Poles. For example, there were two Jewish-owned groceries, a Jewish tailor, an Armenian restaurant, an English barber, an Italian-owned liquor store, a French-Canadian grocery, and a Chinese laundry. On Mill Street across from the textile mills, most small businesses were run by Jews and Armenians, although several Polish businesses—including two groceries, one blacksmith shop, a restaurant, a bakery, and an insurance agency—had been established. By 1935 Polish small-business entrepreneurs completely dominated the neighborhood commercial establishments.

Women recalled the old-world Polish quality of the neighborhood

4. Imports ruined the Rhode Island lace industry after the war, and this plant was closed in 1921.

of their youth and contrasted it with the later results of urban renewal—parking lots, unused spaces, and a few newly built concrete-
block businesses. Mrs. Roskowski gave the following description:

> Now, it's not like it [was] any more, . . . when the houses were crowded
> here, one next to the other. . . . Now it's all parking lots. . . . But there
> used to be houses where people lived upstairs and downstairs. There
> were furniture stores, clothing stores, dry goods [stores], and a variety
> [store]. So, for example, when they were selling records . . . this man
> had his door open and played. . . . You could hear around the corner.
> People were making beer there, too, so they went to one [store] to buy
> some spices for the beer and made beer at home. And when you were
> buying something, it was out of a barrel, not like now [when] it's pack-
> aged. But one could buy four, five pounds and put it into a sack. And
> there were Polish bakeries . . . not Polish because there were Jews who
> had them. They spoke Polish. You bought [herring] from them. A half of
> a cow was hanging [in the shop].[5]

Later in the same interview, Mrs. Roskowski mentioned the presence of Jewish peddlers as well as Jewish small businessmen who sold
produce to Polish wives and mothers: "Then they were bringing fish
to your home. This man had a small truck and blew his horn and
everybody knew that it was the fisherman. Another one was carrying
apples and yelled 'Jablka! Jablka!' My father-in-law told me that one
used to come with buttermilk. He yelled 'Buttermilk' but nobody
came out. So somebody told him to yell 'Maslanka,' and when he did
this, people came from all over."

Some families lived in the large, brick commercial blocks on Central Street or in the frame houses along Cross Street, both in the
Pulaski Square area. Others lived in two- and three-family houses in
the small streets near the square and on High Street, which ran north
and south the entire length of the neighborhood. Families were
densely packed into these houses since many took in boarders; conditions were crowded in an era without plumbing and other amenities.
Mrs. Wendoloski remembered the neighborhood not by evoking the
image of a village as French-Canadians had done but using the image
of a ghetto:

> On that spot, we lived there . . . when we were small. And I remember
> we had a fireplace. There were two floors and we got burned out, and

5. Quotations for the section on the Polish community come from oral-history interviews conducted by Ewa Hauser during 1977 as part of her dissertation research.

there was another family downstairs. . . . We moved to the house on the back, and we lived in one of these tenements. . . . We lived on the left side. There was a stable with horses. It was awful because, you know, we had no screens in the summer. There was no garbage collection in those days. So in the summertime it was terrible, because we lived on the side with the stable. . . . We had no bathrooms. . . . We had to . . . my mother used to boil the water, warm it, and get the tub out, and each one of us washed, like that. . . . You don't know when you're growing up that this isn't the way to live. . . . You're happy. . . . It's just like now when they say "the ghetto." . . . Certain people live in ghettos; well when they came from Poland, Polish people lived in ghettos. Because you couldn't get a tenement in a nicer place. Besides people weren't looking for nicer places because they came from Poland. It was . . . you know, "roughing it."

Polish immigrants were concentrated in one neighborhood partially because French, Irish, and English populations already dominated other parts of the city. This concentration provided the spatial context for building a set of cultural institutions that created an ethnic identity for Polish men and women. Polish immigrants in 1915 were young families or single individuals; they were peasants, mainly from Gali-

More of a ghetto than a village: view of back yards in the Polish neighborhood near High Street, Central Falls, around 1912. Lewis Hine photograph. Slater Mill Historic Site, Pawtucket, R.I.

[111]

cian in Austrian-dominated Poland, although some came from Russian Poland. Nationally, voluntary associations, which were founded by Poles in the decades before World War I, mobilized American Polonia to work for the restoration of the Polish nation-state. Even in Central Falls, voluntary associations had a double-edged purpose: to help immigrants grapple with industrial life and adapt themselves to the American situation and to weld together Polish immigrants on the basis of nationalistic sentiments.

Most of these associations were started and led by men, but because several societies were related to both work issues and the establishment of religious institutions they touched the productive and reproductive roles of women. The first Polish organization in Central Falls was the St. Joseph's Brotherly Aid Society established in 1900. It was the precursor of both the local Polish Catholic parish and the Pulaski Mutual Aid Society. This male organization, named for St. Joseph, a patron of workers, focused on the need for insurance, particularly sick benefits, in this new working-class community.

Although there were elements of class interests in the founding of the St. Joseph's Brotherly Aid Society and other organizations, the images remembered by members of the Polish community concern national sentiments and the process of becoming an ethnic group within America. The *Jubilee Book*, written during the 1950s, emphasizes the transition from peasants to American citizens: "This society was created by simple folk, so to speak, who came here from under a thatched roof in Poland, . . . and when they found themselves on free American soil, they soon understood and felt the need to organize (the need that could not have been fulfilled in Poland) to help each other, to educate each other, and to prepare themselves to be future defenders of the Fatherland [Poland] as well as wise citizens of the adopted country" (Pulaski Society 1954; translation by Ewa Hauser).

In retrospect, the need to organize immigrants from various villages, and even regions of Poland, into a cohesive unit was also noted: "Creation of this society was caused by a need to bring closer together the country men newly settled in Central Falls—those who came either from other Polish communities in America or as new immigrants from different parts of Poland . . . also with an aspiration for an independent Poland from which they came." Three other organizations also built on nationalistic sentiment to unite members of the new immigrant neighborhood. A branch of the Polish Falcons, a male paramilitary organization, was founded in 1908. Some immigrant volunteers joined General Haller in France to fight for Polish freedom during World War I. The *Jubilee Book* notes: "The Falcons were the most active young organization. Gymnastics and singing were especially [important]. [The organization] renewed the life of local Polonia through exercises, singing, marches, celebrations, balls, meetings, lectures, frequent travel to contests, frequent theatrical performances, and collection of funds for the armed struggle. Thus this organization contributed greatly to the well-being of the Fatherland." A similar organization was the Union of Polish Young, which "through physical exercises, celebrations, meetings, theatre performances, parties, fund raising for the military struggle and Polish independence . . . rendered great services to the Polish cause."

Finally, the Society of Polish Knights was founded by several families including some of those involved in the St. Joseph's benefit society. It was part of the Polish National Alliance, which provided life, accident, and other insurance benefits for its members. In 1910 the group built the first Polish National Home in Rhode Island called Pulaski Hall. Pulaski Hall became the center for nationalistic demonstrations as an announcement in *The Pawtucket Times* noted:

> Celebration of the announcement that Russian Poland would be set up as an independent Kingdom [*sic*] will be held by the Polish people in this city tomorrow. The ceremonies will begin with a high mass. . . . Rev. Kluger, the pastor, will be the celebrant and will also preach a sermon appropriate to the occasion. A parade will follow the mass and the line of march will be through Clay Street to Broad Street, to Central Street, to Mill Street to the Polish National Hall, where a meeting will be held. (*The Pawtucket Times*, November 11, 1915)

Pulaski Hall was also used during the same period as a meeting place for strikers: "For the second time within ten months the plant of the Royal Weaving Company is at a standstill as a result of a strike by practically all of the 500 to 600 weavers. A committee of men and women employees went to see the Manager, Joseph Ott, and presented him with their demands. They wanted more money, ranging from an increase of .5 cent per yard to 1 cent. The strikers met this morning in Pulaski Hall and will meet again tomorrow" (*The Pawtucket Times*, November 9, 1916).

In contrast to the French community, where small businessmen, doctors, and the priest organized the cultural institutions that created an ethnic community, working-class men seemed to take the initiative in the Polish case.

Ewa Hauser argued that peasants from Galicia were very conscious of the class structure of their native society and in many ways resisted re-creating a hierarchy in the American context. In the French community there was conflict in the religious sphere with the Irish-dominated church over cultural control of the parish. Polish parishes in the United States experienced similar dissension in the 1890s and early 1900s. There is also evidence that Polish parishioners in Central Falls resented the authority of the priest much as they had the coalition between clergy and nobles in Galicia (Hauser 1981:291). The conflict between parishioners and the local priest led to a split in the local church and the creation of two religious groups in the community.

The Polish parish was founded in 1904 after members of the St. Joseph's Society petitioned the bishop of Providence. When a census revealed that there were two hundred Polish families in the Central Falls area, the bishop accepted the petition and assigned a German-Polish priest to organize the new parish. In 1907 Father Kluger purchased the Temperance Hall and had it renovated. It became St. Joseph's Church, named for the patron of the Polish benefit society. Rufus Stafford's mansion was purchased in 1909 to be used as a rectory, and additional land was purchased in 1915 to build a new brick church for the parish, which had by then grown to more than sixteen hundred individuals. Before the church was started, however, the old bulding was destroyed by fire on Easter Monday, 1915. The new church was then built on the old site, and enough of it was completed so that Easter services could be held in the church hall in 1916.

One faction broke away from the parish in 1916 with the cooperation of Father Switala, a young priest, who had come to assist the German priest Father Kluger. Parishioners thought that the older priest was too authoritarian and that they were paying too much out of their meager paychecks for the support of the church. As the daughter of a couple in the breakaway faction explained: "you had to buy little cards to go to confessions and pay five dollars for these cards a month. Imagine . . . they were making three dollars a week. Ya, there are lots of facts that nobody writes about, but I think [they] should be out because it should be known how these poor people lived. They came from one servitude in Europe and came to another servitude here."

Another parishioner in the dissident group analyzed the situation as follows:

> They were very dictatorial at the church, you know. The priests at that time were expecting to have people kiss their hands. . . . And some of the people came in . . . some of them were not educated. Most of them came . . . from the farm, from the country, and a lot of them were on that level, what I guess they call serfs. They used to work for the estates. . . . They were just breaking away from that. However, they were very uneducated. By "uneducated" I mean nonschooled. They were intelligent, hardworking people, see. So, all they knew was what they thought, see. And then they were expanding a little bit intellectually because a few of these groups came in . . . and they organized these different groups. And the church, after a while liberalized, especially after our church came in.

The dissidents founded an independent parish, which the church refused to recognize. Apparently changing his mind, Father Switala was persuaded to return to the church and was transferred to another parish. The independent group then contacted the Polish National Catholic Church (PNCC) and applied for affiliation, which they received in 1918.

The PNCC had started in a Scranton, Pennsylvania, Catholic parish in 1898 when another young priest and his parish broke with the Catholic hierarchy in order to retain financial independence, control over their parish, and the right to choose a pastor. The situation was very similar to what occurred in Central Falls eighteen years later. The PNCC was eventually able to build a new church uniting eastern and midwestern parishes that held similar views.

The PNCC embodied opposition to Irish control of local parishes and to the ultimate authority of the pope. It attempted to establish a more democratic governing structure by instituting general rather than individual confessions, allowing priests to marry, altering the sacrament of confirmation, and giving parishes the right to choose their own priest. The PNCC was instrumental in forming an ethnic consciousness based on nationalistic sentiments among parishioners. Mass was celebrated in Polish, the Polish flag was used as a sacred symbol, and attention was paid to Polish culture heros in addition to Roman Catholic saints (Kubiak 1970).

The Central Falls PNCC parish was founded with perhaps two

hundred local families. Land was purchased and a church building completed in 1925. A school was established, but it lasted for only a few years since the expenses of building the new church made it difficult to finance the school as well. At the same time, the Roman Catholic parish continued to expand. A school, which had been started in Temperance Hall before it burned, was later reestablished in the parish hall after a new church had been erected. By 1921 a building for a convent and a new house for the rectory had been purchased. The old rectory (formerly Rufus Stafford's mansion) was then renovated to make a new and larger school.

Thus between 1915 and 1925 members of the Polish neighborhood were still forming ethnic institutions that defined themselves in opposition to the French-Canadians, Irish, and English and that even divided their own community. Although men were responsible for the founding and leadership of most of the voluntary organizations and benefit societies, they were established with no professional elite other than priests and nuns. In contrast to the French neighborhood, which had been established in the 1870s and which by 1915 had a small group of small businessmen, contractors, doctors, and pharmacists, the Polish neighborhood was dominated by working-class people. Although not in leadership positions, single women and young wives and mothers were heavily involved in Roman Catholic church activities and in the founding and maintenance of the new PNCC parish. Ties to Poland, strong until the end of World War I, and ties within the neighborhood were reinforced by the new institutions. In addition to emphasizing similarities in language and cultural background, these ties provided an ethnic identity in opposition to those of other ethnic groups in Central Falls.

Economic Niches and Family Developmental Cycles

By 1915 not only were women living in culturally distinct neighborhoods, but the families of each neighborhood were occupying separate niches within the local mill economy. As we saw in examining the process of immigration, families came as units or as part of a family network. In the Central Falls mill economy, these families were the units that allocated labor to productive and reproductive activities. Husbands were the primary breadwinners in households across ethnic groups, but the particular jobs they were able to find and keep depended on when they migrated, the jobs available outside the mills, the skills they may have brought with them, and the positions that were already monopolized by men of other groups. Most sons and daughters over fourteen years of age went to work for wages. Some sons got jobs at unskilled levels in the mills, others worked for machine shops, and still others were employed in the building trades, depending again on which jobs were already occupied by men of other ethnic groups. Working daughters of all ethnic backgrounds tended to have the same kinds of jobs (winding, spinning, twisting), although Polish women were most able to get jobs as weavers in the silk mills.

The labor of wives and mothers was the most variable. Certainly, they performed most of the housekeeping and child-care tasks in the household, but they were also able to take in boarders to add cash to the family income, and some worked for wages. How the labor of married women was allocated depended on when a particular ethnic population arrived in Central Falls, the availability of fellow immigrants as boarders, and the wages that their husbands commanded.

Family strategies for allocating members' labor and for coping with the local mill economy varied for all groups with their stage in the developmental cycle of domestic groups (Fortes 1958). Young couples with children under fifteen were in a different position from those with unmarried, older children over fifteen who could work for wages. But even for families at each of these two stages of the domestic cycle, the labor of husbands and wives was differentially allocated according to the wages husbands commanded, the availability of boarders, and the willingness of wives to work for wages outside the home.

Neighborhood Composition: Mature and More Recent Ethnic Populations

The three Central Falls neighborhoods in 1915 selected for study represent a different ethnic composition: French-Canadian, English-Scottish-Irish, and Polish. As table 1 shows, the dominant population in each neighborhood accounts for 60 to 80 percent of the sample. However, because of the earlier arrival of the French-Canadians and the English-Irish, and later arrival of the Poles, the age structure and household composition of each neighborhood is different (see population pyramids, figures 1–5).

The French-Canadian population in 1915 was a "mature" immi-

Table 1. Ethnic composition, Central Falls sample neighborhoods, 1915

| | French-Canadian neighborhood | | | | English-Irish neighborhood | | | | Polish neighborhood | | | |
| | Individuals | | Households | | Individuals | | Households | | Individuals | | Households | |
	Number	Percent	Number	Percent	Number	Percent	Number	Percent	Number	Percent	Number	Percent
French-Canadian	**468**	**81.8**	**105**	**82.7**	130	13.8	29	13.6	44	6.0	10	8.3
English-Scottish	19	3.3	3	2.4	**452**	**47.9**	**102**	**47.8**	27	3.7	5	4.2
Irish	27	4.7	7	5.5	**284**	**30.1**	**63**	**29.6**	20	2.7	9	7.5
Polish	0	—	0	—	27	2.9	4	1.9	**516**	**69.8**	**74**	**61.7**
Russian Jew	12	2.1	2	1.6	8	0.8	1	0.5	55	7.4	8	6.7
Syrian	22	3.8	6	4.7	0	—	0	—	0	—	0	—
U.S. parentage	15	2.6	2	1.6	32	3.4	8	3.8	35	4.7	8	6.7
Other*	9	1.6	2	1.6	11	1.2	6	2.8	42	5.7	6	4.9
TOTAL	572	99.9	127	100.1	944	100.1	213	100.0	739	100.0	120	100.0

Note: Boldface figures highlight the dominant ethnic groups in each neighborhood.
*In the French-Canadian neighborhood, "Other" includes French, Belgian, Austrian, Armenian, and Lithuanian; in the English-Irish neighborhood, it includes one German, three Belgian, one French, and six Greek individuals and, in terms of households, it includes one French, three Greek, one German, and one Belgian household; in the Polish neighborhood, it includes Italian, Armenian, German-Austrian, and Chinese.

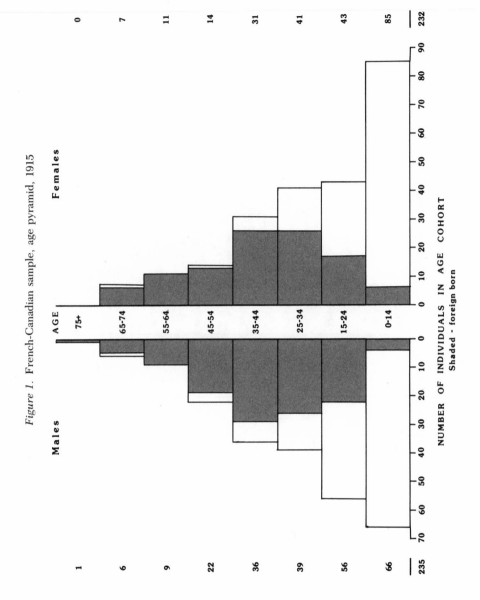

Figure 1. French-Canadian sample, age pyramid, 1915

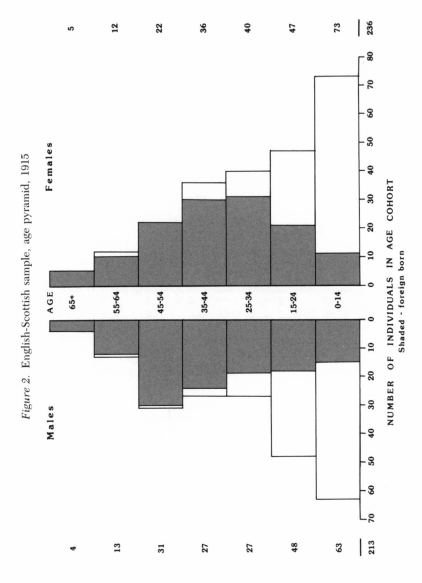

Figure 2. English-Scottish sample, age pyramid, 1915

Figure 3. Irish sample, age pyramid, 1915

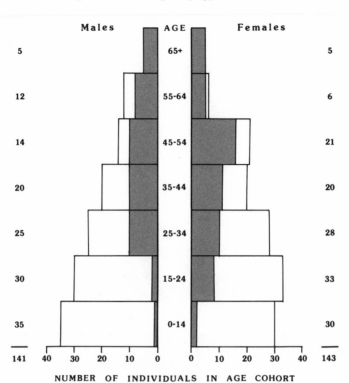

NUMBER OF INDIVIDUALS IN AGE COHORT
Shaded - foreign born

grant population, one that had immigrated during the early life of the older adults and with most children born in the United States. The majority of adults over twenty-five were born in French Canada, and a large proportion of those under twenty-five were born in the United States. Most of the immigration to the United States occurred between 1870 and 1890, although there were still individuals and families who arrived after 1900 (figure 1).

The English-Scottish age pyramid has many of the same characteristics (figure 2). Most men and women over age twenty-five were foreign born. A larger proportion of children were foreign born than in the French-Canadian sample, indicating that many families in this neighborhood were more recent immigrants from England and

[121]

Figure 4. Polish sample, age pyramid, 1915

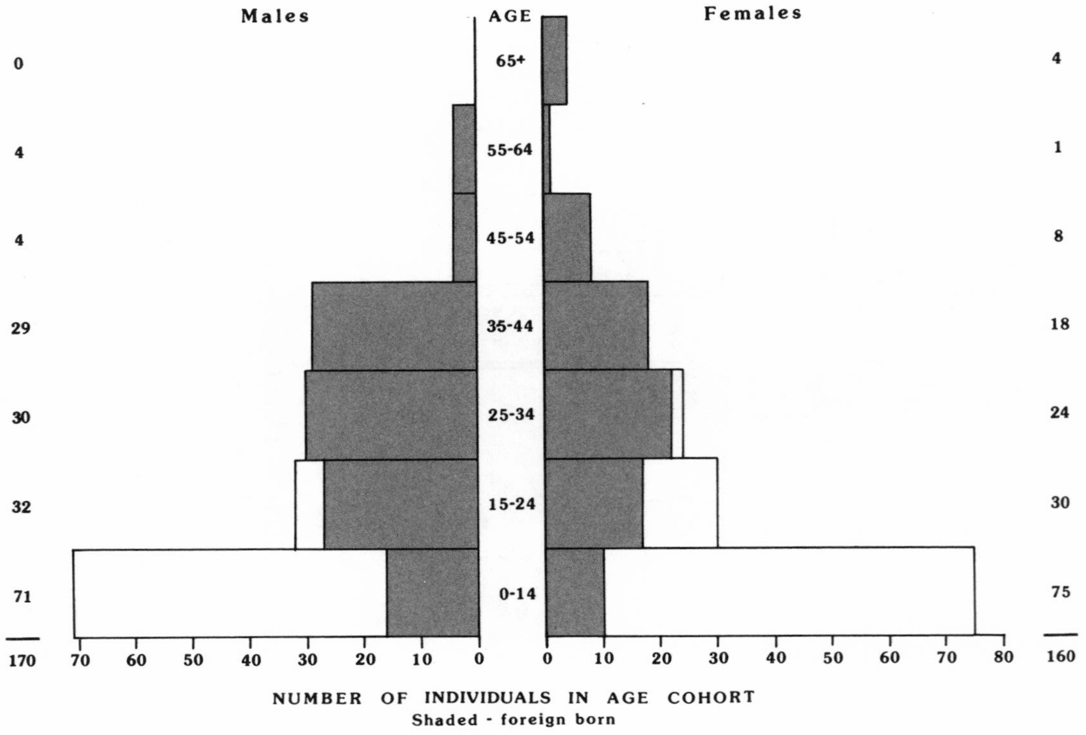

Figure 5. Portuguese sample, age pyramid, 1915

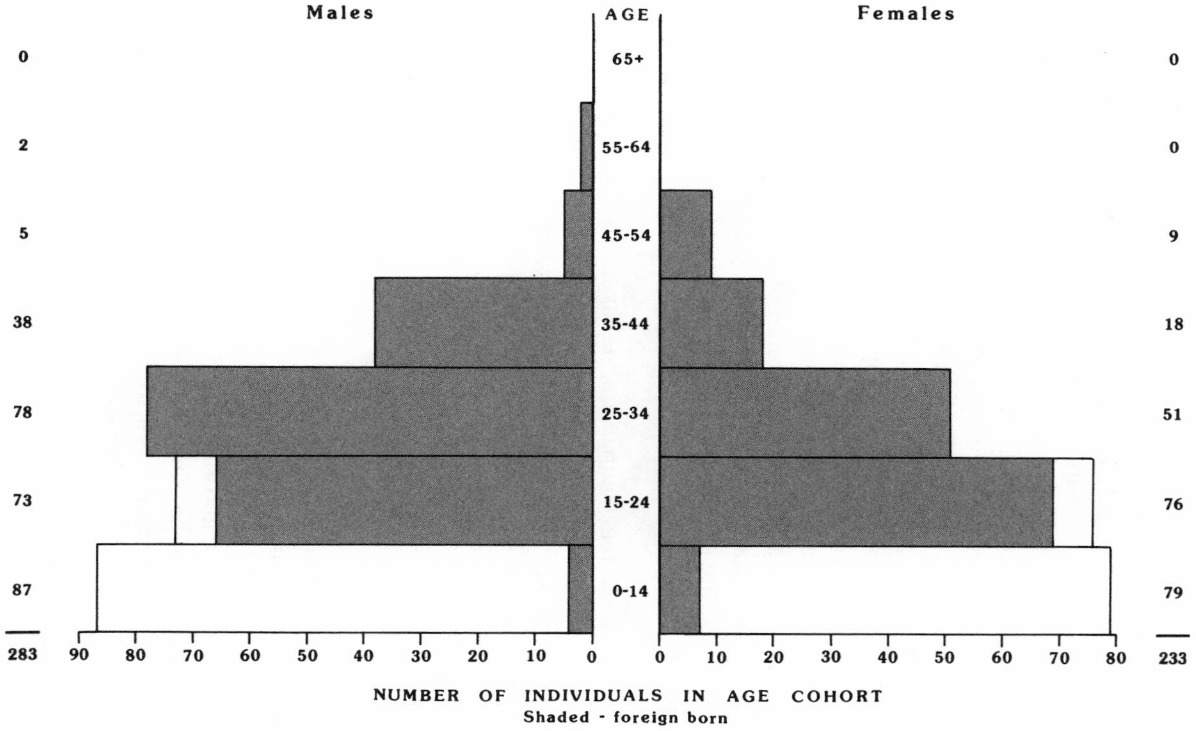

Scotland. There were more women than men in the twenty-five- to forty-five-year-old age span and a greater proportion of middle-aged individuals in this sample than in the French sample. The Irish population pyramid (figure 3) has these same characteristics to an even greater degree. The Irish sample, however, includes some United States-born individuals between the ages of forty-five and sixty-four, children of Irish parents who migrated before 1870.

The Polish population, in marked contrast to the other three, represents a recent or "young" immigrant population (figure 4). The overwhelming majority of adults, and of those between ages fifteen and twenty-four were foreign born. Those born in the United States were mainly children under fourteen. In addition, the pyramid is "truncated," with very few Poles in the sample over forty-five years of age. This was a neighborhood of virtually no old people. The numbers of males in the fifteen to twenty-four and twenty-five to thirty-four age groups were greater than the number of females, indicating that more young adult males were migrating than young adult women. This is reflected in the overall sex ratio of the sample, which is composed of about 55 percent males (n = 283) and only about 45 percent females (n = 233).

To broaden the comparison, I have also included a Portuguese population sampled from Pawtucket, the neighboring town, where the Portuguese were scattered in several areas. Like the Poles, the Portuguese were a newly arrived "young" immigrant population with relatively few older people in the sample (figure 5). Almost all over age fifteen were foreign born, and male adults outnumbered female adults.

Family and Household Structure in Mature and Recent Immigrant Populations

The productive and reproductive labor of immigrant women needs to be analyzed in the context of the family and household. Census data alone, however, do not tell us how decisions were made within the family. We must infer that wives and daughters consented to or were instrumental in developing strategies for coping with the industrial environment. The three strategies that most involved women were: (1) adding relatives to the nuclear family either to bring in cash if the relative worked or domestic help if they did not; (2) taking in boarders, which also added cash but entailed more domestic labor on the part of the wife; and (3) working in the paid labor force, an option taken usually by teenage daughters but also by some married women.

An examination of the family and household structure in the three sample neighborhoods confirms that these strategies were differentially distributed among French-Canadian, English, Irish, and Polish households. Table 2 shows that most French and English-Scottish families were nuclear or "simple," being composed of a husband, wife, and children or a widow (or widower) and children.[6] Relatively few families were "extended," including additional relatives of either spouse, or "multiple," including at least two related couples of different generations, such as an older couple living with a married child and grandchildren.

In contrast, in the Irish sample a greater proportion of families were "extended" or "multiple." The Irish clearly had chosen to expand the household pool of productive and reproductive labor by bringing in relatives. Many of these adults worked for wages and were able to add to the family income in exchange for their room and board. Many of the additional women (elderly sisters of one spouse, a niece, or a mother-in-law) could also have provided labor in the home in the form of cooking, cleaning, and child care.

In these three samples only 11 to 14 percent of the households contained boarders, which indicate how rare this strategy was among the French, English-Scottish, and Irish. In the Polish neighborhood, however, 66 percent of households had boarders. More than 80 percent of the sampled Polish adults were living in households containing a family plus boarders. Thus many Polish women could augment family income by offering lodging to newly arriving immigrants, a strategy that was not so readily available among populations that had immigrated earlier.

Irish women were most likely to be members of households that added relatives and Polish women most likely to be members of households that took in boarders. All families with children over fifteen years of age sent sons and daughters to work for wages, but this was most common in the "mature" immigrant populations represented by the French and English-Scottish samples (table 3). This strategy was most available to those families with older children in the mature stage of the developmental cycle.

6. I constructed table 2 following David Kertzer (1977) in his revision of the categories developed by Peter Laslett in working with European materials.

Table 2. Household structure in four ethnic groups, 1915

| | French-Canadian | | | | English-Scottish | | | |
| | Nonboarding | | Boarding | | Nonboarding | | Boarding | |
	Number	Percent	Number	Percent	Number	Percent	Number	Percent
Solitary individuals	10	9.5	—	—	12	11.8	—	—
Coresidential siblings	2	1.9	—	—	1	1.0	—	—
Simple family (including widows)	75	71.4	12	11.4	60	58.8	10	9.8
Extended family	2	1.9	—	—	12	11.8	2	2.0
Multiple family	4	3.8	—	—	5	4.9	—	—
TOTAL	**93**	**88.5**	**12**	**11.4**	**90**	**88.3**	**12**	**11.8**
TOTAL HOUSEHOLDS	105	99.9			102	100.1		

Note: Boldface highlights differences between neighborhoods in the proportion of boarding and nonboarding households.

Young married couples in the first phase of the developmental cycle quickly established themselves in their own tenement apartment. Relatively few young couples remained in the parental household when they were married—only four of fifteen French couples, five of seventeen English-Scottish couples, and four of nine Irish couples. This stage was followed by new families in which children under fourteen years of age were not employable. A third stage began when the oldest child reached fourteen and could leave school to work in the mills or at other wage jobs. In this phase, a couple (or widow or widower) could count on the incomes of daughters and sons as they went into the labor force.

In a fourth phase, grown children began to marry and move out. Household size diminished, but the incomes of maturing daughters and sons were still available. From census data we cannot tell how many children in a particular household had already married and established a new residence. Married sons and daughters rarely lived at the same address, and married daughters took their husbands' names and thus could not be linked to their parents' households. However, since the number of children for couples and widows with several working children was fewer than that of families in the previous phase, it is likely that this category included families where one or two children were already married. During the final phase, an older couple or widow-widower lived alone or in some cases with a married child.

	Irish				Polish			
	Nonboarding		Boarding		Nonboarding		Boarding	
	Number	Percent	Number	Percent	Number	Percent	Number	Percent
Solitary individuals	5	7.8	1	1.6	5	6.8	—	—
Coresidential siblings	3	4.7	1	1.6	—	—	—	—
Simple family (including widows)	27	42.2	5	7.8	18	24.3	42	56.7
Extended family	16	25.0	2	3.1	2	2.7	5	6.8
Multiple family	4	6.3	—	—	—	—	2	2.7
TOTAL	**55**	**86.0**	**9**	**14.1**	**25**	**33.8**	**49**	**66.2**
TOTAL HOUSEHOLDS	64	100.1			74	100.0		

Table 3 shows the contrast between mature and young immigrant populations in the possibility of sending daughters and sons out to work. Thus 31 percent of the French-Canadian and 30 percent of the English-Scottish families had children fifteen years or older who were working in the paid labor force, and another 31 percent of the French-Canadian and 20 percent of the English-Scottish families had young children (under age fifteen) not yet able to work for wages. Only 9 percent of Polish families (both those with and without boarders) had working children over age fifteen. The Polish proportion of married couples with young children—those in the second phase of the developmental cycle—was much greater—59 percent—pointing to the youthfulness of the population and its recent immigrant status. However, most of these young families (thirty of forty-two, or 71 percent) were taking in boarders. Families with boarders amount to 66 percent of all of the Polish families in the sample. Thus French and English families were more likely to be at a stage in the family cycle where daughters could be sent out to work, while Polish women were wives in households at an earlier stage of the cycle and instead were taking in boarders. The availability of boarders was greater in the still-immigrating Polish population. The most economically vulnerable group was probably those young French and English-Scottish families consisting of a couple and young children, where the household was dependent on the wages of only one individual.

Not all newly arrived "young" immigrant populations used the strategy of taking in boarders. Table 4 shows the family and household structure for the fifty-nine Portuguese families from Pawtucket. Most

[127]

Table 3. Developmental cycle of sample families in three ethnic groups, 1915

	French-Canadian				English-Scottish				Polish			
	Families		Families with boarders		Families		Families with boarders		Families		Families with boarders	
	Number	Percent	Number	Percent	Number	Percent	Number	Percent	Number	Percent	Number	Percent
Married couples without children	11	10.5	2	1.9	8	7.8	—	—	—	—	4	5.4
Married couples with small children	32	30.5	3	2.8	20	19.6	3	2.9	14	18.9	30	40.5
Married couples with children over fifteen No children working	—	—	2	1.9	—	—	—	—	2	2.7	2	2.7
Some children working	18	**17.1**	2	1.9	12	**11.8**	2	2.0	1	1.4	3	4.0
Married couples with all children over fifteen Most children working	8	**7.5**	—	—	11	**10.8**	4	3.9	1	1.4	—	—
Widows with small children	—	—	1'	1.0	—	—	—	—	—	—	1	1.4
Widows with some children working	5	**4.8**	2	1.9	5	**4.9**	1	1.0	—	—	—	—
Widowers with some children working	1	**1.0**	—	—	4	**3.9**	—	—	—	—	2	2.7
SUBTOTAL	75	71.5	12	11.4	60	58.8	10	9.8	18	24.4	42	56.7
Other families (extended, multiple, solitary, coresident siblings)	18	17.1	—	—	30	29.4	2	2.0	7	9.4	7	9.4
SAMPLE SUBTOTAL	93	88.6	12	11.4	90	88.2	12	11.8	25	33.8	49	66.1
TOTAL NUMBER OF HOUSEHOLDS	105	100.0			102	100.0			74	99.9		

Note: Figures in boldface sum to 30.5 and 31.4 percent of the French-Canadian and English-Scottish households, respectively. They emphasize the larger proportion of families in the middle stages of the family cycle in these two groups.

Table 4. Household structure and developmental cycle of sample Portuguese families, 1915

Household type	Families		Families with boarders		Simple family type	Families		Families with boarders	
	Number	Percent	Number	Percent		Number	Percent	Number	Percent
Solitary individuals	0	0.0	0	0.0	Married couples	5	8.5	—	—
Coresident siblings	0	0.0	—	—	Married couples with children under fifteen	25	42.4	7	11.9
Simple families	37	62.7	10	16.9	Married couples with some children working	11	18.6	3	5.1
Married couples	5	8.5	1	1.7	Married children with most or all children working	1	1.7	—	—
Extended families	5	8.5	0	0.0	Other families	6	10.2	1	1.7
Multiple families	1	1.7							
TOTAL	48	81.4	11	18.6	TOTAL	48	81.4	11	18.7
GRAND TOTAL	59				GRAND TOTAL	59			

Note: This sample is not from a single neighborhood; given the small number of Portuguese in Central Falls and Pawtucket in 1915, we attempted to pull together the data on every Portuguese family in Pawtucket that could be located in the 1915 census books. This sample of 59 households and 330 individuals represents 87 percent of the 379 Portuguese listed in the general tables in the 1915 census.

were nuclear or simple families, but only 19 percent took in boarders, a proportion slightly larger than in the French and English groups but much smaller than in the Polish sample. Most Portuguese families were young—54 percent with children under age fifteen—but only 12 percent of them were taking in boarders. The Portuguese like the French and English young families were probably dependent on just one male wage earner.

Women of different ethnic backgrounds were part of families that used different strategies to allocate female productive and reproductive labor. The developmental cycle of the family and the time of arrival of an immigrant population were important factors in shaping and limiting the use of these strategies (tables 2, 3, and 4). Next, to gain a fuller understanding of the allocation of women's labor, I will examine the jobs that husbands and sons were able to command in the mill economy, the work daughters and married women did in the mills and in the home, and the way in which boarding fit into the family economy.

Work and Family in a French-Canadian Neighborhood

Most of the French-Canadian families in our sample were nuclear families living in three- and four-decker housing. Only six families were "extended" or "multiple" in form.[7] Many of the nuclear families

7. There were only six nonnuclear families in the sample. Two were extended families. One, at the third stage of the domestic group cycle, contained a nephew living in a family of ten children, where six were already working to supplement the father's income. In the second case, an older aunt, at the second phase of the cycle, was living in a nuclear family where the husband was the sole support of the family and where she provided perhaps domestic labor but not a wage income. Three multiple families were all organized around nuclear families at the third or fourth stage of the cycle, where there were children over age fifteen, most of whom were working for wages. In each case, one of the daughters had married, bringing a son-in-law and wage earner into the household. None of these three couples had had children by 1915, perhaps a time when they would find a separate place to live. The one three-generation multiple family was an unusual case, composed of an older widow, her employed son, and his sixteen-year-old daughter, who was also working. Perhaps the son had been widowed or separated from his wife and continued to support his daughter as well as his mother. These six cases illustrate both a family's willingness to support older and younger relatives as well as provide a temporary home for young married couples in exchange for additional cash income and the additional domestic labor of the married daughter.

were at the stage of development where they could send children of working age into the paid labor force.

The occupations of the French-Canadian males in the neighborhood sample show that by 1915 they had come to occupy a distinct niche in the local economy, one that brought families who depended on one or two male incomes a comfortable, but not affluent, working-class income. Most French-Canadian men (70 percent, or 126 men) held jobs in manufacturing, grouped into three distinct types of occupations: textile jobs (26 percent), other manufacturing jobs (18 percent), and individual occupations including the building trades (27 percent). Textile employment did not dominate the lives of French-Canadian men in the same way it did in other ethnic groups. Textiles was more important in women's work, where forty-four of fifty-six women (79 percent) who worked for wages were employed in textile-mill jobs.

Thus by 1915 French-Canadian men had been able to find jobs in machine shops and had been able to translate their carpentry skills into the construction jobs made available by the general expansion of housing that took place in Central Falls between 1880 and 1915. Furthermore, French-Canadian men were able to obtain the higher paying jobs (i.e., those that paid more than fourteen dollars a week in 1915) in textile mills, machine shops, and building trades.[8]

Among French-Canadian men employed in the textile industry, the sample included two overseers, five loomfixers, and eleven weavers in the cotton industry and a weaver and overseer in the silk industry. All of these jobs averaged more than $16.00 a week. Among those in other manufacturing jobs, there were sixteen machinists probably earning from $11.00 to $24.75 a week. However, the real advantage of French-Canadian males was their position in the skilled trades. In our sample there were seventeen carpenters, three painters, two stone

8. The 1915 Rhode Island census contained information only on the type of job each man held, not his weekly wage. Wage data were obtained from the State of Rhode Island, *Twenty-Ninth Annual Report, Commissioner of Industrial Statistics.* I used the tables on "Rates of Wages and Hours of Labor per Week Prevailing in Rhode Island Industries, December 31, 1915" (Rhode Island 1916:11–22). I also consulted the State of Rhode Island *Report of Commissioner of Labor, 1916–1919*, and used the tables "Comparative Rates of Wages and Hours of Labor Prevailing in Rhode Island Industries, December 31, 1915–December 31, 1919" (Rhode Island 1921:88–100). These are statewide figures and can be used only as an estimate of the actual wages earned by Central Falls workers. The estimate of fourteen dollars a week average wages comes from the statistics collected by the office of the Commissioner of Labor using a sample of twenty-four thousand persons in Providence acquired along with the 1915 state census (Rhode Island 1921:223–28, 249–60).

masons, and two plumbers. In 1915 carpenters earned between $13.85 and $25.42 a week, while painters earned between $20.00 and $24.00 a week. Stone masons earned between $19.80 and $24.20 a week and plumbers between $19.20 and $24.75 a week. These jobs were higher paying than those in textile mills or machine shops except perhaps for overseer and second-hand positions. Overall, 60 percent of the French-Canadian male sample were in high-paying jobs and had better than average incomes relative to the local Central Falls working class (see table 5).

Many of the French-Canadian men holding unskilled and low-paying jobs were young men, that is, sons living at home with their parents. Sons were more likely to hold the least-skilled jobs in textiles, machinery, and building trades, while fathers were more likely to hold the more highly skilled, higher paying jobs (table 6). This trend is clearest in textiles, where single, young men were doffers, spinners, yarn carriers, cleaners, and laborers, and married men were more likely to be loomfixers and overseers. There were nearly equal numbers of single and married men in weaving, which meant that young men were able to obtain some of the higher paying jobs in the mills.

Nevertheless, there was still a substantial number of married men (twenty-four, or 26 percent of the married male sample) who had low-paying jobs. Among them were six men with wives and children working as laborers, a twiller, or a bellhop. These families, surviving on one male income, were the most vulnerable of the sample. In six other families where men held low-paying jobs as spinners or laborers, children worked to augment family income, and in three more, the husband's income was supplemented by taking in boarders and sending sons or daughters out to work.

In general, French-Canadian fathers and husbands held relatively high-paying jobs in textile mills, machine shops, and the construction industry. Yet for many families, these incomes were supplemented by strategies that allocated sons and daughters to productive work for wages and wives and mothers to the additional reproductive work entailed in taking in boarders. Not every family was able to take advantage of these strategies, but those who had children of working age certainly placed them in the paid labor force. Virtually every French-Canadian son or daughter over the age of fifteen was a wage earner. Fewer wives and mothers, however, were able to take in boarders.

Table 5. Jobs held by French-Canadian males, 1915

	High-paying jobs (more than $14/wk.)			Low-paying jobs (less than $14/wk.)	
	Number	Percent		Number	Percent
Textiles					
Weaver, loom-fixer, overseer	22	12.2	Laborer, doffer, spinner	24	13.2
Machine or iron works					
Machinist	19	10.5	Laborer, operator	13	7.2
Individual occupations					
Carpenter, painter, plumber, printer, tailor	35	19.3	Construction laborer	13	7.2
Other jobs					
Salesman, merchant, barber, teamster, driver	33	18.2	Pedler, street laborer	15	8.3
TOTAL (n = 181)*	109	60.2		65	35.9

*Seven (4 percent) have no occupation.

Table 6. Single and married men's jobs, French-Canadian sample, 1915

	Single		Married	
	Number	Percent	Number	Percent
High-paying jobs				
Textiles	6		16	
Machine and other manufacturing	7		12	
Individual occupations (including				
building trades)	16		19	
Other	16		17	
TOTAL	45	24.9	64	35.4
Low-paying jobs				
Textiles	16		8	
Machine and other manufacturing	10		3	
Individual occupations (including				
building trades)	7		6	
Other	8		7	
TOTAL	41	22.6	24	13.2
Males with no occupation	2		5	
GRAND TOTAL	88	48.6	93	51.4

Boarders and Women's Reproductive Work

In the French-Canadian household sample, there were only 12 of the 105 households that contained boarders in 1915 (11 percent). Many of these boarders were single males (nine of twenty French-Canadians and two Portuguese boarders). Two were single females and nine were members of the three family units who boarded with French-Canadian households. The predominance of single males in the boarding population supports the point made earlier that men often migrated first, leaving families behind until they found jobs and decided that permanent migration was a good strategy. For one of the family units, Edward Fleury and his two sons, boarding provided the female reproductive labor (housekeeping and cooking), which was unavailable in his own widower family. For a young couple with a six-month-old baby, the Perreaults, boarding may have been a temporary situation at a time when the wife's energy was taken up with a young child but before they could establish their own household. The Pa-quettes, who had a three-year-old daughter and who boarded with Jeanne Archambault, a widow, may have been recent immigrants hoping to start their own household. For Mrs. Archambault's other two boarders, two single young women employed as a winder and an inspector in the mills, boarding was probably the only option if they had no kin in Central Falls.

In households where women expended their energies providing for boarders, most either had husbands with low-paying jobs, were childless and had the space and time to take on paying boarders, or were widows who lacked the financial support of a mature male. For example, Heloise Mercier, whose husband, Armand, was a low-paid laborer at odd jobs, ran a boarding house for single men. With the help of her stepdaughter, she provided room and board for a Scottish-Irish couple and for four French-Canadian and two Belgian men who ranged in age from nineteen to thirty-eight and who worked as weavers, loomfixers, painters, and laborers. The age and occupation of these men suggests that they were married and intended to bring wives and families to Central Falls or hoped to marry and settle in the community.

Six other nuclear families also took in boarders. In the Moreau and Michaud families, the fathers (a machinist and a weaver) had relatively well-paying jobs. The sixty-year-old boarder in the Moreau household may have been Mrs. Moreau's Irish mother. In the Michaud household the boarder, a Belgian woman of twenty-five employed as a spinner, may have found her way to this household through community contacts with Mrs. Michaud, who was also Belgian. The extra cash income might have been a welcome addition, even if offering housing to a fellow countryman may not have been a necessity. In two other households the fathers were laborers, and each had a working son (one a laborer and the other a machinist). Nevertheless, adding a single male boarder to the household would have helped financially and would not have been an excessive burden for the wife. Finally, the Brouillard family, with three young children and a husband who was a polisher, took in Edward Fleury and his sons, and the Vanasse household offered lodging to the Perreaults, the young couple with a six-month-old baby mentioned above.

In addition, two childless couples took in boarders. The Chabots supplemented the husband's income as a peddler by housing two young French-Canadian males, and the Chapdelaines provided room and board to a United States-born couple who worked in a lace mill. These wives, with no children and with space in their flats for additional people, were able to afford the extra effort of cooking, cleaning, and washing for single males or a couple.

Finally, three of the eight widows in the sample took in boarders.

These women had fewer working children than did those widows who did not take in boarders. Elise Gautier, who had five children including an eighteen-year-old son who was a doffer, took in two young Portuguese male boarders, while Adele Henault worked as a weaver in a cotton mill as well as taking in a male boarder. The third widow was Jeanne Archambault, who housed the Paquette young couple and their three-year-old daughter and two single French-Canadian women.

Not all widows or wives whose husbands had low-paying jobs opted for the strategy of taking in boarders. Immigration to the United States from Canada was declining, and there were relatively few single men and even fewer young women or young families in need of lodging. This lack of potential boarders might explain why only three of thirty-five young families with only a single income took in boarders. Yet three of eight widows (37.5 percent) adopted this strategy, suggesting that there was some connection between economic need and women's use of their own reproductive labor to gain cash income. For these three women and for four women with husbands and working children, taking in boarders was one way to supplement the wages of working children when husbands were deceased or had low-paying jobs. Others in the same stage of the domestic cycle may have had to be content with the wages of their sons and daughters since the pool of potential boarders was disappearing.

Women's Productive and Reproductive Work

Women's work in connection with the developmental cycle of the family had two distinct phases: as daughters women worked for wages outside the home, and as wives and mothers they worked inside the home to raise a large family. Table 7 shows that 38 percent of French-Canadian women in our sample were working for wages, but the overwhelming majority of these women (85 percent) were single, young daughters who worked in mill jobs. Most worked in relatively low-paying "female jobs." About 35 percent of them were spoolers, and others were doffers, inspectors, or winders or operated a warping machine, thread machine, or spinning machine. Relatively few women, only seven, were weavers, and three of them were among the few married women workers in the sample who worked outside the home for wages. Most of the working daughters probably earned nine to ten

Table 7. Women's labor-force participation, French-Canadian sample, 1915

Labor-force participation	Single		Married (no children)		Married (with children)		Married with children (no spouse)		Total	
	Number	Percent	Number	Percent	Number	Percent	Number	Percent	Number	Percent
French-Canadian										
Paid	48	84	3	20	4	6	1	11	56	37.6
Unpaid	9	16	12	80	64	94	8	89	93	62.4
TOTAL	57	100	15	100	68	100	9	100	149	100.0
Non-French-Canadian										
Paid	7	58	2	29	0	0	1	50	10	27
Unpaid	5	42	5	71	16	100	1	50	27	73
TOTAL	12	100	7	100	16	100	2	100	37	100

Summary

Of all paid French-Canadians,
  85% are single
  91% are childless
    (5% are married but childless)
  9% have children
Of all unpaid French-Canadians,
  77% have children
  23% are childless
    (12% are married but childless)

Of all paid non-French-Canadians,
  70% are single
  90% are childless
    (20% are married but childless)
  10% have children but no spouse
Of all unpaid non-French-Canadians,
  63% have children
  37% are childless
    (21% are married but childless)
Only 37.6% of all French-Canadian women are working, compared with 48% in the Polish sample.

dollars a week at their mill jobs, slightly more than an entry-level sweeper or doffer but less than their brothers who were working as carpenters, machinists, or even laborers.

Marriage for French-Canadian women, which often did not occur until women were in their midtwenties, quickly brought children and retirement from the paid labor force. Of eleven women in households composed of married couples, six were young couples without children. Half of these women were still employed, but the category is so small that it suggests that women, once married, began their families quickly. Few married women with children, only three of seventy, were working outside the home. French-Canadian married women worked long hours at home to support large families of five to seven children. Between the ages of twenty-five and thirty-four, women were raising two or three young children. By the next phase of the family cycle, there were three or more children in the family, and some sons or daughters were beginning to work for wages outside the home. Later, only one or two children were living at home, and most were working to support the family. Some families at this stage were headed by widows whose children were wage earners or who themselves may have been working or taking in boarders.

A clearer picture of the allocation of the labor of fathers, daughters, and sons working outside and widows, wives, and mothers working at home can be seen by examining three families who lived in a three-decker tenement located across the street from the French parish church. On one floor lived a forty-eight-year-old widow, Alice Giroux, with her four grown children who had not yet married. The two unmarried sons, ages twenty-five and twenty-three, worked as a plumber and carpenter. One daughter, Marie, age twenty-eight and separated from her husband, worked as a cop spooler in a cotton mill, and the other, Louise, age twenty-nine and single, was a stock clerk in a knitting mill.

On another floor lived the Lefebre family with seven children. The father, Phillipe, age forty-two, was a laborer. His wife, Marguerite, was not employed for wages, but the oldest son, age twenty, had a well-paying job as a weaver in a cotton mill. The nineteen-year-old brother was a yarn carrier in a cotton mill, a low-paying, entry-level job, and the seventeen-year-old son was a laborer at a glass works. The sixteen-year-old son was a stair builder working in a carpenter shop, and the next son, age fifteen, worked at odd jobs in a grocery store.

Working daughter seated at the end of her spinning frame, around 1912, Pawtucket, Rhode Island. Lewis Hine photograph. Slater Mill Historic Site, Pawtucket, R.I.

The only daughter was not old enough to work for wages, nor was her youngest brother.

A third family in the house, the DeRoche's, included a couple, ages forty and thirty-two, with four children. The father, Paul, worked as a molder in an iron foundry, and the oldest son, Jean, age eighteen, did odd jobs. The daughter, age seventeen, was a spooler at a cotton mill. The younger daughters, age fourteen and six, were too young to be employed, and the wife, Yvonne, who was perhaps a stepmother to the older children, worked in the home caring for the family.

All of these families were at the third and the fourth stage of the family cycle with some or all of the children in the paid labor force. All of the mothers engaged in housework to support the labor of their sons, daughters, and husband, unless widowed. The sons in these families held a variety of jobs in mills or in the building trades, while girls worked in the cotton mills.

Three families in a three-decker house several blocks away give us a sense of how younger and older families managed. The thirty-two-year-old father in the LeClair family was a machinist; his wife, Denise, age thirty-three, was working in the home, and they had three young sons and a daughter ranging in age from one to eight years. In the Martineau family in the same tenement, Wilfred, the thirty-three-year-old husband, was a wood turner in a carpenter shop. He was married to Yvonne, who at twenty-five years of age worked at home caring for two sons, age eleven months and three years.

The third family in the house was headed by Arthur Patenaude, a sixty-three-year-old stone contractor. His wife, Anna, sixty-two, was not working in the paid labor force. They had five children, all in their twenties. One daughter was married, and she and her husband, a teamster, lived in the household. Another son-in-law was also in the household and worked as a machinist in a machine shop. None of the daughters worked for wages but presumably took part in the cooking, cleaning, and laundry work generated by such a large household. The family benefited from the wages of two sons, ages twenty-five and twenty-three, one working as a stone mason for his father and the other as a weaver in a textile mill. In this tenement, Robert LeClair and Wilfred Martineau were younger men with families who had relatively high-paying working-class jobs when their children were still young and their wives took responsibility for reproductive work in the home. In the older family, Arthur Patenaud's high-paying position as a stone contractor was supplemented by the wages of four young males, also in relatively high-paying jobs.

Women's own accounts of their lives also emphasize the divided nature of women's work—as young daughters in the mills and as wives and mothers in the home. Oral-history interviews with French-Canadian women, tinged with present-day nostalgia, show us both how women culturally constructed their work experience and how their work fit into the family economy. Of four French-Canadian women from Central Falls interviewed in the University of Rhode Island Oral History Project, all quit school at age fourteen or sixteen and worked at the Coats and Clark Mills. They lived outside the boundaries of our sample French-Canadian neighborhood, and each had considerable contact with English and Scottish young women. Their fathers may have been in more difficult financial straits than some in our neighborhood sample, but the importance of their work for their family was indicative of the situation for French-Canadians in general. All viewed their work for wages as an outcome of financial need, and all reported living at home and handing their wages over to their mothers. They also stressed the difficulties that their parents faced because of illness, death, or low-paying work.

Rose Forcier was born in Central Falls in 1893 and at age fourteen went to work at Coats and Clark, "because I had to," she explained. "My father was sick. At fifty-two he wasn't working any more so we supported the family. I had an oldest brother who was a silk weaver. We gave up our pay (to my mother) until we were twenty-two years old." Her first job was tending the "doublers," machines that made the roving after the cotton was carded. She made $6.20 for a week's work of fifty-four hours, turning over to her mother all of her pay, except for twenty cents spending money and ten cents for her weekly church contribution. Rose explained, "My mother never worked. In them days very few mothers worked. They stayed home and did their cooking and laundry and all that stuff. We used to help at home too, when we'd come back, and at night we used to help with the ironing, but then we used to wear so many aprons and petticoats at that time."9

Another French-Canadian woman, Emily Desrosiers, was the oldest in a family of eleven children. Her father was a "traveler" who finally settled in Rhode Island, worked in insurance, and when that failed, learned carpentry. She mentioned that her father was ill as well. Emily started work at Coats and Clark when she was sixteen years old. Following a typical female work history, she started out as a winder making $4.00 a week. Then she became a spooler and worked at the thread mill for twenty-seven years. She, too, turned her pay check over to her mother, keeping twenty-five cents a week for spending money. She said, "They gave you two weeks to learn before you went on piece work. If you worked five or six years you could make $8.00 or $8.50 or $9.00; $8.00 or $9.00 was good money."

When World War I began, more people were hired, and she taught other girls how to work the machines. She described the ethnic diversity of the shop:

I knew all the girls. I worked with French . . . lots of English, Scots. They didn't hire a whole lot of French girls. There was another Emi-

9. The quoted material in this section is from the University of Rhode Island Oral History Project, Mill Life Series, 1970–76. Interviews were conducted with mill workers in 1975 and are available from the Special Collections in the University of Rhode Island library.

Women workers leaving the Coats and Clark Mill, around 1900. Courtesy of the Rhode Island Historical Society.

ly. . . . She had some of the English girls, some of the Scots girls. I had some too. They spoke English, but they came from Lancashire. That's how I started because I could speak French. We had mostly Irish, French, Scotch, and English. . . . Nobody complained. The Scottish and English girls put up with a lot. We got along with them. There were a few that wanted to make trouble. They wanted us to get into the union . . . fifty cents a week.

A third woman, Paulette Fortier, went to work at Coats and Clark at fourteen years of age. Like Rose, she said, "I had to go to work. There were seven of us in the family. . . . My father didn't make much money. If he made $7.50, that's as much as he made in a week."

Paulette quit school at age twelve to help her mother: "Because my mother used to go out washing and cleaning and everything like that so I stayed home, which I needed somebody to be taking care of me, you know, because I was only small. And there was five of us . . . five kids." Her mother did the washing at home, and Paulette would go out and pick up the laundry from the customers. Beginning employment at Coats and Clark in 1908, she was first a sweeper, earning $4.24 a week for a fifty-six-hour week. Then she became a second girl or helper, and finally she tended machines. She worked for twelve years and quit in 1920 to marry and begin raising a family of eight children. She returned to work in 1947 after she was widowed.

A fourth example, Yvonne Doucette, came from a smaller family of only three children. Her father was a millwright, and they built their own house in the northern section of Central Falls. Her family was better off than those of the other three. Yet she, too, quit school and worked at Coats and Clark from the time she was fourteen to sixteen years of age. She gave her reason for going to work as, "I didn't like school I guess. It's as good a reason as any." She worked as a rewinder, earning ten to twelve dollars a week between 1920 and 1922.

The 1915 census data and these examples show different family and household structures with French-Canadian husbands and fathers being employed in a range of jobs from skilled, well-paying positions to that of common laborer. Many occupied relatively high-paid jobs in the construction trades, a particular niche in the local economy generated by Central Falls's expansion as a mill town. By and large the skills of wives and mothers were needed in the raising and care of from three to seven children. Even comfortable families sent sons and daughters out to work at the age of fourteen. These young women were universally employed in "female" jobs, and they defined working as a "financial necessity." They turned over their pay to support the domestic labor of their mothers, and they probably continued to help with chores in the home. When they married they left the paid labor force and took up domestic responsibilities in their own households. These family strategies for women were also typical of other mature immigrant populations during the same period.

Work and Family in the English Sample

Compared to French-Canadian men, English and Scottish men from our next neighborhood sample were more highly concentrated in textile jobs (48 percent compared with 25 percent among French-Canadians). They also held more jobs in machine, iron, and other manufacturing industries (27 percent compared with 18 percent among French-Canadians) (see table 8). But English men lacked access to the skilled building trades that gave older, married French-

Table 8. Jobs held by English and Scottish males, 1915

	High-paying jobs (more than $14/wk.)			Low-paying jobs (less than $14/wk.)	
	Number	Percent		Number	Percent
Textiles					
Weaver, loomfixer, overseer, mule spinner, printer	21	14.1	Laborer, doffer, spinner, carder, cleaner	51	34.2
Machine or iron works					
Machinist, iron molder, grinder	26	17.4	Laborer, apprentice	12	8.1
			Other	2	1.3
Individual occupations					
Carpenter, painter, bricklayer, mason, electrician	15	10.1		0	0.0
Other jobs					
Store owner, clerk, fireman, teamster, policeman	11	7.4	Store clerk, janitor, street repairer, chauffeur	8	5.4
TOTAL (n = 149)*	73	49.0		73	49.0

*Three (2 percent) have no occupation.

Canadian men incomes of more than fourteen dollars a week. The English niche in the local economy lay in their ability to command some of the high-paying jobs in textiles where they were overseers, foremen, mule spinners, loomfixers, and weavers and in their skill as machinists in the machine-tool industry. In addition, a number of English men had their own businesses or professions including a grocery-store owner, a manufacturer of ice cream, a real estate agent, and a music instructor.

As in the French-Canadian sample, married men in the English sample were more likely to command the higher paying jobs, and single men (usually sons) were likely to be in unskilled jobs, particularly in textile mills where they were doffers, carders, and laborers (see table 9). In contrast to the French-Canadian males, where 60 percent of the men, both married and single, held high-paying jobs, only half of the English men had access to employment paying more than fourteen dollars a week. This difference can be accounted for by the concentration of French-Canadian men in the skilled jobs of the building trades.

Contrary to the overall position of the English and French-Canadians in New England, the English men in Central Falls's local economy, were no better off than the French-Canadian men, and perhaps they were slightly worse off. This was particularly true of the married

Table 9. Single and married men's jobs, English-Scottish sample, 1915

	Single		Married	
	Number	Percent	Number	Percent
High-paying jobs				
Textiles	4		17	
Machine and other manufacturing	13		13	
Individual occupations (including building trades)	9		6	
Other	5		6	
TOTAL	31	20.8	42	28.2
Low-paying jobs				
Textiles	29		22	
Machine and other manufacturing	7		7	
Individual occupations (including building trades)	0		0	
Other	3		5	
TOTAL	39	26.2	34	22.8
Males with no occupation	3	2.0	0	0.0
GRAND TOTAL (n = 149)	73	49.0	76	51.0

men with low-paying jobs (48 percent compared with 26 percent of the French-Canadian men). Six men with young children were the only wage earners in their family, employed as a laborer, box maker, carder, splitter of yarn, and clerk in an oyster house. Others hàd older children who could supplement their low-wage incomes. Although men with high-paying jobs also sent sons and daughters out to work, the additional income from children was undoubtedly more critical to low-paid fathers who worked as laborers, spinners, and finishers.

As one Englishmen conceptualized the importance of working sons and daughters:

> It was an economic thing because one man's pay could not furnish any of the luxuries, if it did furnish the necessities. So, ah . . . to get along with children coming every so often [the family] needed more income and that was the way it was. Now my first pay was an eight-hour-a-day job for $7.43 a week. . . . This system of the oldest child going to work as soon as he was fourteen was brought over by the English people. Of course, the other . . . they imported all the nationalities at one time. . . . In fact the Blackstone Valley was a melting pot of nationalities because of this . . . this reason. Now, when the English got used to the country and learned its ways, they wanted more money, and so they would recruit from other countries that had textile industries.[10]

Taking in Boarders

British and Scottish wives were only rarely able to pursue the strategy of taking in boarders, since the decline in immigration, which came with a "mature" population of established families, resulted in few single individuals who were in need of a place to live. The twelve households with boarders constituted only 12 percent of the British-Scottish sample, a proportion similar to that of families with boarders in the French sample. Boarders were predominantly single individuals, often foreign born, who lived with a nuclear family. They did not cluster in one sex or age category. All were employed and through board and room payment contributed to the income of the host families.[11]

10. This quotation is from an interview that is part of the University of Rhode Island Oral History collection.

11. There were five women boarders: two young women, two women in their forties, and an older woman of seventy-five. There were eight male boarders, including five young men, two older ones, and a thirteen year old. There was one couple boarding with a family.

The families who took in boarders ranged from older couples and an older widow to nuclear families and a younger couple who provided lodging for a father-in-law. The nine nuclear families were split between four in which the husbands had relatively high-paying jobs (machinist, fireman, dyer, and teamster) and five in which the husbands had low-paying jobs (two spinners, a yarn weigher, a watchman, and a bleacher). Two female heads of household (a single mother and a widow) took in individual male boarders as well. The single mother worked as a weaver in a cotton mill, but her mother provided the household labor that supported her working son and a male boarder. The widow lived with her employed twenty-nine-year-old daughter and took in a fifty-three-year-old male boarder.[12] In these last two cases as well as in some others, the small size of the family left space that could be used by a boarder. Wives and mothers in these households thus provided domestic labor not only for their families but extended that labor to gain cash income for the family. For English families the boarding strategy was not as prevalent as that of sending daughters into the mill labor force. Even in these twelve boarder households, there were ten wage-earning daughters (winders, spoolers, and speeder tenders) contributing to household income.

English Women's Work inside and outside the Home

English daughters, like their French-Canadian counterparts, constituted the largest portion of English women working for wages. Most single women in the English-Scottish sample were wage earners, resulting in a labor-force-participation rate for single women (86 percent) that was equal to the French-Canadian sample (84 percent) (see table 10). Slightly greater percentages of childless, married women and of mothers had jobs in the paid labor force compared to the French-Canadian sample. Overall, the labor-force-participation rate was higher among English-Scottish women than among French-Canadian women (48 percent compared with 38 percent), but families in both groups allocated female labor in the same manner. Young, unmarried women lived at home and worked in productive jobs outside the household, while married women with children provided the reproductive work that involved raising children and maintaining the labor of husbands, older sons, and daughters.

12. The twelfth household was composed of an extended family, that is, a nuclear family plus the wife's father and one male boarder.

Table 10. Women's labor-force participation, English-Scottish sample, 1915

Labor-force participation	Single		Married (no children)		Married (with children)		Married with children (no spouse)		Total	
	Number	Percent	Number	Percent	Number	Percent	Number	Percent	Number	Percent
English-Scottish										
Paid	56	86	6	46	7	11	8	42	77	47.8
Unpaid	9	14	7	54	57	89	11	58	84	52.2
TOTAL	65	100	13	100	64	100	19	100	161	100.0
Irish										
Paid	55	83	2	18	1	3	4	31	62	51.2
Unpaid	11	17	9	82	30	97	9	69	59	48.8
TOTAL	66	100	11	100	31	100	13	100	121	100.0

English daughters, like French-Canadian women, were employed almost entirely in textiles. Seventy-nine percent of the seventy-seven employed women in the sample worked in textile jobs, mainly as spoolers and winders but often as carders, speeder tenders, and spinners. A number of women had jobs at the Sayles Bleachery located within walking distance of the sample neighborhood. Most of these women were earning seven to ten dollars a week in these "female" jobs, less than the earnings of young English men who worked as laborers but an amount similar to that of those sons who worked as doffers or cleaners.

Like French-Canadian mothers, English-Scottish women had large families of five to seven children before the family was completed. Women in their late twenties and early thirties worked at home caring for their growing families, which by that age numbered around three children. At the next stage of the domestic cycle, the families of women in their late thirties and early forties had neared completion. Daughters and sons could contribute to the family income, while mothers continued to do the reproductive work of shopping, cleaning, cooking, and other chores. Women in their later years had few house-

Card-room hands: working daughters and working sons at the Lonsdale Mills, Lonsdale, Rhode Island, a British working-class community. Lewis Hine photograph. Slater Mill Historic Site, Pawtucket, R.I.

hold members to care for, since older children had married and moved away to form their own families. However, some of these women faced widowhood when the support of working children and income from a boarder or perhaps a wage-earning relative ·were important for family maintenance. Exceptions to this cycle were the six English women who continued to work after marriage but before bearing children and the seven who worked even though they had children. Four widows were also employed, two as housekeepers. The proportion of married working women, 13 percent, was higher than the national average at the time (which was between 3 and 5 percent) but still only a minority. Most women who worked for wages were daughters living at home.

Work and Family in Irish Families

Irish men held a place in the Central Falls local economy very similar to that of the English. Although not as concentrated in the textile industry as the English, Irish men did hold almost the same proportion of jobs in machine shops. They had more jobs in transport, service, and sales occupations than the English but very few of the building trades jobs, which were monopolized by the French (see table 11).

Irish men proportionately held more low-paying jobs than did English men (see tables 8 and 11). Furthermore, single Irish men were more likely to have low-paying jobs as laborers in textile mills, in machine shops, and with the railroad, despite the fact that the Irish had been long-term members of the community (table 12). Although there was a small Central Falls Irish elite composed of grocery-store owners, steamfitters, toolmakers, policemen, and firemen, there was also a large population of low-paid laborers, weighers, dyers, cotton helpers, wagon drivers, and other unskilled workers among the Irish.

Boarding in Irish Households

Taking in boarders was a strategy utilized by women in nine of the sixty-three Irish households in our neighborhood sample (14 percent), a proportion similar to that with the French and English. The boarders in these households were primarily single young men and wom-

Table 11. Jobs held by Irish males, 1915

	High-paying jobs (more than $14/wk.)			Low-paying jobs (less than $14/wk.)	
	Number	Percent		Number	Percent
Textiles					
Foreman, weaver, clerk, mule spinner, dresser tender	7	6.9	Laborer, winder, cleaner, carder, spinner	28	27.7
Machine and iron or other manufacturing					
Machinist, molder, grinder	20	19.8	Laborer, speeder	11	10.9
Individual occupations					
Blacksmith, painter, plumber	5	5.0		—	—
Other jobs					
Grocer, clerk, teamster, motorman	8	7.9	Janitor, waiter, railroad laborer, chauffeur	16	15.8
TOTAL (n = 101)*	40	39.6		55	54.4

*Six (6 percent) have no occupation.

Table 12. Single and married men's jobs, Irish sample, 1915

	Single		Married	
	Number	Percent	Number	Percent
High-paying jobs				
Textiles	3		4	
Machine and other manufacturing	8		12	
Individual occupations (including building trades)	1		4	
Other	4		4	
TOTAL	16	15.8	24	23.8
Low-paying jobs				
Textiles	19		9	
Machine and other manufacturing	8		3	
Individual occupations (including building trades)	0		0	
Other	12		4	
TOTAL	39	38.6	16	15.8
Males with no occupation	2	2.0	4	2.0
GRAND TOTAL (n = 101)	57	56.4	44	43.6

en, although there were also two old male boarders and one Polish family. In the Irish sample there seems to be a more definite correlation between family need and a woman's efforts to add to family income by taking in boarders. Of the boarder-taking five families with male heads, four of the men were employed in low-paying jobs or had no occupation. In the four female-headed households with boarders, three were headed by widows, and a fourth was composed of two sisters who had taken in a Polish family. Thus in eight of the nine households, one or two boarders could compensate for either a man's low pay or the lack of a male breadwinner.

Women's Work inside and outside the Home

Given the similar position of Irish and English men in the labor force, it is not surprising that a similar proportion of Irish and English women worked for wages in 1915 (51 percent of the Irish and 48 percent of the English sample) (see table 10). Compared with English women, fewer Irish married women were working outside the home, but more Irish widows were employed in wage jobs. Among both groups, most female wage workers were single and living at home. These working daughters held jobs primarily in textile mills, although 23 percent held service, clerical, and sales jobs. The women in service jobs include six women employed as housekeepers (10 percent of wage-earning Irish women). This is a larger proportion than other ethnic populations and indicates that even in 1915 the historical pattern of paid domestic work remained an occupation filled by Irish women.

Married Irish women worked mainly in their homes taking care of their husbands and children. In about a third of the households, their domestic labor supported other relatives as well. Most of them were employed siblings of either the husband or wife who presumably added to family income. For Irish wives, work in the home to support an employed relative was a more prevalent strategy than taking in boarders. Sixteen households included such relatives. Three of these households were caring for a parent: a father, father-in-law, or mother-in-law of the household head. Two of these parents also worked for wages. In a fourth household, a brother-in-law who had his own barbershop was included in the household along with his two children. In a fifth case, a widow living with her daughter and son-in-law was being supported by her three working daughters. In ten households, by far the largest number, employed brothers or sisters of the household head or his wife added to the family's income. The one exception was a widow who presumably provided the domestic labor for her brother-in-law, who was a shoemaker, and his son, who worked as a chauffeur. Except for some of the elderly parents, relatives who lived with couples or widows brought an extra wage to the household. In eight of the sixteen households, those headed by a widow or a male holding a low-paying job or unemployed, the additional relative's wage was welcomed. In the other eight, where fathers had high-paying jobs, additional income added to the comfort of the family, but the obligation to help a single relative could have been the more important factor.

Most wives and mothers in the second phase of their family domestic cycle were taking care of two to three children, and in the third phase their families had grown to three, four, or five children. By this stage, daughters were old enough to leave school and enter the paid labor force.

Oral-history interviews with Irish women show that they, like their French-Canadian counterparts, viewed their wages as important for the support of their families. They may have remained unmarried longer (as suggested by the greater proportion of Irish single working women in the twenty-five to thirty-four age range in our sample), and some may have even remained single throughout life. For example, Katherine O'Brien, whose grandparents immigrated from Ireland, worked as a young girl at Coats and Clark and later in several bleacheries. She remained single and supported her mother, "but I brought my pay home until I got my pension, and my mother was [still] living. And I brought that home and gave it [the pension] to her too. But she did the best she could with it. We didn't want for much. No, she tried to give us everything she could."[13]

Mary McCabe, who worked at several mills as a spooler, also gave her unopened pay envelope to her mother. She got fifty cents spending money and later, when she was older, she received one dollar a week. Her father died when she was just three years old, so the income that she, her two brothers, and her sister generated was cru-

13. In this section I have used data from oral histories on Irish women which were collected between 1973 and 1975 and are from the University of Rhode Island Oral History Project, Mill Life Series, 1970–76.

cial to the family. Her aunt lived in the household with them. Mary, like Katherine, remained single and cared for her aged mother.

Other women lived in extended families. Maureen Reilly, whose mother died in childbirth, was cared for by her maternal grandmother. Although her father, who owned a liquor store, did not want her to work, she did, secretively at first, so that she could buy things for herself. She reported thinking, "There's this girl and I thought . . . gee, she's working and getting all nice clothes and everything, and I wanted the same things." She left school to work in a dye works. Later she worked a silk mill and gave her salary to her father, a custom her own children continued when they went to work. Like many women in our census sample, she quit work when she married.

Louise Healey was also brought up in an extended family. Her parents died when she was young and she went to live with an aunt and uncle and seven cousins. In 1913 when she was fourteen years old, she began working in the packing room at Coats and Clark. She worked there until she was about twenty-one, when she left because she was ill. When she returned to work, she was employed in the winding room. She also left her aunt and uncle at this time to live as a boarder. As she explained, "When I was twenty-one, I went on my own. I left my aunt. It was getting too hard for her [she was pregnant again]. I went to live with people named Garrahy." She paid board and had her own bedroom. She lived with them until she married and quit work at the age of twenty-nine.

For these Irish women, as well as for daughters in other "mature" ethnic populations, work in the textile mills was a common experience. Irish husbands and fathers were less well off than English and especially French-Canadian fathers. Of the three working-class samples, French-Canadian families were in a slightly more comfortable position. In none of the groups was the male wage enough to support a growing family. Sons and daughters universally quit school at fourteen to work in the mills. Mothers worked at home raising large families of four or five children, reproducing the next generation of industrial workers as well as providing sustenance and care for their husbands and children. A few were able to take in boarders or perhaps a relative in the Irish case, adding to family income, but boarders were not numerous in mature immigrant populations. Most adults were involved in their own nuclear families and lived in their own tenement apartments.

Work and Family in the Polish Neighborhood

The productive and reproductive labor of Polish women was allocated in a strikingly different way than in any of the "mature" ethnic populations. This was due to the recent arrival of the population and to the economic niche that Polish men held in the local Central Falls mill economy. The Poles came to Central Falls while the cotton industry was as its peak and when firms specializing in silk or in mixed silk-cotton goods were still growing. The more skilled jobs in many of the mills were held by the English, Irish, and French-Canadians, leaving the heavier, less-skilled jobs to the newer immigrants: Poles, Syrians, Italians, and Portuguese. Unlike the French-Canadians who had arrived thirty years earlier and who were able to take advantage of the building boom by becoming carpenters, painters, roofers, and other skilled craftsmen, Polish men came to a neighborhood that was already built and to a location where the building trades already were monopolized by French-Canadians.

In 1915 Polish men were overwhelmingly employed in the textile industry, although a substantial proportion of men (forty-two, or 21 percent of the sample) were employed in the iron and wire mills. Within the cotton mills Polish men were largely laborers, carders, pickers, and weavers. Only one male was a loomfixer, and there were no Polish second hands or overseers. Although weaving paid as much as sixteen dollars a week in 1915, working as a carder, picker, or laborer yielded only ten to eleven dollars a week. Consequently, 54 percent of Polish men were earning wages below fourteen dollars a week or had no occupation, and only 41 percent were earning above fourteen dollars a week (see table 13).[14]

Polish single men, like other young males, were in low-paying jobs, but in contrast to many French-Canadian sons who worked in the building trades, Polish single men were doffers, carders, pickers, and spinners or laborers in machine shops or in iron and wire mills. Equal

14. These data coincide with a wage survey of twenty-four thousand male heads of households in Providence in 1915. In this survey 64 percent of the men born in Austrian Poland earned below fourteen dollars a week as did 69 percent of the men born in Russian Poland (including Jews as well as Catholics). In the survey Syrians and Italians were at the bottom of the wage hierarchy, with the Portuguese next, and Russian and Austrian Poles and Jews above them. Irish men stood at the midpoint and French-Canadians, along with northern Europeans, were in the upper portions of the wage bracket (Rhode Island 1921:224–25, 249–60).

Table 13. Jobs held by Polish males, 1915

	High-paying jobs (more than $14/wk.)			Low-paying jobs (less than $14/wk.)	
	Number	Percent		Number	Percent
Textiles					
Loomfixer, weaver, silk weaver	52	26.5	Laborer, picker, doffer, carder, spinner	63	32.1
Machine and iron or other manufacturing					
Machinist, machine hand	12	6.1	Laborer	32	16.3
Individual occupations					
Carpenter, baker, fireman, plumber, building contractor	8	4.1		—	—
Other jobs					
Musician, priest, life insurance agent	9	4.6	City laborer, grocery clerk, bartender	10	5.1
TOTAL (n = 196)*	81	41.3		105	53.5

*Ten (5 percent) have no occupation.

proportions of married and single Polish men were weavers, but many other husbands and fathers had the same low-paying jobs as single men (table 14). Polish men and women were able to gain employment as weavers in the silk mills near their neighborhood, but wages in the silk industry in 1915 were lower than in cotton. Thus the picture

Table 14. Single and married men's jobs, Polish sample, 1915

	Single		Married	
	Number	Percent	Number	Percent
High-paying jobs				
Textiles	24		28	
Machine and other manufacturing	5		7	
Individual occupations (including building trades)	4		4	
Other	2		7	
TOTAL	35	17.8	46	23.5
Low-paying jobs				
Textiles	29		34	
Machine and other manufacturing	21		11	
Individual occupations (including building trades)	0		0	
Other	4		6	
TOTAL	54	27.6	51	26.0
Males with no occupation	8	4.1	2	1.0
GRAND TOTAL (n = 196)	97	49.5	99	50.5

emerges of the more precarious economic situation of both single and married Polish men within the local economy. More men were pickers, carders, and laborers than in other ethnic groups, and given the young age of the population, few married men in 1915 had sons and daughters old enough to send into the mill economy.

The young Polish wives and mothers thus allocated their labor in response to husbands' low-paying jobs. They took in boarders to add cash to family income or worked in the mills. Single women could not afford to live alone, and as new immigrants they often had few close relatives in the community. For them, boarding was a way of managing on low wages.

Polish Women as "Hostesses": The Importance of Taking in Boarders

In our neighborhood sample of seventy-four Polish households, there were forty-nine households with boarders, twenty without, and five solitary individuals. "Hostesses," the female household managers responsible for caring for the boarders in these households, included forty-five married women (forty-two with children) and five single women (mostly daughters in their teens).[15]

Many hostesses were women who had infants or school-age children. They often cared for married boarding couples in which the wife continued to work. As table 15 shows, those women who continued to work after marriage were boarders, while those who did not work often took in boarders.

By taking in boarders young mothers could supplement the family income and care for their children at the same time. Mrs. Szymanski described a woman who took in boarders in the company house where she lived in a Massachusetts mill town. As a young woman with children, she became a hostess rather than a mill worker:

She came the same time that I did, but she came with her husband and family, and she couldn't go to work because she had one child and was

---

15. The term *gospodyni,* translated as "hostess," was used in Poland for the female head of a household in a wealthy peasant family. She was responsible for the care of the house and feeding and clothing the family—a sort of manager of the domestic sphere. This term was carried over to the United States, where it was applied to wives who took in boarders and performed domestic tasks in an urban rather than a rural context.

[157]

Table 15. Married Polish women: Boarding and wage work in the Polish neighborhood

	Paid Work		Unpaid Work at Home	
	Number	Percent	Number	Percent
Boarding	24	77.4	10	13.7
Hostesses	7	22.6	43	58.9
Independent nuclear families	0	0	20	27.4
TOTAL (n = 104)	31	100.0	73	100.0

expecting another. He got a job in this factory and applied for the house, and the company rented him a huge house. There were eight rooms for rent upstairs, and downstairs they had one for themselves and a big dining hall and kitchen. Everybody who lived there had to bring his own food from the store and she cooked it. She cooked the same food for everybody, telling what everybody had to get for the next day so it was easier for her.[16]

It was standard practice for the hostess to provide coffee but ask boarders to purchase food for her to cook. She did the laundry (bedding and perhaps clothes for the boarders) and the housecleaning, although female boarders often helped with this chore on Saturday afternoons.

Mrs. Bielecki described her godmother's role as hostess, giving a good example of a woman who took in boarders and also worked in a mill—a set of tasks that took superwoman qualities:

Usually, men came here and left behind their wives and children. He just came to make some money here. He would buy some pork fat. . . . They counted every cent then. . . . And the hostess would get up at 3 A.M. and make a huge coffee pot. She was giving the coffee free. It was included in the board and the pork fat everybody bought; and she fried it for him and he ate it on some bread. They had to raise money to pay for the board. One of these women was my godmother, so I know it well. . . . She came from the [old] country in very hard times. But she was very optimistic and knew how to foresee things. She came along and married soon and brought over her mother. . . . Anyway, my godmother was a clever woman. Somehow she gathered money and bought two houses and had lots of boarders. She got up early and gave them all coffee. She had only one daughter. Then she herself went to work from 7

16. Quotations in this section are from the oral histories collected by Ewa Hauser in 1977 from Polish women.

A.M. to 6 P.M. It was in 1908, 9, 10, or 11 up to 1924. She died in 1924. After she came back from the factory she had to fix supper for everybody. They ate, and then she had to clean up the dishes, and on Saturday she washed the sheets, and on Sunday she was a godmother. She had over one-hundred godchildren.

In the period 1902 to 1911 when wages were between three and seven dollars a week, most boarders paid three to four dollars a month to the hostess. Older female children and the women boarders often helped with the chores. Recalling her mother's boarders, Mrs. Nowak said, "Even I cooked for them. We had to. Where was he suposed to go? He bought his food in a store and we fixed it." Sometimes boarders helped with the housework: "They helped in doing laundry. Some women helped more. When I was boarding before I got married, I always helped to wash the dishes. The hostess liked those who helped her and those who didn't help were looked at [askance]. . . . I boarded only for two years [after her parents had returned to Poland], then I got married, had my own house and my own children."

Women's Paid Labor in the Mills

The labor-force participation rate among Polish women (48 percent) was greater than for French-Canadian women (38 percent) but about the same as English-Scottish (48 percent) and Irish women (51 percent). Although a greater proportion of wage-earning Polish women were single, they were not daughters living at home. Most wage-earning single women (thirty-six of forty-three) were boarding with unrelated Polish families. Certainly, some of these women were sending money to Poland to assist their families there, but in the United States context, they were self-supporting, paying for their board and room from their wages (see table 16).

Furthermore, Polish women did not drop out of the paid labor force at marriage as did their French-Canadian, English, and Irish counterparts. Of married women without children, 62 percent (sixteen out of twenty-six) had a paid job—a far greater proportion than in the other three samples. Furthermore, 15 percent (eleven of seventy-three) of married women with children were employed outside the home, a large proportion compared to the few working mothers among the

Table 16. Women's labor-force participation, Polish sample, 1915

Labor-force participation	Single		Married (no children)		Married (with children)		Married with children (no spouse)		Total	
	Number	Percent	Number	Percent	Number	Percent	Number	Percent	Number	Percent
Poles										
Paid	43	86	16	62	11	15	4	80	74	48
Unpaid	7	14	10	38	62	85	1	20	80	52
TOTAL	50	100	26	100	73	100	5	100	154	100
Non-Poles										
Paid	16	57	1	17	3	10	1	17	21	30
Unpaid	12	43	5	83	28	90	5	83	50	70
TOTAL	28	100	6	100	31	100	6	100	71	100

Summary:

Of all paid Poles
  58% are single
  76% are single
  81% are childless
  80% are childless
    (22% are married but childless)
    (5% are married but childless)
  20% have children
  19% have children but no spouse
Of all unpaid Poles
  79% have children
Of all paid non-Poles
  66% have children
  34% are childless
  21% are childless
    (12% are married but childless)
    (10% are married but childless)
Of all unpaid non-Poles
Nearly half of all Polish women older than fifteen years of age are working.

French-Canadian, English, and Irish. For Polish women, remaining in the paid labor force was a response to the relatively low-level jobs of their husbands. Since most young married women (nine of eleven) were boarding with a family, the hostess relieved the working wife of many domestic responsibilities. Wage-earning wives were weavers, carders, and spinners for the most part. In some cases their incomes probably equaled that of their husbands and helped prepare for the day when they could rent a tenement or buy a house of their own.

Oral-history accounts give us insight into the career patterns of Polish daughters. They often came as single immigrants, started at entry-level jobs, and then became spinners or weavers. Others who had jobs in cotton mills in other communities learned silk weaving upon coming to Central Falls.

Mrs. Nowak first worked at a thread mill. She was a trainee for several months and then worked on looms. She made seven dollars a week in 1915. When she got married in 1917, she was making ten dollars a week, a low wage for that year since wages were rising during World War I.

Mrs. Malinowski recounted the series of jobs she had before marriage: "Later on I worked on looms, but at first I swept floors in a factory. Then I was a spinner. It was in Central Falls. I made three dollars a week [around 1915]. . . . They were paid very little then. I learned cotton. It was a little better paid . . . four or five dollars a week, but we had to work longer. . . . Everybody was poorly paid, but men could work in the machine shops, and then they made more money."

When they first arrived, Mrs. Bielecki's parents came to Central Falls and learned silk in a few weeks. "It was very difficult. They were trained without any pay and had to have someone who kept them then [gave them board]. When they started to be paid, it was three or four looms to be tended. They made three or four dollars a week and had to work hard to pay for the room." Mrs. Szymanski first worked in a cotton factory in Massachusetts as a young single woman. "I came to Central Falls in 1916 and got a job on the spot because there were all these silk factories here. They paid better. When I learned the silk, I preferred it to cotton and never returned to Massachusetts, even though I had my whole family there and friends. But the work was much better for me."

Some women came to Central Falls as young children and at fourteen became working daughters contributing to family income in much the same way that French-Canadian, Irish, and English daughters did. Mrs. Nowak worked at the Greene and Daniels Mill when she was twelve years old and earned $3.30 a week. She got her job through her father. "My father worked there and my mother and my brother. So when my father brought me and said I was his daughter, they looked at me and saw what kind of work he did. He saw that I was a child, so he gave me a job to learn" (i.e., an unskilled, entry-level job).

Women who worked after having children managed child care in a variety of ways. There were eleven of these women in the neighborhood sample. Several examples in the oral-history interviews give us insight into how women in these circumstances coped. A good deal of domestic labor was shifted to daughters in the family when they became old enough to handle chores. Once mills began running two shifts in the 1920s, mothers could work different hours than their husbands did so that the children would not be left alone.

Mrs. Nowak, who worked after each of her nine children was born, used both arrangements. Her daughter said, "I was like the babysitter. I was taking care of the little ones." Mrs. Nowak herself added: "I went to work during the night. I came home at 5 A.M. I started work at 7 P.M. until 5 A.M. I came home, set the fire in the oven. My husband got up to go to work, and I gave the kids breakfast, combed them, looked after them so they could wash and went to school, whoever was at school. The smaller ones stayed at home. I slept then."

Mrs. Polacek's mother, who was separated from her husband, worked as a weaver in textile mills during Mrs. Polacek's childhood. There were three children in the family, Mrs. Polacek and two brothers. They lived with her maternal grandmother, but at an early age Mrs. Polacek had considerable domestic responsibility. "My grandmother took care of us sometimes and . . . well, we were on our own. I had to take care of my brothers and I was the housekeeper. I was eight years old. And I had to have things ready. She'd come home [her mother], and I had to have the house clean and I'd have supper started. She would pick up the meat."

Mrs. Roskowski came from a large family where both parents worked. When asked if her mother continued to work while the children were being born, she replied:

Yes . . . in between. I don't think she had too much of a span. Because her children were born . . . like a year and a half apart . . . and two years, the next one, or maybe 18 months. . . . My mother would go and work a little bit, you know, she would take another shift. My father worked in the daytime, and she'd take a second shift. And he'd be home shortly, and maybe the oldest would stay (I was the oldest you know). . . . We would stay and manage to take care of the children until my father came, but that didn't last too long because she would be ready to have another baby. But I think she stayed bringing up the last one until the boys got older and went into the service. Then she went to work for a number of years. My mother and father were weavers in the end. They did different jobs.

To conclude our survey of the Central Falls Poles in 1915, let us look at the variety of strategies for allocating male productive and female productive and reproductive labor in eight households found in one frame house. Four of them had boarders and four did not. In the first nonboarder household lived Edward Kozak, thirty-five years old and a teamster for an express company. His wife Stella, twenty-nine years old, remained at home caring for four children, ages five to twelve. In a second household, Stanley Kovacs, also age thirty-five, was a weaver in a cotton mill. As in the first family, here, too, his thirty-year-old wife, Wanda, worked at home tending their three young children. A third father was a bartender, but his wife worked as an inspector at a lamp works. They had three children, a daughter seventeen years old who was not working for wages; a son, eight; and a daughter, two. The older daughter probably provided most of the domestic labor for the household.

In the fourth nonboarder household, Walter Kulas headed a nuclear family during the stage in the life cycle when his sons were old enough to work. Kulas was forty-six years old and worked as a laborer in an iron mill. His wife, Sophie, was forty and did not work for wages. Two sons, ages twenty and sixteen, were doffers in a cotton mill. Although Kulas's wage was probably low, perhaps twelve dollars a week, there were the two other wages of five to seven dollars each to supplement his income and help support Sophie and the two youngest children in the family.

The four families with boarders in this tenement were composed of young couples in their late twenties and early thirties. Three of the four husbands had jobs as carders in cotton mills, earning only about ten to twelve dollars a week. All of the wives had very young children. Taking in boarders undoubtedly augmented their husbands' low income. These families included that of Kasimir Nimiroski who was twenty-five years old and worked as a carder in a cotton mill. His wife,

Jenny, was twenty-eight years old and cared for their two-year-old boy. Their eight boarders included a married couple in which the husband was a laborer in a wire mill, five single male boarders, and one female boarder. The unmarried female boarder worked as a weaver in a cotton mill, and the men were laborers, pickers, and a weaver. The hostess, Jenny, may have been assisted by the boarding wife, since the domestic labor required to care for eight adult boarders was extensive.

A second family with boarders consisted of Frank Werbicki and his wife, both age thirty-four, and their two sons, ages one and four. He worked in the carding room at a woolen mill, while she provided domestic labor for her family and for the married couple and the single woman who boarded with them. The couple both worked in a carding room in a cotton mill, while the single woman was a cotton weaver. Thomas Marszalek, age thirty-four, and his wife, Anna, age twenty-eight, headed a third household who took in boarders. In addition to caring for three young children, Anna provided domestic labor for the couple boarding with them, a twenty-eight-year-old husband who worked as a carder in a cotton mill and his wife who was a cotton spinner. The last household in the tenement was that of John Rozak, thirty, also a carder in a cotton mill; his wife, Mary, age twenty-nine; and their two small children, ages two and five. Mary took in three single boarders: a man, age twenty-one, who was another carder; a woman, age twenty, again a carder in a cotton mill, and a second woman, age eighteen, who worked as a knitter in a stocking mill.

Thus Polish women provided productive and reproductive labor for households that were structured differently from those of the French, English, and Irish samples. Very few single women (only four of fifty) were working daughters who brought home paychecks to supplement the industrial wages of their fathers and brothers. Most single women were themselves living as boarders and paying part of their wages to a family where a young mother provided domestic labor for the household. Many married women were in this situation as well, since they continued to work in the mills after marriage but before having children. Young mothers were not only caring for their children but were doing cooking, laundry, and cleaning to maintain several boarders in addition to their own nuclear family. These family strategies for the allocation of women's labor were a response to the recent immigrant status of the Polish population, to their confinement to an established neighborhood now abandoned by the elite, and to the low-level jobs

Polish men were allotted within the gender and ethnic hierarchy in the mills of Central Falls and Pawtucket.

Contrasting New Immigrant Strategies: The Portuguese

Not all new immigrant populations adopted the same strategies in allocating women's productive and reproductive labor as those of the Poles. A sample of Portuguese families from Pawtucket illustrates a second set of strategies for coping with the industrial milieu.[17]

Most Portuguese migrated either as nuclear families or as single adult males. Virtually no single women migrated. Women were involved as wives and mothers, not as young working women who might board in others' homes. Twenty percent of the Portuguese households (eleven of fifty-five) took in boarders, a higher percentage than in the French, English, and Irish samples but not as high as in the Polish case. Fifty-eight percent (thirty-two of the households) were composed of young couples with children, but less than 2 percent of the families had reached the stage where all children would be working in the paid labor force. Although some families (26 percent) had children old enough to be working, in most households the father was the sole wage earner.

Compared to the other groups living in Central Falls, the Pawtucket Portuguese were in the most difficult situation within the local economy. Some families lived scattered through the western side of Pawtucket and were thus close to several mill complexes, but many families were not near mills. The Portuguese seem to have just begun to penetrate the local textile labor market, since only 38 percent of the ninety employed men in the sample were employed in textile jobs. More important, Portuguese males were seldom employed in the machine shops or building trades, important sources of high-paying jobs for French-Canadian, English, and Irish men. Instead, Portuguese men worked largely in coal yards, produce houses, or slaughter houses or in small grocery, fruit, fish, or bakery shops. A significant proportion worked on farms as laborers (see table 17).

17. In 1915 there were only 7 Portuguese immigrants in Central Falls but 379 in Pawtucket. Our sample, the result of a search of the 1915 state census books, includes a total of 330 individuals in fifty-nine households, or 87 percent of the population. In 1910 in Providence there were 2,190 Portuguese and by 1915 there were 3,737 (Rhode Island 1921:216). This indicates a rapidly increasing immigrant population, which reached 10,499 for the whole state in 1915.

Table 17. Jobs held by Portuguese males, 1915

	High-paying jobs (more than $14/wk.)			Low-paying jobs (less than $14/wk.)	
	Number	Percent		Number	Percent
Textiles					
Foreman, weaver	7	7.5	Laborer, doffer, picker, carder, spinner, speeder tender, spooler	28	30.1
Machine and iron or other manufacturing					
Fireman, blacksmith	2	2.2	Laborer, coal-yard worker, jeweler, rolling mill, electric- and gas-company worker	14	15.0
Individual occupations					
Baker	1	1.1		—	—
Other jobs					
Slaughterhouse (butcher)	6	6.4	(Laborer)	3	3.2
Sales and shops (fruiter, butcher, grocer, fish shop)	4	4.3	(Produce, oyster house, fertilizer dealer)	8	8.6
Transport	—	—	(Wharf, highway, teamster, chauffer)	5	5.4
Service	—	—	(Boat cook, hotel chef)	2	2.2
Farm (owner, foreman)	3	3.2	(Laborer)	7	7.5
TOTAL (n = 93)*	23	24.7		67	72.0

*Three (3 percent) have no occupation.

Most of these jobs were low waged. Consequently, the proportion of low-paying to high-paying jobs for men was three to one, even greater than the three to two ratio for the Polish sample. In the textile industry, young single Portuguese men were combers, speeder tenders, spinners, carders, and doffers, while in other industries they were laborers. Forty-six percent of the single men were laborers (seventeen of thirty-seven), as were 32 percent (eighteen of fifty-six) of the married men. Two-thirds of the married men held low-paying jobs such as speeder tender, picker, driver, and teamster (table 18).

Even the high-paying jobs that Portuguese men held were not the same kinds available to French, English, and Irish men. For example, there was only one machinist in the sample and no carpenters, bricklayers, or masons. Among the textile jobs, there were only two weavers, one mule spinner, and one foreman. This is very different

Table 18. Single and married men's jobs, Portuguese sample, 1915

	Single		Married	
	Number	Percent	Number	Percent
High-paying jobs				
Textiles	4		3	
Machine and other manufacturing	—		2	
Individual occupations (including building trades)	—		1	
Other	$\underline{1}$		$\underline{12}$	
TOTAL	5	5.4	18	19.4
Low-paying jobs				
Textiles	17		11	
Machine and other manufacturing	2		12	
Individual occupations (including building trades)	—		—	
Other	$\underline{13}$		$\underline{12}$	
TOTAL	32	34.4	35	37.6
Males with no occupation	—	—	3	3.2
GRAND TOTAL (n = 93)	37	39.8	56	60.2

from the large numbers of weavers among the French and Polish samples, and the number of loomfixers, mule spinners, and overseers in the English sample. These Portuguese men were in much the same situation as were Portuguese men during 1915 in Providence, where a wage survey showed that only 24 percent were making more than fourteen dollars a week. The Portuguese were indeed at the lower end of the working class scale, holding a position only above Syrians and Italians in terms of wages.

The Labor of Portuguese Women inside and outside the Family

Since most Portuguese women immigrated as young mothers, their time and energy was spent in the domestic labor necessary to raise their children and cook and clean for their husbands. There were thirty-two households composed of nuclear families with all children under fifteen years of age. Many of these women were in their late twenties and had already had three of four children. Seven of these women took in boarders to supplement family income, and two worked for wages. Since almost half of these families had husbands who were laborers, they were undoubtedly pressed financially.

Those fifteen families who had children able to work were in better

[167]

financial condition. There were only two working mothers in this group, but this amounted to 15 percent of the total, a much larger proportion of working mothers than in other ethnic groups. In three of these families wives took in boarders, and in six families there were working daughters who were employed in textile jobs.

There were seven extended and multiple families in which several of the young wives worked in the mills or took in industrial homework. In one case the mother-in-law provided child care while the wife worked as an inspector in a braid mill. In other families, women worked at home as lace clippers. Fátima Cabral and her sister Delfina Gomes were lace pullers who worked at home where they could supervise the three young Cabral children. The two older daughters worked as spoolers in a cotton mill. The husband and his brother-in-law were butchers in a slaughter house. In another extended family, the husband's mother worked as a lace clipper at home, and the husband's sister was employed as an inspector at a lace mill. The wife and a second sister provided domestic labor for the extended-family household. Extended families, as in the Irish case, provided a larger pool of wage laborers, drawing on wives, sisters, mothers-in-law, or nieces to work in mills or as industrial homeworkers.

Overall the labor-force participation rate of Portuguese women (table 19) was lower (36 percent) than that of Polish, English, and Irish women. Yet a larger proportion of married women were earning wages owing to the opportunity to do industrial homework (18 percent). Portuguese women used a range of strategies that differed from those of Polish women. Since there were virtually no single women who migrated alone and since most women were young wives and mothers, they had to deal with their husband's low position in the local labor force by taking in boarders, by expanding the household so that more female relatives could help with domestic chores or engage in wage labor, and by taking in homework from the local lace mills. As daughters reached fourteen, they, too, went into the mills, but for most Portuguese families this did not happen until the 1920s. These Portuguese daughters, however, would be particularly active in the general textile strike of 1922 in Central Falls and Pawtucket.

Conclusions

As migrants were brought into the Central Falls mill economy, they formed separate and distinct ethnic neighborhoods. Central Falls

Table 19. Women's labor-force participation, Portuguese sample, 1915

Labor-force participation	Single		Married (no children)		Married (with children)		Married with children (no spouse)		Total	
	Number	Percent	Number	Percent	Number	Percent	Number	Percent	Number	Percent
Portuguese										
Paid	15	83.3	3	60	11	20	1	20	30	36.1
Unpaid	3	16.7	2	40	44	80	4	80	53	63.8
TOTAL	18	100.0	5	100	55	100	5	100	83	99.9

women thus assumed French, Irish, English, or Polish identities. Families in each neighborhood adapted to industrial capitalism by carving out different niches in the local economy. This meant that fathers and sons from each ethnic group often held very different wage jobs and that the allocation of women's labor diverged. The major contrast was between women in the "mature" ethnic populations and the newer immigrants. In the former, young unmarried daughters worked at middle-level jobs in the mills as spinners, winders, twisters, and sometimes weavers. Their mothers, and the wives and mothers in younger families, labored at home to support the family's wage workers and raise the children. In contrast, in the new immigrant Polish community, married women expanded their households and took in boarders, while single women and childless, married women worked in the mills and boarded with other families instead of setting up their own households. Women were hostesses and wage workers rather than wage-working daughters and housekeeping mothers. In the Portuguese population, extended families allowed some young mothers to work for wages in the mills or, more commonly, to take in industrial homework. Other Portuguese wives gave domestic support to relatives or boarders who were working outside the home. The segregation of ethnic communities and the dissimilarity among distinct family economies had implications for women's resistance strategies as the mill economy declined in the 1920s and 1930s.

[4]

The Decline of the Textile
Industry and Women's Resistance

In 1915 most working women in Central Falls were single, either daughters living at home or single boarders living with nuclear families. There were a few working married women in the Polish neighborhood, but these women were largely boarders and without children; widows and a handful of mothers worked for wages in other neighborhoods. Women were divided by ethnicity, living in ethnic neighborhoods and participating in religious and other nonwork institutions that reinforced women's identity as French, English, Irish, Polish, or Portuguese. The restriction of immigration in 1924, however, stopped the flow of newcomers and served to homogenize the experiences of both older and newer ethnic groups. Thus as the newer ethnic communities of 1915 matured, they began to resemble more and more the French-Canadian, English, and Irish populations in terms of demographic structure and household composition.

After World War I, women in Central Falls ethnic communities began to be subjected to the forces of economic decline in the textile industry. The rise of the silk industry, however, and the continued hiring in the thread mills and bleacheries of neighboring Pawtucket meant that jobs were available to Central Falls daughters until the mid-1930s. But women increasingly faced more difficult conditions at work, owing to the implementation of the speedup (tending faster machines) and the stretch-out (tending more machines). These tactics were part of management's response to the downward spiral in both the cotton and silk industries. Women were able to unite across ethnic boundaries and become important participants, though not leaders, in the textile strikes of 1922, 1931, and 1934 in Central Falls.

As the Depression of the 1930s wore on, families' allocation of productive and reproductive labor changed radically. Unemployment was widespread through all ethnic communities, and the strategy of sending sons and daughters into the paid labor force no longer brought financial security to Central Falls families. Boarding declined as a way in which wives could add cash to the family income, since the flow of immigrants had ceased. Daughters still tried to find employment, and more mothers worked for wages or took in factory homework as families struggled against hard times. The 1920s and 1930s were decades of change since the decline of the textile industry affected women's strategies both at work and at home.

The Decline of the Cotton Industry and the Rise of the Silk Industry

Beginning in 1915 the New England textile industry geared up for wartime production. With the government buying 75 percent of what was produced, woolen mills expanded 35 percent to fill military orders. Cotton mills sprang up, especially in the South, to meet the demand caused by the decline in British exports. The increased production became excessive in the immediate postwar period.

Highly fragmented and competitive, the industry did not adjust readily to this decreasing demand. Not only were there different sectors—cotton, woolen, silk and rayon, knitting, and "narrow fabric" mills—but within each one there was a complicated division of labor between production and marketing. In the cotton industry, for example, spinning was done in one set of mills, weaving in another, and dyeing and finishing in a third. Mills did not sell directly to each other or directly to wholesalers or retailers but rather to a complex and often chaotic web of intermediaries (Dunn and Hardy 1931:15).

The industry's dependence on middlemen to link stages of production and to distribute goods contributed to a boom and bust cycle. Anticipating a rise in the price of cotton, for instance, converters, jobbers, and garment makers would rush to place orders, generating an illusory demand. Soon there would be huge inventories and overloaded warehouses. To pay their creditors, manufacturers would begin dumping goods on the market and would take heavy losses. Prices would fall and the cycle was ready to begin again (Dunn and Hardy 1931:15; Murchison 1930b:72).

The boom days that had started during World War I continued with minor recessions during 1919 and 1920, but in 1921 the cotton textile industry went into a depression that marked the end of an era (Pope 1942:217). Then came a resurgence and continued rush to overproduce, leading to a peak production year in 1923. Since this was largely production for markets that had disappeared, warehouses became overstocked, and a sharp decline followed in 1924. The years 1927 and 1929 were relatively profitable, but on the whole the industry was on the decline. In Rhode Island in 1923 there were eighty-one mills employing 33,993 workers. By 1929 there were fifty-five mills in opeation employing 21,833 workers, and by 1933 only forty mills had survived, with 13,077 workers.

Looking only to their short-run interests, New England's mill-owning families maximized profits, squeezed as much out of their workers as possible, and ran their factories into the ground. The cotton industry in New England did not "run away" to the South in these early years of the textile recession. Instead, mills in New England were liquidated as the southern industry was able to recover from slumps and continue to expand.[1] In the South mill owners were investing in new plants and improved machinery, which helped give them a competitive edge (Pope 1942:219).

The southern cotton-textile industry achieved lower production costs than that in New England not only because improved equipment was used but because labor was cheaper. Male weavers in the South earned twenty-one cents an hour less than their northern counterparts in 1924; female weavers earned seventeen cents an hour less, and female spinners, nineteen cents an hour less (Abramson 1936:54). There was an abundance of nonunion labor in the South, the standard of living was lower, and longer work hours were permitted. Most workers lived in mill villages, which allowed mill owners to control worker culture and encourage antiunion sentiment. Encapsulated mill

---

1. In 1922, 84 percent of the southern spindleage was controlled by southern capital, with only 11 percent by northern capital and 3 percent by New England mills. In 1928 only eighteen New England cotton mills had southern branches, and the total by 1944 was still only twenty-five.

villages offered little in terms of job alternatives, and workers were obliged to accept low wages and the fifty-six-hour week. (See Dunn and Hardy 1931:113; Abramson 1936; Murchison 1930a; Lahne 1944.) Wages may have tipped the balance toward the South in the early years of the textile depression, but the structural weaknesses of the New England industry and the antiquated and outdated plants underlay its inability to recover from the downturns of 1921 and 1924. Overproduction after World War I was perhaps the immediate cause of the textile depression. However, the fragmentation of production and the archaic marketing system of New England's cotton-textile industry made it impossible to adjust to decreasing demand by limiting production. After taking huge profits during the war and running their mills into the ground, many mill owners liquidated their textile interests and invested their money elsewhere. Manufacturers who continued to produce during the 1920s turned to cost-cutting techniques to survive.

A popular tactic at first was to cut wages. Robert Dunn and Jack Hardy reported that between 1920 and 1928 mills decreased wages by 30.0 percent, and cuts between 1928 and 1933 were even greater. In Rhode Island, a year after a 22.5 percent wage cut, mill owners announced a further cut of 20.0 percent to take effect on January 23, 1922. There is some evidence that these cuts were planned in advance by mill owners at a meeting in Boston. At the same time, the work week was increased from forty-eight to fifty-four hours, perhaps to compete better with southern mills. The measures resulted in a nine-month strike in the Pawtuxet Valley and in the Central Falls-Pawtucket area. The 1922 strike eventually spread to Massachusetts and New Hampshire and was one of the largest in textile history.

Following that episode and the downturn of 1924, surviving companies began to reorganize and modernize the industry. A national manufacturers' association, the Cotton Textile Institute, was founded in 1926. Its purpose was to gain cooperation among mill owners in solving the problems of overproduction. Industrywide statistics on production, sales, and stocks were collected for members. The association discouraged selling goods below cost, and they set up the Cost Section to help mills figure exact expenses. During the early 1930s, the institute promoted a fifty-hour week for the North and a fifty-five-hour week for the South as a control on production. They also proposed elimination of night work for women and children, not on humanitarian grounds but because this would decrease the number of workers in mills and hence their productive capacity. These voluntary measures were only mildly successful and, in fact, gave a short-run advantage to firms that did not comply.

With the association unable to control competition, individual companies sought to gain an advantage by enhancing efficiency and adopting "scientific management techniques" to rationalize production. Mills hired agencies like the Barnes Textile Service of Boston, which specialized in industrial engineering. Such organizations analyzed production and suggested changes in the number of machines to be run by each worker as well as alterations in the physical layout of equipment. These changes, plus increased use of improved picking machines and drawing frames, the superspeed warper, the Barber-Coleman automatic spooler, and the Draper Model X automatic loom all "streamlined" production by eliminating workers.

The labor force was affected in three ways: (1) new equipment eliminated human labor, (2) routine tasks were shifted from higher to lower paid workers, and (3) workers were required to tend more machines on the basis of time and motion studies. This last change, the "stretch-out," was the bane of the worker. Sometimes instituted after careful observation such as in the Pequot Mills in Salem, Massachusetts, in 1929, it was more often baldly announced by a new superintendent without the benefit of the time studies as at the Loray Mills in Gastonia, South Carolina in 1928, a mill owned by the Manville-Jenckes Spinning Company of Rhode Island (Pope 1942:230). In either case, workers lost jobs, and those that remained had to work harder, tending more machines, or accept less-skilled, lower paying jobs. The stretch-out did reduce payrolls during the textile depression, but it was resisted by workers, including many women as well.

Mergers also brought reorganization of production. Mergers were readily executed in the 1920s after several years of decline. The first were horizontal: the conglomeration of mills in the same phase of the production process. But beginning in the 1930s, more mergers were vertical, joining distributors and manufacturers or mills in various phases of production. Mergers frequently led to the closing of older mills, while more efficient mills continued to operate. Some mergers, especially in the late 1920s or early 1930s, consolidated holdings in both the North and the South. New England mills might then close while southern mills continued to operate.

The 1920s Depression and the Rise of the Silk Mills in Central Falls

Following the recessions of 1920–21 and 1924, half of Rhode Island's cotton-yarn spindles stopped producing. In Pawtucket, Darius Goff and Sons, which had employed nine hundred people, was sold to bondholders in July 1924. The Dexter Yarn Company was also liquidated in 1924, and the Slater Mills, which had employed two hundred fifty, were closed in 1925. Yet as the cotton industry, particularly cotton spinning, was beginning to decline in Pawtucket and Central Falls, silk mills were expanding and moving in.

Early in the twentieth century the silk industry had been centered in Paterson, New Jersey, but by the early 1920s it began to move into small towns in Pennsylvania and to New England. This move was accompanied by corporate concentration. Paterson had been a highly competitive environment with many small, family-run mills that operated on commission and frequently changed hands (Copeland 1935:1). As the larger firms expanded, they relocated production in small towns. These firms included Cheney Silk in South Manchester, Connecticut, which employed forty-five hundred by 1919; Sidney Blumenthal and Company, which employed twenty-five hundred at its plant in Shelton, Connecticut; and Corticelli Silk, which had three thousand workers in five mills in Massachusetts and Connecticut.

The move out of New Jersey in part resulted from the gains made by silk workers through strikes and union militance. Paterson had been the scene of several important strikes beginning with the International Workers of the World (IWW)–organized strike of 1913 and ending with the 1928 strike of the Associated Silk Workers. By the end of the 1920s, union militancy had temporarily blocked a speedup, won a shorter work week, and obtained higher wages for Paterson silk workers.

In Rhode Island the expanding silk industry was centered in Central Falls and Pawtucket. The raw silk was produced in Japan and China, while the "throwing," or silk spinning and weaving, was done in the United States, sometimes in separate mills. In Rhode Island most companies were of medium size and produced about 10 percent of the broad-silk yardage and most of the cotton and silk mixed goods (U.S. International Trade Commision 1926:95, 98, 104). Some of these silk firms had been in business since the end of the nineteenth century. They were the mills that were employing Polish and Syrian immigrant men and women in 1915. Other companies such as the Jenckes Spinning Company and the Lorraine Mill began to specialize in silk weaving during World War I. The Lorraine Mill, whose records were used in chapter 2 and appendix A, had once specialized in cotton and worsted cloth but by 1931 was producing "the finest colored cotton and rayon dress goods of various kinds, shirtings, cotton and silk and cotton and worsted mixtures, as well as all silk shirtings and dress goods" (Rhode Island, State Bureau of Information, 1930:242). The Waypoyset Mill founded in 1907 in Central Falls was another locally financed mill that expanded as the demand for silk and rayon cloth increased.

Large corporations that had conglomerated in the expansion of the 1920s also located mills in Rhode Island. The General Silk Corporation, a chain of twelve "throwing" mills operating in several states, also had a weaving mill in Central Falls and one in New Bedford. It was reorganized financially in 1927, possibly with the help of the Cheney family, giving stockholders enormous profits. By 1929 the company had supply offices for purchasing silk in Japan and China, employed more than four thousand workers in fifteen mills, and accounted for 8 percent of the silk throwing in the United States. It also was notorious for initiating the speedup policy in its New Bedford weaving plant where workers had to run twelve looms instead of four or six. A technological innovation made the work load possible—on paper—but when operating with poor quality silk, weavers were hard pressed repairing breaks on such a large number of machines (Hutchins 1919:84). General Silk eventually became General Fabrics, and its Central Falls weaving mill was the scene of the 1931 strike discussed in this chapter.

The expansion of the industry also brought a number of small firms from Paterson to Central Falls between 1924 and 1928. Three silk firms moved into the vacated Darius Goff Mills. Cadillac Silk of Paterson moved into the Dexter Yarn Company mill and Chelsea Silk of Paterson into a former Jenckes Company mill. Hamlet Silk used part of the Slater Yarn Company mills. Several new silk companies incorporated in the 1920s, many of them locating in the original cotton mills along the river in Central Falls. In the meantime, the Royal Weaving Company expanded, moving out of the Central Falls mill and adding a new weave shed at the mill complex in Pawtucket.

Most of the silk mills in Central Falls and Pawtucket wove mixed goods or silk broad fabrics. Women made up a large proportion of this

Skein winding to spools at the Royal Weaving Mills, a typical woman's job. Many Polish women worked at this mill, where the skeins of fine silk thread were placed on a "swift" and wound off onto bobbins. Courtesy of the Rhode Island Historical Society.

labor force from the mid-1920s into the 1930s. In the smaller companies, women were 50 percent of the work force, while at larger firms like the Royal Weaving Company and the Waypoyset Mill with more than one thousand workers, women made up from 53 to 60 percent of the labor force.

The heavy concentration of women in silk production was apparantly a result of the high number of fine threads per inch that skein winders, creelers, and weavers dealt with. Some women indicated that their husbands found working with silk threads irksome and chose to find jobs outside the silk mills. Certainly, the manufacturers thought that women were better able to do the work because of their dexterity and patience. However, considering the lower women's wages in other mill jobs, women were probably more willing than men to do tedious silk-weaving work.

Women soon experienced the effects of the stretch-out and the speedup. Mrs. Wendoloski contrasted work conditions at the beginning of the 1920s with those of the 1930s:

At the next stage of the process, women also tended the huge silk-warping machines that wound the bobbins of silk that became the warp. Royal Weaving Mills. Courtesy of the Rhode Island Historical Society.

We had a good boss, you know. He didn't mind, you know, as long as the looms were running. We used to go to the sick room and talk and bring things. We crocheted, embroidered, or something, you know, while the work was going well. It was much easier. . . . Today . . . it's a rat race. Today, when I got through weaving, they were giving us a room with four looms. Then there were six looms. Well, there is somebody going to be out of a job. Well, I wasn't out of a job, but they put me on another floor, and they gave me four looms that I was familiar with and two, what they call box looms—you can make fancy cloth on it . . . you know designer. All right, I couldn't stop those looms. I couldn't do anything with them. Anyhow, that was awful.[2]

The speedup and stretch-out eventually drove Mrs. Wendoloski out of weaving and back to drawing-in, which she found much easier to do. "They wanted to speed up a little bit. It was going into that kind of

2. Quotations in this section are from oral-history interviews conducted with Polish women by Ewa Hauser in 1978.

[179]

thing. And when they did that, they gave me six looms. I couldn't. I went back drawing-in. I went back. I got a job in Central Falls. . . . That was what they called National Fabrics, and I was working there and I enjoyed it."

The expansion of silk in Rhode Island and in Central Falls cushioned the area from some of the effects of the textile depression in the 1920s. However, in both cotton and silk mills women workers from various ethnic backgrounds felt the full force of management's efforts to deal with the depression: wage cuts, speedup, and stretch-out. Women, as well as men, often responded to these tactics with increased militance.

Women's Strategies of Resistance and the Textile Strikes of the 1920s and 1930s

As women and men experienced the effects of the textile depression, they resisted management's strategies with walkouts, strikes, and other forms of opposition.[3] In the following sections, I examine three strikes in Pawtucket and Central Falls: the general strike of 1922, the Royal Weaving and General Fabrics Strike of 1931, and the general strike of 1934. The participation of new immigrant working daughters was extensive, but there is also evidence of interethnic and intraethnic conflict. Women's activities were often overshadowed by those of male union organizers or male workers. Resistance was tempered by the historical context of the strike, the organizing philosophy of a particular union, and the tactics used by management or government. Women were sometimes, but not always, able to bridge the ethnic divisions that separated them or to circumvent the dominant role men played in worker-management conflict.

3. Evidence for these resistance strategies comes from newspaper accounts of strikes and walkouts. The oral-history interviews cited in this chapter tell us that women workers often experienced difficult working conditions, including the stretch-out. However, there is little mention of women's informal strategies or ways in which they might have quietly resisted a supervisor's authority, pay cuts, or the effects of the stretch-out. Even the strikes are hardly mentioned in the oral histories available to us. Hauser (1981:chap. 6) argued convincingly that Polish interviewees blocked conflict out of their accounts of both religious life and work life, so the view of the community's history as presented to an outside anthropologist was substantially at variance with newspaper accounts of that history. Thus I have relied on newspaper accounts, public records, and interviews with labor organizers to give some idea of how women workers participated in the increasing labor militance of the period.

Since its beginnings, the textile industry in Rhode Island has been characterized by worker militancy and women's participation in resistance, notably in the Pawtucket weavers' strike of 1824, strikes in the 1850s, and the Knights of Labor activities of the 1880s (see chapter 2). However there were difficulties in forming permanent labor organizations. Women, including recent immigrant women, often participated in strikes, but like male immigrants, they were least involved in labor unions. From the 1850s the union movement in textiles involved the male-dominated skilled crafts, particularly mule spinning and loomfixing. The United Textile Workers of America (UTW), founded in 1901 and headed by John Golden, was essentially a conservative craft union. The UTW funded few organizers since craft locals objected, and they supported relatively few spontaneous strikes. The UTW became notorious for undercutting more radical unions that organized ethnic minorities on an industrial, rather than a craft, basis. The UTW was, in addition, a male-dominated union. It played an important role in the 1922 and 1934 strikes, but its conservative philosophy had an impact on the participation of women, particularly in 1934.

Women's involvement in strikes and walkouts did not begin with the textile depression and the 1922 strike. Data collected by the Rhode Island Commissioner of Industrial Statistics between 1887 and 1894 and between 1901 and 1919 indicates that women were involved in many labor incidents.[4] Almost all plants where Central Falls women worked experienced one or two strikes between 1901 and 1919, with an estimated 5 to 10 percent of the textile labor force involved in strikes in any given year (Ferguson 1940). Three examples illustrate women's participation. In 1901 seventy-five women and several males—all carders—went on strike at the U.S. Cotton Company in Central Falls in response to a 10 to 14 percent wage cut. The "trouble" was adjusted the next day, and the strikers returned to work with a 10 percent raise in wages (Rhode Island 1902:125–26). At American Hair Cloth, also in Central Falls, 200 employees struck in July 1907 when they were required to run ten, rather than eight, looms. The

4. There are difficulties with these data. Employers were not required by law to report strikes, forcing the Bureau of Industrial Statistics to rely on newspaper accounts, probably resulting in an undercount. The reason for strikes or their outcome were unclear, and the gender and ethnicity of strikers were seldom reported. I have thus assumed that a strike of mule spinners, back boys, or loomfixers involved men; that walkouts of weavers included women; and that a strike of twisters or spoolers was predominantly female.

company locked them out and shut down the mill. In August the strikers were offered a 10 percent increase in wages and were permitted to run only eight looms. Some strikers voted to accept the offer, but others remained out, later returning to work with no further gains (Rhode Island 1908:1106). The outcome of these two successful strikes was less typical than was the strike at Coats and Clark in September 1906. The demands of the male "back boys" for increased pay were met to avoid shutting down the mill, but the next day five hundred female twisters demanded increased wages as well. Women in the winding room walked out a week later. The strike was eventually broken, and the women returned to work without a raise in pay (Rhode Island 1907:23).

Later strikes offer evidence of ethnic conflict as well as ethnic cooperation. At the Royal Weaving Mill forty female warper tenders struck because a woman from Poland was hired. The management refused to discharge her, and the women returned to work a few at a time (Rhode Island 1908:1090). Although this indicates prejudice against the newly arriving Poles, a few years later there were signs of ethnic cooperation. In January 1916 a strike of female and male weavers at the same mill presented a multiethnic committee of strikers to confer with management. The committee included two members from each of seven nationalities: English, French, Swedish, German, Polish, Syrian, and Armenian. The weavers requested a pay raise of 1.5 cents a yard and returned to work after receiving an increase of 0.5 cent a yard. (A 1915 weavers' strike over a similar pay demand had been crushed.) In February more conflict broke out when the management retaliated against some of the strikers. About two hundred fifty weavers and two hundred fifty spoolers (mainly women) went out on strike and another "one hundred girls" struck two days later, stating that their demands for increased wages and better working conditions had not been met. In late February "these troubles were adjusted," and the management agreed to take back all workers involved in the strikes (Rhode Island 1921:126–27).

In some of these cases and in the overall record there is extensive evidence of the harshness of mill owner countertactics. Mill agents and supervisors, particularly at the Royal Weaving Mill, refused to deal with strikers, tried to hire other workers, discriminated against workers by not taking them back after a strike, and held out as long as possible instead of negotiating with strikers. In the Coats and Clark case, as well as in some of the Royal Weaving conflicts, mill managers were able to break strikes. Without permanent labor organizations to provide strike pay, negotiating experience, and other kinds of support, workers were in a weak position. It was not until the 1922 strike that widespread resistance was organized. Only after the 1934 strike was an effective organizing drive mounted in the textile industry.

The 1922 Strike and Ethnic Militancy

The 1922 strike was a widespread, virtual shutdown of the New England textile industry. It started in Rhode Island but soon became a massive, regionwide response to employers' wage cuts and other tactics for dealing with the 1921 recession. On January 19, 1922, several Rhode Island mills announced that, effective January 23, they would cut wages by 20.0 percent and at the same time increase the work week from forty-eight to fifty-four hours. This followed a 22.5 percent wage cut during 1921. The announcement appears to have resulted from a meeting of Rhode Island mill owners in Boston on January 4, 1922. The strike began with a walkout of weavers at the Royal Mill owned by the B. B. and R. Knight chain in the Pawtuxet Valley south of Providence.

The strike included semiskilled women workers from new immigrant groups. Luigi Nardella described how it started:

> Yeah, my oldest brother, Guido, he started the strike. Guido pulled the handles on the looms in the Royal Mills, going from one section to the next shouting, "Strike! Strike!" But I was the one who had to go out and bring in the support. When the strike started we didn't have any union organizers. But we had gotten the mills out, one after the other. We got together a group of girls and went from mill to mill, and that morning we got five mills out. We'd motion to the girls in the mills, "Come out! Come out!" Then we'd go on to the next. (Nardella 1978:156)

The strike began in the Blackstone Valley north of Providence on the same day, where it was spearheaded by the skilled male workers (mule spinners, back boys, and beetler operators at a bleachery). It was organized by the UTW, which held open meetings of weavers, loomfixers, and other workers, but did not launch a mill-to-mill callout involving women. Mills in Pawtucket and Central Falls did not close until the next week. By February many women were picketing and demonstrating in front of the mills, among them women from the

Pawtuxet Valley strikers in southern Rhode Island collect funds to aid the 1922 strike effort. Scott Molloy Labor Archives.

expanding Portuguese community in Pawtucket. Police were present at a demonstration on February 20 at the Jenckes Spinning Company in Pawtucket when one thousand workers demonstrated with drums, whistles, and cymbals, and two Portuguese strikers were arrested (Jaffee 1974:chap. 1, 15).

On the next morning crowds gathered again at the Jenckes Mill, but the police were there with riot guns. A "self-appointed leader," a young woman among a large group of women strikers, blew her whistle, and the crowd surged toward the mill. Newspaper reports and a subsequent investigation produced several contradictory accounts of what happened next. One paper reported that the mayor had read a section of the "riot act," warning the crowd to desist from further violence. Another asserted that the mayor had pleaded with the police not to use firearms against the crowd but in so doing gave permission to shoot as a last resort. Apparently, the woman leader attempted to grab a policeman's night stick, and he was rescued by a guard from the nearby mill. The crowd in reaction began to shower the police with a barrage of rocks and clubs. In the ensuing tumult, the police fired on the crowd, killing a young Portuguese man, João Assuncão, who was apparently delivering groceries to a family who lived near the mill. They also wounded eleven men, many of them Portuguese, and two

[184]

Women carrying flag at a demonstration in the Pawtuxet Valley during the 1922 strike. Scott Molloy Labor Archives.

Portuguese women, Emilia D'Concencão and Mary Almeida (*Providence Journal*, February 21, 1921:1).[5]

Several young female mill workers testified at the investigation of the shooting. Eighteen-year-old Mary Tavares, who reported to picket duty at the Jenckes Mill every morning, testified that she heard the mayor give the order to shoot. Aurora Fernandes said that she saw a policeman grab a woman by the chest and knock her down. A nineteen-year-old from Valley Falls, Virginia Almeida, possibly the young woman who led the march toward the mill, maintained that a police officer struck her with a gun and club as she was trying to cross the street. Isabel Honoratos testified that the mayor did not read the "riot act," the section of the General Laws of Rhode Island warning people to disperse from a potentially riotous situation. "Then I heard a voice," she said. "I think it was the mayor's saying 'shoot'" (Jaffee 1974:chap. 3, 30–32).

5. In the historical account of Rhode Island strikes I have used real names of individuals as they appeared in newspapers and other public documents.

Funeral for João Assunsão, a young Portuguese man killed when police fired on a crowd of strikers at the Jenckes Mill in Pawtucket during the 1922 strike. Scott Molloy Labor Archives.

Testimony was given in Portuguese. The investigating coroner claimed that Isabel Honoratos could not speak English and hence could not have understood anything the mayor might have said. She countered that "shoot" was one of the few English words she understood. UTW organizer John Thomas suggested that the linguistic and cultural gap between the strikers and the mayor may have been a factor in precipitating the incident. Many in the crowd, he said, probably did not even recognize the mayor and could not understand the "riot act" read in English (Jaffee 1974:chap. 3, 31–32).

The funeral for João Assuncão was a demonstration of solidarity among a number of union and ethnically affiliated groups in the Pawtucket area: "Several thousand strikers, including prominent representatives from both the labor and ethnic organizations of the city, joined in the procession behind the casket of João Assuncão in a demonstration of sympathy. The funeral was arranged jointly by local Portuguese societies, Thomas McMahon of the UTW, and the Portuguese Vice-consul" (Jaffee 1974:chap. 1, 18).

Employers also attempted to use ethnic associations for their own end. In mid-April officials from a Pawtucket mill sent letters to striking Polish operatives announcing a meeting for a "strike vote" in Pulaski Hall in Central Falls. Organizer Thomas arrived at the hall with picketers, stating that the report of a meeting on a strike vote was false (*The Pawtucket Times*, April 17, 1922:1).

During late February 1922 efforts to settle the strike ended in failure, and the mills reopened, guarded by troops and the police. Picketers attempted to dissuade scabs from entering the mills, and there were continual reports of violence and arrests during March and April. In one incident a deputy sheriff shot a Portuguese male picketer outside the Jenckes Mill. The picketer was then brought to court for arraignment while still bleeding and in weakened condition (*The Pawtucket Times*, April 25, 1922:1).

Although the incidents at the Jenckes Mill illustrate Portuguese participation in the strike, accounts of arrests in Pawtucket indicate the wide ethnic diversity among striking workers—Portuguese, French, Polish, Armenian, and Italian.[6] The strike generated support across ethnic boundaries, but it also brought conflict within ethnic groups, often between strikers and nonstrikers. In the Pawtucket area Portuguese male strikers were arrested for attacking other Portuguese men and hurling rocks at their home. An Armenian or Syrian striker was given sixty days for assaulting an Armenian woman when she tried to enter a mill to work, even though he claimed that she had threatened him with a knife. Other, more persuasive evidence of conflict within ethnic communities comes from the southern part of Rhode Island.

There is also evidence of conflict between ethnic groups, particularly between French-Canadian residents and Polish or Portuguese workers. In April 1922 Stanislaw Dumraski of Central Falls allegedly hurled stones and broke several windows at the home of Exsilde Brunelle, a French-Canadian. Paul Pipin, another French-Canadian, declared that during his wedding on May 1, he was met outside the church by twenty to twenty-five Portuguese who crowded around his car (*The Pawtucket Times*, May 19, 1922:2). Yet French-Canadians and Portuguese also cooperated within the ranks of the strikers. Joseph LaChappelle, a French-Canadian picket captain who led some of the demonstrations in front of workers' homes, denied using the

6. The Italian population of Pawtucket and Central Falls was extremely small, and Italian participation and leadership were most pronounced in the southern part of the state where there were numerous Italian mill workers.

word *scab* but claimed that some of the Portuguese who were picketing with him might have used the word *crab* (*The Pawtucket Times*, May 25, 1922:10; both incidents cited in Jaffee 1974:chap. 3, 45).

During the spring of 1922, several strikers, primarily Portuguese men, were arrested for carrying weapons while trying to prevent others from entering the mills. Two incidents involved women. On April 19 two women strikers, Gracienda Augusta Perreira and Gremlinda Augusta, were held on two hundred dollars bail and charged, respectively, with possession of a club and "reveilling" (creating a disturbance). In another case, Sadie Argencourt, a French-Canadian, was fined twenty dollars and costs for the reveilling, apparently because she had been jeering and yelling "scab." Thus women were active in picketing and even used militant tactics such as carrying clubs and yelling at strikebreakers.

The UTW pursued less militant strategies during the strike then did the Amalgamated Textile Workers, the union that operated in the southern part of Rhode Island. The UTW, however, was forced to deal with the new immigrant groups whose own militancy surfaced during mass picketing held outside the closed mills. In February Portuguese UTW organizers were brought to Pawtucket to direct the Portuguese strike effort. Foreign-language meetings were held first for Portuguese and Italian workers and then for Greek and Polish speakers. In March Polish-speaking strikers from the Royal Weaving Mill met in Pulaski Hall to have the situation explained to them in Polish before deciding whether to join the UTW (*The Pawtucket Times*, March 3, 1922: 1). Finally, the local picket captains in Central Falls were French-Canadian and English, and multiethnic committees were organized to end the strike at several mills.

Ethnic associations, particularly among the Portuguese, organized relief activities in conjunction with the UTW. Tom McMahon praised the work of Portuguese women, for example, in soliciting funds in New Bedford and other textile centers (*The Pawtucket Times*, March 3, 1922:1). In March Portuguese societies staged a play and donated the proceeds to the Blackstone Valley strikers (Jaffee 1974:chap. 2, 43). On the whole, however, the UTW ran a centralized effort. It did not mobilize ethnic organizations in Central Falls and Pawtucket as did the Amalgamated Textile Workers in southern Rhode Island.

The strike dragged on through the summer of 1922. Finally, in late August the mills in Lawrence, Massachusetts, agreed to restore the old wage scale. On September 12 the mills in the Blackstone Valley returned to the old wage scale and the forty-eight-hour week. In Central Falls and Pawtucket, however, mill owners were only willing to restore the old wage scale on a fifty-four-hour-a-week basis. More workers returned to the mills, and owners and agents discriminated by not rehiring workers with records of union or strike activity. Susan Jaffee concluded:

> Even if only the basic "bread and butter" wage and hour demands of the strikers are considered, the hard-fought, over nine-month-long textile strike of 1922 was, at best, a "mixed bag" success for New England workers. The results became even more tenuous when one considers the drive for the most rudimentary form of union recognition, non-discrimination. When manufacturers did not give organizations and committees of workers an outright rebuff, they attempted to bypass them and erode their support by opening the mills under conditions of their, the owners', choosing. (Jaffee 1974:chap. 1, 75)

For women, the 1922 strike was a watershed, indicating that women, particularly immigrant daughters, were willing to take an important role in labor-management conflict. Many participated in the initial walkout, and women continued to be active during the months of picketing. The militance of young Portuguese daughters is particularly interesting since in 1915 the Portuguese population was not yet fully integrated into the mill labor force (see chapter 3). Seven years later, as more families immigrated and as daughters in other families grew older, women had clearly taken jobs in the nearby Jenckes Mill. Their wages were crucial to family survival in households where the men were employed in low-wage jobs; hence they were willing to take a militant stand against wage cuts.

Incidents of both ethnic cooperation and ethnic conflict involved women as well as men. Interethnic cooperation occurred mainly through union efforts to communicate to workers of diverse ethnic backgrounds or to use ethnic associations for fund raising, places to meet, or the organization of a funeral. There were undoubtedly severe splits within ethnic neighborhoods over support of the strike, with some workers returning to work when the mills reopened while others continued to picket. Women from different ethnic groups participated in picketing and mass meetings, acting on identities as "working girls" rather then siding with antistrike sentiment in their own neighborhood. Participation was shaped by the male-dominated UTW. On the whole, more men were involved in reported violent incidents, and the strike leaders, UTW organizers and officers, were all male, primarily from Irish or English backgrounds. The militance of women from the new immigrant groups, however, would reappear in later strikes, particularly the Central Falls–Pawtucket strike of 1931.

The 1931 Silk Workers' Strike

The 1931 strike at the Royal Weaving and General Fabrics mills was generated by the issues of speedup and stretch-out, rather than a combined wage cut and increase in hours as in the 1922 strike. The walkouts at the two mills resulted from organizing efforts of the Communist party–affiliated National Textile Workers Union (NTWU), whose philosophy and tactics were different from those of the UTW. The strike was led not by males but by a young woman organizer, Ann Burlak, often called "the Red Flame" in newspaper accounts.

The strike at the General Fabrics Mill started on May 8, 1931, because of a proposed increase in the work load. The strike at the Royal Weaving Mill began on June 24, when two hundred box-loom silk weavers (including many women) walked out in reaction to a proposed one cent a yard decrease in the piece rate.[7] This amounted to an 18 percent wage cut affecting seven hundred to eight hundred box-loom weavers. Strikers also wanted an end to the fining system and a limit of four placed on the number of looms operated by a weaver. Sympathy strikers were added to the ranks, and when the mill was closed two days later, an estimated 50 percent of the employees supported the strike. Stella Stawarz, a Polish worker, was said to have brought the box-loom workers out on strike (*Providence Journal*, July 24, 1931).

Ann Burlak, the young Pennsylvania-born woman of Ukrainian descent, was one of four NTWU organizers. In a 1976 talk she described her tactics:

> The workers were of many nationalities; I don't know the proportions but there were many Polish workers. There were French-Canadian, English . . . and the strike took place over the usual thing: the wage cut

---

7. The no. 5 mill, which included the weave shed, the rayon spooling department, and the warping department, and the no. 7 mill weave room were all involved in the strike. The strike originated in the no. 5 and the no. 8 mills, both of which employed box-loom weavers.

and stretch-out: doing more amount of work for the same pay, you know. So, the workers came out on strike. I think it was in May 1931 and since they were in the NTWU, immediately we began to apply those methods that I told you about: all workers organized in one local, mass picketing to keep the mill shut down, campaign to rally the community behind the strike, because, unless you had the community support, it would be very difficult to conduct the strike. You needed all the community support because all power of the state and the city was lined up on the side of the employers. (Burlak 1976)

Several of the ensuing demonstrations became scenes of conflict between police and strikers. At a mass meeting on July 9, state police read the riot act to the crowd of two thousand strikers, who then charged police lines and hurled rocks and garbage. Police retaliated with tear-gas bombs, some of which were thrown back at them by angry strikers. Hundreds of panes of glass were broken in the mill windows, and the General Fabrics Mill remained closed for some time. In Burlak's words:

Ann Burlak, often called the "Red Flame," addressing a crowd of two thousand workers in Pawtucket during the 1931 silk workers' strike. Wide World Photos.

[191]

One of ten strikers arrested, including four women, when workers clashed with police at the Royal Weaving plant, July 13, 1931. Scott Molloy Labor Archives.

One day they put police with machine guns on the roof of General Fabrics and we heard them talking that, "We will shoot to kill if the massive picketing won't stop." But the mass picketing went on, trying to keep it very peaceful. When they began to bring in scabs, they brought them in in what is called a Black Maria; the scabs didn't want to come in on their own, so they were picking them up in these police wagons and taking them in. They had rows set up to keep the strikers away from the front door of the General Fabrics Mill, but somehow when the scabs came in, the rows didn't hold all those strikers and their friends, sort of gave way . . . and the strikers got to the scabs and well, we convinced quite a few of them. (Burlak 1976)

On July 10, a large demonstration took place at the Pawtucket City Hall where Ann Burlak was found guilty of assaulting a strikebreaker. Strikers were teargassed as they crossed the police line. On July 13, when strikers were prevented by police from picketing at both mills, workers held a mass meeting, which was broken up by the police. Abe

Harfield, one of the NTWU organizers, was arrested, and Burlak was detained. Eventually, she was arrested and taken to the East Boston immigration detention station, pending a hearing to deport her. Burlak's description of the incident follows:

> I came from Ukrainian background and I do speak Polish . . . not terribly well. Sometimes I used to explain things to the General Fabrics workers in Polish because they didn't understand English sufficiently, so they decided that "So she speaks Polish, she must be an alien" and therefore we were. One day during the strike I got a word that there was a warrant for me and I didn't know. . . . I haven't broken any laws . . . but sure enough. . . . I thought it would be best if I stayed with friends, so I stayed with different families of strikers and the police were wondering, where is Ann Burlak? But after three days, they caught up with me. . . . Three detectives arrested me. And I said, "You have a warrant?" And they said, "We don't need any warrant for you. The Federal Government has one." I tried to reason with them, but of course, I was picked up and thrown into a car. Then I found out that I was arrested as an alien and held for deportation to Poland. You know, you are innocent until proven guilty, but it doesn't apply to immigrants. In the immigration (situation), it's your case to prove that you aren't an alien. I was arrested and taken to East Boston where there was an immigration station and held there for a week. (Burlak 1976)

Eventually, Burlak was able to produce her baptismal certificate from a Ukrainian church in Pennsylvania. She was released and a hearing was scheduled for July 16. Beginning July 14, after the usual vacation break between July 3 and 13, the Royal Weaving Mill was opened, and workers began to return to work. The agent first opened the cotton mill, the carding room, and the spinning room, all sections where workers had not originally participated in the strike that largely focused on issues for silk weavers.

At another demonstration on July 24, strikers attempted to bring their demands to the mayor of Pawtucket. A large demonstration proceeded to City Hall, while others attempted to march past the Royal Weaving Mill. Harfield was unable to see the mayor, others were refused entrance to the City Hall, and demonstrators approaching the Royal Weaving Mill were dispersed by the police. Harfield, however, released a list of demands to the press, which included the right of workers to picket the mills, the cessation of police interference and arbitrary arrests, and the withdrawal of the "shoot-to-kill" order. Strikers also requested that they have the use of public buildings for their meetings and that money expended on maintaining armed force against the strikers be used for a strike relief fund (*Providence Journal*, July 24, 1931:1).

At the General Fabrics Mill, the management refused to deal with the NTWU strike committee of thirty workers. The plant manager of the mill remarked, "The so-called committee is a part and representative of the National Textile Workers Union which is the type of Communistic organization that we cannot recognize and deal with" (*Providence Journal*, July 16, 1931:1).

A citizens' committee was formed to attempt to negotiate a settlement, working with Anna M. Weinstock, a commissioner of conciliation for the United States Department of Labor. Included in the committee were the acting mayor of Central Falls, the police commissioner, a Pawtucket city councilman, the president of the West-Side Polish-American Citizens' Club, and members of the Republican Club, the Central Falls Aerie of the Eagles, the Kosciuszko Polish-American Citizens' Club, the Central Falls Polish-American Citizens' Club, and the Polish National Alliance.

Five Polish representatives were from the established part of the Polish community. The strikers refused to meet with the citizens' committee and instead demanded to meet directly with the mill management. That Polish-American groups played a mediating role, working with local government and police figures, suggests that some Poles had assimilated into the Central Falls power structure. By 1931 their ethnic institutions included the "respectable" segment of the community that wished to distance itself from worker militancy.

Three Polish women were arrested during the strike on July 16, 1931, along with four men while driving in a car filled with stones and a pile of "Communist circulars." They included Rose Okulaski, age twenty-six, of Pawtucket, who had been arrested previously, and Jennie and Anna Brack, ages twenty and twenty-three, of South Attleboro, just north of Central Falls. A young Polish woman, Mary Kalenkeiwicz, age sixteen, also of South Attleboro was struck twice in the abdomen with the nightstick of a Central Falls policeman and was hospitalized for several days. Hospital officials claimed that her condition was not critical and that there was no external evidence that she had been struck in the abdomen, but she refused to leave her bed when discharged. Militant activity on the part of Polish women was similar to that of Portuguese women in the 1922 strike.

Another common feature with the 1922 strike was intraethnic group

Workers at the Royal Weaving Mill, November 1931, four months after the 1931 silk workers' strike. Workers include many men and women from the Central Falls Polish and Syrian communities. Courtesy of the Rhode Island Historical Society.

conflict between women who took opposite sides in the 1931 event. Red paint and crude lettering was daubed on the porch of Mrs. Franz Moeckel and her daughter Elizabeth, employees in the rayon department of the Royal Weaving Mill. The women had returned to work when the mill reopened claiming, "Our department was not in the strike; nobody asked to go out. It was only the raw silk workers" (*Providence Journal*, July 16, 1931:1). The Moeckels reported that they had found a small shoe print in the fresh earth under the porch and blamed the vandalism on other Polish women. Windows in a number of area homes were also broken that night.

After the demonstration of July 24, more and more workers returned to work. Mill owners continued to refuse to negotiate with strikers at both mills, and the strike was eventually broken. Despite its failure, the 1931 strike involved many women. It represents the most prolonged militant labor activity in the history of Central Falls and of the adjoining Pawtucket neighborhood where the Royal Weaving Mill was located.[8]

8. In 1930 the Royal Weaving mills employed 705 women and 390 men in mixed-goods production. In April 1933 the General Fabrics work force was composed of 236 women and 200 men according to the Department of Labor industrial statistics.

[195]

It is difficult to determine how much female participation was related to Ann Burlak's role and the NTWU's philosophy of industrial organizing, mass picketing, and efforts to mobilize different ethnic communities. Whatever the effects of these efforts, women were clearly important in initiating the strike, in leafleting, in helping to lead the march past the Royal Weaving plant, and even in acts of violence in response to police brutality and to other workers returning to the mill. Women overcame ethnic separateness to participate in common strike-related activities. Although most of the arrests involved men, several women of Polish background were jailed as well. The Polish women emerged as activists, much as the Pawtucket Portuguese women had been militant during the 1922 strike.

The 1934 Strike

Evidence for active female participation and leadership is harder to find in the general strike of Labor Day, 1934. This strike was orchestrated and led by the UTW and is noted for the violence between strikers and the National Guard. With the passage in 1933 of the National Recovery Act, which set up the National Recovery Administration (NRA), minimum wages and maximum hours were established for each industry, and workers were guaranteed the right to organize and bargain collectively with employers. Textile workers flooded into the UTW, and its membership went from 27,500 in 1932 to 270,000 in 1934 (Brecher 1972:168).[9]

However, the promises of the NRA failed to materialize. Although the minimum wage was set at thirteen dollars a week in the North, the act failed to prevent the stretch-out or the firing of workers who joined the union. Of 544 complaints investigated by the Cotton Code Authority by November 1933, 459 were dismissed. Workers charged that the work load had been increased anywhere from 33 to 100 percent, and forty thousand union members had been discharged by the summer of 1934 (Ferguson 1940:121). Also in the summer of 1934, General Johnson, head of the NRA, reduced work hours to thirty a week, with no increase in pay, amounting to a 25 percent cut in wages. Southern locals were particularly incensed by the failure of the NRA

9. Ferguson (1940:119) cited UTW figures as thirty thousand members in Rhode Island in 1931 and thirty-five thousand by July 1934.

to protect their interests. At the UTW convention in August 1934, southerners pushed for a general strike to be called if the National Labor Relations Board (NLRB) was not able to negotiate a change in the situation.

A formal strike call was issued on Saturday, September 1, 1934. The following Tuesday (the day after the Labor Day holiday) the UTW claimed that 300,000, or about 50 percent of the textile workers in the country, had stayed away from work. In Rhode Island, the union claimed that 22,329 workers stayed out the first day, and by September 7, 29,000 of 50,000 mill workers were on strike. By September 15, due to mill closings because of conflict between strikers and non-strikers, 43,000 workers were out. The UTW used a number of strategies to mobilize workers and to draw public attention to the union's cause. Frank Gorman, first vice-president of the union and chair of the Strike Committee, added an air of mystery and sense of clear organization by issuing a series of "Sealed Orders" to locals during the course of the strike. The union also used "flying squadrons" to close the mills, a tactic very similar to the "iron battalions" that had closed the Rhode Island mills during the 1922 strike (Brooks 1937:109–10).

In closing the mills the UTW focused on the skilled workers, particularly the loomfixers. Thus in mills where the loomfixers were organized, but others were not, a mill could be closed down, since owners had a difficult time finding replacements. Employers began to request that local officials send in the police, and even the National Guard, to keep mills open. The first injunction against mass picketing in Rhode Island was issued on September 6 in Pawtucket. In Saylesville, near Central Falls, union effort focused on the closing of the large Sayles Finishing Plant. On September 7, one thousand pickets descended on the mill, attempting to close it. Deputy sheriffs kept them on the move, and officials said the mill would continue to operate.

By September 11 National Guard troops had arrived to protect the plant. In response to management's failure to close the mill, at the end of the day shift, strikers smashed the gate and overturned a gate house. They seemed likely to take possession of the mill but were driven back in to the nearby Moshassuck Cemetery by police and soldiers using tear gas. Eventually, 280 National Guardsmen arrived in trucks and were met by paving stones hurled by the strikers. The battle continued on into the night. By the next afternoon the crowd had grown to five thousand, and again they charged the troops. *The Pawtucket Times* reported the story as follows:

Fifteen guardsmen when cornered in Moshassuck cemetery this afternoon by several hundred persons armed with sticks and rocks shot into
the crowd and critically injured William Blackwood, 10 Humes Street,
Pawtucket, and Charles Gorsey, 18, 643 High Street, Central Falls. . . .
Before the guardsmen fired they attempted to disperse the crowd with
tear gas bombs and warn the mob, but the gang refused to get back and
when an attempt was made to rush the guards, they fired into the
gathering. . . . Following four days of sporadic violence during which
more than 50 persons were injured, 20 arrested and unestimated
damage caused to property as deputy sheriffs, state police and military
men repelled charge after charge by frenzied mobs, new trouble had
been feared in strife-torn Saylesville as 1,200 national guardsmen converted the area around the Sayles plant into a veritable "war zone." (*The
Pawtucket Times*, September 12, 1934:1)

The governor declared martial law and tried to get federal troops to
assist in restoration of order. When this failed, he prevailed on the
Sayles management to close the mill on September 13. In the meantime, President Roosevelt had appointed a three-man board of inqui-
ry, headed by Governor Winant of New Hampshire. The UTW offered to submit all issues to the Winant Board for arbitration, but the
organization of mill owners, the Cotton Textile Institute, refused to let
the government "interfere." In Central Falls, American Legion vet-
erans were given nightsticks, clubs, and blackjacks and patrolled the
streets after the 9 P.M. curfew. During the next week factories began
to reopen, despite the pickets, as a back-to-work program spread

During the 1934 strike, on September 11, National Guard troops drove a crowd of strike sympathizers down Lonsdale Avenue, and they then gathered at the corner of Dexter Street. The crowd was later attacked and five individuals including two women were injured. Scott Molloy Labor Archives.

National Guard and strikers during the 1934 strike. On September 12, the crowd cornered fifteen guardsmen in the Moshassuck cemetary, and guardmen shot into the crowd. *Providence Journal-Bulletin.*

[199]

Funeral for Charles Gorcynski, a young Polish mill worker, shot by National Guard troops on September 12. Several thousand Polish-American friends, strikers, and sympathizers gathered around the automobiles parked near his home, next door to the church. Scott Molloy Labor Archives.

around the nation. The Sayles Mill reopened on September 19, and nine hundred workers returned despite heavy picketing. Clearly, the union was beginning to lose the strike.

Finally, on September 20 the Winant Board sent its report to the president. Although the board was sympathetic to the strikers' grievances, it made only weak recommendations: that a new impartial grievance board be established, that the stretch-out be supervised by the Textile Labor Relations Board, and that a study be made of earnings and wages and the enforcement of the code minimum. Most important, they recommended that the UTW not be recognized as the collective bargaining agent for the industry. None of these proposals supported union demands for an end to the stretch-out, for enforcement of minimum-wage standards, and for union recognition. The UTW nevertheless declared this a victory and called off the strike on September 22.

The union, in fact, won very little except an investigation into employer practices. When the NRA was declared unconstitutional in 1935, even the regulation of the stretch-out went by the boards. Without national-level union recognition, many UTW workers were locked out when they returned to work. The UTW claimed that twenty-five thousand workers had been discriminated against including fifteen thousand local strike leaders who were blacklisted (Ferguson 1940:135).

Elizabeth Nord, a silk weaver of English descent from Pawtucket, was a vice-president of the weavers' union and later on the UTW executive board. She worked in the southern part of Rhode Island during the strike and was discouraged by the results. In the end, she thought the strikers lost; so many were fired and there was no way of reinstating most workers, even though a National Board of Review was to have processed the firings fairly. The main issue had been the work load, and, here, the strike brought no concrete improvements (Nord 1976).

The evidence for women's participation in this strike is slim; certainly, women walked out of the mills in great numbers. However, photographs of the crowds at the Moshassuck Cemetery and during the attack by the National Guard are filled with men and young boys. Women may have avoided such violent confrontations in comparison to the marches and mass pickets of other strikes. Perhaps the "top-down" structure of the strike organization and the limited participation of women at the national levels of the UTW meant that women had little to say about strike organization and were able to take few leadership roles even at the local level.

The Depression and Family Strategies

Changes in the conditions of production brought on by the lengthy downturn in the textile industry and management's efforts to cope with the decline through wage cuts, speedup, and stretch-out brought resistance on the part of women and men in the workplace. The convulsions felt in the productive system, especially during the 1930s, spilled over into the family as households faced mill closings, layoffs, and part-time work. The reallocation of productive and reproductive labor by families during the depression can be thought of as "coping strategies"—ways of grappling with the diminished availability of em-

[201]

ployment. The expansion of the silk industry shielded Central Falls and Pawtucket from the recessions of 1924 and 1927, but by 1936 even silk production was in severe decline.[10]

Nationally, the Great Depression began with the fall of the stock market in October 1929, and the decline continued until 1933, when official unemployment figures reached 25 percent, representing an estimated 12.8 million people, the highest number in United States history (U.S. Bureau of the Census 1975:135). The economy revived in 1936 and 1937 when unemployment rolled back first to 17 and then to 14 percent (U.S. Bureau of the Census 1975:135). However, official figures underestimated the number of unemployed, so although a 1937 "voluntary" census of unemployment counted 7.8 million, the actual figures may have been closer to 10.8 million (Garraty 1978:169). In 1938 and 1939 another downturn took place, and only the outbreak of World War II brought the great Depression to an end (Garraty 1978:167).

Mill closings indicate a steady decline in the employment possibilities in Central Falls and Pawtucket even during the early 1930s. A number of medium-sized silk mills closed between 1929 and 1932, and two large cotton firms (the Lonsdale Company and the Jenckes Spinning Company) began closing mills and consolidating operations. For example, Penikees Silk Mill, which in 1928 employed almost 800 workers including 368 women, closed in 1929, and Salembier and Clay, which employed 120 male and 102 female workers, was shut down by 1930. Two small mills, one employing 196 workers and the other 43 workers, disappeared by 1931.

By 1935 the occupational structure of Central Falls had diversified slightly, but textiles was still the dominant industry employing 42 percent of the male and 71 percent of the female wage earners. In comparison to 1915, there were more jobs in 1935 in trade, food industries, domestic service, and the professions. Within the textile industry, silk mills employed 39 percent of women workers, and the thread mills, including the giant complex at Coats and Clark, employed 33 percent. The remainder worked in cotton mills (16 percent) and in dyeing and finishing or worsted and woolen mills.

10. The best data for the 1930s come from the 1935 Rhode Island State Census. Due to funding problems the census was not actually conducted until January 1936, the beginning of a period of upswing in the context of the decade as a whole. However, the census contains important data on employment and unemployment for 1935 and gives clear evidence that 1935–36 was still a period of hard times in Central Falls.

However, not all of these women textile workers were steadily employed. Although the national unemployment estimate for 1936 was 17 percent, 20 to 30 percent of the Central Falls female textile workers were unemployed depending on the sector of the industry. Between 20 and 40 percent were working part time, leaving half or less working full time. Even full-time employees may have been working less than a 40-hour week at times during the 1930s. In 1935 silk workers of both sexes were working 36.2 hours a week for $15.44, and cotton workers were working 37.5 hours for $13.79. In contrast, in 1931 silk workers averaged 45.0 hours a week for $22.29. Clearly, not only was there considerable unemployment and part-time work, but even full-time workers suffered a decline in wages.

In the meantime, two of our three sample neighborhoods, the French and Polish, maintained their ethnic character. The English-Irish neighborhood became more heterogenous and by 1935 included substantial proportions of French-Canadians and Poles.

The French neighborhood changed least between 1915 and 1935. French-Canadians were still in the majority, although their proportion in the neighborhood decreased from 82 to 68 percent. The number of households remained steady, 108 in 1915 and 105 in 1935. In the meantime, the number of Syrian households had increased from 6 to 13 and the 7 Polish families that entered the neighborhood by 1925 increased to 12 by 1935. On the other hand, there were fewer English and Irish households by 1935.

In the Polish neighborhood in 1935 the number of households in the sample dwellings had decreased, indicating that some individuals and families had moved out. Between 1915 and 1925 the proportion of households containing boarders decreased from 66 to 28 percent. In 1925 there were very few fifteen to twenty-four year olds in the sample households in the neighborhood. Oral-history interviews indicate that this was the period when young married couples were leaving the neighborhood along with middle-aged couples—both groups finally able to purchase houses in Pawtucket or South Attleboro. Despite these changes, the neighborhood remained predominantly Polish.

The Coats and Clark neighborhood also declined in population from 215 households in 1915 to 159 in 1935. This neighborhood, which had never been characterized by the population concentration and institutions of one ethnic group, was now even more ethnically diverse. The English-Scottish population was cut in half to only 21 percent of the sample of individuals and 25 percent of the households. The Irish

[203]

population declined from 30 to about 10 percent. The number of French-Canadians at first declined from 136 in 1915 to 125 in 1925 but then increased to 181 in 1935 to comprise 26 percent of the sample. Likewise, the number of Poles in the neighborhood increased from 27 (3 percent) to 118 (17 percent). The net result was that by 1935 the neighborhood had equal proportions of Poles, American-born, French-Canadian, and English households, with the Irish a declining fifth group. Population pyramids for these groups show a decreasing number of children of English-Scottish and Irish descent. Young English or Irish families may have left the neighborhood, but others might have been classified by census takers as Americans.

French-Canadian Women and the Depression

Women in the 1935 French-Canadian sample were part of very different family economies than women in the same neighborhood in 1915. Men in French families no longer had a place in the building trades since the building boom of World War I had ended. The proportion of men engaged in carpentry, masonry, and painting had declined from 18 to 6 percent, and most of them were over thirty-five years of age. Laborers in the building trades disappeared altogether. Textile mills and machine shops still employed roughly the same proportions of men (28 percent in textiles and 12 percent in iron and steel fabrication). However, those out of work, working on a relief project, or with no occupation had risen from 7 to 29 percent. In stark terms, the place that young or middle-aged fathers had held in the building trades was exchanged for unemployment among sons and older men in the neighborhood. Furthermore, a third of employed males were working part time. Part-time work was especially prevalent among textile workers, who were fairly evenly distributed among cotton and silk mills.[11]

The allocation of women's productive and reproductive labor was influenced both by the employment situation of fathers and sons and by the employment opportunities, or lack of them, for wives and

11. Of the eighty-seven employed men, fifty-eight were working full time and twenty-nine part time. Ten of the twenty-two unemployed were between the ages of fifteen and twenty-four, and seven young men were still in school. Almost all of the men over fifty-five were out of work or on relief projects or listed no occupations.

daughters. Employed women were still predominantly young, unmarried women living at home who had jobs in textile mills. Thus 65 percent of the employed women were working in textiles. The majority (twenty-five of forty-one female mill workers) were employed in the silk industry, primarily as winders. Many were working part time including eight of the fourteen winders. However, the proportion of married women working for wages had increased fivefold between 1915 and 1935 from 4 to 21 percent. In addition, more childless married women were employed (46 percent compared to 27 percent in 1915). Simultaneously, fewer single women were employed (65 percent as opposed to 89 percent in 1915). Overall, the female labor-force participation rate was unchanged (38 percent in 1915 and 39 percent in 1935). The major impact of the Depression was that daughters living at home were less likely to find employment, while wives were going to work in greater numbers. The strategy of sending daughters to work in the mills was being replaced; now all adults sought employment.

This change can be seen by examining the allocation of labor in particular households. Male and female workers in textiles were more affected by the Depression in 1935 than those in other occupations. Almost every textile worker family had faced a situation during 1935 where at least one member of the family was unemployed for several months.

Some women worked part time as did twenty-four-year-old Gisele Bertran who was a knitter in an elastic mill. In January 1936 her husband, Eugene, age twenty-six, was employed as a laborer in an elastic mill, but he had been unemployed for seven months in 1935. Gisele reported being unemployed for eleven months of the previous year and had perhaps found her part-time job in December in response to her husband's lack of work. The couple had four children including a baby of six months. In other families, men were in jobs that allowed them to support young families without their wives working outside the home (e.g., a toolmaker, baker, laundry owner, and salesman).

Some teenage daughters were able to remain steadily employed, but others were working part time or were out of work in 1935. In the Houde family, the three oldest daughters, ages twenty-three, twenty-one, and seventeen, had been employed full time during 1935 as winders at the Weyposset silk mill in the neighborhood. Their father, Roland, a machinist in a cotton mill in the neighborhood, worked full time for twelve months in 1935. The nineteen-year-old son was employed as a machinist in a machine shop, and the mother provided the reproductive labor at home to support the family. Clearly, in this family sending daughters to work remained a viable strategy.

At the other end of the continuum was the LaChappelle family. The father, René, was a milk dealer who had been out of work for twelve months. His daughters were all working but only part time. Bernadette, age twenty-nine, a part-time winder at Coats and Clark, had experienced a period of seven months unemployment during the previous year. Her sister Marguerite, a reeler at Coats and Clark, was employed in January 1936 but had been out of work six months during 1935. Yvonne, the twenty-one-year-old daughter, was working as a winder in a silk mill in the neighborhood but had been unemployed for nine months during the previous year. The mother was a housewife taking care of the family's reproductive needs.

Layoffs and shortened hours hit families in a random but devastating way. Even in a household with an employable father and several teenage children, the family could not count on jobs for even one or two potential wage earners during the Depression years. The 1935 census was taken in January 1936 during a relative upturn. Unemployment had been more serious in 1933 according to the the low employment statistics recorded in the State Factory Inspection records. It would rise again in 1938 when the Waypoyset and Royal Weaving mills, the area's two largest employers, closed and the next recession hit. Even so, in 1936 young families could no longer count on the husband's steady employment, and families at a later stage of the household developmental cycle could no longer depend on their unmarried children being able to secure regular employment in the textile industry. Wives often sought employment to fill in the gap, but widespread unemployment meant a lowered standard of living. Families could no longer control which members were employed and which were not.

As one French-Canadian male woolsorter, interviewed as part of the University of Rhode Island Oral History Project, recalled the situation in Woonsocket: "Where I was working then . . . they shut down and they used to open up and call us for one day, two days, and then two or three weeks off, five weeks, six weeks. And you'd go to the next one [the next mill] and ask for a job; it was the same thing, you know. You couldn't . . . there wasn't hardly anything at all, see."

Polish Women and the Depression

The situation was even worse in the Polish neighborhood. As I have already described, the neighborhood was less densely populated, and the "young" ethnic population had developed into a "mature" one. Although in 1915 there were mainly young families in the neighborhood (virtually no one was over the age of forty-five), by 1935 more than half (56 percent) of the households contained children of working age. There were six older married couples whose children had presumably married and left to form new households. Only twelve households (15 percent) contained a couple and young children. There were also many more fragmented families: widows, widowers, and married women whose spouses could not be found in the census records. These figures profile a population with grown children who were either working or had married and moved to new neighborhoods.

Among males, both fathers and sons, unemployment was rampant. As in 1915, men were primarily employed in textiles (23 percent as opposed to 11 percent in other manufacturing jobs). More men were employed in nonmanufacturing jobs, particularly as truck drivers or in personal service as bartenders, barbers, restaurant workers, or window cleaners.[12] Also, many more sons (15 percent of all males in the sample) remained in school, a possible response to the lack of employment in the mills. Most important, 31 percent, or 41 of 135 men, were out of work, a much larger percentage than the 17 percent male unemployment figure for the French-Canadian sample. In sum, whereas in 1915 Polish men had been weavers, carders, and laborers in cotton and silk mills, or laborers in machine shops, by 1935 many were shut out of their customary jobs. Of the fifty-four young men between the ages of fifteen and twenty-four, sixteen were employed, eighteen were unemployed, and twenty were in school. Clearly, sending young sons out to work was not a viable strategy for most families.

The same was true of young daughters. The proportion of single working women in the sample had dropped from 86 percent in 1915 to 67 percent in 1935. In 1915 working daughters had largely been new immigrants living as boarders with other Polish families. In 1935 sin-

12. Some personal service jobs might have opened up because of the high unemployment rate in textiles and could have been filled by former textile workers.

gle working women were daughters in households where they were helping to contribute to family income since fathers, brothers, and even mothers faced shortened hours and layoffs. About twenty percent of the single women reported they were out of work, and 8 percent remained in school. Their brothers experienced higher levels of unemployment and were even more likely to stay in school, indicating that Polish families were more willing to educate sons then daughters. In contrast to 1915, in 1935 there were few young, childless, married women in the sample and many more married women with older children. A greater proportion of married women were employed outside the home (30 percent in 1935 compared with 15 percent in 1915), and even more women who were accustomed to working were seeking employment in January 1936.

As in the French-Canadian sample, most employed women in the Polish sample (both single and married) had jobs in textile mills, two-thirds of them in silk mills. Many had greater experience in the silk industry and were weavers rather than winders, the typical female job in the French neighborhood. Polish women tended to learn silk weaving and remain in the mills through their childbearing years, especially when textile employment became harder for husbands to find. Six of the nine weavers in the sample were married, indicating the larger number of Polish women now continuing work after marriage. Female labor-force participation was lower in 1935 than in 1915 (13 percent compared with 48 percent), but twenty-two women were out of work, sixteen of them former textile workers. Under full employment, 56 percent of the women in the Polish sample would have been employed in textiles. If one looks only at married women with children, 41 percent of Polish women would have been working under full employment, but only 28 percent of the French-Canadian women would have been working.

In sum, the unemployment rates for men, married women, widows, and single women were all higher in the Polish than in the French-Canadian sample. The impact of unemployment can be seen by examining how particular families allocated productive and reproductive labor. Since relatively few families in the sample were young couples with children, I have chosen my examples from households with children of working age.

Miriam Gorcynski, the fifty-six-year-old mother of the young man who was killed in the 1934 strike, was a cotton weaver. In January 1936 she was out of work but had been employed for twelve months

[208]

the previous year. Stanley, her husband, age fifty-eight, was an unemployed cotton weaver who had been out of work during 1935. The oldest two sons were also skilled textile workers but unemployed. Stanley Jr., age twenty-four, was a silk weaver who had been out of work for six months, and Frances was a loomfixer in the silk industry and had been unemployed for all of 1935. (Charles, the deceased son and silk-mill worker, would have been twenty.) Mary, the seventeen-year-old daughter, worked sewing tape and had been employed seven months during 1935. No occupation or schooling was listed for the sixteen-year-old daughter; the two youngest girls (ages fourteen and ten) were still in school. Thus in a family of eight with five employable adults, only one daughter was working full time in January 1936. The mother had been employed full-time during 1935, and two sons had contributed wages for part of the year. Stanley's older brother Joseph, age fifty-two, who lived next door, was not much better off. He was an employed weaver in a cotton-tape mill, but he had been out of work for four months during 1935. Both his wife, a doffer in a cotton mill, and his nineteen-year-old son, a laborer at odd jobs, were unemployed and had been out of work the previous twelve months.

It is difficult to find in the sample another household with both school-age and working-age children in which the situation was any better. Theresa Lukowicz was a full-time mother and housewife, and her husband was a weaver who had worked twelve months of 1935 at the Royal Weaving Mill in Pawtucket. Her oldest son, age seventeen, was still attending school, as was her fourteen-year-old daughter. The husband's wage supported a family of four whereas in better times at least two would have worked.

In the Lithuanian Michalek family, the forty-four-year-old wife and her nineteen-year-old daughter worked part time (probably at home) stringing tags for a print works. They had each been employed only four to five months during 1935, whereas the father, a machinist, had been out of work for the entire year. The seventeen-year-old daughter was in New York working as a housekeeper for a private family, and the remaining three children (ages fifteen, fourteen, and eight) were still in school. There was also a three-year-old in the house to be cared for. Seven persons subsisted on the part-time industrial homework done by the mother and daughter.

Data on industrial homework collected by the Women's Bureau of the Department of Labor in Rhode Island in 1934 indicates that women in thirteen households in Central Falls and Pawtucket (including three Lithuanian and seven Polish families) did tag stringing in their homes. At 1934 rates families were paid ten to twelve cents for three hours' work; tag stringing contributed between $2.00 and $3.00 a week to family incomes. Since a number of unemployed family members also participated, tag stringing might have contributed as much as 60 percent of the family income. In this study, family income averaged about $13.68 per week, just above the minimum wage established by the NRA for one wage earner in the textile industry. Clearly, households that did tag stringing were in desperate straits.

In the thirteen households where all children were age fifteen or older, only two fathers had been employed full time in 1935, and one of them worked in his own bakery. There were six mothers who had textile occupations, but five were either out of work or had been unemployed between two and nine months in 1935. One of the better-off families was that of Anna Grocki, a silk weaver who had been employed three months during 1935 and was still working in January 1936. Her husband had worked five months as a silk weaver, and her twenty-three-year-old daughter had been employed as a quiller in a silk mill for four months. They were able to let their twenty-one-year-old son remain in college.

Even widows with children of working age were in difficult situations, especially if their children were employed in textiles. Mary Sklarski's daughter and son were employed full time in a drugstore, which gave her household the security of two incomes. More typical was Stella Lizak, who had four daughters over age twenty and two sons still in school. The girls were all employed part time, three in silk mills (as a weaver, a twister, and a drawing-in girl) and one in a local box factory. All had been out of work during 1935 for periods ranging from four to eight months. Again, even in households with potentially large numbers of working daughters, the strategy of wage employment was frustrated by the shortage of mill jobs.

Oral-history interviews also give a clear sense of the Depression's impact on women's lives. Mrs. Szymanski described her situation:

We both worked before the Depression, and we bought a home and went into debt. When the Depression broke out . . . it's unbelievable how hard those years were, because today I can't believe how we lived through it. I lost my job and papa lost his job. Papa didn't work a whole year and I, about a half a year. We had little Viola and Broniu then [the two younger children]. I had to be away from them, running around for work. There were two hundred, three hundred people around one factory, looking for work. Maybe one person would be hired where some place was running a bit, but almost every place was closed. People wandered around those factory walls looking for work all day, day after day. There was no help. If you were Irish or French and had someone in the city [government], then you could get some help or some kind of job. But of the Poles, nobody even went [for help]. . . . I don't know how we lived. We went into debt up to our ears . . . and then when things started to get better, well we paid off our debts, where it was most urgent.[13]

Another Polish woman expressed her willingness to work after marriage but also recounted the difficulty of getting a job or bringing home much pay, especially in the years before the NRA set minimum wages in the garment and textile industries. Lillian Jankowski explained:

I got married in 1936. . . . I didn't work and I worked on and off. . . . Not all the time and not often. It was Depression and there wasn't that much work. We were lucky if one of us worked; [we] could make it. Many people lost their houses then. . . . It was very difficult. Only when Roosevelt came and he made the NRA, they had to . . . you should ask my sister-in-law. She will tell you. She got two or three dollars a week where she was working. It was that sweat shop, you know. . . . And where I worked, I made more money.[14]

Mothers who continued to work used several strategies to care for their children. Mary Bielecki left her older daughter at home to take care of the younger children. Mrs. Szymanski's husband worked nights while she worked days after their first child was born in the early 1920s. Other women, like Mrs. Wendoloski, worked during the day and had their mothers live with them to take care of the children.

Housing became a problem since families had little money for rent or lost recently purchased houses. As Mrs. Szymanski said: "There was no money to pay for renting. Who is going to rent to you when you come to him and have no money to begin with? He'd rather let it stand empty, right? That was unbelievable. . . . Many houses stood

13. These quotations from Mrs. Szymanski were part of an oral history collected by her daughter as part of a University of Rhode Island extension course. (See Phillips 1977.)

14. Quotations from Lillian Jankowski and Mary Bielecki in this section are taken from oral-history interviews collected in 1978 by Ewa Hauser.

empty because two or three families would live in one home. Children moved in with parents or parents with children, all jammed together, so they could live through this Depression."

Other families could no longer count on renters to help pay the mortgages on their two- and three-decker houses. Mary Bielecki remembered:

> There wasn't much money in the house ever. Those people upstairs . . . well they paid if they had work, but when they were out of a job, they didn't. . . . But mother had to pay taxes. She cashed in her life insurance to make sure to pay her debts. Because she was very proud, she didn't want to give up. So nobody would say that Poles couldn't make it. How do you say in Polish "proud"? My mother sewed. . . . She always sewed my clothes. . . . I was well dressed. She also sewed for other people to make some money but she didn't have that much time. . . . The factory job was more stable.

Other women also used this tactic to bring in extra cash. After losing her factory job, Mrs. Szymanski worked full time at home making clothes.

> Then I worked on my own. I had to cut the fabric and had to make the suit all by myself and finished to give to the customer. That's taking a lot of time, and each suit has to be different. I liked it, but I had to take care of my family. . . . I didn't have time to clean my house or cook; my husband would come from his work hungry, tired, and my daughter was still at school. . . . We are just about to sit and eat and somebody [wanting their clothes] is at the door or calls. . . . I worked like this for three years, so I almost had a nervous breakdown, and the doctor told me that either you close it up or you are going to get sick, seriously sick.

Polish women, both wives and daughters, tried to help their families in various ways during the Depression. Many daughters were unsuccessful in finding and maintaining mill employment, and about 20 percent were out of work, despite their skills. Married women and widows, including experienced weavers, spinners, doffers, and dressmakers, also tried to find work and could not. Some daughters did find jobs outside textiles, as housekeepers, salesgirls, or stenographers, but nearly half the working single women had to be content with part-time employment. One of every two employed married women was also working only half time. Even more married women who would have preferred to work were full-time homemakers. Some may have been able to bring in extra cash as Mrs. Szymanski did through her dressmaking business. Other families went into debt, cashed in their insurance, and struggled to make ends meet with a very depressed standard of living.

English and Irish Women and the Depression

Many English women were in households that suffered less during the Depression. In our third sample neighborhood the proportion of English and Irish families had declined as the population aged, and by 1935 there were only forty-four English-Scottish households and fifteen Irish families. In the English sample, many were couples or widows with children of working age (nineteen households) or older couples whose children had all married (nine households). In the Irish sample, five households were couples or widows with working children, and five were solitary older couples or single elderly people. The American-born portion of the sample (thirty-nine households) included many couples with English or Irish surnames and accounted for a significant proportion (forty-one percent) of young couples with children under working age.

The relatively skilled position of older English men shielded them somewhat from the effects of the Depression. In 1915 many in the neighborhood had been machinists or skilled textile workers. In 1935 they were still the jobs held by English fathers, whose jobs ranged from millwright, foreman, and weaver in cotton or thread mills to machinist, bricklayer, plumber, and baker outside of mills. A number of men were able to get service jobs within the mills as a watchman, inspector, or elevator man. In four instances men went from relatively skilled positions as machinist, spindle setter, and dyer to elevator man, card grinder, and manager of a saloon. Among the forty older men in the sample (married, widowed, and single) eleven were out of work, physically incapacitated, or on relief. Although this was an unemployment rate of 28 percent, the rest had full-time employment as a printer, compositor, plumber, fireman, machinist, and foreman.

In addition, households in this sample were relatively small, ranging from one to three children. Evidently, the few younger couples were having smaller families, and some children of the older couples may have already married. There were relatively few young sons, only twelve, of working age in this sample. Some of them remained in

[213]

school, and others were working part time in textiles or in jobs outside of textiles. Only two were out of work, a doffer and a laborer for a junk yard.

Women in these families were often able to find work or stay in school and secure a diploma. The overall labor-force participation rate for women was 39 percent, only slightly lower than the 44 percent for Polish women. However, given the smaller size of the sample and its smaller household size, there are some important internal differences. Of the eighteen single women, only 39 percent were working for wages, compared with the much larger proportions in the French (68 percent) and Polish samples (65 percent). Some, 33 percent, were staying in school compared with only 13 percent of the French daughters and 8 percent of the Polish. Fewer of the English daughters than the Polish daughters reported that they were out of work—11 percent of the English daughters compared with 20 percent of the Polish daughters. Of the married English women 39 percent were working for wages and 60 percent were at home full time. Only one was out of work compared with 17 percent of the Polish wives. Some of the English wives were undoubtedly working so that their daughters could stay in school.

The English households were in a more comfortable position than their Polish and French counterparts. Bessie Holt worked part time in Coats and Clark while her husband was employed full time as a watchman in a silk mill. Their only daughter living at home was fifteen years old and attending tenth grade in school. Faye Pierce was a full-time homemaker and probably helped care for her eighty-seven-year-old mother-in-law in addition to doing other household chores. Her husband, Edward, was employed full time at Coats and Clark as a machinist. Their twenty-four-year-old son Earl had a steady full-time job at a barbershop, but their nineteen-year-old daughter, previously employed as a feeder at a thread mill, had been unemployed for an entire year. Even though in normal times the household would have been able to count on three full-time pay packets, they were fortunate to have wages from two full-time adults (one skilled) during 1935.

Other families were less fortunate. Robert Henderson was a weaver at a cotton mill and unemployed for six months of 1935; his wife, Grace, was a full-time housewife and their daughter Maryann, previously a doffer at a thread mill, was also out of work and had been unemployed six months during the previous year. Thus although there were two potential workers in the family, this household had lost all obvious sources of income in January 1936.

But most of the sons and daughters over eighteen were able to find at least part-time work. In some families the wife was working as well. Among the better off was Thelma Davis, who worked full time as a weaver at a cotton mill during 1935. Her husband was employed full time as a baker, and her daughter worked part time as a cotton weaver in the same mill as her mother. A son, age fourteen, was in ninth grade. The daughter had been employed only four months during 1935, but the household had been able to count on two wages even during her layoffs. At the other end of the continuum was Edith Cook's household. She was a full-time homemaker with five children at home. Her husband, a fireman at a nut and bolt mill, had been out of work for twelve months. There were two unmarried older daughters, Samantha (age twenty-nine), employed as a twister in a silk mill, and Lily (age twenty-two), a baller in a thread mill. Both were employed part time in January 1936 and had worked only four months during 1935. Three other children remained in school, including an eighteen-year-old son and sixteen-year-old daughter. Thus only two part-time female salaries supported a family of seven.

English households seemed somewhat better off than Polish families and were in a position similar to that of the French-Canadians. However, with generally smaller households, they may have been able to manage better when only sons and daughters worked part time or when fathers were laid off. Mothers were willing to work for wages, even in the households with daughters and sons of working age. Polish mothers were willing to work, too, but were unemployed more often than their English counterparts. The English households in dire condition during this period were older couples and solitary widows who may have had to depend on married children in other households for some support. For example, Thomas Bradbury was a clerk at a thread mill who had been unemployed for a year. His wife, Alice, who listed no occupation, also had no work.

Conclusions

Militant resistance in the workplace and coping with unemployment at home were the twin realities for Central Falls women as the textile depression continued to deepen during the 1930s. Whereas during the previous hundred years there had been a steady expansion of the textile industry, beginning in 1920 its New England branch faced decline and crisis. Structural weaknesses in the productive system as it had been developed by Rhode Island capitalists were largely responsible for decline; as industrialists cut wages and transformed the production process to cope with their deteriorating market situation, workers resisted their tactics with walkouts and strikes. Central Falls and Pawtucket were somewhat shielded from the textile recession because of the expansion of silk production during the late 1920s. However, by the mid-1930s even the silk mills were forced to lay off workers and curtail working hours or go out of business. The two largest mills, the Royal Weaving Mill and the Waypoyset Mill, stayed open the longest, but in 1938 both closed their doors, ending the era of silk production in Central Falls.

Data from the 1935 Rhode Island census reveal strategies women and their families used in coping with unemployment in the reallocation of productive and reproductive labor. Options open to members of each ethnic group depended to some extent on the economic niche they had occupied in previous periods. The jobs and wages that men could maintain during this period were especially important in determining how important women's employment would be. English families were cushioned somewhat from unemployment since many fathers had skilled textile jobs that were not reduced as quickly in the decline. English wives were more successful in holding jobs than their French-Canadian and Polish counterparts and hence could support their teenage daughters who remained in school. In contrast, French-Canadian men had lost their privileged position in the building trades when construction came to a standstill during the Depression. Daughters were having a difficult time keeping jobs in textile mills. More married women probably sought work both in response to their husbands' unemployment and to their children's periods of part-time work or layoff. The strategy of sending sons and daughters into the paid labor force, a predominant theme among French, English, and Irish families in 1915, was no longer viable in 1935. The more general strategy was for all adults to seek work.

Polish families were hardest hit. With both men and women tied to the textile industry, more people were out of work. Daughters could not find employment nor could many married women who wanted to work outside the home. Polish immigrant women who had worked in the mills when young continued to seek work during the textile decline but had the most difficulty in actually retaining a job. Oral-history accounts from Polish women describe the difficulties of the Depression for many families.

Even though some French-Canadian and English families were better off, it is important to emphasize that the difference was not great. Central Falls working-class families suffered through hard times as mills closed and jobs disappeared. The last years of the Depression marked both the closing of an era for Central Falls and the beginning of a new trend. The demise of the silk industry meant that textile employment was primarily available only at the large Coats and Clark, Saylesville, and Lorraine mills outside Central Falls. An increasing number of married women were working, a trend that would continue during World War II and afterward. Thus we see in this period of turmoil and transition the beginnings of the transformation of the female labor force from working daughters to working mothers.

PART III

Working Mothers, 1940–80

[5]

The Transformation of the Central Falls Economy and the New Women Immigrants

The 1940s and 1950s serve as a bridge between the era of working daughters in the Central Falls economy and that of working mothers. So, too, this chapter serves as a bridge in my analysis of immigrant women and their families: between history and ethnography, between the experience of pre-1924 immigrant groups and the Portuguese and Columbian immigration of the 1960s and 1970s, and between immigrant daughters working in large cotton and silk mills and immigrant mothers employed in a variety of industrial jobs in small family-run businesses that have replaced the textile giants of the past.

Many of the themes that I have emphasized in previous chapters will recur in this and the next two chapters. These themes include the importance of the economy in shaping the conditions for incorporating immigrant groups, the establishment of economic niches as immigrants are differentially recruited to industrial jobs, the use of family strategies in the process of immigration and the allocation of productive and reproductive labor, and the expression of resistance as women workers cope with management tactics on the job.

Using interview data from fifteen Portuguese and fifteen Columbian immigrant couples as well as my experience working in an apparel plant, I will be able to present very different insights into production and reproduction in the contemporary period. The interface between family decisions to immigrate and the needs of firms can be more clearly established than was the case with French-Canadian, English, and Polish immigration. The use of kin networks in immigration can be more concretely traced then was possible with the French-Canadian and Polish oral histories. The actual decision to send women into wage employment and its repercussions for the allocation of housework and child care can be analyzed. Finally, the day-to-day kinds of resistance that women employ on the shop floor can be examined. Thus I am able to go beyond a description of strikes and walkouts to a more subtle analysis of worker-management conflict and interethnic communication between women workers. In some respects the next three chapters will contain a richer and fuller account of immigration, work, and family lives. I will, for example, be able to say much more about family ideology, about the views husbands and wives have concerning their family roles, and about ways that women on the shop floor talk about their experiences. On the other hand, without the preceding historical account of the lives of Central Falls French-Canadian, English, Irish, and Polish working daughters, the continuities with the past and the discontinuities embodied in contemporary experiences would not be as apparent. The historical long view makes it possible to see how these similarities and differences are linked to change in production and to see how women have actively responded to their situation within a political economy.

The Transformation of the Post–World War II Rhode Island Economy

To understand how Portuguese and Colombian families came to Central Falls and why wives and mothers took wage jobs in local factories, we must first examine the changes that took place in the Central Falls economy between 1938 and 1965 and then the more recent changes in United States immigration policy. The history of the textile industry between 1940 and 1965 is, again, largely one of decline, though in these decades woolen and worsted mills, rather than cotton and silk, were hardest hit. Although some of the reasons for the continuing decline were similar to those that caused the recession of the 1920s and 1930s, the historical context was different. In Central Falls the post-1950 decline was coupled with an aging labor force and with the survival of some synthetic and narrow fabrics mills that managed to modernize and preserve their markets. It was these mills that eventually provided jobs for new immigrant Portuguese and Columbian mothers.

With the closing of silk and rayon mills in the late 1930s, the Rhode Island textile industry suffered badly. But during World War II, production again expanded, and wages increased. Beginning in 1937 the Textile Workers Organizing Committee (TWOC), with money from the CIO, was able to organize the industry so that by 1947 65 percent of Rhode Island textile workers were unionized. The war was a time of increased production and profits for owners and of wage gains for workers. By 1947 workers were earning more than one dollar an hour, much higher then the minimum wage of thirty-two cents an hour mandated by the NRA (*Providence Journal*, November 11, 1943:1; March 15, 1947:10).

During World War II rayon, woolen, and worsted production expanded, but after the 1947 postwar peak, even these sectors faced a severe decline. As a last blow, Korean War contracts went to southern mills. Between 1951 and 1957, sixty-four mills in Rhode Island closed, and about twenty thousand textile workers became unemployed. Mill owners pointed to the lower wages in the South, where in 1952 textile workers earned between forty and forty-seven cents an hour less than in New England. As the president of the Rhode Island Textile Association said, "Yankee ingenuity can overcome 10 cents, but not 50 cents," arguing that it was impossible to survive in the face of the wage differential (*Providence Journal*, January 27, 1952:10).

United States Senate subcommittee hearings indicated, however, that there were several additional factors at work. First, foreign competition was putting American firms out of business. United States tariff reduction, in effect, subsidized foreign production; cotton was being sold to foreign mills at reduced prices; and assistance to Japan was rebuilding its textile industry (U.S. Senate 1958:8–9, 574). Second, the industry as a whole was consolidating into giant firms that had their own selling houses, large research budgets, the latest in marketing techniques, and mills in both North and South. Small New England firms without these resources were severely handicapped. Finally, New England mills were not producing products with the newest fibers, nor were they installing the latest machinery (U.S. Senate 1958:345–47).

Mill liquidation was seen as a profitable answer for those who failed to modernize. Speculators, financiers, and second-hand machinery dealers could make money quickly through liquidation, whereas mill

Triple-decker housing in the French-Canadian neighborhood, 1980s. Courtesy of Margaret Randall.

owners who had made big war profits were encouraged to sell since the capital-gains tax was significantly lower than the personal income tax structure (U.S. Senate 1958:345–47). The forces at work in the textile depression of the 1950s were strikingly similar to those in the 1920s—overproduction and profit taking during a war period, with mill owners failing to modernize and thus losing out to southern competition after the war.

Some of the larger companies that acquired smaller mills were nonetheless responsible for their liquidation. Textron, for example, founded by Royal Little in Rhode Island in the 1940s, bought the Jenckes Mill in Pawtucket, the site where Portuguese women protested during the 1922 strike described in chapter 4, and a number of the Brown family mills in the Blackstone Valley. In 1953 Little sold the Blackstone Valley mills to a realty corporation, which closed them,

Jeanne and Julianne Delise, a French-Canadian couple in their Central Falls home. Courtesy of Christine Corrigan.

laying off more than nine hundred workers. This was only part of Little's strategy of closing old mills. His subsidiary, Amerotron, sheltered the parent company, Textron, from the textile-inherited losses, leaving it free to diversify. Eventually, Amerotron liquidated all of its New England holdings and later abandoned textiles completely (Dunwell 1978:164).

The largest closings occured in 1953, when the Atlantic Mill in Providence laid off 2,300 workers, and the Lorraine Mill in Pawtucket closed, putting 1,337 out of work. That year textile unemployment reached 6,000. One-third of those laid off were between fifty and sixty-five years of age; 80 percent could not find work (*Providence Journal*, November 14, 1952:19). Three years after the Atlantic Mill closing, the female ex-employees were more likely than the men to be still unemployed; if employed, they had reduced incomes. Thus women, many of whom had remained in the work force all of their lives or had returned after their children had grown, were more severely affected than men, with many being forced out of work altogether (U.S. Senate 1958:621–31).

Other mill closings followed in the late 1950s and early 1960s. Another thirty-seven hundred jobs were lost in finishing, many when the Sayles Company closed its mills. Then, fourteen hundred jobs were terminated when the Berkshire Hathaway plants in Rhode Island closed. Older women were an important segment of the work force that lost their jobs. Rose Green, for example, looked on the Sayles Glenlyon plant where she worked as a second family. "I don't have a day's regret for the years I spent at Glenlyon," she said. "I'm only sorry it had to stop" (*Providence Journal*, February 9, 1958:M31). Some companies, specializing in fiberglass or wire and cable production, moved into vacated mills, but they did not employ ex-textile workers like Rose Green (Hodgins 1958).

The firms specializing in synthetics or narrow fabrics did manage to survive in Central Falls and Pawtucket. Some were larger firms (once

The Fales house, built by mill owner D. G. Fales in the 1860s and owned by a Polish family in the specialty-food business in the 1980s. The Polish-American presence is still felt in this neighborhood despite urban renewal and outmigration. Courtesy of Margaret Randall.

family owned) that had grown profitable enough to be bought out by conglomerates. Others were small, family-run companies with a "rolled-up shirt-sleeves" style of management (*Providence Journal,* December 2, 1961:B22–23). Synthetics firms had started as silk mills and converted to synthetics in the postwar years. They employed between fifty and one hundred workers, including a large number of male weavers, in a labor force that was often 60 percent male. Narrow fabrics firms, most with less than one hundred fifty employees, had a work force that was 70 percent female and 30 percent male.

As their native-born work force aged, three of these firms turned to new immigrants. Carter Textiles (a pseudonym), the first example, was started in 1921 by a Jewish weaver in Paterson, New Jersey. In 1928 one of his sons moved the family mill to Pawtucket and then in 1933 to a site north of Central Falls, where they were still located in 1977. Carter Textiles continued to weave silk in the postwar period but by

Women at the Polish Picnic, St. Joseph's Parish, Central Falls, 1980s. Courtesy of Christine Corrigan.

1971 had "invested in new looms and other processing equipment and switched to synthetic fabrics" (*Providence Journal*, March 1, 1971:B10–11).[1]

Liberty Silk, a second example, was started in 1917 by an Italian immigrant who first lived in southern Rhode Island but who later was able to acquire silk looms from the Jenckes Mill in Pawtucket when it converted to cotton tire fabric during World War I. Angelo Gelardi, the owner, located in Central Falls in 1918 and later moved into the Royal Weaving Company's weave shed across the street in 1930, a site his firm still occupied in 1977. Always specializing in silks (crepes, shantung, and crepe de chine), Gelardi was able to survive the Depression, although he had to close between November 1936 and 1937. During World War II he produced parachute cloth. After the war he returned to silk production, mainly for men's neckties, although his workers also produce a variety of synthetic fabrics.

Marshall Webbing is a third example, in this case a narrow fabrics firm that survived and expanded. Narrow fabrics firms directly profited from the Vietnam War. By 1966 many of these mills were making belts, bandoleers, knapsack straps, tent webbing, and boot laces, all on government contracts. One Central Falls firm also supplied elastic bandages. Marshall Webbing was founded in 1937 by Mr. Marshall but was sold in 1952 to an owner of Italian descent. In 1975 it employed 275 workers and produced automobile seatbelts. The owner had done well enough to purchase a plant in Arkansas, which produced hardware for webbing machinery. A fourth firm, also specializing in narrow fabrics, was founded in 1952, employed 130 workers in 1977, and produced elastic braid for lingerie, swimwear, and shower caps. This company also had a plant in Alabama and in Puerto Rico, with main offices in New York.

As early as 1956 mill owners were commenting on the lack of skilled labor, finding weavers, loomfixers, and spinning-frame operators all in short supply (*Providence Journal*, March 11, 1956:S3, 7). A decade later the same situation continued:

> Textile industry spokesmen in every segment of the industry made it clear that job openings were going begging for lack of takers. On the basis of their complaints, it was apparent that the state's textile work force would be somewhat larger if the workers could be hired. The

1. In this chapter and in chapter 6, I have used pseudonyms for mills that were still in operation in 1977 and for individual managers.

common complaint is that there are no skilled textile workers available and what is available in the unskilled category is generally undependable. In almost a chorus, mill men agreed that they are scraping the bottom of the Rhode Island's worker pool, that what is left of the unemployed must be unemployable. (*Providence Journal*, September 5, 1965: B4)

Some accounts suggested that textile workers were urging their children to look for jobs outside the industry, which had been plagued with reduced hours, layoffs, and liquidations for twenty years (*Providence Journal*, October 25, 1964:B25).

The shortage of labor pushed some mill owners to modernize, "to make up for the man that isn't there" (*Providence Journal*, September 29, 1968:B14–15). One mill in 1968 installed high-speed water-jet looms that were five times as productive as shuttle looms. Another mill introduced the Leesona Unifill with the fast Draper X-3 shuttle loom, which needed less maintenance and was adopted because of the shortage of loomfixers. For most mills, this produced only a standoff, with the new machines barely making up for lost workers.

Despite modernization, these small firms were still vulnerable to fluctuations in demand. In 1971 the synthetic industry lost 2,100 jobs, partially due to foreign competition and partially due to new preferences for double knits (*Providence Journal*, April 4, 1971:I12–13). With a decline in Vietnam War government contracts and in automobile industry orders, narrow fabrics hit a low point between 1972 and 1974. Finally, the entire Rhode Island textile industry suffered during the 1974–75 recession, when employment dropped to 11,800, the lowest figure since 1947. Despite some recovery, when our study was conducted in 1977, the textile industry remained unstable, with new mill closings and layoffs.

In the years of relative prosperity between 1965 and 1970 several synthetic mills recruited skilled mechanics and loomfixers from Colombia. The narrow fabrics mills during these years began to use Portuguese immigrants to fill semiskilled jobs. It was ironic that an industry that had long suffered decline should suddenly experience a labor shortage in these few short boom years. Given the financially precarious nature of the firms left in textiles, it would have been difficult to increase wages or to spend a great deal of effort in training a local labor force, especially since many young Rhode Islanders had already been turned away from the industry because of its reputation for instability. The situation was ripe for the recruitment of a new wave of immigrant workers.

Factors Supporting the Recruitment of New Immigrants

As a few mill owners began to recruit Colombian males for skilled textile jobs, wider changes in the Central Falls economy and labor force created conditions favoring the hiring of even more Colombian and Portuguese men and women. The growing mix of industries in Central Falls continued to favor semiskilled female labor, but the outmigration of younger families from the town left a gap soon to be filled by newcomers. Changes in United States immigration policy encouraged and shaped the new stream of immigration from Colombia and Portugal.

Between 1930 and 1970 Central Falls lost 7,000 residents: population dropped from 25,898 to 18,716.[2] Most of those who remained were in the older age brackets since families with young children moved to the working-class suburban towns north of Central Falls. The labor force declined by 4,000, most of this in textile jobs. Other manufacturing jobs, which in the 1930s were located in machine shops and other textile-related firms, by the 1970s were in metalworking (including wire processing), electrical machinery, apparel, and jewelry plants.

As in the textile industry, Central Falls apparel, jewelry, and wire-processing firms were either small family-run companies located in old textile mills or larger firms that had been acquired by conglomerates in the 1970s. The insulated wire and cable plants employed a male labor force, but other firms tended to hire women in semiskilled jobs. In jewelry, women typically were hired for "bench work" (soldering, racking, stringing, and hand painting). Men held the higher paying jobs in plating and casting, but the labor force of a particular firm was between 40 and 60 percent female. The city's largest apparel firm hired a labor force that was 90 percent female in its sewing department. In a host of miscellaneous industries housed in old mill

2. By 1980 the population of Central Falls had further dropped to 16,995, a decrease of 10 percent. This total includes 1,769 Hispanics (10 percent), of which 37 were Mexican-American, 339 Puerto Rican, and 1,385 "other Hispanic" and predominantly Colombian.

complexes (including a toy firm, a candy company, and a cosmetics-container plant) women were hired in assembly work and packing.

Thus jobs in textile mills and machine shops disappeared during the postwar period, but firms that moved into Central Falls, as well as the mills that survived, hired women in substantial proportions. Female labor-force participation in Central Falls remained high and continued to increase, despite the aging labor force. Between 1930 and 1950 the Central Falls female labor-force participation rate hovered around 42 percent, higher than the Rhode Island rate, which grew from 30 percent in 1930 to 35 percent in 1950. By 1960 the female labor-force participation rate had climbed to 46 percent in Central Falls, even as the total population was getting older and younger families were leaving the town. Married women with children were probably returning to the mill labor force or continuing to work through their childbearing years.[3]

This change is confirmed by the 1960 census, which showed that 30 percent of Central Falls women with children under age six were employed, compared with 25 percent in Rhode Island and in the United States as a whole. The working mother was becoming part of the female labor force, a trend substantiated in oral histories from Central Falls Polish women who worked through the 1950s. Certainly, Central Falls and Pawtucket employers, whether in textiles, jewelry, or apparel, were in need of female workers. They were becoming accustomed to employing married women workers, but with the general aging of the labor force, there was room for new women workers. Newspaper articles talked about replacing the "man that wasn't there" in textiles with new machinery, but there was also a need for replacing the "woman that wasn't there" as well.

The Role of Immigration Policy

The recruitment of immigrant labor would not have been possible without the major changes in United States immigration policy, which came in 1965. These changes occurred simultaneously with the build-

3. The evidence for this is indirect since United States Census data in the decades between 1930 and 1960 do not give labor-force participation rates by age, marital status, or age of children, and there were no Rhode Island censuses after 1935.

up of the Vietnam War and a general expansion of the manufacturing economy.

The 1965 Immigration Act lifted the quotas that had made it so difficult for southern Europeans to immigrate to the United States after 1924. For the Eastern Hemisphere (including European countries like Portugal), the act established a maximum of 170,000 immigrants a year, a 20,000 country-by-country ceiling, and a preference system. First preference was given to children of American citizens and second preference to spouses and children of resident aliens. Sixth preference was given to workers with skills that were in short supply, according to a list certified by the secretary of labor (Kubat 1979:56–57). For Portuguese immigrants the 1965 act's emphasis on family ties became the major basis for recruitment.

The Western Hemisphere regulations that pertained to Latin American countries did not include a preference system or a country-by-country ceiling. A Western Hemisphere limit of 120,000 immigrants a year came into effect in July 1968, tightening up what had been a very fluid situation between 1965 and 1968. Without the ceiling, proportions of immigrants by country were based on previous applications, and visas were considered in the order in which they were made. In contrast to Portugal, in Latin America close relatives of immigrants often had to wait a long time for their visas to be processed. Furthermore, beginning in December 1965 labor certification, proof that the immigrant had a job waiting, was required, a provision that favored skilled workers (Kubat 1979:57). The requirement of certification and the lack of a preference system encouraged illegal immigration from Latin America. This was less common in Central Falls than elsewhere, however. Here early immigrants between 1965 and 1968 came on contracts and could later bring relatives through the preference system. The 1976 Immigration Act brought the regulations for both hemispheres into alignment by establishing a 20,000 per country ceiling and a preference list for the Western Hemisphere. Labor certification was needed for only third and sixth preference, and Latins could change their immigration status from tourist to resident without returning to their native country. However, after 1976, labor certification from both hemispheres had to be in the form of a job offer, making it more difficult for those without relatives already in the United States to immigrate (Kubat 1979:58–59).

For Colombians, changes in immigration policy made immigration increasingly more difficult. Loomfixers and weavers fit under the Department of Labor's criteria for certification, which made recruitment easy until the 1968 ceiling of 120,000 came into effect. Between 1968 and 1976 the lack of a preference system and the length of time required to get a visa encouraged illegal immigration, and the additional restrictions on labor certification after 1976 tightened the situation even more.

In contrast the Portuguese families we interviewed in Central Falls had not been recruited on labor contracts (with one or two exceptions). There were few policy changes affecting Portugal, and most Portuguese were able to obtain visas through the preference system. There were always openings available within the twenty thousand-person quota for Portugal. Between 1965 and 1977 a chain migration process was well underway, providing a pool of Portuguese labor to Central Falls employers.

These employers saw a number of advantages in recruiting immigrant labor. John Gelardi, the first Central Falls employer to visit Colombia and hire workers, pointed out how difficult it was to recruit a local work force:

> The industry has a very bad reputation because they remember the closing of mills that hurt the local economy so badly during the 30s, 40s and 50s. Another thing is that a worker has to be trained in textiles, maybe as much as six months . . . and people don't want to train for so long for an unstable job or one where they have to work so hard . . . and the work is hard. On the other hand, the Colombian textile industry has a very good reputation, to the point that it is considered an honor to work for the biggest companies. In Colombia, the mills hire their weavers young . . . at the age of 18 or 20, whereas in the United States it is rare to find a weaver under 25 years of age.[4]

Employers were enthusiastic about both Colombian and Portuguese workers. One mill owner called Colombian workers "willing and conscientious," and the president of a small webbing company said that if there had not been an influx of Portuguese in 1970–71, they probably would have closed down and gone South. "Nobody wants to do weaving except the Portuguese," he commented. If the

4. The interviews with John Gelardi and José Cruz (pseudonyms) were conducted by Mercedes Messier in 1977 and are part of the Spanish Oral History Project at the Central Falls library. Carter Textiles, Liberty Silk, and Marshall Webbing are also pseudonyms.

firm could have gotten more Portuguese, it would have expanded production and started a third shift. At another webbing company, the general manager said they would love to have more Portuguese employees. "They are hard workers," he explained.

Both Colombians and Portuguese are aware of their reputation as hard workers. For example, Yolanda Cardoso, who worked at a firm where workers sealed packages of thread by running them through an oven, said: "They gave us that machine [the oven] because we are able to produce a great deal. The Americans give very little production in that task. The Americans take a long time between pressing one pack and the next. Instead, we are very fast while we are there. The machine keeps moving all the time when we are working there. The Americans take it very easy. . . . That's why they prefer Latins who work more and try very hard to do a good job. The Hispanos are better workers."

The mixed industrial economy of Central Falls as it had evolved during the postwar period created the conditions for hiring immigrant labor. During the boom years of the Vietnam War, small textile firms faced with an aging labor force needed skilled male labor, while other firms welcomed immigrant women to fill their semiskilled jobs. The reasons that immigrants were willing to come to New England and take these positions in the Central Falls economy lie, however, in the economies of the "sending" countries from which they came.

The Economy of Two Sending Societies: Colombia and the Azores

Like earlier female immigrants to Central Falls, Colombian and Portuguese women came to Rhode Island as part of a family strategy to better their lives. Whereas French-Canadian, English, and Polish immigrants were pushed out of nineteenth-century economies, Colombian and Portuguese immigrants came from economies shaped by developments within twentieth-century capitalism. Underdevelopment in Colombia created massive urbanization and an overcrowded service sector, making immigration attractive even for skilled workers and professionals. In contrast, the underdeveloped nature of rural Portugal, particularly in the Azores, Madeira, and Cape Verde, provided the same impetus for immigration to the United States it had in the early part of the century.

Within the past forty years, Colombia has experienced a decline in the rural population and phenomenal urban growth (partially from migration and partially from population increase). Capital-intensive productive techniques in agriculture and mining pushed people out of primary production with only a fraction being absorbed in the newly mechanized agricultural enterprises or in the modernized and capital-intensive manufacturing and service sectors (Chaney 1976b:109). Agrarian reform in the 1960s did not slow urban migration because there was not sufficient land to give enough peasants plots of viable size. Furthermore, "La Violencia," a period of widespread conflict between liberal and conservative guerilla bands from 1948 to 1959, drove many families into the cities, particularly in the departments of Tolima, Valle, Caldas, and Antioquia.

Since many of the immigrants to Central Falls were from Antioquia, it is not surprising that "La Violencia" was important in family migration histories. Guillermo Lucero's father sold a small ranch he had in Santo Domingo, Antioquia, deciding to leave for Bello, a sector of Medellín, the capital city of Antioquia: "He sold it . . . [the ranch] for nothing. . . . Imagine, he sold it in 1962. Today a ranch like that is worth a million pesos, but my father sold it. . . . He gave it away. And he did it because . . . there was a lot of violence around there . . . people killing, looking for other people to kill."[5]

Few of these urban migrants were absorbed into the industrial sector of urban economies. Most were drawn into the service sector and into marginal jobs. Estimates of unemployment and under-employment run as high as 20 to 25 percent of the work force (Chaney 1976b:109). Some urban workers migrated to Venezuela to seek work, and others went to Panama and Ecuador. Among our sample of Central Falls Colombians, Eduardo Olivera's father, a loomfixer, migrated to Venezuela in the mid-1960s to work in the textile industry. Eduardo followed in 1965 and worked for a large Venezuelan firm for four months on a tourist visa before returning to Barranquilla to work in another firm in the Colombian textile industry.

Ironically, however, United States immigration policy led to the recruitment of professionals, technicians, and skilled workers rather than from workers in the overcrowded and underpaid service sector. Whereas professionals and clerical workers were a significant propor-

5. Comments from Colombian immigrants come from interviews conducted by Ricardo Anzaldua and Aida Redondo as part of our NIMH project. In utilizing pseudonyms I have not tried to replicate Columbian names but have used general Hispanic names, which may be more common in Mexican or Puerto Rican populations.

tion of those who migrated during the 1950s, the proportion of crafts-men and operatives increased during the 1970s, with the combined total of these groups reaching 71 percent of the Colombian immigra-tion (Cruz and Castaño 1976:54).

C. I. Cruz and J. Castaño argued that Colombian migration to the United States is not prompted by unemployment alone but by the search for occupations more gratifying in terms of income and social status (1976:74). One of our interviewees, Fernando García, stated clearly that the standard of living to be achieved in the United States was better than in Colombia. "One lives better here than there. The country [United States] is more industrialized, and one can have many things that one can't over there. . . . One would have to earn one of the larger salaries in order to have what one has here . . . obtaining a stove, you know? A gas one . . . or a refrigerator, that requires a large outlay you know? . . . Here [United States] it's easier to get things, and everything [is] on credit."

Most Colombians migrated to the New York City area, particularly to Jackson Heights in Queens. The New York Colombian population is much larger than any in New England, is much more diversified, and represents a larger segment of families from professional and technical backgrounds. Nevertheless, many Colombians in New York work in factories and service jobs, as restaurant workers, construction em-ployees, janitors, and parking attendants (Chaney 1976b:120). In con-trast, the unique history of Colombian recruitment in Rhode Island has drawn immigrants from only two cities (Barranquilla and Medel-lín), with both men and women employed in the textile industry. As in the New York population, female labor-force participation here is higher among Colombian women than for the United States as a whole, making the *ama de casa*, or housewife, almost unknown (Chaney 1976a:114–15). Both populations are made up of young indi-viduals and families, who were motivated to immigrate by a desire to improve their economic situation.

Rural underdevelopment, rather than urban overdevelopment, characterizes the economy of the Azores. These islands off the coast of Portugal have been exploited by the mainland economy, which re-tained control over essential institutions and obtained a large propor-tion of the islands' surplus from taxes, tariffs on exported goods, and absentee ownership. Several of the seven Azores islands, and es-pecially São Miguel, have been dominated by large landholders, re-ducing most agriculturalists to small holders, renters, or day laborers.

The 1965 Agricultural Census showed that that 80 percent of the land in the Azores was held by individual families, but 75 percent of the holdings were not large enough to support the families that worked them. On São Miguel the proportion of insufficient holdings was higher, land was more heavily concentrated in the hands of large landowners, and more families rented, rather than owned, their land.

In 1975, because of the largely underdeveloped industrial sector (only 17 percent of the labor force), half of the paid labor force was employed in agriculture and a third in services.[6] Azorean women worked in their homes at both productive and reproductive tasks. They grew food in the family garden, tended animals, or helped with the harvest. They also processed food, washed clothes by hand, and cared for their children. Only 11 percent of Azorean women were in the paid labor force, and of them, 47 percent were in service jobs, most of them in domestic service. Only 26 percent of the female labor force was employed in the industrial sector and those jobs were in small dressmaking, embroidery, and knit shops or in a larger brewery, tobacco factory, or milk-processing plant.

Given these conditions, it is not surprising that seventy-five thousand Azoreans immigrated between 1960 and 1970, about 54 percent to the United States and 43 percent to Canada. Immigrants from São Miguel made up one-half to three-fourths of the total Azorean outmigration.

Like the Colombians, Azoreans made it clear that immigrating to the United States was part of a family strategy of bettering their way of life (*A melhorar a vida*). A woman from Terceira, Luísa Carvalho, stated the matter very well: "There we are raised as poor people. We immigrated for this reason: because we have the need to improve our standard of living. There the economy is very low right now. It's not that my land isn't beautiful, because it's absolutely marvelous. If we had the standard of living that we have in the United States, no one would ever leave. I think most people feel the same way. We arrive here in order to improve our lives."[7]

6. This compares with 30 percent in agriculture, 35 percent in industry, and 31 percent in services for the whole of Portugal, stressing the more underdeveloped nature of the Azores. For the United States, in 1970, 4 percent of the population was in agriculture, 35 percent in industry, and 60 percent in services (Brettell 1982:23).

7. Comments from this and other Portuguese immigrants quoted later in this chapter come from interviews conducted by Rebecca Matthews, Carlos Pato, John Sousa, and Filomena Silva. I have used Portuguese pseudonyms throughout this chapter and chapter 6.

The theme of economic improvement emerges as the main reason for immigration. Immigration is itself a family strategy, a means of bettering the economic situation not only of the parents but of the children as well. In this sense, family strategies were similar to those of earlier French-Canadian, Irish, English, Polish, and Portuguese immigrants. Like the earlier populations, the new immigrants entered into the process of chain migration where kin networks played a crucial role in early adjustment. As local populations of Colombians and Portuguese grew in Central Falls, these families, like their predecessors, began to form and participate in ethnic community organizations and institutions.

Patterns of Migration and the Importance of Kin

Portuguese and Colombian women in our study entered the United States during roughly the same period, but different modes of recruitment meant that the importance of kin networks and the formation of their respective ethnic communities have also been different. Historically, we have seen that the earlier migration to Central Falls of the French-Canadian, English, and Irish gave them a different place within the working class than the Polish and Portuguese who arrived later. The different times of arrival, because they meant differing access to jobs and housing, also had consequences for household structure and the allocation of productive and reproductive labor.

In the contemporary period, Colombian and Portuguese men and women have been recruited to different sectors of the local economy, but this has not produced differences in household composition and the allocation of productive and reproductive labor. Some income differences, however, do result from this recruitment to different "economic niches." The greatest contrast between the two populations is in the process of chain migration itself and its impact on creating a network of kin that families can use after arrival in the United States.

In the first stage of immigration, individual family members arrive in the host country and then begin the process of reassembling their own nuclear families—wives and children or parents and siblings. At a second stage, these kin bring additional relatives. A wife, for example, will encourage her mother, sister and husband, or brother and family to immigrate to the United States; a man will bring his spouse's parents a few years after he has arrived. This second stage extends migration outward in a "migration chain" as more immigrants continue to recruit their own close relatives. This same process occurred in the past, as the French and Polish oral histories discussed in chapter 2 show, but its impact on family strategies for adapting to a new environment becomes clearer with contemporary Portuguese and Colombian interview data. The emphasis of United States immigration policy on labor contracts (which recruit initial family members) and on the preference system (which reunites families and continues to bring immigrants through a kin network) clearly has shaped contemporary immigration to the United States.

The Colombians were first recruited specifically for textile work. Men were hired, and their wives and children immigrated later. By 1977 many of the families we interviewed were still the only ones from their respective kin networks in Central Falls. In contrast, although a few Portuguese immigrants came on labor contracts, most came to join relatives already in New England. Kin were thus important in their adaptation to the new situation. Rather than initially clustering in one industry, the Portuguese were spread over a number of industries: jewelry, wire-processing plants, apparel, and textiles, although none of the men commanded highly skilled jobs in textiles. Portuguese male wages were generally lower than Colombian ones, and the need for a wife or teenage child's additional income was greater. Portuguese families also tended to be older than Colombian couples, had more children, and were often able to count on the wages of an older child as well as the husband and wife. Colombian couples had younger children, more need for child care, and no teenage children who could become wage workers. By 1977 both the Portuguese and Colombians were in the stage of bringing close relatives through the preference system. Eventually, the differences between Colombians and Portuguese will disappear as the Colombian community ages and reaches the second stage. Also, as the local textile industry continues to decline, Colombian men and women will undoubtedly find jobs more frequently in jewelry, apparel, and other light industries.

The Colombian migration can be traced to 1964–65, when John, the son of Liberty Silk's owner Angelo Gelardi, obtained visas for the first three workers: two weavers and a shift supervisor. As he described the process:

I am a partner in "Remaches Industrializados," and I went in 1961 to visit Colombia and returned in 1964 to direct my father's textile mill. When I arrived, my father told me of a serious shortage of weavers and loomfixers in Central Falls. . . . I had known of a large textile mill located in the same block as my business in Colombia . . . so I went back to Colombia to interview people regarding the possibility of coming to the United States to work and found a large demand for visas to enter and work in this country. I was at first afraid to bring people over whom I didn't know, but I decided to take a chance, sending letters requesting visas for three persons: the supervisor of a shift and two weavers. These were young men between twenty and twenty-five years of age when they came.

These initial immigrants came from Barranquilla as did the fourth immigrant: a mechanic who had worked at Celta, a large textile firm. José Cruz's account of his immigration is as follows:

Mr. Gelardi sent me a letter [without our knowing each other] saying that he wanted my services as a mechanic in this country. That proposal confused me, because I had never thought of leaving my country. I was a real homebody, with lots of kids and all that, but I accepted, and I came. I arrived August 30, 1965, and so I'm about to complete twelve years. . . . My friends kept saying, "Why are you going to the United States? You don't even speak a word of English. You'll kill yourself there, and they'll pay you very little. And they might not treat you very well." So I thought a lot, but I thought that it might possibly be better for me with such a big family, that I might be able to raise them better, because there would be broader services for them here: education, work, and so on. I came here with three dollars, and I didn't even know Mr. Gelardi when I arrived in Boston. He went to meet me with two other guys who had already come two months before, but they weren't mechanics, but weavers. I arrived at 3 A.M. and they took me to their apartment. . . . I went to sleep, and the next day, I went to the factory, and it was really strange to me, everybody speaking English, and I didn't understand a thing, and the cold weather had already begun.[8]

Soon other synthetics firms in Central Falls and Pawtucket began to recruit weavers and loomfixers, going to Medellín, Antioquia, one of the other textile centers. John Gelardi described what happened:

Personally, I think I have brought about one hundred. But what happened was that some of the workers we brought were very good, very

8. The first mechanic, the shift supervisor mentioned by John Gelardi, had apparently been dismissed and was leaving for California, so José Cruz ended up staying in his apartment. The company had contracted him for $2.20 an hour, but since his predecessor had not worked out, they paid him only $1.80 an hour, because "they thought I wouldn't be any good, either."

acceptable, and well trained, so we wanted to bring more, as did some of the other, larger mills here in Central Falls. So they sent people to Colombia to interview prospective workers as well. So everybody began bringing their own personnel. I was the first, but there was never a shortage of workers. We never had to fight over them . . . and there was always a lot of people. I remember one occasion when I arrived in Medellín [the Colombian textile industry is centered in Medellín, even though the first workers we brought over here were from Barranquilla] . . . so the other factories went to Medellín to find workers, and I went there, too, to find workers experienced in the operation of a certain machine, of which there are none in Barranquilla. We put an ad in the newspaper stating that some Americans would be interviewing at a certain hotel and that those interested should appear for an interview at 10 A.M. That morning, I went out to breakfast, and when I returned, there was a line blocks long waiting for the interviews to begin, and we had to interview all day.

In the early years of 1964–67, obtaining visas for workers was a simple matter, as Gelardi explained: "In those days, the government required only a letter stating that there was a job offering for the individual which would keep him from depending on public assistance . . . a question of three sentences. In one or two months, the visa was sent [in 1965]. But in 1967 preference for Latin Americans was ended by the Johnson administration, and they began to be treated like immigrants from anywhere else . . . like Europe. Now there is a lot of paperwork involved."[9]

Between 1967 and 1972 Central Falls and Pawtucket companies continued to recruit, often employing some of the first immigrants to do the actual traveling and interviewing. Worker-recruiters used their own contacts with relatives, coworkers, and friends, so that many Colombian men who came after the initial year reported that either their relationship with a worker-recruiter or a friend was responsible for their initial job offer and their immigration.[10]

In our interviews we collected data on five instrumental tasks that are critical to setting up a life in the United States: (1) arranging for

9. John Gelardi is probably talking about the transition period between 1965 and 1967 before the ceiling of 120,000 for the Western Hemisphere went into effect. After July 1967 it was much more difficult for Latin Americans to obtain visas. After 1976 labor preference had to be in the form of a job offer.

10. Labor recruitment using the sixth preference undoubtedly dropped off due to the decline in the synthetics industry around 1971 and the adverse effects of the 1974–75 recession on textiles. After 1972 most Colombians came on visas arranged through their relatives rather than through labor contracts.

immigration, (2) obtaining housing on arrival, (3) finding the husband a job, (4) finding the wife a job, and (5) arranging for child care.

For Colombians, employers and friends, rather than kin, played a crucial role in helping to find jobs, housing, and child care (for details see appendix C). Of the fifteen families we interviewed, eight men had come on work contracts with textile firms, and another had arranged his own visa as a skilled machinist. Another two men may have come on textile contracts.[11] Four families immigrated to New York City or Connecticut on a tourist visa rather than a labor contract, representing a different kind of immigration history.

For those men who came on labor contracts, access to a job and housing came through the recruiting process. Most often a worker-recruiter was the key contact. In fact, two of the early workers, including one who became a worker-recruiter, came from Medellín but had worked for a large textile firm in Barranquilla, giving them contacts in both cities. The example of Alvaro Rodríguez, a Colombian recruited from Barranquilla, will illustrate the common pattern of finding male jobs and initial housing.

In 1967 Alvaro received a letter from a friend who worked as a maintenance mechanic for Phoenix Textiles in Central Falls. The friend asked him if he would like to immigrate and work for the company as a mechanic's helper. He accepted. The company then sent him papers, and four months later he was in Central Falls. He stayed with José Cruz, who was working for Phoenix and who often traveled to Colombia to arrange work contracts for Colombians with the firm. (A number of immigrant men had stayed with José during the initial months of their employment while looking for other housing.) Alvaro then found a small furnished apartment and lived there for eight months, until his wife, Aida, arrived. Then they moved to a second apartment, where they lived until they could find a suitable place, a third apartment where they stayed for two years. When their child was born, they moved to a fourth apartment, where they were interviewed in 1977. They chose this apartment since Aida's sister and family had arrived and they were able to rent two apartments in the same house. The sister was then able to provide baby-sitting for the new baby. Although Alvaro was at first dependent on his employer

11. These two husbands were both weavers for one of the big textile mills in Medellín. However, we were unable to complete interviews with the husbands in these families, and only a few details of their work histories and immigration experience could be gained from the wives' interviews.

and connections through work for housing, he later used impersonal sources of information (signs in windows, for example) and kin connections in making decisions about housing and child care.

For the four Colombian families who did not come directly to work in textiles in Central Falls, strategies for finding the husband's job and initial housing were very different. In these cases the husband, and often the wife, overstayed on a tourist visa and subsequently had difficulty obtaining a resident visa, often because of "undocumented status."[12] For these families, friends, rather than employers and work contacts, played a crucial role in the early stages of finding the husband's first job and initial housing. Otto Fernández came to New York City in 1972. He found a job through a Colombian friend and stayed in an apartment with another friend who later returned to Colombia. His wife, Isilda, joined him in New York. After several months, they came to Central Falls at the suggestion of another Colombian friend.

Fernando Martínez from Barranquilla, who was unemployed in 1968, came with a *compadre* on a tourist visa to New York City and found a job through friends. He worked eight months and returned to Colombia to obtain a resident visa in 1969. He used his training as an electrician, a letter of recommendation from a Colombian employer, and an affidavit of support from a New York Colombian resident to obtain the visa. By August 1970 he was able to obtain a resident visa for his wife, María Elena, and their three children. They lived in Queens in the Colombian community until 1974 when Fernando lost his job as a porter in an apartment complex. They were encouraged by Colombian friends who had already moved to Central Falls to come and look for jobs. Leaving their children with María Elena's mother in their New York apartment, they came to Central Falls and were able to find two jobs and eventually an apartment. In both the Fernández and Martínez families, connections with Colombian friends were crucial, but impersonal sources of information about housing and jobs (such as "For Rent" signs) and applications at various firms were also important.

Like the women whose husbands immigrated on labor contracts,

---

12. The proportion of this type of migration to Central Falls in the 1970s may have been greater. However, because of the sensitive issues surrounding the status of undocumented workers, we did not attempt to interview more of them. All of these families had been able to get a resident visa or were in the process of doing so by 1977, the time of our study.

wives in these four families immigrated later than their husbands. Friends were important in finding their first jobs in Central Falls, and this continued through their years in the city. In two cases, the husband was the key contact in finding a job for his wife. Although Magdalena Valdéz's husband worked for wire and cable companies, he took her around to various textile firms when she was out of work to help her find a job. More typical was the case of Amelia Escobár. When she arrived in Central Falls in 1969, she met Ramona Duran, who worked at the local toy factory. Ramona, also from Barranquilla, was a friend of Amelia's husband's brother-in-law, one of a network of Colombians from Barranquilla that had developed by then. Ramona took Amelia to the toy factory and helped her to apply for a job. She became friends and socialized with the other fifteen Latin Americans working there. Since many of the Colombian women we interviewed remained in textile work until 1977, friends within the Colombian network of textile workers continued to be a source of information about jobs after layoffs and plant closings.

Kinship was most important with respect to child care, with most couples working on alternating shifts to provide child care within the nuclear family. (Other strategies that couples used in initial child care and changes they made over their first years in Central Falls are explored in detail in chapter 6.) In some households nonnuclear kin became involved in child care for several Colombian families. In the Rodríquez and García families, the wife's sister was able to provide child care for one period, although both of these families have also solved this problem by working on different shifts. In the Cardoso family, the wife's aunt provided child care, and in the Sánchez family, the children were sent back to Colombia to stay with the husband's mother. Finally, in the Martínez family, María Elena's mother visited Central Falls periodically on a tourist visa to baby-sit while the wife worked. Other families hired Colombian women, often a neighbor or friend (the Fernández, Escobár, Pino, and Gallegos families). This was not always the first arrangement but one that developed after the husband and wife had been in Rhode Island several years. When children reached school age, a couple often returned to alternate shifts or both worked the first shift, dispensing with baby-sitters except for a few hours between shifts or after school.

Colombian men and later their wives had virtually no relatives in the United States when they arrived. Employers, coworkers, and other Colombians (usually from the same city) first met at work and were crucial in helping to find housing, jobs, and extrahousehold child care. Even by 1977 most Colombian families we interviewed had very few relatives in Central Falls. Only in Ricardo Sánchez's family had his parents and most of his siblings immigrated by 1977, brought over by the younger brother who was the first to immigrate. Several families were in the process of helping parents or siblings immigrate through the preference system. The Oliveras were obtaining a visa for his parents, and the Luceros were bringing Flor's mother to the United States. Finally, María Elena Martínez's mother was living with the family, Yolanda Cardoso's aunt was residing in their apartment, and Isilda Fernández's sister had recently arrived in Central Falls at the time of their interview.

In most families there were frequent phone calls and letters to relatives in Colombia. Many couples were sending substantial amounts of money, expecially to parents. Many wives felt isolated and lonely without contact with female kin. Even husbands complained of the difficulty of coping without a network of kin. Eduardo Olivera said:

> My problem in this country has been that we are only my wife and I. We don't have . . . a single relative in this country. So since . . . she and I both have to work, . . . she works one shift and I the other . . . so there is no time. There is no time to go to school, because if possible, English classes could be attended . . . then there would be no one to care for the children. She is working. . . . That is the problem. . . . Like before I was working in the morning and she was working in the afternoon, so there was no way in which I could go to . . . any place, because if in the afternoon, I was able to attend some school, she was working and . . . there was no one to care for the children.

Portuguese Immigration and the Role of Kin

Representing a second stage of the "chain migration process," the Portuguese families we interviewed in 1977 had a very different set of first experiences in the United States. Kin were much more important in arranging for the initial visa and housing than was true for the Colombian families. (See appendix C.) Among the eleven Azorean and four Continental families interviewed, many siblings on one spouse's side of the family were living in New England by 1977. Members of the other spouse's kindred had often immigrated to Canada or California or remained in the Azores. Thus for each couple members of one kindred provided support in the initial stages of immigration and were still important for visiting and occasional exchanges of goods and services. In turn, some families were arranging the papers for other relatives to immigrate to the United States. Most husbands and wives had three to six siblings each, providing a potentially large network of kin if they had immigrated to southern New England.

Most Azorean families were able to immigrate using the preference system established by the Immigration Act of 1965. The Portuguese use of the phrase "arranging a *carta de chamada*," or "letter of call," to describe the visa-application process. Among the eleven Azorean families interviewed, a whole range of kin connections had been used. For example, Alicia Pacheco's sister, who was married to an American citizen, was able to sponsor the family's immigration. Eduardo Dias's mother had been born in New Bedford. "She went back when she was seven years old. . . . My mother's parents—neither one was born here [in the United States]. They were born there [in the Azores]. When they felt like it, they came to this country and here they had two daughters. They had my mother and her sister." Thus Eduardo's mother, at a much later age, was able to use her citizenship to bring Eduardo's older brother to the United States. The mother remained in the Azores, but three years later, the brother was able to provide an affidavit of support for Eduardo and his family.

Overall, links through the husband's kin seemed slightly more important than those through the wife. In seven of the eleven Azorean families, immigration was arranged through the husband's parents or brother, and in four cases the wife's relatives initiated the procedure. In two of these four families reliance on kin had been combined with work contracts. Eugênia Nunes's father immigrated on a work contract in 1968 when she was a young woman. He was able to bring the family to the United States in 1969, and Eugênia herself obtained a contract to work in a bridal shop. After seeing a picture of António Nunes and corresponding with him for two years, Eugênia married him, and he was able to immigrate because of her resident status. Paulo Mello's parents immigrated first, via his father's sister. However, his parents did not learn English and could not become citizens. But they were able to get a work contract for Paulo to work in a textile mill in New Hampshire. He disliked the situation very much because of the cold weather and his difficulty with English. He soon returned to Bristol, where his parents lived. Unable to find employment there, he came to Central Falls where he was able to get a job.

Of the Azorean families, only the Carvalhos came without the aid of kin. Manuel Carvalho was able to arrange a visa himself, since he had been a tailor and was able to come through the sixth preference. The Carvalhos utilized a friendship network in acquiring housing and jobs. Nonetheless, Luísa Carvalho had a well-developed analysis of how difficult it was to rely on friends:

> You can be quite sure that many people are friendless here. People still aren't well prepared to be friends with one another. They come here with little culture. They are used to always being with family. Look, at home I was like this (holding up two fingers together) with my family. We were three sisters, but it was as if we were one. It was the same with my brothers. We lived as a very united family. *Viviámos assim uma família muita unida.* When we came here, this was very tyrannical, tyrannical, tyrannical. It's the most bitter thing about this land. . . . The other problems, we can face—the family together or by talking we can solve them. But the problem of friendships is not solved here. In this country, it isn't easily dealt with.

Three of the four Continental families also came on work contracts between 1969 and 1979. Like the Colombians these families were the first in their respective kin networks to come to the United States. The Paivas both immigrated on work contracts with Central Falls textile mills but later found jobs in a wire and cable and an electrical-cord plant. Joaquim Machado immigrated on a work contract to a plant in Connecticut that made guitars. Arturo Santos was able to arrange a work contract in Washington, D.C., through his sister who was working for a United States senator. The Santos household subsequently moved to Central Falls through friends of Arturo's sister, and the Machados came because Virginia Machado had an uncle in the area. The Mendes family came to Central Falls through Maria Lídia Mendes's sister. Even where work contracts were important in the initial migration, contacts with relatives were part of the migration process for the Continental families and relevant to helping them find jobs and housing in Central Falls. In addition, women's connections were important in three out of the four families. The fourth family, the Paivas, are much like the Carvalhos, isolated from their own network of brothers and sisters, but both families in 1977 were in the process of bringing over a sibling.

A variety of kin ties were used in dealing with the five tasks connected with settling in the United States. Carlos Almeida's family immigrated with a visa arranged through his parents, but the couple's first jobs were found in Woonsocket through a company foreman who happened to be from their home town in the Azores. Their housing was arranged through a woman who knew Carlos's mother. Their Woonsocket house had very little heat, and their baby suffered during the cold winter months, so Carlos's sister found them jobs in Central Falls. They located an apartment in Central Falls through a newspaper ad. The older daughter provided child care in Woonsocket, but after the family moved the husband and wife worked on different shifts.

Although sponsored by a relative, many husbands and wives in the years following migration began to find jobs through coworkers, through advertisements in the newspapers (often seen by relatives or coworkers), or through unspecified word of mouth and signs in shop windows. Sometimes husbands encouraged their wives to work in the same firm, especially in the jewelry industry where men and women are employed in equal numbers. Using these more diverse sources for job information, however, did not mean that kin ties became irrelevant. For many they continued to be a source of information and support.

As an illustration of this process, Viola Gomes held six jobs between her arrival in the United States in 1968 and our interviews in 1977. Her first job was in a shop making billfolds where her brother's wife worked. She was laid off after one year and found a job on the second shift at a shoelace factory through a newspaper advertisement. Viola worked the second shift and was laid off after three months. In 1969 she went to work for a braiding company owned by a Portuguese man. She found this job through the mother-in-law of the man who put up the money for their transportation to the United States. She left work during the fourth month of her pregnancy and stayed at home for two years. Returning to work in 1972, she worked first shift packing jewelry. Her sister had an in-law working in the plant and showed Viola the newspaper advertisement for the job. She left the job when her boss was unsympathetic to her absences due to visits to the doctor.

In 1975 she went to work for another braid company after seeing a "Help Wanted" sign on the door. She worked there for two years on the first shift until an arm infection forced her to quit. Several months later, her husband found her a job at the jewelry factory where he worked. She left the job because the boss blamed her for work that had been poorly completed. Throughout this work history, we see how Viola Gomes first relied on kin ties in finding jobs but subsequently used a variety of means: advertisements, kin of friends, a sister, her husband, and even a "Help Wanted" sign. Kin and other connections within the Portuguese community were not set aside as potential sources of job information, but rather, other, more impersonal, sources were added.

While Colombian couples in 1977 were bringing their siblings and parents to the United States and reconnecting their kin networks, Portuguese families were experiencing the dispersal of their kin. A couple and children were often separated from their initial sponsors due to the vagaries of finding and keeping jobs in the depressed New England economy. Most men and many women experienced repeated layoffs as well as sickness, difficulties with coworkers, and conflict with a particular boss or supervisor. Siblings were scattered over the several towns and cities in New England where there were substantial Portuguese populations. Thus a couple may have moved to where another sibling lived in order to get a new job or better housing. Alternatively, they might have migrated on their own to find employment or housing using information from a more distant relative (a cousin) or a coworker.

Not only have kin dispersed, but tensions have developed over the sharing of resources and the exchange of goods, services, and support. Most Portuguese families are under financial stress, especially during the first few years in the United States. Husbands and wives earn low wages, and couples must pay off substantial debts incurred for plane fares, furniture, and a car in addition to managing the weekly expenses of rent, food, and the ever-rising heating bills. Portuguese families do not like to be in debt and prefer to pay cash. It takes a number of years for a family to be able to buy a house even in working-class areas where three-decker frame housing is still relatively inexpensive.

Under these circumstances, some families experienced considerable conflict in the late 1970s. For example, José Ferreira said of his family:

> You know this was a poor family, and once this family came to America, money got to their heads. . . . There were several brothers and sisters, and we never had any trouble . . . nothing. All married, on good terms with all. But ever since they came over to America it's been hell. . . . Nowadays I don't want to owe any favors to anyone, not because I am rich. It's because I already know what it is to live owing favors to others.

[249]

I already lived here in America with my brothers as a favor; it was the worst time I ever lived.

The Costas had difficulties with the wife's relatives rather then the husband's. Luís Costa loaned his wife's brother $400 for a plane ticket to come to the United States. This has not been repaid nor has another loan made to a second brother-in-law. Ida Costa implied there were conflicts: "My brothers and sisters are ultimately very disunited . . . that is, they speak to each other, but they don't visit each others' houses. . . . Well, I am going to speak frankly, I've at times more confidence in friends than in my own family. I do because in my life, I'm always trying to do the best for my family, and my family now hasn't returned this kindness."

Other families have remained united and visit and exchange goods and services often. For example, the Estrellas, a young couple, visit Amélia's brother and family in Canada each summer. Victor's parents, two brothers and a sister, live about fifteen miles from the Estrellas, and they visit regularly on weekends. Amélia Estrella explained: "My brother-in-law showed up here on Friday. We don't have regular days of getting together. Saturday, Sunday, yesterday down there, today all day. . . . You know, his brother works the night shift and is at home during the day and they are trying to finish his house . . . cleaning the yard, cutting the grass, because his house has a fireplace and he has a cousin who has some trees and they cut wood for the winter."

The Nunes are another family that interacts frequently. Eugênia Nunes's parents and married siblings live about fifty miles away, but the Nunes see the parents almost every weekend for the family Sunday meal. António Nunes's sister is Maria Luísa Mello, another woman we interviewed. The Nunes and Mello families see each other often and have become close. "Every week, starting about a year ago, we used to have dinner at Paulo Mello's father's house. We four families got together: four couples, his father and mother, Paulo himself, another brother who lives nearby, and we. We are only acquaintances, but we were accepted just as if we were their children. About three weeks ago we went for a ride to New Bedford, to a feast; then we ate there and then we went for another ride, far away. Yes, we have a good atmosphere."

In between these extremes in visiting patterns are the habits of the Dias family. Eduardo Dias has two married sisters and a married brother who live near Central Falls, but his wife Emelinda's relatives have remained in the Azores. When the Dias family first arrived, they stayed with Eduardo's brother and then with one of the sisters. Eduardo described the changes that have taken place in visiting since their immigration.

> We used to visit one another, but lately no; you know, they also have their lives, taking care of things, and we can't be always looking for them. Well, on special occasions, then we visit; we exchange visits. . . . They used to come over to the house and we used to go over there, but for quite some time, they stopped doing it. They stopped looking for us and we have been doing the same. . . . We don't know what is the reason. Sometimes it's outsiders, because of a word used in a conversation, they make a big thing out of it. People stop seeing each other, and it's a shame seeing families not being as close as they should be.

On the other hand, Eduardo thought that his family members would turn to one another for assistance. "When we have some special need, some great need of anything, they always help us."

Many of the Portuguese families were at the stage in their developmental cycle where they had teenage children. With five to seven children in tow, visiting with other families took more planning and preparation than it would have taken for a young couple with one or two children. Maria Cecília Ferreira, who explained that she rarely visited her two sisters because of her large family, expressed a philosophy of "everyone in their own home." This phrase was used by many couples, indicating both a strong ideology of family self-sufficiency and the economic pressures separating kin. Economic forces have scattered families and pushed individuals to work different shifts and overtime hours. Free time to visit dwindles to a few hours on Sunday. As Maria Cecília said, "Everyone in his own home. The visits are when we can, and if we can't, we talk by phone and see if anyone needs anything. That is, here there is no time to visit a lot of people."

Whereas Colombians often felt isolated and without the help of kin, Portuguese families had the benefit of siblings and parents to ease their adjustment to New England. However, the New England economy has had an important impact on Portuguese women and their families. By 1977 most families were finding themselves spatially separated as layoffs and employment opportunities sent families to other towns and cities. Conflict over resources has emotionally separated some families, although others have remained united even under these conditions.

[251]

A Colombian restaurant, Dexter Street, 1986. Small businesses are a concrete indication of the Colombian presence in Central Falls. Courtesy of Stephen Cabral.

Community Formation and Women's Ethnic Identity

In addition to kin networks, friends, and employers, women's strategies for dealing with immigration have been affected by the growing number of ethnic institutions. In the early twentieth century immigrant women were part of concentrated ethnic neighborhoods and participated in ethnically defined organizations, the most important of which was the local parish or church. Women's social identity was defined by ethnic rather than class institutions, although many of them (benefit societies, credit unions, ethnic hospitals) were important in providing women with ways of coping with industrial life.

Similar processes are at work for Portuguese and Colombian women but in a different historical context. Both populations are dispersed

In the Colombian market, Washington Street, 1986. Courtesy of Christine Corrigan.

throughout Central Falls, although many live in three-decker houses inhabited by two or three Colombian or Portuguese families. There are no Portuguese or Colombian neighborhoods, but there are a number of stores, restaurants, and other small businesses in Central Falls and in Valley Falls, which cater to either Spanish- or Portuguese-speaking clientele. As the only Spanish-speaking population in Central Falls in the 1970s, the Colombians began to form their own institutions. The Portuguese, in contrast, entered an area where two older Portuguese populations (Azoreans in Pawtucket and Continentals in Valley Falls) had already formed an extensive number of Portuguese institutions. They included two Catholic parishes, a club that sponsored a Portuguese school, and several social clubs. Both the parishes and two of the clubs sponsor annual Saints' Day festivals.

Colombian community organizations began with the establishment of a Spanish mass at the Holy Trinity Church and with the founding of a community organization that helped to lobby for better social services for the growing Colombian community. In 1977 between three

[253]

Portuguese daughters carry the figure of the Virgin in a parish feast day procession, East Providence, 1977. Portuguese participation in public ritual is a visible sign of the community's strength in many towns in Rhode Island, including Central Falls and Pawtucket. Louise Lamphere.

hundred and five hundred families were part of this Apostate parish (one not located in its own church facilities), although some families attended the Catholic church nearest their home or sent their children to the closest Catholic school. The Colombians have organized two social clubs and a soccer team. Although these social organizations and the community organization are led by men, women are often important participants in organizing social events. Some women are also very active in church activities. However, a number of interviewees mentioned the division (and often rivalry) within the community between those from Barranquilla (*Costeños*, or those from the coast) and those from Medellín (*Antioqueños*, or those from the state of Antioquia). As Hector Pino commented: "Here the Colombian community is divided for all practical purposes in two groups . . . people from the coast and people from Antioquia. . . .

Well, the people from the coast . . . try to stay away from the Antioquians. And the three families that live in this building are all from the coast. They don't have much to do with Antioquians. They keep themselves more or less divided from us."

In contrast with the high level of participation among the Colombians, the Portuguese families we interviewed participated rarely in either parish or social-club events.[13] In this respect our Portuguese sample may be unusual. However, it is also the case that the pressures of the dual-worker family life leave little time for extra activities, expecially if they are not located in the same neighborhood. Participation was often activated by kin ties. The Pachecos belonged to the Holy Ghost Brotherhood in the town where Alicia Pacheco's sister lives, some thirty miles away. The Carvalhos belonged to the local Madeiran club, which they joined through their landlord who had been president for three years. The Costas were members of the Portuguese Club partially because Ida Costa's brother-in-law was president. More typical of this sample of Portuguese immigrants was the statement by Sergio Gomes, who said, "My club as you know, is my home," referring to the time he spent renovating his two houses, time that others might have spent on church or social club activities.

Nevertheless, most women did attend mass whenever they could and registered their children for catechism. Although the Portuguese women we interviewed were not as active in parish or community organizations as the Colombian women, they did participate in some Portuguese cultural activities.

For Colombian women, community organizations have provided a pool of acquaintances and friends, as have contacts at work that create ethnic networks. Speaking little English has perhaps kept women in a Spanish-speaking world, but it has also provided them with an ethnic identity and continuity with their lives before immigration. For Portuguese women, kin networks have been more important in maintaining an identity, although the presence of a larger Portuguese community and Portuguese institutions makes it possible for Portuguese women also to move in an ethnic world outside the workplace. Although the residential situation contrasts with that of the French-Canadians, Poles, Irish, and English in the early decades of the twentieth century, women's contacts outside the workplace, like those of early immigrants, are ethnically defined.

13. This contrast may be a byproduct of the way we recruited participants in our study. Colombians were contacted through the Colombian community organization, and Portuguese families were contacted through the schools.

Conclusions

In the decades between 1940 and 1970, changes in the Central Falls economy continued to encourage female labor-force participation and the tranformation of that work force from one dominated by working daughters to one primarily of working mothers. After the final wave of recession in the textile industry, small family-owned mills that specialized in synthetics and narrow fabrics persisted while jewelry, apparel, and other light industries moved into vacated mills. Cable and wire-processing plants and electrical-fabricating firms also opened up in the area. Many of these firms still depended on female labor to fill their semiskilled assembly jobs. Daughters and married women from French-Canadian, Polish, English, and Irish backgrounds were leaving Central Falls or were taking jobs in clerical and service work in surrounding areas. Some women from these ethnic groups continued to work in industrial jobs as they got older and after their children had grown.

As the Central Falls population aged, the remaining textile mills experienced a shortage of skilled male labor and actively recruited in Colombia for mechanics and weavers. This was in part possible because of changes in the immigration laws, which also brought more Azorean and Continental Portuguese to southern New England. Women accompanied their husbands or followed them within a year or two, taking jobs after they arrived in Central Falls. Portuguese and Colombian immigrants differ in the ways in which they were recruited, in the niche in the local economy they came to occupy, and in the role of kin networks as a source of support. Colombian women at the first stage of the "chain-migration process" were isolated from kin, whereas Portuguese women, at a second stage, were able to utilize kin ties for jobs, housing, and child care. Yet by 1977 many were finding that economic pressures had created conflict and separation within their kin networks.

Both Colombian and Portuguese families were similar in the extent to which wives took jobs in the paid labor force. The next chapter explores the rationale behind the "working-mother" strategy and its impact on the allocation of productive and reproductive labor in the family. Family strategies for coping with a full-time working mother not only necessitated a change in the allocation of reproductive labor but challenged traditional notions about the family.

[6]

Working Mothers and Family Strategies in Colombian and Portuguese Households

During the decades when working daughters dominated the female labor force, family strategies for allocating productive and reproductive labor did not change the gender division of labor in the home. Daughters handed over their pay to mothers, who used the cash for the running of the household. Daughters retained some money for church and leisure activities but continued to support their mothers by helping out with household chores such as washing and ironing. Nor do we have any evidence that male authority in the household changed in response to the daughter's employment. Daughters developed their own autonomous sphere at work and many participated in strikes and other types of workplace militancy. We do not know if these challenges to workplace authority spilled over into the home. Only with the advent of the wage-earning wife and mother have substantial domestic transformations emerged. This chapter examines these new arrangements in the allocation of productive and reproductive labor among Colombian and Portuguese immigrants.

In probing the new set of strategies of working immigrant wives we particularly sought out dual-worker families with young children. Since the burden of reproductive labor is greatest for these families and since a forty-hour work week creates a substantial need for replacing the mother's labor, we thought these families would have experienced the greatest change.

[257]

Unlike the historical data, which allowed us only to outline variations in wage-labor arrangements within households, intensive interviews have provided richer data. Our interviews focused on the actual
allocation of household and child-care tasks, on how decisions were
made, and on how husbands and wives viewed recent changes in their
roles. We were able to study the cultural construction of family roles
and reproductive work, topics about which census data only hint. The
comparison of Colombian and Portuguese families allows us to understand differences in the timing of each ethnic group's incorporation
into the local economy, the "economic niche" a group comes to occupy, and persisting cultural differences.

As in the historical cases, the allocation of female labor to wage jobs
is a response to the male's position in the local labor force. Where
French-Canadian, Irish, English, and Polish families needed the
wages of working dughters, so Colombian and Portuguese families
have needed the wages of wives and even daughters over the age of
sixteen. Interview data also give us a sharper picture of how female
wage-labor allocation decisions are influenced by a husband's wages as
well as periods of unemployment due to layoffs, plant closings, and
health problems.

Men's Jobs in the Central Falls Economy: Colombian and Portuguese Immigrants

The Colombian husbands who had come on labor contracts were
still largely employed in the textile industry in 1977. Those who had
come on tourist visas or who were able to arrange their own visas were
by 1977 employed in local wire and cable plants, a machine shop, and
a toy factory. Several husbands had moved from one textile company
to another following economic crises among the firms that employed
them.

José Cruz, one of the first immigrants, explained why he had left his
first employer, Liberty Silk:

> Well, I quit, because many times the factory has had certain crises. I've
> quit temporarily, but not even that . . . really because I've continued
> working part time: five or six hours working somewhere else, because I
> was a mechanic for two years at Waldorf Mills . . . full time there and
> five or six hours here. I was a mechanic for Jerome Textiles for about six

months, but then Liberty Textiles called me back to work full time. (Interviewer: What were the crises that the first company experienced?) Well, few sales, which is something that happens in textiles. So, in certain small factories, they make only what had been ordered and don't inventory anything. So when the factory has a lot of clientele, there is never a lack of work, like we are now working twelve hours.[1]

During late 1976 and 1977 a number of firms in Central Falls and Pawtucket were in economic difficulty. Two of the largest firms in the area had closed after the 1974–75 recession; they were purchased by larger corporations that moved south. During our interviewing, another plant closed in which members of three of our fifteen Colombian families worked. By the end of our research, there were rumors that a fourth plant was about to close.

Eduardo Olivera expressed his disappointment in the textile industry in the area:

Because textile firms are disappearing here, in this state more than anywhere else, now it's my lot to look for another vocation . . . or because just a little while ago, this afternoon, my wife told me that they are closing or closed another company. . . . And I think that the company where I went to work might be possibly closed very soon, too. . . . The owner died a year or two ago. . . . He was the one who . . . ran the business and the sons, I think that one is in New York, and the other is over here, and he has a little heart trouble, and since he has another business, he can't work so much, so possibly . . . they might close it.[2]

In contrast to the Colombian males, only one of the fifteen Portuguese husbands interviewed worked in a textile mill, but five were employed in wire-processing or metals firms, three worked for jewelry firms, one was a solderer for a trailer repair firm, and another was an auto mechanic at a gas station. Three were employed in cleaning, warehouse, or junkyard jobs, that is, in low-wage service occupations. One was permanently disabled but had worked four years in a tool and fastener firm; another was unemployed.

1. The quotation from José Cruz is from an interview conducted by Mercedes Messier in 1977 that is part of the Spanish Oral History Project at the Central Falls library.
2. Quotations from Colombian husbands and wives throughout the remainder of this chapter are derived from interviews conducted by members of our NIMH project: Aida Redondo and Ricardo Anzaldua.

The Portuguese husbands were earning less than the Colombians. The lowest-paying jobs were in jewelry firms and in cleaning and warehouse employment. Portuguese male earnings ranged from $2.36 to $6.50 an hour in 1977. (The 1977 minimum wage was $2.35.) Their average wage was $3.70 an hour, whereas Colombian men averaged more than $4.00 an hour. Portuguese family incomes in 1977 ranged between $10,900 and $20,000 a year. (The United States median income was $26,000 for a family of four.) Colombian families were slightly better off with incomes ranging from $11,440 to $22,000. It is important to note that these incomes were from households in which the wife and often a teenage child were employed in addition to the husband. Some men worked substantial amounts of overtime; others worked eleven- and twelve-hour shifts. One husband held two full-time jobs to make ends meet. In a number of Portuguese dual-worker families, household income fell below $13,273, or in the range of the lowest 40 percent of family incomes in the United States for 1977. Certainly, for both Portuguese and Colombians the husband's wage alone would not have supported the entire family.

Family Ideologies and the Reallocation of Reproductive Work

The cultural conceptions surrounding the roles of husband and wife, parent and child, include a number of key concepts that together can be thought of as an ideology about family. For Colombian and Portuguese couples, they included conceptions of the husband as the economic provider, notions surrounding male authority, ideas about gender differences in personality and behavior, and concepts of respect, especially between children and parents. As we discussed these conceptions with women and their husbands in 1977, we learned that these notions were in flux. In our interviews we discovered that family ideology was changing in response to immigration, the wife's employment, and other experiences in the United States.

The ideology surrounding family life for Portuguese and Colombian couples showed both similarities and differences. For both groups, the husband was seen as the head of the household and the primary provider. In other words, he is engaged in productive work outside the home. The wife was viewed as the primary child raiser and specialist in domestic chores such as cooking, cleaning, laundry, and sewing. Her work was reproductive labor in the home. Within this similar pattern, the interviews emphasized different themes.

Our interviews with Portuguese families revealed that most couples had taken part in a lengthy, chaperoned courtship, and that the role of father-provider was still strongly articulated by the husbands. Since rural values of hard work and family self-sufficiency were emphasized for both men and women, women's labor-force participation was rationalized as consistent with these goals. It did not alter the husband's position as provider and head of the household. Portuguese husbands and wives emphasized that respect for authority and for parents is consciously taught to their children. Children's behavior, especially that of young girls, is carefully watched over and controlled. Underlying this is the notion that men are stronger, and women need to be protected.

Colombian men also felt strongly about their roles as providers, but they were less able to reconcile the wife's wage work with their role as provider. This was revealed in their initial opposition to the wife's employment, a topic I will return to. However, they emphasized their authority in the household to a lesser degree than did Portuguese husbands. Colombian men seemed less interested in their control over the wife's paycheck or over household decisions in general. Instead, a male's ability to socialize on his own and have his own autonomous sphere outside the house was viewed as important. Interviews with Colombian parents also revealed a concern with respect for parents and for parental control over children. Although they emphasized gender differences, Colombians described them in terms of a male's "rougher" and a woman's "softer" and more compliant personality. Parents were concerned to teach their children Latin customs, to control carefully the behavior of their children, and to bring them up with the proper respect for their heritage. These similarities and differences will become clearer as we now examine the interview data.

Most of the Azorean couples we interviewed had gone through a traditional upbringing and courtship. Young women were carefully watched and not allowed to walk unchaperoned in public places. Maria Cecília Ferreira, who was forty-three in 1977 and from a village in São Miguel, provides a good example of the way in which a traditional courtship progressed. She had known her husband, José, since childhood. By age fourteen, she knew she liked her husband, who was then twenty-one years old. Once they began courting (became *namorados*) the relationship was closely supervised. They would talk formally to each other on Sunday afternoons. The duration of the encounter was supposed to be for an hour, but it usually lasted most of the afternoon. She would come to the window in the front part of the house, and he would speak to her from the sidewalk. Occasionally, they would meet in public, especially during feasts, but that was frowned upon by the parents. At no time were they allowed to be alone. In the Azores, the young man must have the father's permission to court "at the window." Only after he has approached the father a second time and been granted permission to marry the daughter may the young man enter the home.

Courting may be interrupted by immigration or a couple may begin to court by mail, first exchanging pictures and then, after receiving permission from the father, exchanging letters for an extensive period. As Amélia Estrella, age thirty-one, described her situation:

> He was courting a girl in my town and when he went there, he saw me and that was it. You know, he courted me for nine months there and then he came here to America. He was here for two years and a half. My father consented to the wedding, and he returned there for the marriage. After we were married, I came back [to the United States] with him. . . . Before he came here, he talked to my father, and everything was set so that I could receive his letters. But before he left he had set the time [for the wedding]—two or two and a half years.[3]

For Portuguese men, the authority of the father in the courtship of a daughter is only one aspect of paternal authority. The core of the man's authority stems from his role as provider. His sacrifices and hard work are for the family, and he in turn demands their respect. The commitment to hard work was verbalized by José Ferreira: "I can do any kind of work here in America. Any kind of work, that doesn't matter . . . nothing. No, the Portuguese, the Azorean, he is used to heavy work; he knows what work means."

Manuel Lopes commented on his role as head of the household: "As long as they live under my wings I am the boss [i.e., the one who gives the orders is me]. No authority will boss my kids around because I am working. I am sacrificing my body to feed them, to clothe them, to get

---

3. Quotations from Portuguese husbands and wives in this chapter come from interviews conducted by Rebecca Matthews, Carlos Pato, John Sousa, and Filomena Silva as part of our NIMH project.

them shoes, and to provide a bed for them to sleep in. . . . I'm not going to be sacrificing myself and watch them at the age of fifteen or sixteen going out for two or three days without coming home. If they ever did that, they would never step back into this house."

The role of provider is also bound up with notions of hard work and the self-sufficiency of the family. Sergio Gomes, an older man, said that from the time he was married, he never received any family help. "I struggled all along" (*Eu é que lutei sempre*). Luís Costa said: "To tell you the truth, I like any kind of work, as long as I can do it, any kind of work. It's my thinking that what I want is to be busy working. It's true, that's our security, but to be honest, many people are not like that because I know. But me, I like to be working."

Women also utilize notions of hard work and self-sufficiency when discussing productive and reproductive labor, both before immigration and in the United States. Work is not equated with either wages or the male-provider role. Thus the reallocation of women's labor to wage work is consistent with the overarching commitment to self-sufficiency and hard work. Azorean and Continental women arrive in the United States expecting to work for wages, and husbands have neither blocked their employment nor felt it threatened their position as head of the household.

In discussing their relationship with their children, Azorean parents emphasize the importance of the "respect" they believe children should give to their parents. Sergio Gomes summarized the Azorean custom: "There we used to ask for our parents' blessing [kissing their hand] in the morning, very respectfully, everything. . . . We used to talk in a lower voice than our parents."

The Gomes family had spent sixteen years in Brazil. They thought that American culture emphasized entirely different relationships between children and parents than did Portuguese or Brazilian cultures. Sergio Gomes noted the following differences:

There [in Brazil] is much more respect for many things. That is, in Brazil, it is not already as respectful as in São Miguel, but in America, it is much worse; there is no comparison. Because in Brazil, my daughters at the age of my younger ones today never spoke in a raised voice to me. Today, no, or because I don't want them to watch TV or because I don't want them to play ball in the street . . . they say that I am different from other fathers. . . . My uncle told me, "You should have never come from Brazil. The person who comes to America to educate their kids only ends up with uneducated children."

Underlying parental notions about the socialization of children is a sense that there are important differences between males and females: that men are stronger and women need to be protected. Fathers were particularly explicit about these differences. As Sergio Gomes said, "The boy, as a man, has another kind of freedom. The woman not as much. The man knows how to defend himself, to take care of himself, and the woman, no." Luís Costa echoed these sentiments. "The man is always a man. He has more opportunities, so we let him go out more than a girl. A girl should be kept more at home, because the woman is always weaker than the man." Most fathers thus were careful to keep daughters close to home. As António Nunes said, "Age doesn't count. Until they get married, they are to stay at home." If they have a boyfriend, "they can talk at the window or the porch. But it must always be at home."

Amélia Estrella explained that it is important to teach both boys and girls to be well behaved and to be obedient to their parents. José Ferreira emphasized the importance of respect in his philosophy of child rearing. "We don't need to hit them; the child more or less follows the father's words, as long as they are polite words, words of obedience, words of respect, the child will follow also that road."

Colombian couples also thought there were important differences between boys and girls. They tended, however, to put this in terms of boisterousness and rebelliousness versus docility. They did not stress the need for greater freedom for boys and the importance of parental chaperoning or control for girls, as did the Portuguese.

Lidia Olivera, a Colombian mother of three boys, said that the "male is stronger and more coarse, while the female is more 'domestic.'" Her husband, Eduardo, also agreed that males and females have different ways of acting, and hence the parent should teach them different things. "To the boy, one should always be giving him the idea of doing something that is productive, so that he becomes accustomed to working, and to girls that they always be, more than anything else, careful of the house and that they help with the household chores."

Magdalena Valdéz said that "girls are more quiet than the boys, and the treatment for girls is much, much softer." Her husband believed that the most important thing a parent can teach his children is how to behave and to respect his or her elders and superiors. "There is nothing more beautiful," Magdalena's husband, Alberto, said, "than to see a child who knows how to behave with and be polite with adults."

These differences between boys and girls translate into different male and female adult behavior. Hector Pino said: "The man is going to be out on the streets more than the woman, the woman is easier to control than the man. The man . . . goes out and he meets a friend, and there he goes. . . . If one is not watching him, he'll go and make bad friendships, and so he can get really messed up. On the other hand, the girls can be controlled more easily and kept in the house."

These different tendencies create an association of men with power and the ability to "command" and women with duty and obedience. As Álvaro Rodríguez described the male role in Colombian society: "It's a right of feeling oneself to be a man, a male. Well, he thinks himself more powerful, right? From the time the [little boys] begin to understand things, it remains their role to be more powerful than the woman. One can speak to a man more comfortably, you know? And more confidently. . . . One must treat a woman more sweetly, more respectful, you know? On the other hand, one can treat a male more roughly, right?"

Yolanda Cardoso, who reported a great deal of equality and shared responsibility within her family, was sensitive to the way in which boys were socialized into the male values of Colombian culture. She said that "the boy is more rebellious than the girl, and a lot has to do with the way boys are brought up." Since they tell their sons not to cry, "they grow up very macho. Machismo is what we are teaching them when we say things like that to them."

Some women thought that it was important to accept the male role as head of the family and as the one who made important decisions. Amelia Escobár reported that if her husband had asked her to return to Colombia to put the children in school there, she would have gone. "If he had asked me to go, my duty was to obey. The husband is the one who commands the house," she explained.

Both Portuguese and Colombian couples see their families as very different from American ones. The Nuneses viewed the Portuguese family as a unit. They saw Americans as more permissive with their children and noted that husbands and wives engaged in different leisure-time activities. As António Nunes said: "Americans have a different life from ours. We are more the type to stay home. For example, . . . if I want to go out, I'll go with my wife. Americans, no.

[265]

The wife goes one place and the husband goes some place else. I don't buy that idea. Either we go out together or I stay home." His wife, Eugênia, had a similar analysis of American families: "A husband goes out with the wife of another; for example, they exchange couples. These are things which are different from the Portuguese couple. The Portuguese, we are brought up husband and wife. We, where one goes, the other goes. Now, here the woman, if she feels like it, she will go to the barroom. The wife goes on Thursday and the husband goes on Friday. I find that very different."

Colombians, since men often socialize outside the home in male groups without their spouses, did not emphasize the family as a unit. They did, however, point to the more "liberal" nature of the American family, focusing on both differences in authority patterns and sexual permissiveness. Otto Fernández said: "There is more freedom [in American families]. . . . Here the law supports the woman more, you know? So the woman wants to be going out, to give the orders. . . . The man then no longer gives the orders, but the woman, right? In Colombia, it's different. In Colombia, it's the man who gives the orders." One of the wives, Yolanda Cardoso, saw the contrast as follows: "The American family is more liberal, they are different. The wives are more liberated. . . . I agree that women should be more liberated, but as long as they are not unfaithful to their husbands. I agree with women's liberation in many ways, by all means. The American family is different than the Colombian family. To start with, they get married two or three times, right? The Colombian women have more difficulty with this because of the way we are brought up and because of our customs."

The Portuguese and Colombian couples all thought that it was important to transmit the familial values of respect and obedience to their children. They worried about the negative influence of American society in this regard. As Consuelo Sánchez summed up the situation from her perspective as a Colombian mother:

The difference [between being a mother in the United States and in Colombia] is that one has to be very alert with the upbringing of the children. In the long run they as children with Latin parents are learning the Latin customs at the same time they are going to American schools, and there they learn American culture. We have to be very aware so that they don't lose the Hispanic culture and that, at the same time, learn how to respect American culture while they are learning it. . . . American children even when they are very little they want to tell their parents what to do and feel that they are very authoritarian themselves. Instead we Latins even after being married, we still have to obey our parents. In my opinion there are a lot of differences in bringing up a family between the two countries.

Both Colombian and Portuguese couples conceive of relations between husbands and wives, parents and children, in similar ways. The husband is the head of the household and enjoys the respect of the wife and children. Respect and obedience to elders and particularly the husband-father are important values. Women are to be accorded respect as mothers and as wives, although this presumes that they defer to their husbands and act properly and modestly themselves. Portuguese men and women emphasize the importance of hard work and family self-sufficiency, a legacy of their rural heritage. Colombians emphasize what they see to be the inherent personality differences between the sexes (the male being more powerful, more agressive, and the female more domestic and docile), and the Portuguese emphasize the way in which norms and values have influenced behavior (men have more freedom, while women are in the home and need to be protected).

The ideology surrounding family relationships seems to have changed, however, to accommodate the wife's employment in a way that is compatible with the husband's authority and his provider role. For Portuguese families, this accommodation has been easier because of an emphasis on family self-sufficiency and the notion that women are as committed to hard work as men. Other notions concerning gender differences and the importance of respect and obedience have changed little, although parents often feel the American situation has a corrupting influence on their children. Family ideology provides a point of reference for comparisons with American family life and for interpretations of their own situation. Behavior, and particularly the allocation of productive and reproductive labor, has changed more than ideology. This is evident when we examine how Colombian and Portuguese families make the decision that the wife should seek employment outside the home.

The Wife's Employment as a Family Strategy

Among contemporary immigrant families, wives and mothers, not daughters, are wage laborers. As we have seen, this shift in the allocation of productive labor within the Central Falls working class has been supported and encouraged by both employers and couples themselves. We now turn to examining how this strategy of reallocating the wife's labor has affected conceptions of familial roles.

In the Colombian case, some wives arrived a few months after the husband's initial migration and others several years later. Soon after her arrival, the couple decided that it would be advantageous for the wife to work outside the home. These were not easy decisions. There was extensive opposition from some husbands to the wife's employment. According to Consuelo Sánchez, "My husband didn't like me going to work and leaving the children alone, but this poverty made us accept it." Her husband, Ricardo, also commented that he did not like the idea because it was not the custom in their own country. Only necessity obliged him to conform to the new situation. Otto Fernández, who was unemployed at the time of our interviews, also thought that his wife's working was a necessity. He expected that she would return to work after having her baby, but he hoped this would not be for long. "Well, it would be good that she return for . . . well for four or five months, and after that, no. Yes, because it will be harder then; there will be two children to watch."

Nilda Valencia also said that her husband opposed her working. When she realized that one salary wasn't enough to support her family, she thought, "I am going to work to help him out." Resisting the idea, he worked two jobs so that she could stay home and take care of their daughter.

Hector Pino was perhaps the most adamant that his wife not take a job. He said he was very upset because he was raised with the idea that married women do not work outside their homes. But when he thought about it, he decided that the financial obligations of raising a family would be too heavy to undertake alone. His wife, María, reported that she wanted the experience of working since her father had not allowed her to. Moreover, she wanted to send money to her sisters in Colombia and to save for future expenses. She opened a savings account and convinced her husband to let her deposit money monthly. "He says that it is better for him and the children if I am not working. He says that the more money we make, the more we will spend. If I quit I would like to baby-sit, then, because I won't be able to collect [unemployment benefits]. So I can have some money coming in. Whatever I make I can save. What I make is for me. I am saving some money, and when I have enough, I will buy a car or a house, we are not sure yet."

Eduardo Olivera had perhaps the clearest perception of the tie between a Colombian husband's position as head of the household and his desire not to have his wife working: "Over there, one isn't accustomed. . . . In our country the wife is not accustomed to working, because it's a dishonor. The guy who gets married and his wife still keeps on working, it's like a dishonor [*deshonra*] that the wife has to keep on working . . . as many people would probably say, to keep on supporting part of the household obligations." The notion of husband as provider is bound up with conceptions of manly honor—an ideology that ratifies the assignment of the husband to productive work and the wife to reproductive labor in the home.

In other Colombian families, the decision for the wife to work for wages was a joint one. Economic reasons were the primary motive, but immigrants also realize that ways of doing things in America were different. They soon met a number of Colombian working wives who could convince the new immigrant wife of the advantages of wage work. Reproductive tasks like cooking, shopping, and laundry are not nearly as time consuming and laborious in the United States as in Colombia, potentially freeing women for wage labor. Employment could compensate for a woman's isolation from a network of kin, neighbors, and friends. In Colombia such women would have been available to a wife who focused her energies on reproductive activities. In New England, with dispersed households, few nearby relatives, and other Colombian women already in the labor force, the housebound wife was essentially isolated.

Gabriel Escobár described his wife's situation: "I tell you that, here in the house, a person alone in the house all day long . . . from the beginning of the day to the end, he'll go crazy. There are four walls—from here to here, over to there, and from there to here. On the other hand, when working one sees different people, talks to them. And her, for example, I agree that she should go out more, because she has that diploma and is a secretary." Amelia agreed but emphasized finances: "When I came here, my husband said, 'Here the husband's salary is not enough.' 'Well,' I said, 'If everybody works here, I'll work too.'" Amelia, unlike most other Colombian wives, had been employed before marriage as a secretary in a large firm.

Colombian couples see the advantages of a strategy of having more than one wage earner in the family. Since employers recruit married as well as single women, such a step makes sense, even if it means rearranging cultural conceptions of the husband's provider role. Husbands may continue to cherish the hope that their wives will not have to work, but they adjust ideology to fit their new situation. Wives were concerned about their husband's low earnings and were "willing to help out" or adapt to "customs" here. The isolation of reproductive work in the new environment was often another incentive for the employment strategy.

Among Portuguese men there was much less resistance to the wives' employment than among Colombian men. As many interviews revealed, the dual-worker strategy was identified as an obvious necessity. José Ferreira said, "From the Azorean end, they always depend on work. They [Azoreans] continue working . . . want the work and want the money. Without the work, the money doesn't come." Some women, like Maria Cecília Ferreira, had worked on their own land, keeping gardens, raising chickens, or even doing heavy agricultural work. She commented that she had "always thought of working" (i.e., considered herself as someone who worked), suggesting that values of hard work could be readily transferable from an agricultural to industrial context.

Like their Colombian counterparts, Portuguese women emphasized the financial reasons for employment. Maria Cecília commented, "With only one paycheck it isn't enough." Her husband, José Ferreira, concurred: "We have to have the money, [so it is necessary] for all of us to work, isn't that so?" Emelinda Dias echoed these sentiments: "We only had one salary and with one salary we couldn't live well. We never had large paychecks, only small ones. It was necessary to live very modestly with the salary he got. So we never had sweets or such things." She used the idiomatic expression that when she worked, "Things keep running" (*Às coissas irem*). "Because I am working, things are much more together in our life and so I keep on working. When we are both working, we can pay for the things that we owe, but if we aren't working, we can't pay for the things that we owe."

Using similar language, Fátima Almeida commented that when both husband and wife are working, "Things go well" (*Às coissas correm bem*). As Alicia Pacheco put it, "It is that here in America, both have to work. If they don't work, we cannot lift our heads, isn't that so?"

Some couples were particularly articulate about the higher cost of living and the debts that began the moment one arrived in the United States. Ida Costa said: "What I find, . . . how can I say it? One knows that in the beginning we find big problems. We arrive, from the beginning we have to start buying our things and a house with [many] people with only two checks, it is a little hard. There I didn't work; here I have to work. I have to come home and take care of my life. One knows that my daughters help me a bit, but I still have to orient things, and sometimes I don't feel like it."

Like the Colombians, Portuguese husbands and wives have experienced repeated layoffs and unforeseen major expenditures. Health problems, industrial accidents, and even an apartment fire made wives' wages critical to family survival. Wives saw themselves as important wage earners during these periods. The Dias and Pacheco families provide good examples of how the husband's work status and the wife's labor-force participation interact.

When Eduardo Dias first arrived in Rhode Island in 1966, he went to work in a textile firm. "I got sick, I got very sick. Of course, when I arrived in this country I didn't get along with the climate. I swelled— swollen all over. I got that big sickness and I didn't work for a month. Then when I went back, they didn't want me, and they told me to stay home and then, if they needed me, they would call me again." Emelinda Dias found employment with the same firm and continued working while he was incapacitated with the skin disease. Eduardo found a job at another textile firm where he worked for six years. During this period the couple had two more children, and Emelinda was employed for several short intervals. Eduardo was laid off in 1974 and later went to work washing dishes in a restaurant. He quit for a better paying job in a jewelry factory but suffered a severe burn when molten glass splashed over his arm and part of his body. Unable to work for a whole year, the family survived on unemployment and the three thousand dollars that he eventually won from the company. He returned to the webbing firm where he had worked for six months. In the meantime, his wife took a job on the second shift, which lasted four months. He was again laid off and finally found a night job as a janitor in a large discount store. At the same time, his wife secured a much more stable job on the first shift as an inspector at the webbing company.

The Pacheco family also had to deal with health problems. Tomás Pacheco first worked for a tool and fastener plant when he immigrated to New England in 1968. His wife, Alicia, worked a few weeks at a rubber toy manufacturing firm, two years at a webbing firm, and two years at a jewelry-casting company on the second shift. She quit the second job to have a baby and began a third job when the child was a year old. The major crisis in the couple's life was Tomás's heart attack in 1972, which totally disabled him. Alicia then stayed out of work for several years to take care of him. "Alicia was home to take care of me, because I couldn't. Alicia had to stay home, which means, she lost her job because of me. So I was counting on getting some relief from welfare. The rents [from the apartments upstairs] were to pay the house mortgage, as they still do, since the house is not yet paid. So I got some help; they used to give me $286; from that I had to take money for the food and the rest of the expenses." It took Tomás several years to get social security disability payments. After three years Alicia was able to return to work; however, she had to leave employment again to take care of her husband following a stomach operation. She returned to work at the same jewelry firm where she was employed off and on for three years. Just before our interview, during a layoff, she found a job with a larger jewelry firm, with the help of the Rhode Island Department of Employment Security.

These two cases show how women's productive labor is shaped by the husband's employment. Men's work histories are filled with job changes. Many of them are the result of the layoffs prevalent in the declining economy in which small textile firms are often on the brink of closing and in which jewelry and apparel production is seasonal. Men also are forced out of jobs for health-related reasons or may quit to take a better paying job. Women suffer job loss through layoffs as well, but their reproductive work at home may also compel them to leave jobs. Thus Alicia Pacheco left wage jobs when she had to care for her disabled husband or when she had a baby. Likewise, Amélia Estrella anticipated finding a job on another shift, once her husband was reemployed, so she could take care of the children. In the era of working daughters female employment added to the family income but did not change the organization of household reproductive labor. In the present era of working wives, there is a "fine tuning" of a family's allocation of productive and reproductive labor.

The cultural construction placed on a wife's employment echoes the realities of male wage and employment patterns. Both husbands and wives talk about the financial necessity of women's wage work and emphasize that one male paycheck is not enough. The fact of female employment brings about an adjustment in the conception of how reproductive labor is allocated in the family. Colombian men were more resistant to changing their notions of male and female employment than either Colombian women or Portuguese husbands and wives. Several connected a man's inability to be the sole provider with dishonor, but others, like many Portuguese men, had begun to stress "necessity." Both men and women, especially the Portuguese, emphasized the importance of hard work for family members regardless of gender and age. Many saw the "environment" as different in the United States, rationalizing the wife's employment when there were many other working wives, including some from their own ethnic background.

The jobs that Colombian and Portuguese women held were financially necessary but often entailed long hours and difficult working conditions. As we shall see, the work women did outside the home altered their reproductive labor inside the home. Thus a description of their paid jobs is important for understanding the entire context in which women experienced productive and reproductive labor.

The Realities of Productive Work

Like their husbands, Colombian wives were concentrated in jobs in the textile industry. Ten of the fifteen women we interviewed were employed in spinning, thread, braid, or weaving mills as spinners, winders, twisters, braidertenders, warpers, or quality-control inspectors. Four wives worked in toy, jewelry, or jewelry-box factories, and one filed order forms for a stationery company. Wages for these women were low. Those who worked for the jewelry-box company made $2.30 an hour, and those in textiles made around $3.00 an hour. The average hourly wage for the fifteen women was $2.89 an hour. The highest paid workers were the quality-control inspectors who received $3.45 an hour and the stationery-company employee whose white-collar job paid $3.85 an hour.

The Portuguese women were less concentrated in the textile industry. Five of the fifteen Portuguese women tended braiding or skein-winding machines and inspected products in small textile firms. Six women worked in jewelry or jewelry-packaging plants, two were employed by a company that packaged liquids in aerosol cans, one worked for a metal-stamping plant, and one was employed in a candy factory. Portuguese women were making between $2.07 and $3.75 an hour in 1977, with an average of $2.70 an hour, or only $0.40 above the minimum wage.

Even though Colombian women thought the main advantage of their jobs was the pay, they knew full well that their wages were low. Francisca Balboa, who worked for $2.30 an hour at the jewelry-box company, said:

> They pay so little to start; they pay $2.20. They always say they are going to increase the wages, but they never do. They raised the salaries of the mechanics and the bosses, but not us. . . . Sometimes I get discouraged with the salary, but it is not worth it to change for five or ten cents. So I would rather stay where I am and keep trying to get a full-time job back [in the same plant]. This job is easy and I do it sitting down. It is not as other factories where the job is hard, for instance the toy factory.

Francisca and the Portuguese women who worked for other jewelry firms thought their jobs were relatively easy. Women who worked in textile plants experienced a different situation. Their attitudes toward work were formed in the concrete conditions of small, antiquated, spinning and weaving mills where one worked forty to forty-eight hours a week tending machines. As a machine tender, a woman spent all day on her feet much of the time bent over to piece ends or change bobbins. Rooms could be hot and humid, depending on the kind of fiber being processed. There was also the danger of catching a hair or a hand in the machine.

Aida Rodríguez, who filled bobbin batteries for looms, said:

> What I don't like about the job is that I have to walk. My job is to walk all day long. I have to tend fifty-three looms. What I like about the job is that I have been able to make many friends. I don't speak English that well, but there I have been able to talk with Americans, even if I have to speak broken English. But they understand me and I understand them. I get along with everybody, with the bosses and all. I haven't had any problems. The advantage I have there is that I can go to Colombia any time I want. They will give me permission. And I will be able to come back. The disadvantage is a lot of work and no money.

María Pino, who worked as a winder in a spinning mill, reported difficulties changing the spools on her machine, dropping one on the floor and getting the threads all tangled. She found the work very tiring. "There is nothing good about working. I don't like to kneel down, when I have to change the bobbins. That's very tiresome," she

Women working in a modern spinning mill, Central Falls. Courtesy of Stephen Cabral.

said. Flor Lucero, a twister in the same spinning mill, had a similar reaction to her job:

> In that factory one works like a mule. To start with they don't even pay holidays. That's why my husband doesn't want me to go back to work there. [She was on sick leave the week of her interview.] Every day

"What I don't like about the job is that I have to walk all day." Women in the 1980s, as in the early twentieth century, are on their feet all day as they tend spinning machines. Courtesy of Stephen Cabral.

when I leave work I am so dirty that not even the flies get near me. I look just like a mechanic. They pay three dollars per hour regardless of the shift you work. One is not even allowed to sit down to eat for twenty minutes without being scolded. One cannot stop the machine for a minute because they said one is not going to give good production.

With the exception of Margarita García, who worked for the stationery firm, the Colombian women all complained about low wages or poor working conditions. As Amelia Escobár, who worked at a toy factory, summed up her situation, "I work only because of the money. Do you know what it is to have to work eight hours there? There is nothing that I like about my job. Nobody likes to work. Work was made for a donkey to do."

The Portuguese women who worked in textile firms also complained of working on their feet all day. As Maria Luísa Mello said, "I like to work there because I am used to it, but it is hard to work there, you walk all day. I like it, but we are better [off] at home. . . . I get home tired, when you have to prepare the food, the clothes, taking lunch. Life in America is like this. We have a little something, but you have to work."

Working in jewelry firms is seen as much easier, especially in the view of two of the Azorean Portuguese wives who had worked on the land before they immigrated. Most who worked in jewelry firms polished jewelry after casting, strung jewelry on racks, did linking or gluing, or prepared pieces for plating. Ida Costa described how she cleaned jewelry. "It comes 'bruto' (unfinished). The earrings . . . and we clean it so that after it goes to the machines to polish, we are cleaning. It is earrings, bracelets, those necklaces—all kinds—that have to pass through our hands. We use a file, a knife . . . and pliers." Maria Cecília Ferreira, newly arrived in New England, said, "I prefer it here . . . because here it is lighter work. There, we work with a hoe in hand, with so much sun. . . . Here I don't dislike it. I never had another job."

Not all Portuguese women had good experiences working in small jewelry firms. Viola Gomes left her job because a boss blamed her for the poor work actually done by another gluer. However, none of the Portuguese husbands or wives working in jewelry companies commented on any of the health and safety hazards that are prevalent in the industry, such as working with dangerous chemicals, inhaling fumes, or exposure to asbestos.

Conditions experienced by the two women who worked in the aerosol-spray-packing firm entailed more obvious hazards. Both reported that the factory had "exploded," that there had been a fire in the plant and four people had died. Josefina Santos operated a machine that put valves on the cans. She sat on a line all day. "Sometimes if I want, I can move around. They don't want us to sit, but now the temperature is . . . like yesterday it was ninety degrees. Let me tell you something. This factory exploded a year ago in January. They made repairs, but for us it became worse. . . . It isn't the work, but the temperature inside the factory. . . . They say that they are going to fix it. . . . That's bad for us, that humidity."

Maria Lídia Mendes, who worked on second shift in the same company, talked about the discrimination against Portuguese workers.

> In the factory, also, we feel inferior. Or they make us feel inferior. I have a feeling that they make fun of us. Because of the way we pronounce the words. . . . It's always a Portuguese who goes to work there (by the hot furnaces). They are the ones that always have to sacrifice. We don't know how to defend ourselves. If one of them feels that we are not doing what we should, whether we are or not . . . they think that they are right. . . . They think we are bad people or something. And we are getting angry. For example, if one of the machines stops for some reason, if you are American, you can stay sitting until it starts. But if you are Portuguese, they'll tell you to grab a broom. And I say why are we always sacrificed? Because the Americans earn as much or more than we do. And we are all children of God. They are flesh and blood like we are. But the Portuguese are always the ones sacrificed. I don't like it.

Portuguese and Colombian women in textile jobs faced difficult conditions and low pay, while those working in jewelry factories complained little and saw their jobs as relatively easy even though not well paid. Their employment was seen as vital to the maintenance of the household and necessary in the American situation. Once the wife was working new considerations appeared in the daily management of the household, particularly in terms of child care and the organization of household tasks. The reallocation of reproductive labor by working immigrant women is perhaps the most significant consequence of their full-time productive labor outside the home.

The Working Mother and the Reallocation of Child Care

As Portuguese and Colombian women began to take wage jobs in Central Falls in the late 1960s and early 1970s, the gender division of reproductive tasks in the home also began to change. The set of activities that altered the most was child care, particularly among families with children under school age.

[278]

Most husbands and wives reallocated the reproductive labor of child care by working different shifts and sharing it. Husbands took on new levels of responsibility for child care. In some respects this is an outcome of the wage structure of the jobs husbands and wives hold. The low combined income of a working couple prevents them from using day-care centers. A day-care fee of $35 a week in 1977 would have come from a woman's take-home pay of between $80 and $105 a week. Even for the Colombian couples who had hired baby-sitters, the fee of $15 to $25 a week was a substantial amount. The Portuguese and Colombian women said that they would be ready to use a close relative for day care, but many Colombian families had few such relatives in the United States, and in Portuguese families sisters and sisters-in-law were also employed outside the home. The strategy of coping with child care by working on different shifts was, therefore, the most feasible arrangement.

The strategy is also shaped by the character of the local economy in which many firms operate on two or three shifts. The textile industry and insulated wire plants all involve heavy machinery, which is more profitably operated around the clock. Textile firms began operating two and three shifts during the 1920s and 1930s when the maximum work week was reduced from fifty-six to forty-eight hours a week, making it possible to run more than one shift. The forty-hour week mandated during the 1930s made a three-shift system possible, even though many plants were not able to operate on a twenty-four-hour-a-day basis until after the Depression. During World War II and in the postwar period, a move to three shifts became advantageous. In the Central Falls jewelry industry, a second shift was often added during the busy seasons in the 1960s and 1970s, especially for small detail work assigned to women.

A couple's stage in a family developmental cycle and the age of their children also affected the two-shift strategy. Most couples worked on different shifts unless there were older children to mind the youngest after school. For those with young children, fathers arriving home at 7 A.M. after the third shift often woke their children and prepared them for school. Some fathers also looked after a young child during the day, catching naps whenever possible. (Appendix D shows the child-care arrangements made by eleven Azorean and four continental Portuguese families in 1977.)

Filomena Paiva had the following explanation for working alternate shifts as a strategy for coping with child-care responsibilities. "Unconnected shifts. My husband was working in the morning and I was working second shift. It had to be that way. It was a necessity. I would have liked to work together [at the same time] but at that time, to pay a baby-sitter, when we were both earning so little, it wasn't possible. So we tried to solve the problem. One on one shift and one on another."

Working on different shifts was especially difficult if one spouse worked on the night shift and had to look after the children during the day while trying to get some sleep. Husbands seemed less tolerant of this situation. Eduardo Dias preferred to have his wife care for the children or to pay for a child-care center. "I think [a center is] better, because the mother isn't here and of course I'm a man. It makes a difference in the home life, having to take care of the children." He described the problems of trying to sleep after working an all-night shift and watching three children, ages nine, seven, and six.

> I would like to get another job, because, you see, this shift is very bad for me. She goes to work in the morning, and I go from 11 P.M. to 7 in the morning. Then I have to be back home to get the kids ready for school. I send them to school, but of course, I lie down. But at 11 o'clock I have to get up again to take [the six year old] to school, so I go with him. At 2, I have to go get him. Sleeping like this has caused my head to feel very strange and about two or three days ago, I felt something. . . . I had dizzy spells. . . . Maybe I'll sleep, but I'm always thinking about them because they are still young.

Nine of the fourteen Colombian families also used the strategy of working alternate shifts to accommodate child care within the nuclear family (see appendix D). The same combinations found among Portuguese families were apparent. Like Eugênia Nunes, a Portuguese mother, Consuelo Sánchez, a Colombian, worked the third shift while her husband was employed on the first shift. In three other Colombian families, as in four Portuguese households, the father worked the third shift, and the wife was employed on the first shift. In four more families, one parent worked the first shift and the other the second shift. Compared to the Portuguese families, Colombian couples were at an earlier stage in their family cycle. They were more likely to have infants or toddlers, while in many Portuguese families the youngest child was already six or seven years old. Fewer Colombian families could rely on older schildren as supplementary baby-sitters.

In talking with parents about these arrangements several issues emerged: (1) the preferability of parental care, especially the mother's, over care by a nonrelative; (2) the negative experience with baby-sitters (usually Colombians) and the negative appraisal of child-care centers; (3) the difficulties of finding child care to cover the hours in which parental shifts overlapped.

In the Sánchez family, in which Ricardo worked the first shift and Consuelo worked the third, Ricardo clearly preferred that his wife care for their three children (ages ten, six, and five): "I feel that the children should have their mother's care more than anything else, and I don't agree that . . . their mother be at work, or in the street, always leaving their children alone. . . . I am not a believer in that. I would like it if she were at their side, so that . . . they be . . . as correct in their manners as possible." Consuelo took care of the children during the day, and her husband took care of them during the afternoon until she left for work on the third shift. When the children were young, he was working the first shift and she was employed on the second shift. When he began to work overtime, there was no one at home between 3 and 6 P.M. Consuelo described the difficulties: "I tried different people to take care of them and I paid twenty dollars or so [a week for them] to be baby-sitters from 3 in the afternoon to 6 o'clock. They wouldn't take good care of them or wouldn't give them food. They cut themselves [while playing] or something wrong was always happening. So I was having so many problems taking care of them and working that I decided to send them to my mother." The children stayed with their grandmother in Colombia for almost three years, returning in early 1977 when the youngest was five years old.

Of the remaining six families, four had a female relative or Colombian friend to care for the children, and two had older children who were able to care for the youngest after school or in the evening while the parents were at work. The Rodríguez family used Aida's sister Carmen as a baby-sitter, which was very convenient since she lived downstairs. The Escobár family had also used Carmen as a baby-sitter several years before, when they had lived in the same tenement.

Among couples using baby-sitters, comments by most husbands and wives indicated that a relative or woman of the same ethnic background was the most suitable substitute for a mother's care. Others felt that a husband's care was better than trusting a stranger or someone who did not share one's own attitudes about child rearing. Thus some families were not satisfied with baby-sitters who were not relatives. María Pino said of a Colombian woman friend who cared for their children while the parents worked second shift: "[My friend] is a very nice person and she takes good care of them. However, when I am home, by 9 P.M. they are bathed and in bed. Sometimes we get home at 11 and they are still up. I don't think that's right. The next day they have to get up very early and they are very small to go to bed so late. It's a problem. One is locked up in a factory and doesn't know what they are doing." Most said they would not use a day-care center, although this decision may have been based on familiarity with Colombian day-care centers, which are used only by the very poor and reputed to be inadequate. Experience with United States day-care centers often changes these attitudes.[4] Nilda Valencia, for example, believed that a day-care center would be a good choice because of the experience of a friend: "She pays fifteen dollars and my friend told me they are very nice. If I have to decide between a day-care center and a Colombian lady to take care of my child, I would choose a day-care center. Because the Colombian woman might have other children of her own to take care of, and she would neglect mine. At least that's my opinion. Instead, in a day-care center, they would have to take care of them all the same way."

Some Portuguese couples also believed that child care should be provided primarily by the mother. Tomás Pacheco, for example, was disabled and did a great deal of the child care while his wife worked but still thought that the situation was not the best: "A working mother can never properly care for the children as she does if she were home, unless she herself had her mother living there. With the mother out working, the child can never receive the care as if she were there. The child can get it from the father, but [care] from the father never replaces the mother's care." As Louísa Carvalho said, "There's always something missing when a mother isn't at home."

Portuguese parents had attitudes similar to the Colombians about the use of baby-sitters and day-care centers. Few had any real knowledge of child-care centers in the United States. Some based their comments on the few child-care centers (*creches*) in the Azores, which are often thought to be only for the poor and as providing only custodial care. Manuel Lopes was one of the few parents who had used a day-care center, but when the staff neglected to change his daughter

---

4. Unfortunately, in 1977 no day-care centers in Central Falls or Pawtucket were bilingual or bicultural or made any effort to provide a milieu compatible with Portuguese or Colombian family life.

when she accidently wet her pants, he took her out of the center, caring for her during the day after he returned home from working on the third shift. On the other hand, when Virginia Machado moved to Pawtucket, she looked for a day-care center because she and her husband were working the same shift and they had two small children. She finally found one, but they charged thirty-five dollars a week, a fee she could not afford. "If there was a cheaper day-care facility, it would be good especially for the immigrant when he arrives here. Since I've been here in the United States, I've noticed that there's a real need."

In general, the reallocation of labor surrounding child care through shift work must be seen as part of a couple's juggling two wage jobs and dealing with layoffs and health problems or beginning a new job. At one point a couple may opt for one form of child care by working on different shifts. At another time hiring a baby-sitter or asking a mother or sister may seem like the best strategy (if both have relatively high-paying jobs or if a relative is available). In some instances the husband insisted that the wife change her job to be at home during the day, and at other times the husband stepped in to care for a child. In still other cases, when the husband was laid off, the wife found employment and the husband took care of the children. Men have thus changed their behavior. They have become more involved in child-care tasks.

Changes in the Allocation of Household Tasks

Fewer changes have taken place in the reallocation of reproductive labor concerned with the daily maintenance tasks that we label "housework." In both Portuguese and Colombian families the traditional division of labor is still followed as it was before immigration. Wives were responsible for cooking and cleaning while the husband took care of household repairs and the car. In some cases, the husband also held the major responsibility for the finances, but here as in some other household chores the wife's employment had brought changes. Some of the reallocation of housework involved the labor of children, primarily daughters, a strategy that might have been used in the preimmigration situation in which the wife was not working for wages. In many families, the husband did some housework, but the extent varied considerably. Portuguese and Colombian men engaged in more household activities than they had before immigration, partially because the structure of these chores is different in the United States. Few Azorean and Colombian women drive cars, so the couple often shopped jointly for food and clothing. The husband also took the washing to the laundromat. Some Portuguese husbands made beds and participated in housecleaning, and a few Colombian men did vacuuming and even cooking.

Some examples illustrate this variation among Portuguese couples. Eugênia Nunes reported that on Saturday mornings, after she came home from night shift, she went to bed and slept until 10 A.M. When she got up, António would have the house cleaned. Tomás Pacheco, who is disabled, had taken over many of the household chores during the daytime, although he still felt uncomfortable in this role:

> In here, it has been slightly different because she had to work and she couldn't look after the children. . . . I'll tell you frankly, I used to change diapers for my children. . . . But I'm not ashamed to say that I changed diapers, and what's more, I also washed them and ironed them before putting them on my kids. . . . It's the life of an immigrant. And I'm not ashamed of it. . . . Just today . . . she made her bed . . . our bed. But most of the time, I'm the one who does it. I clear the table, set it, you know, put the things she wants on it, all straight, or I put things away. I can't do as good a job a she does; I can't do it because let's face it, a woman is a woman and a man is a man. But at least she arrives home and doesn't see . . . a shoe over here . . . a towel over there. No, nothing is out of place. I help her in what I can. That's life, all that is part of life.

A third husband wanted to decrease his participation and return to the more traditional division of labor. He had been taking care of his children while his wife worked the second shift. He said he was *saturado* ("He'd had it"), and he encouraged his wife to change to the first shift, using a neighbor as a baby-sitter.

In many Azorean families, the husband was clearly still in charge of the finances. The older children usually followed Azorean custom of giving their paychecks to their father. In the American context the son or daughter might pay the bills, because they spoke English; yet the father remained in charge. José Ferreira described how financial arrangements operate in his family with an employed wife and sixteen-year-old son: "No, I am the one who is in charge of the money. We all do it together. I come home, I tell them what's what, you see, but they do the same to me. For example, if the son goes shopping with his brothers, he must tell me what was spent." Manuel Lopes used a similar system. "He [his seventeen-year-old son] comes home first, puts the check on the table or over there. . . . He puts it down first; then later he cashes it. Yes, he cashes it; I give him my check; he cashes it. The bills—I give him the money; then he leaves, pays everything, brings back the change and there is never any problem."

In other families decision making on financial issues was a joint effort. Manuel Carvalho handled the finances, according to his wife, but they cashed their checks together and then decided how to spend the money. In the Nunes family (a younger couple), Eugênia, reported that António took care of the money. Nevertheless, they put their paychecks together to pay all bills and what was left over was theirs to spend jointly. António said: "Until this day, I never decided anything without talking it over with her together. And I enjoy it this way, because we can't blame the other. If it's good, it's for both of us and if it's bad, the same."

There was also wide variation among Colombian husbands in undertaking household tasks that would have normally been labeled "women's work." For example, Aida Rodríguez had the following cryptic remarks about her husband's participation, "Nobody takes him away from the TV. . . . He doesn't help around the house for anything. . . . And I have to fight with him so that he will wash a plate. No, that one is very lazy."

Amelia Escobár faced much the same situation:

> When I come back from work, I cook and do some washing [by hand] and clean the house. On Fridays we all go to the laundry. The little girl helps me a little in the kitchen. I make her do it so she will learn. He doesn't help at all. In the laundry, he brings the bag and that's all. . . . Every Saturday I do the same thing . . . clean the house, cook, do some washing. Last Saturday, we went to a dance. In general, I stay home all the time, by myself. He goes out by himself. He either goes to the track or goes out drinking.

Others, like Isilda Fernández, had received more help from their husbands since they began working outside the home: "Many things have changed since I started to work. He picks the baby up. However, I am the one who does most of the kitchen and household chores. I continue being in charge of the kitchen. The majority of the household chores are my duty. My husband helps me a little and my little sister [who had just arrived in the United States and was temporarily living with the family] helps me once in a while." It is apparent that the husband's initial involvement in reproductive labor may come in the area of child care, while the wife continues to do much of the work involved in transforming purchased commodities into meals or maintenance work such as cleaning and laundry.

As in the Portuguese families, older children in a number of Colombian families had an important role in chores. In the Pino family with three children—two daughters of thirteen and twelve and a son of nine—each week, one girl did the kitchen and the other cleaned and made the beds. The boy vacuumed the floor. The husband had been involved in some of the housework, but his involvement was being replaced by the daughters as they were trained in female work.

In perhaps the most egalitarian example, Flor Lucero was responsible for the household chores, but with considerable help from her husband, Guillermo. At the time of our second interview, she was on pregnancy leave from her paid job and was doing a larger share of the "female" chores, while Guillermo took charge of the money, paid bills, and handled the taxes. In this family, however, the husband did some of the cooking and had helped with the baby. Guillermo also took the children to the dentist or doctor and bought school items for them. The couple shared the discipline of the children and the buying of their clothes. Guillermo commented on their Saturday routine: "The whole day is chores around here. One thing, the other . . . the kitchen over here, fixing clothes, or cleaning around here . . . there is no end to the work. If one sits down, it's because one has to rest, but here there is work all the time. . . . All the time there is something to do."

Almost all of the husbands and wives, Colombian and Portuguese, commented on the double burden that wives face combining productive and reproductive labor at home and in the factory. Most women complained of being tired from holding down two jobs and of the difficulties of leaving children with their husbands, a relative, or a baby-sitter. Filomena Paiva had the most specific analysis of women's "double day":

> In Portugal, I wasn't thinking of this so much because I wasn't working, you know. Things went along, that is, I had the day and it was my own, you know. I think that an operator's job: practically, there are two shifts that you have to do. Because you have to work a shift in the factory and after you have to do the other one. That is, I noticed that I am more tired with more work, you know. I'm not just fatigued by the factory but by the home life as well. It's this that makes the difference.

[286]

Nilda Valencia, a Colombian mother, expressed some of the same sentiments: "Do you know what it is to live eight hours at work, all locked up, and then to come home to be locked up again? When I come home, I still have to cook, fix the house, fix clothing for all to wear the next day. And if I go out for a ride, when I come home I still have all those chores to do, so what time do I go to bed then?"

The fact of the wife's employment and the common pattern of handling child care through working on different shifts has meant, however, that some reproductive labor has been reallocated. Women have also gained more autonomy, or joint responsibility, in financial matters. There is a great deal of variation among the families we interviewed; yet we may conclude that women have a greater say in decisions and men are doing more of the "female" reproductive tasks than in the preimmigration situation. In some families, wives seem to be pressing for more participation, while in others, the necessity of the wife's work on the second shift or the husband's disability has put the man in a position where he has had to do more housework and child care. In sum, the era of the working mother has brought about a reallocation of reproductive labor that did not occur earlier in the century when the majority of working women were daughters.

Conclusions

In examining changing strategies used by Colombian and Portuguese families in allocating productive and reproductive labor, I have emphasized the causal role of the economy. Local firms actively recruited immigrant labor or welcomed new immigrants already in New England and seeking work. Given the gender typing of jobs, there was a need for female as well as male labor. Male wages were insufficient to support an immigrant family. This situation pushed wives and mothers to seek wage employment, with important consequences for the allocation of reproductive labor within the household. Husbands began to participate more in child care and "female" household chores because many couples reconciled child-care needs with the wife's employment by working two different shifts.

An important comparison may be drawn between contemporary wage-earning immigrant mothers and the employed daughters of immigrant families in the years 1900 to 1930. In the earlier period, female labor-force participation hovered around 20 percent, but most women workers were single and young. In 1915 immigrant families sent teenage sons and daughters into the mills and machine shops while wives took in boarders, cared for relatives who were wage workers, and in a few instances took in factory homework. These strategies preserved and intensified a wife's reproductive labor instead of reallocating it among other household members.

The present era thus signals significant changes in the behavior of men and women in terms of work done in the home. The relationship of this new behavior to cultural conceptions is complex. Despite resistance (as exemplified by Colombian husbands) women and men have come to see women's employment as necessary and even appropriate. There seems to have been an easier adjustment for rural Portuguese families in which values of hard work and family self-sufficiency apply to wives as well as husbands and can be transferred to industrial contexts. Other conceptions are still maintained, such as the importance of the husband as head of the household, the emphasis on children's respect for parents, and the stress on gender differences. But even here, I would argue, the position of couples within the local economy is creating changes in behavior. Although cultural conceptions of family roles are altering, change takes place only gradually in some areas. Men seem more resistant to modifying their ideas about male authority than do women, but within each population there is a wide range of variation, both in behavior and ideology. The nature of change is tentative, but clearly, women's employment has gone further in transforming relationships in these immigrant families than it did in earlier generations. Daughters in present-day families, growing up in an era when female labor-force participation is increasing and the working mother is commonplace, may go even further in redefining their family roles as they enter the labor force for an extended period of their lives.

[7]

Women's Strategies on the Job: Informal Resistance in an Apparel Plant

Transformations in the Central Falls economy led to the incorporation of new immigrant workers, including working wives and mothers, in the late 1960s and 1970s. For families, the strategies of immigration and a wife's employment involved the reallocation of productive and reproductive labor within the household. Within the productive system itself, however, there have been fewer changes in women's situation. As large, family-owned textile mills have been replaced by some larger plants (often bought out by conglomerates) and by small family-run firms in a variety of light industries, women are still employed primarily in semiskilled, low-paid jobs.

In examining women's relation to their wage work between 1900 and 1940, I focused on strikes as the major strategy of resistance. This formal, more public form of resistance is easier to document through published sources than are more informal means of resistance. Even oral histories were poor sources of information on resistance, although they provided information about the actual jobs women did, their place in the production process, and how productive labor fit with family life and reproductive work.

The strikes of the 1920s and 1930s in Central Falls were responses on the part of male and female workers to management strategies for dealing with the decline of the textile industry. They were militant attempts to reverse wage cuts, oppose the stretch-out and speedup, and protest against the government's inability to improve working conditions under the National Recovery Administration (NRA). This public form of militance was no doubt underpinned by more informal strategies women used on the job, both to create ties with one another and to resist management. However, these informal strategies are more difficult to document historically than they are in the contemporary period.

Women's resistance grows out of the concrete conditions of women's productive work. Others (Tentler 1979) have argued that women's commitment to marriage and family leads them to see themselves as temporary workers and hence to remain complacent about their work conditions. I suggest that the presence or absence of resistance has more to do with the particular conditions on the shop floor and with management's strategies for controlling labor than with women's family ties. Attitudes and values that come out of women's family or ethnic background often change as women are socialized by more experienced workers and they learn the tricks of resistance practiced by other women. Recent immigrant working mothers, like the immigrant working daughters of the past, are divided from one another and from other workers by cultural and language differences. These women need to be brought into the local work culture; ties between women must be forged across ethnic boundaries. Thus women workers' strategies not only need to resist management tactics but they must also bring new workers, including immigrant women, into a women's work culture.

This chapter focuses on the informal strategies of women workers, including Portuguese immigrant women, in a Central Falls apparel plant in 1977. I took a job as a "trainee sewer," and during a five-month period (interrupted by a work stint in the plant's warehouse and a two-month layoff), I was trained to set sleeves on little girls' dresses and toddlers' T-shirts. The plant where I worked, like virtually all garment plants in the country, paid on the piece-rate system.

On the shop floor there is a subtle conflict between management's attempt to control women's work and women's attempts to preserve their own autonomy and maximize their own interests. I discovered workers' strategies for dealing with management policy by watching other women and by taking tips from them. New workers were constantly being hired at the plant and trained as sewers. At each seasonal change in style, production might first decrease as the last orders were filled and then increase as new garments were put into production.

These changes meant considerable shifting of workers from job to job or, worse, layoffs. Both management and workers were continuously socializing new workers to their respective views of work and production. Women workers had four sets of strategies for dealing with shifting management policy: first, socializing new workers in the context of the training program; second, creating ties among workers in the face of ethnic conflict by humanizing and "familizing" the work context; third, socializing new workers to informal work rules within the department; and fourth, outguessing new management policy with regard to the organization of production and worker layoffs.

The Shop Floor

The plant where I worked in Central Falls was established in nearby Pawtucket in the 1930s. The main offices remained in New York, creating a territorial division between the production facilities in Rhode Island and the design and sales portion of the company. The company had a reputation for being a sweat shop, especially in the 1930s, when sewers were paid $3.00 and $3.50 a week until the NRA mandated weekly salaries of $13.00 a week. As one Portuguese worker commented:

> You had to work hard to get that three dollars, and you know, they were very strict. If it wasn't done just right, you'd have to rip it out and you wasn't getting paid for it. It was overalls then; that's what we started on, overalls. That firm had just come in from New York, and you had to work hard, so that's why it was a sweat shop, for fifty-four hours. And you'd work like that and it was bad. . . . And after that, when the NRA came in, then things were better. . . . Of course they raised the prices. . . . I thought I was a millionaire.

Mrs. Okolowicz, a Polish woman who retired in 1978 after twenty-nine years of work for the company, reiterated many of the same feelings: "Oh yes, that was a sweat shop. I was underpaid. You had to put out a lot of garments to make your rate. . . . That was on piecework, you know. They make money like that—the company. They make millions. They could've paid us better. Especially, I worked there so long. You think they'd give me something for working there so long. Nothing! Not even a good watch."

The plant was unionized in 1951. The union negotiates piece rates, protects jobs (laid-off union members are the first to be recalled), gives workers seniority in their specific jobs, and provides small pensions and a medical-care program. In 1977 workers also received eight holidays, a paid birthday, and three weeks' vacation (paid on a percentage of wages earned).

In the ten years before 1977, there were two important changes in the company. First, as the paternalistic owner reached retirement age, he sold out to a large conglomerate. The company had already expanded, through adding a plant in Virginia and a distribution warehouse in Rhode Island. Second, the conglomerate increased the productive capacity of the company by 50 percent between 1974 and 1977, starting a sewing plant in Alabama, a knitting mill in New England, and a sewing operation in Puerto Rico. After 1977, a second warehouse was added in Rhode Island, as well as another plant.

As more of the older workers retired, rather than reduce or end production in this plant, the management was able to hire recent Portuguese and Latin American immigrant women, through the process described in chapter 5. This infusion of new immigrant labor made it possible to retain many of the older, experienced workers, some with twenty-five to thirty years with the company, who were also adept in the most skilled operations, for example, those involved in making girls' dresses.

The plant is located in a three-story brick mill that had been owned by one of the silk companies involved in the 1931 strike. One Polish worker commented on the irony of once being a silk weaver in the same building where she was employed as a sewer in the 1970s. The plant has a number of conveniences (including a cafeteria) that made it one of the better places to work in Central Falls. The offices for the plant were located on the first floor and the cutting of garments was done on the third floor. Most of the sewing operation took place on the second floor, which contained seven departments. Three additional sewing departments were located on the third floor and two at the back of the offices on the first floor.

At first sight, the vast second-floor room seemed chaotic—filled with sewing machines whirring away, chutes of cut and partially sewn garments in brightly printed colors, and between two hundred and three hundred women. However, there was order in all of the chaos. Work came down from the cutting room in lots of 80 to 120 dozen garments. At the row of machines close to the back of each department, women performed the first operations in the process: sewing the shoulder seams, neck bindings, and collars. As the bundles progressed to the front, some women attached labels and then others joined the tops and bottoms of girls' dresses. Different workers set the sleeves and seamed the sides. Finally, across the center aisle, the garments were hemmed, pressed, folded, and pinned. They were then taken off the floor to be boxed and sent to the distribution center, where shirts and pants were assembled into outfits, and orders from across the country were filled.

The lots were divided into bundles of 2.5 or 5.0 dozen garments, with smaller packs of sleeves, collars, sides, and other unsewn parts. On each bundle, a "ticket" specified the operations that had to be done to make a complete dress or T-shirt. Each operation had a number, and each style of garment had a pay rate for each operation. For Operation 37, "set sleeves" for example, the piece rates varied depending on the size of the garments in the bundle and on whether the garment was a dress or T-shirt.

Piece rates were based on the decimal system so that they would be easy to computerize. The system used in the Central Falls firm seems similar to that used to calculate rates in other large firms in the United States. It is a system that also seems designed to baffle workers, since the garments were batched in dozens and most sewers kept their eyes on a clock that ticked away in 60-minute hours. In the official system, however, the hour was divided in one hundred parts, so that 10 minutes was really 0.167 of an hour. Thus a piece rate of 0.073 meant that an operation had to be performed on a dozen garments in 4.38 minutes if the sewer was to earn $3.31 an hour in 1977 or $4.05 an hour in 1979—the "base rates" on which the piece rates were figured. Following the example of our training instructors, I always used a pocket calculator (at home) to figure out how well or how badly I was doing, and I marveled at other women who seemed to be able to translate all of the decimal figures into real dollars and cents. I figured that to earn the minimum wage in 1977 ($92.00 a week before deductions) by working all day on the same T-shirts with a rate of 0.073, I would have to sew a dozen garments (setting two sleeves each) every 6.3 minute, completing 76 dozen garments each day. Even workers who were fast had difficulty "making money." I was always impressed by the Portuguese woman sewing sleeves at the machine in front of me who said she sewed more than 110 dozen pairs of sleeves a day,

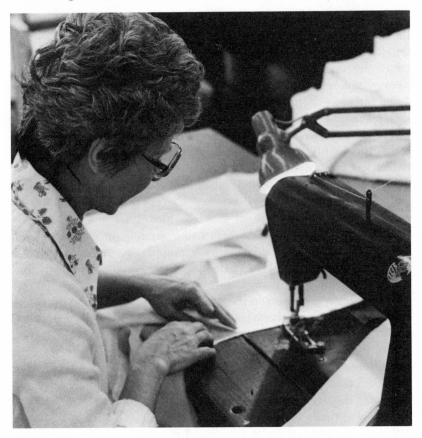

Sewing under the piece-rate takes skill and hand-eye coordination. Courtesy of Bronwen Zwirner.

while I was struggling to top 70 dozen. She worked with "the precision of a machine," and yet she probably was making only the base rate of $3.30 an hour (or $132.00 a week before deductions in 1977).

Women had several strategies for dealing with the piece-rate system, as I outline below. However, new workers first encountered management's views and organization of work as part of the training program. Only later did they begin to discover alternatives as they got to know older employees and were transferred from the training program to the shop floor.

Socializing the Worker through the Training Process

The conglomerate initiated a training program in January 1976 to standardize training in plants throughout the company. Each of the sewing operations was categorized as an A, B, or C job. A sewer was trained for an A job (neck binding, collars, sleeve bindings) in six weeks, for a B job (labeling) in twelve weeks, and for a C job (setting sleeves, seam sides, hemming) in eighteen weeks. Management used the program both to give the skills needed to become a sewer and to instill the correct attitudes toward work and toward the company. Training also provided a method of weeding out workers who "did not fit," those who had difficulty gaining the skills or who exhibited the wrong attitudes.

The training supervisor and her three bilingual assistants gave new employees a battery of tests and assigned them to a particular job. One of the training assistants taught the "new girl" a job (for example, setting sleeves) according to a prescribed method worked out by the supervisor. After about a week, they placed the trainee in her future department, where they continued to monitor her work by an efficiency chart tied to her machine.

Use of bilingual instructors made the training program an extremely effective way of integrating Portuguese women into the production system. Since the trainer could act as a mediator if the "new girl" made mistakes that affected the work and wages of others, the program reduced conflict with older workers. It also helped control the high turnover rate by spotting and encouraging "good workers" and replacing with a minimum of disruption those who left.

Throughout the training program, the supervisor and her assistants worked toward reinforcing the "company line" about work. Lucia, a second-generation Portuguese woman and supervisor of the program, believed she was training women to work as efficiently as possible, which was in both the company's and the workers' interest. "Let's face it. It's for the company, but it helps the girls make more money too." She explained that the company wanted to improve production and to save wasted motion. "You see some girls who *look* like they are working hard," she told me while imitating a woman shaking out a garment before sewing it, looking as if she were rapidly working, "but they are really wasting a lot of time. Others hardly look like they are working: it's almost automatic. *And* they are the ones that are making money."

"Making money" was the code word in the culture of both management and workers for making more than the minimum wage—in 1977 a vast terrain above $2.30 an hour and an amount that was limited only by a worker's lack of experience from management's point of view. Lucia was always pointing out women who were doing well. After my fifth day at work, she told me I was improving (up to 37 percent efficiency) and that she was "proud of all my girls." "That little Spanish girl reached 100 percent and graduated [from the training program] just a couple of days ago." Christina, one of the instructors, told me about a woman who had just started the week before and was already up to 88 percent efficiency and already making $22.00 a day. Accounts of women who were able to "make money" were held up as the ideal, and making money was the prize to be won by any worker who applied herself to the task at hand.

The training program during the peak of the season handled a large number of women, most of whom did not stay. For example, two of us started work on February 2, another six started the next Monday, and fourteen showed up on Valentine's Day to be trained. Some women lasted only a few days. One, I remember, said that she purposely had done badly on the tests they gave her the first day. She wanted an easy job, and she received one: gathering sleeves. She found it boring and did not show up the next day. Another trainee had worked for the company before, in the section where machines automatically embroidered designs on to the clothes. She had not had previous experience with sewing, and her reactions to the first day's tests were that they were "bullshit tests, just like in grammar school." These women clearly looked with skepticism on the training program, the management ideology of hard work, and the constraints of sewing; they quickly left the job.

Management might use workers' personal qualities, as well as their inability to keep up with the pace of the training program, to discourage unpromising trainees. Alice, a heavyset woman, was having a difficult time learning to set sleeves. Her efficiency had been up to 19 percent (about right for the second week of training) but had dropped to 11 percent when she received a difficult batch of sleeves to set. During the next week, she was called down to the nurse's office and told to take two baths a day and to use a particular deodorant since her body odors had been so offensive. Alice explained that because of her weight she perspired a lot and most deodorants did not work. She could not take a bath every day, and with the weather as cold as it was, she did not want to catch a cold. "The awful thing is, they don't tell you directly; they told the nurse. It really hurt." After she got home, she cried. She left the job soon after, convinced that her boyfriend, who encouraged her to quit, would help support her, with the help of her food stamps.

Another example was Cindy, a young woman who had started the training program before I did and who was still in the training area long after I had been assigned to a department. On February 11, she said that she was still in the same place and did not know why. "I really don't care how fast I go and sometimes I'm just fed up with the whole thing," she said. Two weeks later she had done several bundles of shirts all wrong and had to do them over again. The next day she was "hauled down to the office" and told that she "must not want her job." If she did not improve, they would let her go. She was furious at the training supervisor, Lucia, who had stood quietly behind the production manager while he talked to her about her behavior.

Cindy said that if she was doing something wrong, "I'd like to hear it from the bitch herself. That bitch, I could punch her in the mouth. I've never met anyone like her. But then I'd lose my job for sure." She *had* done the shirts wrong but said that the instructor had not checked her work. "They" also complained that she took too much time off from work and was always in the ladies' room. "Well," Cindy said, "they told me that whenever I wanted, I could get up and go to the bathroom and have a cigarette." She insisted that she did not do this too often, but her supervisor countered, "She's in there all the time." The production manager gave her two days to shape up. He said he would see on Friday if she still wanted to keep her job. On Wednesday she was working hard and had done twenty-nine dozen sets of sleeves by the end of the morning. Cindy continued to work until the layoffs a week later but declined to work at the warehouse and did not reappear in June when we were called back to the sewing operation.

The training program effectively weeded out workers like Alice and Cindy who were having difficulty working fast enough and with enough skill and whose demeanor and attitudes did not fit the work environment. Cindy often did not care how hard she worked, and she was defiant, not willing to assume responsibility for her mistakes (which are very common for all workers in the first weeks of sewing). Lucia, the trainee supervisor, always had a cheery attitude and encouraged hard work, "sticking to it." After a week at work, I mentioned during a lunch break that I was having a bad day, repairing a lot of sleeves that I had put on wrong. Lucia said that maybe in the afternoon things would go better. She counseled me always to be optimistic, to "look on the bright side of things." That afternoon I would get paid (my first paycheck) and that would brighten things up.

A week later I stopped by the supervisor's desk to see how I was doing and to explain that my hands were hurting by the end of the day. Lucia explained to me that it takes time to get used to sewing. "That's why we give you several weeks to work up to one hundred percent efficiency," she said. "Your body's not used to it yet. Probably you weren't doing much with your hands in whatever you were doing before. It's just like training for a sport. Your body has to get used to it." She commented that she herself was out of practice, and whenever she went back to sewing, her arms would get sore at first. "Your body has to work up to it," she concluded. All of these comments and pep talks seemed to be aimed at encouraging me to continue to work hard and improve, despite difficulties and setbacks.

Many, like Cindy and Alice, did not stay with the training program for very long. The trainers developed a clear set of attitudes that characterize this kind of behavior—all part of the ideology that encourages hard work and evaluates laziness negatively. During the summer months when the fall-season clothes were being produced the company again began to hire and train new sewers. Again, a number of new trainees failed to show up for the job or lasted only a few days, some it seems because they had genuine difficulties arranging child care. Although the trainers were resigned to such problems ("I guess that's the way it is"), they had little sympathy for other women who quit. "Some of these girls don't want to work," Christina reported. Maria Lucia, another trainer, commented, "About three-fourths of them quit, you know. They get in here and see what it's like and then leave." She thought that the number of Portuguese trainees was lower than usual that summer because "maybe they hear what it's like and don't want to work here." She told of one typical strategy in which new girls call in sick for a week until they find another job and try it out. Then they fail to call in and are terminated. One girl however, quit and went to find another job only to realize that the first job was better; however, the company would not take her back.

Although Maria Lucia said that "the good ones quit and I end up with all the rest," the general attitude among the trainers and the training supervisor was that most girls quit because they "don't like to work." Others were quickly terminated if they stepped outside the rules. Sophie, who started training the same day I did in February, did not return after summer vacation, although she had been making the piece rate. Her husband called in during the first week saying she was sick, but during the second week, nothing was heard from her. So on a day when they terminated four new trainees, Maria Lucia came by and cut down the efficiency chart on Sophie's machine. "Well, you never know," she said, as she perfunctorily eliminated any evidence of Sophie's presence on the floor.

Diane, however, was fired. She had already been trained on several jobs and had requested a more steady job from the manager. She was being "cross-trained" on a new job: seam sides. Her trainer reported that she did not like the job, and "if she doesn't like it, it will be hard for her to do well." Since she had just started this job, Maria Lucia thought it would be unlikely that she could change again. "They can't let everyone change jobs. There are a lot of girls here who don't like their jobs, and if you let them all change . . . it wouldn't work." Diane began to spend more and more time in the ladies' room, and finally, about three weeks later, her floor lady told her she was fired. Diane was still not in the union, since she hadn't completed her training and had not made the piece rate on any of the jobs she had held. Her termination was therefore irreversible. She had not produced as well as others, and her attitude and behavior were much like those of Cindy and Alice. She had managed to last much longer then they had, drifting from job to job until her unsuitability became too apparent to her floor lady. The training program had not initially weeded her out, but her floor lady had.

Although the training program tried to instill notions of "making money" in new trainees and eliminate those who failed to produce, older workers were more cynical about the management view that hard work made it possible to "make money." They cautioned trainees not to accept management ideas, especially after a trainee was assigned to her permanent job on the sewing floor. Mrs. Okolowicz, an older Polish woman, asked how a Polish trainee was doing. The instructor, Christina, said, "She's a smart girl and doing really well." Mrs. Okolowicz retorted, "Pretty soon she'll be working really fast, but *she still won't be making any money.*"

The older workers in my department counseled me about the job itself, how to do it and when not to get discouraged. Rose, who had been setting sleeves for twenty-two years, said, "It's a good little job . . . take your time and the speed will come to you." Several times

Fighting the piece-rate in a New England men's suit factory. Courtesy of Bronwen Zwirner.

when I was having trouble putting sleeves on inside out or not catching the first two inches of the sleeve, she encouraged me, saying that she had had the same difficulties at first. "Just keep going . . . it will come to you." At the same time she made no bones about her feeling that it was difficult to make money. "If you are satisfied with $2.30 an hour, you'll do all right. You really have to push yourself to make more. . . . The one thing about this place is that the work is steady. . . . If you keep improving, it will be okay. As long as you do a dozen or so more each day."

Although the trainee supervisor implied that an average worker was timed in setting the rates, older workers scoffed at this idea. Angela pointed out the management efficiency expert by saying, "That's the one we hate." When I asked whom he timed, she said, "They usually pick out the fastest girl. They're not dumb, you know." A few days later when I had just finished struggling over a batch of sleeves on green-striped dresses, I was relieved to find that the next lot of yellow dresses was much easier, but I was puzzled to find that both styles had the same rate. Angela and Rose agreed about the differences in the two styles. "It's crazy," Angela said. "The engineer is supposed to have a college education, but they don't know what they are doing."[1]

Worker attempts to put "new girls" straight about the realities of the way management enforces the piecework system was illustrated by the following incident. My instructor came by to tell me that my card indicated that I had done only seventeen dozen sleeves the previous day. She thought there must have been some mistake, since I had been doing closer to thirty-six dozen a day. My handwriting had been misread so that, for one style, only two dozen sleeves, rather than twenty-four dozen, had been counted. She wrote this down on her pad and left, presumably to correct the mistake in the office. Angela, thinking that the instructor had been criticizing the level of my work, gave me the following advice: "Don't let her tell you that seventeen dozen isn't enough. She hinted at it, you know. She ought to try it sometime. The girl who used to be at your machine, she used to tell them."

Angela and Rose reminded me that my predecessor had quit because she could not make more than the minimum wage. She had reached a plateau in two or three months and just could not make any more. I explained that I had been told I would be able to make $3.31 an hour (the base rate) by the end of my training period. Angela scoffed at this: "I've been here ten years and I don't make that." Rose said, "You tell them that if an *old girl* who's been here twenty-two years can't make that, then you can't do it." Angela concluded, "You just let what they tell you go in one ear and out the other. Just keep going along as best you can."

The training program had several other functions. It helped to dampen conflict between the new trainees and their coworkers by having someone available to supervise and deal with mistakes. The disruptive potential of these mistakes was made clear to me in March when I was sent to another department to sew side seams on little infant "coveralls," a new and very difficult job for me but one necessitated by the lack of work available to the sleeves-setting girls in my department. While I was trying to master this new job, it turned out

1. The piece-rate system itself pits workers against one another in a competitive race for wages. Women were fairly secretive about how much they are making. I sensed that some of the rates were easier to make than others. In setting sleeves, I was told that Rose made about $3.00 an hour, while Angela seemed to be making closer to the minimum wage. The women sewing tops and bottoms together were reputed to be making $4.12 an hour, or $33.00 a day. The rate on sides was also supposed to be good. "We fought hard to get them a high rate," Anita explained.

that I had made a number of mistakes on sleeves in the same garments a few days earlier. Christina, my training supervisor, said she had heard "a girl over there" saying that I had a lot of repairs, and she was "going to make a fuss about it." Christina helped me find the bundles of sleeves that I had done and helped me check some of them. I was absent the next day, and one of the other trainers checked through the remaining bundles and made the necessary repairs. Trainers, thus, are "go-betweens" in that they try to ease the disruption of a new worker in the department.

There was still some resentment on the part of coworkers against the training program since, no matter how much effort was made, there was some disruption. For example, women in the "seam sides" row in my department, resented Dulce, the trainer, coming to take dresses to be seamed back in the training section. They realized that taking work out of the department cut down on the number of dresses they sewed in each lot, which meant that they would have to lose time by changing thread and starting on a new lot before they would ordinarily have switched thread. Also the dresses were never returned quickly so that the women sewing the next operation received the dresses long after they had changed thread and started on a new lot of garments.

Finally, the training program gave management access to workers who could be easily used on a number of jobs and then laid off during seasonal lulls without the encumbrances of following union rules, since trainees do not become members of the union for ninety days. The large number of trainees recruited during July and August were at first being trained for sewing jobs, but in late July the training department decided to send some to pinning and pressing jobs, since the amount of sewing to be done was declining as the end of the fall season's work approached. The training supervisor explained that they had taken these women off sewing and had put them on pinning since there was a "lot" that had to get out by Saturday and they were needed to pin. She admitted it was a little disruptive, but "the girls were taking it OK."

A few weeks later, Maria Lucia admitted that a young Continental woman, who was just learning to do sleeves and who sat at the machine in front of me, would either be laid off or be transferred to some other work as soon as the fall season ended. Older workers were often cognizant of this tactic and commented on the company's policy of continuing to bring in "new girls" even at the end of the season when there was very little work. By mid-August there was already an apparent lack of work on the second floor. The quality-control inspector told me that they were already laying off women, but "here they are hiring new ones." She gave examples of workers who had been asked to work for the general minimum (80 percent of their piecework average) on a new job or take a layoff. Clearly, the company was more able to get new workers to do pinning and pressing that needed to be done for the minimum wage than it was able to convince older workers to work for less.

In sum, from the management perspective, the training program helped give women workers the appropriate skills and weeded out those who could not acquire those skills fast enough as well as those who did not have the appropriate attitudes toward their work. Older workers often blamed trainees for making mistakes and for making their own jobs more difficult or for interrupting their work by asking for help. They were also careful, however, to socialize trainees to a different view of the work and the piece-rate system. During the first few days at work, the trainee supervisor and her assistants were in frequent contact with the trainees and offered their view of working hard and making money. When the worker was placed in the department, she heard a different opinion: that it would be difficult to make more than the minimum wage and that the piece-rate system often worked against you. Workers were cautioned to be wary of management promises.

Shop-Floor Realities: Dealing with Power and the Piece Rate

As the new trainee shifts from the first few days under the training program to her position in a particular department, she begins to feel the rapid pace of the work and the pressure to produce. The reality of the piece-rate system becomes clearer every day as she tries to keep up with the curved line on the efficiency chart and comply with the wishes of her floor lady and training instructor. Worker strategies involved three issues: (1) coping with the work itself and the mistakes that arise in trying to do the work correctly, (2) dealing with the piece-rate system, and (3) relating to the power and authority of the management—the training instructors, the floor lady, and the male production managers.

To continue to increase in "efficiency" and sew more dozens a day (and eventually "make money"), a sewer has to overcome a whole range of errors, mistakes, and difficulties that can beset her on any particular operation. My field notes are filled with all of the difficulties I had in setting sleeves correctly. A few examples will illustrate the problems that sewers need to overcome. Most sewers, especially those who worked on the three-needle Merrow machines, had to watch out for a "loose stitch"—a stitch where the tension on the threads becomes loose enough so that if the seam is pulled, the threads will pull apart, almost disconnecting the seam. If the woman who turns the dresses or shirts from wrong side to right side catches loose stitches, the seams have to be resewn. At first, I did not even know what a loose stitch was, until one was pointed out by my coworkers. Then I learned that the male mechanic had to be called over to adjust the tension and correct the stitch. If the sewer failed to watch the seams she was sewing, her work would be returned, and she would lose time in repairs.

Another typical problem was that of a broken thread, which meant that the sewer had to stop and, if she had not seen the problem soon enough, rethread her machine, a complicated process on the three-needle Merrow machine. Thread breaks used to slow down my production and add several minutes to the time it took to finish a bundle. Often thread breaks were related to the tension on the thread, something that had to be corrected by the mechanic. Using a heavier spool of thread often solved the problem.

A great deal of time could be wasted locating the right color thread to put on the machine to sew the next lot, pulling unsewn chutes of clothes near one's machine, or sorting out a "lot" by sizes so that each worker could have an equal number of bundles of the various sized garments. When I first started timing my production with a time clock, I realized that I spent one or two minutes of nonsewing time on each bundle doing all of these chores. Other new workers did the same thing. For example, one morning Francine spent almost an hour looking for orange thread for one lot of dresses. The thread broke, and she spent extra time looking for stronger thread and finally called the mechanic to look at her machine for the possible source of the difficulty. Her friend Clara told her at the break, "Get the mechanic to fix the machine for you. Tell him, you'll go home if he doesn't fix your machine." Josie once chided me, "You'll never make any money that way," commenting on all the time I spent pulling chutes over to my machine and sorting bundles out. These comments from older workers help show "new girls" that to make the piece rate, extra motions and activities have to be eliminated.

In sewing sleeves, I learned all of the possible mistakes I could make. One typical error was sewing on the sleeve wrong side out. This easily happened if the sleeves in one lot were stacked differently than in another lot or if the difference between the right side and the wrong side of the material was difficult to see. These wrong-sided sleeves were what kept Francine busy during almost a whole day in June. To make the repairs, she had to rip out the seam and do it all over again. After spending the whole day working on these sleeves, she commented, "I should have stayed home."

Other typical mistakes included stretching the sleeve so some was left over after the seam was completed or catching some of the sleeve material in the seam, leaving a little tuck. Both mistakes meant ripping the sleeve out and doing it over. An easier mistake to repair was not catching the entire sleeve in the seam, leaving a small hole, which could be corrected by sewing over the seam again, without ripping it out. The most difficult sleeves to sew, however, were small, shirred sleeves on baby garments. They were difficult because the actual sleeve was larger than the armhole, and during the process of sewing, the sleeve material had to be gathered. Also the sleeve style was like that of a baby's undershirt and involved a complicated overlay portion. Frequently, I did not get all of the parts caught by the seam, leaving either the thread from a previous operation showing or a hole in the sleeve.

Late on August 1, my floor lady brought over several of the shirred sleeves and showed me that they needed repairs. She said that the "quality-control girl found them," and now they needed to go through the whole lot and find more. I learned later that the lot had been rejected by Quality Control, perhaps the worst thing that could happen to a floor lady. I was able to make some of the first repairs on my break that afternoon, but many more had to be done later. My field notes for that Wednesday read, "Today was wretched. It was the worst day I have had in a long time and put me in a horrible mood. I spent two and a half hours making repairs on the pink and purple shirred sleeves." There must have been one hundred garments to fix.

Most of these mistakes were a result of inexperience and trying to work fast under the pressure of increasing production quotas. The training instructors were usually the ones to step in and watch the trainee work, helping her to correct the mistake. Help sometimes came from other workers who noticed what the trainee was doing and made suggestions for improvement. However, sewers were often reluctant to step in since they always felt the tension of having to keep up with their own work and hence wanted to avoid any disruptions that would slow them down. Rose, just before her retirement, felt free enough to help Vivian, showing her how to sew the notorious shirred sleeves. However, Angela often reminded me that I should call the trainer to get help rather than ask the "old girls" since such questions slowed them down.

As I trained, I soon began to hear conversations during the break indicating that others were having the same difficulty on the same operation. Break times were also times to share feelings about the nature of the work and about the piece-rate system itself.

It was apparent that women had several strategies for dealing with the piece-rate system. They kept track of how many dozen pieces they had sewn each day, and they kept a sharp eye out for rates that were too low for the difficulty of the style. Each worker kept a little notebook in her machine drawer listing the number of bundles finished so that she could accurately fill out her punch card at the end of the day and recheck the amount on her paycheck when she received it on Thursday afternoon. I often talked with coworkers during lunch and the afternoon break when they were adding up their dozens and calculating whether they were "making money" that day.

On the one hand, the number of dozens a woman sews in a day is often a jealously guarded secret. The piece-rate system itself pits one worker against another in a competitive system, each trying to "work for herself." On the other hand, workers are often willing to talk about the difficulties they are having or are willing to discuss the qualities of the job in a general way.[2]

After working for twelve weeks at a production level above the minimum wage, workers were given a "piecework average," a figure that represented their wage when they were put on a new job, if work on their usual job was not available. It was often difficult to get older women to discuss their own piecework average. Rose, who was about

2. Discussing production in terms of "dozens" is an approximation, since the actual wage is calculated by the formula: Dozens × rate (on a given style) × 3.31 (the base rate). However, workers had some sense of how many dozens (given some variation in rates for different styles) it was necessary to produce to make over the minimum wage. One worker told me that the 1977 system was relatively new, and that the rate used to be calculated by the dozen, for example, "twenty-five cents a dozen." Each worker would just figure out the amount she made on that basis rather than "all this adding and multiplying."

to retire, evaded my questions about the exact amount of her piece-work average. She simply said that it was going down, but she did not care much any more, since she was retiring. On the other hand, Anna, an older Portuguese woman who had worked for seventeen years for the company, would tell me how many dozen collars she had sewn during the morning while she was adding up her dozens at lunch time. Clara, who sewed labels, once told me that she was able to do more labels when she worked on shirts rather than dresses, since there weren't so many pieces to tie up and bundle together after she finished. She sometimes could sew two hundred dozen labels on shirts a day (or about $4.95 an hour). But discussing the number of dozens one could do in a day was about as far as most women would go in saying what their pay was.

"New girls," or recently hired workers, were more willing to talk about the piece rate, partially because they were not yet making the piece rate (more than the minimum wage) and partially because they were more willing to discuss difficulties. During one afternoon break, Francine said that forty dozen sleeves was the most she had ever done in a day, and the previous day she had done something like thirty dozen. (It took at least sixty-five dozen to make the minimum wage per hour for the whole day.) "I don't think I'll ever make any money at this job," she concluded. Clara said that Angela "worked here for years and she never made any money." Angela herself said that she had worked hard all one week on dresses with a good rate for the sleeves and had made $3.60 an hour, only $1.30 an hour over the minimum wage.

Sophie, the Polish woman who started training when I did, was frank in telling me how well she was doing, especially in June when she reached 80 percent efficiency and was making $20.00 a day, more than the minimum wage of $18.40 a day. Other younger workers, like Liane, told me that they had worked for the company for a year and still did not have a piecework average. She could make the piece rate on neck bindings and cuffs but not on the other jobs she had done during the year.

Workers, in general, resented the management's enforcement of the piece-rate system, a fact that was obvious when workers commented on the time clock that sat on my machine table. I found it difficult to work faster without having a clock to time me, so I kept the clock there long after the training instructor first suggested it. Angela, when she returned for Rose's retirement party, said, "Oh, they've still got their darn old clocks. . . . Well, don't let them bother you. You just let that go in one ear and out the other. You just keep on doing the best that you can. You'll do all right." Other workers often asked if "they still have the clock on you," indicating that this was management's tactic for making me work faster.

Some workers, however, did try to pace themselves by the clock on the wall. Lena, who was a pinner, told me that she watched the clock nearest to her. She used fifteen minutes as a unit of time. If she didn't have two or two and a half dozen done by the end of the fifteen minutes, she hurried up and worked faster, because she was lagging behind her usual pace.

In general, although workers were protective about revealing their own wages, they were willing to discuss whether jobs were good or bad. "That's a nice little job. You can make money on that," Josie once told me. Workers, especially the older ones, discussed the ways in which working on the piece rate affected their health. Rita, who did a number of jobs as "a utility girl," said that she didn't like to work too fast, for example, sewing one hundred sleeves a day. "It's not worth it," she said, explaining that she did not want to take tranquilizers. "If you work that fast, you get nervous and your heart starts pounding." Jan told me that she was getting an ulcer. She had to take antiulcer medicine four times a day—both pills and liquid. "It's rough. It isn't easy, you know." She explained that her job (sewing elastic between the bottoms and tops of dresses) was not easy: "You have needle holes and you have to get it just right."

Workers were often convinced that once they became good at a job, they were taken off it and forced to learn another one. Josie, who sewed elastic, said that she used to do shoulder seams as well. "But they took me off that, because I made too much money. I could make money with my eyes closed." Francine was convinced that she had made three dollars an hour sewing pockets because the floor lady had tricked the efficiency engineer and had gotten him to time a slow worker. "This place is really a sweat shop," she said. "It's just like a sweat shop. They pay you so little," she commented, also stating that she would never make any money setting sleeves.

Under the constant pressure of working fast, workers tried to insure that their work went through and did not get returned for repairs. They watched that cutting-room mistakes were not blamed on individuals and protested when work was "sectioned," that is, tied in small bundles that contained only a few garments because the material was shaded differently and had to be separated. Often workers colluded in "letting the work go through" or covering up the mistakes of others. For example, those setting sleeves often covered over a poorly done shoulder seam (where the two sides were not joined evenly) by sewing the sleeve on and cutting off the extra piece of material. Once in a while this backfired, when the set sleeve did not look right and had to be discarded or returned for repairs.

One of the "seam sides girls" showed me how to fix sleeves that had been sewn inside out just by redoing the trim rather than ripping out and resewing each sleeve. Sometimes the floor lady was involved, since she often called in the Quality Control personnel to see that a potential mistake did not result in the rejection of the lot after the garments were completed. For example, when one worker discovered that some holiday-season red dresses were actually two colors, they sat in front of the department for several days until the quality-control supervisor had inspected them. Then our floor lady was able to tell us to "let them go through."

Thus workers attempted to protect themselves against management in terms of the way the piece rate was manipulated. They tried to protect their own earnings through careful record keeping and a watchful assessment of the mistakes made by cutters and other workers that might affect their ability to work quickly. Against this pressure to work on one's own and for individualistic goals, women often helped other workers, covering over the mistakes of "new girls," giving tips on how to sew better, or talking about the way in which management manipulated the piece-rate system.

Coping with the piece rate also entailed dealing with various levels of management, the training instructors, the floor ladies at the point of production, and more distantly, the male production manager and the conglomerate in general. Workers often commented sympathetically about the training instructors and floor ladies, especially since the latter were all ex-sewers and had considerable experience as floor ladies (often twenty to thirty years). They contrasted with the "bosses" who did not know how to sew and who, in 1977, represented the increasing control of the conglomerate in ways resented by workers and floor ladies alike.

The training supervisor and training instructors approached the trainees with encouragement and a tone of enthusiasm. Especially if the trainee was compliant, rather than sullen and defiant, training instructors were cheerful, asking each morning, "How are you doing?" and returning at the end of the day to record the number of dozens each worker had completed. By talking to new women about their weekend activities, boyfriends, or family, the three young Portuguese training instructors personalized management and mediated the difficulties of the work and the piece-rate system. Dulce, for example, sided with me against Betty, when I was temporarily having difficulties learning to seam sides in her department. She agreed with me that Betty's demeanor made her nervous, but she encouraged me, saying that "we'll have your work be the best," indicating that she would help me with my mistakes so that Betty would not be able to complain. When my efficiency was not increasing as quickly as it should have been, Maria Lucia quietly reminded me each day how I had done, suggesting that I use a clock and then later agreeing not to count all the time I had taken on repairs against my efficiency rating. She also politely teased me when I recounted my troubles during a morning break: "Excuses, excuses, always an excuse." Thus even her public reprimand was polite and jocular, a comment that I should have been doing better but not a direct reproach. More punitive sanctions (such as firing Cindy) fell to the training supervisor and the sewing director, leaving the training instructors with more informal and "polite" sanctions as their main tools for gaining compliance.

Floor ladies varied considerably in the way in which they exercised power and authority. From the point of view of the worker, the floor lady had several main tasks: (1) to keep the work flowing through the department from step to step in the sewing process so that each worker had sufficient work, (2) to check the work sufficiently so that there were no mistakes that would result in a lot being rejected by Quality Control, and (3) to take sewers off jobs, put them on new work, or lay them off in order to make adjustments to increases or decreases in the amount of work to be done.

The conglomerate company newspaper touted the floor lady's role in the article "Women Play a Growing Role in Management" by acknowledging that the combined years of employment represented by the twenty-eight floor ladies amounted to more than four hundred—"a commendable achievement." They also quoted an anonymous worker as describing the supervisor's role as follows: "It's helping others make a *career* for themselves, as well as earning a living." Workers generally scoffed at this overblown characterization of the floor lady's role, implying that it was not a position of much power or part of a career ladder. One woman said, "I never thought I'd get a laugh out of this paper, but this is sure funny." On the other hand, workers realized that it took skill to be a good floor lady, and they were often critical or full of praise for one set of tactics or another.

Workers are quick to socialize new women into the tactics for fighting the piece rate, and new workers soon learned that training instructors and floor ladies, although often helpful and easy to work with, were part of management. These women were carefully distinguished from the "bosses," or male upper management (the production supervisor, plant manager, and personnel manager), who were more clearly associated with the conglomerate and with recent negative changes for workers. The labor process, the piece rate, and management policy tended to set workers apart from one another. The socialization of new workers to "tricks of the trade" and to a nonmanagement view of work helped to overcome some of the devisiveness of the piece-rate system, but there were also differences in age, marital status, and ethnicity that divided workers. These differences were primarily overcome through informal interaction and strategies I have called "humanizing the work place."

Humanizing the Workplace

During my first few days in the department, I quickly realized that there were relatively stable groups of women who met during the breaks to share a cigarette, take coffee and sweet rolls in midmorning, buy lunch in the cafeteria, or eat a lunch from home while clustered around someone's machine. These groups were formed among workers of the same age and ethnic group who also worked near one another. The major division, between Portuguese and non-Portuguese workers, was created partially because so few of the recent Portuguese immigrants spoke English well, if at all. The few Portuguese speakers who mingled with non-Portuguese were either second-generation women or those whose command of English was fluent.

In some ways these small groups illustrated the ethnic divisions in the workplace—largely between Portuguese and non-Portuguese. But in addition, there were often clusters of Continental Portuguese, as opposed to those from the Azores, and there were several groups of Polish workers, many of whom were first-generation immigrants. Women of second- and third-generation French-Canadian, Italian, Irish, or English background were often part of mixed groups. For

[311]

example, in our row of sleeve setters, Rose (a French-Canadian) and Angela (an Italian) were the center of a little cluster that included another Italian woman (a pinner) and the quality-control woman (whose ethnic background I did not determine). In the department behind me, one lunch group included two Polish women and a French-Canadian. Age was the most important divider among the non-Portuguese. The young, unmarried high school graduates formed a group of their own that included two girls of French-Canadian descent, a second-generation Portuguese, and a girl who said she was of several different ethnic backgrounds—"Heinz 57 varieties," as she put it.

Break and lunch-time conversations were often an opportunity for individuals to talk not just about their work but their personal lives as well. Virtual strangers were transformed into acquaintances and, over a number of years, into friends. Although women did not often see each other outside of work hours, sharing the details of personal lives served to create bonds within the workplace.[3]

On Mondays, conversations often involved events of the past weekend. Some of the Portuguese women discussed attending a *festa*, and others discussed a wedding they had attended or in which they had participated. For several weeks before the plant shut down in July, conversations were heard about vacation travel plans: trips to the Azores or the Continent, a trip to Colorado, a special return to Poland, or even just the possibility of going to the beach. Then the week after the two-week July vacation, workers shared news of their vactions, filling in the details of a trip, merely saying they had a good time, or sharing pictures of family and friends taken during vacation travels.

Workers shared the details of their personal lives as well. Clara revealed difficulties with her boyfriend to those of us who sat out in the hall during breaks, detailing her opinions of his new girlfriend, keeping track of his activities, and later discussing her times with a new boyfriend. Rose told her break group about attending the Jubilee Lunch at her French-Canadian parish, and Vivian commented to her

3. There seemed to be considerable variation in how much coworkers socialized outside work. Rose and Angela had known each other for years but had not visited each other's houses until after retirement. On the other hand, two of the younger workers had apartments next door to each other, Clara and Francine went to the dog races together, and Lena invited Angela to dinner several months after retirement. Several Portuguese women belonged to the same parish and participated in parish activities. In addition, there were a number of relatives (sisters, mothers and daughters, and mothers and sons) who worked in the plant.

Continental friends that her father was extremely lonely since her mother had returned to Portugal for her grandmother's funeral. The clique of younger women, usually over the lunch table in the cafeteria, discussed their experiences of living with their boyfriends or recent weekend incidents including a car accident that left one girl with a black eye. One group of two Polish women and a French-Canadian woman discussed food in endless detail, including favorite dishes, ways of canning and pickling various vegetables, and cooking tips. These conversations built feelings of solidarity within the small groups and dyads that clustered together during breaks. However, there were also conversations that indicated substantial divisions within the workplace.

The most significant division was between the Portuguese and non-Portuguese workers, evident in the anti-Portuguese sentiment expressed in the non-Portuguese groups. A week after I started work, and on one of my first days in the department, Rose and Angela were upset that the two Portuguese sisters sewing tops and bottoms of dresses (the operation just before ours) had not told them they were working on two different lots of the same style dresses. Rose and Angela had inadvertently mixed up the bundles from the two lots and later had to stop work to sort them out into different chutes. After explaining all this to me, Rose said, "I'm glad they are hiring some of our own kind (obviously referring to me). There are too many Portuguese being hired now."

While I was working temporarily at the warehouse, one of the young male workers complained to the union shop steward that a Portuguese woman "smelled bad." During the morning coffee break, one of the French-Canadian women told my Polish friend Sophie and me about it, saying that there was no excuse for that. "Of course, if you are working a job like this where you have to work hard, you sometimes perspire, but it's important to keep clean." Sophie agreed that there was no excuse for body odor and stated, "It is terrible." The French-Canadian woman concluded that she had heard Portuguese women say that they were all brought up to be clean and wash regularly, but she herself did not believe it. Perhaps the clearest sign of anti-Portuguese hostility came one morning when my Polish friend Sophie told a Portuguese "joke": the same kind of joke that has been labeled a "Polish" joke, one that pokes fun at the lack of sophistication and "backwardness" of the ethnic group described in the joke.

There were interethnic tensions around the piece-rate system as well. Employers hired Portuguese women because of their reputation as hard workers, and the Portuguese women fulfilled their expectations. Some workers thus saw Portuguese women as working too hard, sometimes cutting corners to keep their wages up, or engaging in "rate busting." One worker commented that the Azorean woman sewing the elastic band that joined the top and bottom of dresses "ruined that job for everyone." In other words, she worked so fast that the piece rate was lowered, and the workers had to increase their output to make the same pay. "She doesn't miss a dime," and "She makes more money than anyone else on the floor," another worker commented. For their part, Portuguese workers often felt discriminated against and said that American workers do not work hard enough.

The divisions apparent in the structure of break and lunch groups and in attitudes expressed within them were cross-cut by the number of ways in which women joined together around their family roles and life-cycle events. Workers celebrated marriages and the birth of children with showers, usually organized by a group of friends who collected a small amount of money from members of the woman's department or other acquaintances. The organizers then presented wrapped gifts as a surprise during the lunch break. Retirement celebrations were more extensive. Friends brought pastry and baked goods for morning break and a cake for lunch. Orders were taken for a fast-food lunch of hamburgers, cole slaw, potato chips, and pop. Retirements and sometimes showers were organized along department lines, often through the help, and certainly with the knowledge, of a management representative, the floor lady. In both the department-organized and friendship-based functions, the monetary contributions and the signatures on the card cut across ethnic lines.

Leslie's baby shower provides a good example of how such non-work-time events integrated workers of diverse ages and ethnic backgrounds. It was organized by her two friends, who collected the money from women in other departments of various ages and ethnic backgrounds as well as from women in her own department. The friends also bought the gifts: a car seat, a high chair, and a baby carriage. During lunch break, they brought the huge, wrapped boxes down the center aisle and placed them by her machine and waited until she returned from the ladies' room. Halfway down the aisle, she realized what was happening. Perhaps a little embarrassed by all the attention, she let one of her friends begin helping her open the gifts. One of the Portuguese women picked up the yellow ribbon that came off the first package and pinned it on Leslie. She exclaimed "Oh,

Jesus!" on opening the gifts and finally pulled the card out to look at it. She thanked everyone, and newcomers to the crowd peered over others to see what the gifts were. "Let's see what we got you," the woman who served morning coffee said, while Leslie's floor lady looked on. More admirers came by as Leslie's two friends began to stuff the gifts back in their boxes. The buzzer rang, ending the lunch break and sending everyone scurrying back to their machines. Although organized by the clique of young high school graduates, Portuguese women in Leslie's department clearly had contributed to the gifts and stood by admiring them.

Rose's retirement party was an all-day event, and that day our work was almost interspersed between festive breaks. We had prepared for the party by each contributing $1.00 for Rose's gift and $1.50 for a fast-food hamburger lunch, all at times when Rose was not around to find out about the surprise celebration. The events began when our floor lady came around before the morning break and told us that they had the pastry all set out. We were to come to the table at the front of the department before the break, when Edna, the floor lady, brought over a corsage for Rose—with blue bachelor buttons, red carnations, two little pink roses, some bridal wreath, and a multicolored bow. Rose seemed appropriately surprised. One of the young Portuguese women gave Rose a congratulatory kiss, and another Portuguese woman gestured excitedly.

Edna motioned us over to eat the pastry, so we all lined up to get doughnut holes, doughnuts, and homemade coffee cakes. Edna presented Rose with two cards, which she opened. One contained about sixty dollars and was signed "From all the girls in Department #11," and the other contained about the same amount "From all your Colleagues." The department card said, "Use this to kick up your heels and enjoy." Everyone spent the rest of the break enjoying the pastry in their usual groups. Rose was surrounded by her usual clique of friends, discussing the last retirement party, which Rose herself had organized for her friend Angela.

The half-hour lunch break brought another round of partying, with the floor lady's assistant bringing each of us a paper bag with our hamburger. Angela, Rose's friend, arrived to join the party just as the buzzer rang, and everyone lined up near the floor lady's desk to get potato salad, cole slaw, potato chips, and soda pop. Again, everyone sat in their usual groups, but several women, both Portuguese and non-Portuguese, came by to talk with Angela or Rose. Angela had lots of tips to give out about retirement and said that she "missed the people more than the place," but "you get used to it." After lunch, she made the rounds of the department, stopping by each machine and talking to each of her ex-coworkers, whether English or Portuguese speaking. One of the Portuguese workers brought over a picture of her grandson to show Angela. She traded stories about grandchildren with the head mechanic, a Portuguese man in his fifties. Her general comment on leaving was that she "missed all my girls." The mood of the whole day was one of departmental festivity. In contrast to the underlying tensions that had surfaced several times during the spring and summer months between Rose and Angela and some of their Portuguese coworkers, the retirement party was an occasion for crossing ethnic lines and expressing feelings of solidarity even across a language barrier.

On other occasions women brought their family lives into the work situation through showing coworkers pictures of special occasions. These pictures, usually shared during morning or afternoon breaks, enabled women to communicate across ethnic boundaries. Several weeks after I had started work in my department, Anita, an older Portuguese woman who set sleeves at the machine behind me, brought in her family pictures to show me. In my halting Portuguese I had talked with her several times about her children and grandchildren. She carefully showed me each picture and explained who each person was. She was particularly proud of the first-communion pictures of her two granddaughters—a studio picture taken of them in their white dresses with curled hair topped with little white veils. "Two little angels," she said.

At other times women showed family pictures to a wide variety of workers, their closest acquaintances as well as those around them with whom they may have had only a nodding acquaintance. Several weeks after the summer vacation, Vivian brought to work pictures of her wedding, taken during her trip to Portugal, where she married the man she had been engaged to for several years. During the morning break, she showed them to our floor lady and her clique. Then she returned to her own Portuguese-speaking group and turned the pages for them, explaining who the godparents and various relatives were. Several Portuguese women came over from adjacent tables when they saw Vivian open the album, so she started her explanation all over. Sharing the wedding pictures involved women across ethnic lines and seemed appropriate as a follow-up to the wedding present the department had given her two weeks before.

Other forms of social interaction that bound workers together included joking, sometimes with a sexual undertone. This kind of joking often involved women of different age groups, but more commonly took place among members of the same lunch or break group, thus rarely crossing the line between Portuguese and non-Portuguese, partially because of the language barrier. For example, a group of Azorean women in my department who clustered around Serina would erupt in giggles and laughter during an afternoon break, laughing over her account of sexual relations with her husband or surreptitiously looking at some "dirty" playing cards. In the break group composed mostly of Continentals, including several of the pinners, jokes and stories that were not of a sexual nature were often told. When I worked at the warehouse, pinning outfits together, one morning I worked next to several Continental young women who entertained themselves by telling a number of jokes, some sexual and some merely poking fun at situations.

Josie, the Polish-American woman who sat behind me sewing elastic waist bands in the next department, had a joking relationship with two of the younger workers in my department. She often called Danielle "the brat" or yelled over, "Here comes Miss America," when one of them returned from the ladies' room. She also established a joking relationship with me, kidding me for not coming in early to take overtime and saying that I was too lazy.

Joking and clowning were the order of the day on the Friday before the two-week July shut down. Josie was one of the ring leaders. Early in the morning she dangled a rubber spider down my neck. Later she pulled out her metal whistle (which she had had for sixteen years) and engaged in a whistling match with one of the mechanics, who returned her whistles by blowing through one of the thread tubes. Just before the afternoon break, lots of giggling and laughing could be heard across the floor above the noise of the machines. A couple of the Portuguese sewers from the other end of the room were racing back and forth, followed by a heavy-set young Italian woman with a skimpy silk bra tied across her blouse and a pair of silk panties decorated with cherries pulled over her trousers. She had a red ropelike object over her shoulder, which was described to me as "a man's thing," which bobbed up and down as she ran through the rows of machines. Everyone in my department was soon standing on chairs craning their necks to see what was happening. Two of the male managers sauntered down the middle aisle to look. One of them disappeared, only to return with his camera. The Italian woman posed for two or three pictures, which he jokingly threatened to put on his bulletin board.

The general mood during the afternoon break was one of giggling and laughter. Some workers started to leave early around 3:00 P.M., and others quit work and began to clean up their machines and prepare to leave. At 3:50 P.M. (ten minutes before the usual quitting time) the head of the plant announced over the loud speaker as he faced the whole floor, "Let's all go home." This precipitated a rush toward the time clocks so that everyone could punch out. Such joking and "high jinks," which took place before vacations, united women of different age and ethnic groups. Portuguese as well as the non-Portuguese participated in the general atmosphere of play, appropriate to a pre-vacation mood.

The union also helped in some ways to create situations where both Portuguese and non-Portuguese could participate in nonwork activities. The union organized a "Twenty Club" in which each participant contributed one dollar a week for twenty weeks. During each week there was a drawing and the winner received fifty dollars. At the end of the period, just before Christmas, the rest of the money was used for a dinner and dance, with additional drawings of cash prizes. Although organized mainly by non-Portuguese "old girls" who were the most active in the union, the dinner-dance was attended by a number of the Portuguese women and their husbands.

Other events that drew workers from different ethnic backgrounds together were more serious. For example, when Lucille's sister died, we all heard immediately, having already guessed that something was wrong when she failed to show up for work one Tuesday morning. A sheet was circulated for each to sign and put down a contribution (usually twenty-five or fifty cents) for flowers. The following Monday, as Lucille came around to each person delivering their repairs, she thanked each one, greeting many with a kiss, even those who did not speak English well. Such departmentwide expressions of support brought workers of different ethnic backgrounds together.

Celebrating special events and sharing family pictures "humanized" the workplace, bringing family life into the industrial setting. Almost all of the collections were for life-cycle events (weddings, baby showers, retirements, and deaths), some of them specifically celebrating women-centered events (such as a marriage or a birth). In bringing family life into the workplace, women workers made connections with each other, making strangers into acquaintances and, within the circle of one's break group, making acquaintances into friends. In a work setting where the piece-rate system drove workers apart and where ethnic divisions were clear, with interethnic tensions just beneath the surface during everyday work, these events might be termed part of a strategy of worker consolidation.

Socializing the Worker through Informal Work Rules

Another set of strategies that united women involved the informal work rules devised to ensure that the work was divided evenly. These rules arose from the clear understanding that the piece-rate system divided workers and could be used by individuals to "make money" unfairly, that is, at the expense of others. A worker's various tricks for getting more garments completed during the day were seen as "cheating," especially if they had negative consequences for other workers. Forms of cheating included sewing only the small sizes in a lot and leaving the larger sizes for other workers or reporting a fake number of dozens on the work card handed in at the end of the day.

Two informal rules in our department were that only half of the workers on one operation should work on one of the two colors in the lot and that each lot should be completed before starting the next one. These rules may have originally been imposed by the floor lady, since both were relevant to having work flow through the department in an orderly fashion. However, both rules also helped workers share the work evenly. For example, if three of the workers in the sleeves line worked on one of the colors and only one on the second color, in order to finish a lot composed of dresses in two colors, someone would have to change her thread and help work on the second color. This is a time-consuming process that could lower that person's number of dozens completed during a day.

A third rule among those of us who were setting sleeves was that everyone should "work by sizes." Two days after I was on the shop floor, Rose, who had worked for the company for twenty years, told me how to work with different sizes to share the work more evenly. She said, "Well, you do a bundle of size 4 (the smallest size) and then an 8 (the largest size on T-shirts) and then a 5 and a 6 and kind of let

[319]

the 7's go in between. Otherwise a girl might get a whole chute of 6- and 7-sized bundles, and it would take her longer. This way, then, each does her fair share." During my first months at work, the older workers often split up a lot for the whole sleeves line, filling a chute near our machines with the appropriate mix of bundles.

By the end of the summer, however, two of these workers had retired and a third had been moved to another job. Three or four new workers had appeared in the line, leaving only one Portuguese woman and myself with a knowledge of the rule system. A running struggle developed over a two-week period in August shortly after a new Portuguese woman entered our department. Frieda and Vivian, both older women who were new to sewing, had been fighting about the size problem before the new trainee entered the scene. Vivian complained that she always did the larger sizes, which explained her low production (sometimes only twenty-five dozen a day). Frieda accused Vivian of doing all the size 4's in the lot. Other workers suggested that Frieda complain to the floor lady or ask the floor lady to give out the work. An older Polish woman tried to mediate, counseling Vivian to take some of each size and to have the floor lady give her the work. I explained the rules to Amelia, the trainee, as soon as she sat down at her machine, as did one of the older workers who spoke both Portuguese and English. Even the trainee instructor came in to make sure that Amelia understood the rules. Things went fine for several days, until one afternoon when Vivian started sewing sleeves on a lot of pink dresses Amelia had begun sewing earlier in the day. After rifling through the chutes of remaining dresses, Vivian accused Amelia of taking all the bundles of size 4's. Then Clara, the label sewer, checked with the floor lady to make sure there were only four bundles of size 4 in the lot and maintained that she had seen Amelia doing all four bundles of size 4's. By afternoon break, it was clear that she had indeed done all the size 4 bundles, but in the end she admitted only to doing two of them. Finally, I sorted out the remaining bundles so that Amelia would have more 6's and Vivian more 5's, trying to make up for the earlier inequity. Several more instances of Amelia's "mistakes" were subsequently brought to the attention of her Portuguese-speaking instructor, the floor lady, and other workers. She then began to be more careful about the size bundles she took, stacking her garments after completing the sleeves, and not mixing garments from several bundles into the same stack.

A few days later, when another Portuguese worker returned from vacation, the issue of "working by sizes" was still in everyone's minds. When she began to pull a chute of dresses to her machine without first looking to see if she had taken a disproportionate number of size 4 bundles, she was told by two other Portuguese workers to "work by sizes." Insisting that in the department where she had previously worked they had just taken the work "as it came," she nevertheless began to sort her bundles like the rest of us.

This series of incidents shows how women worked to socialize new workers to an informal set of rules that would distribute the work fairly and thus alleviate some of the divisive competition that can develop under the piece-rate system. Both Portuguese and non-Portuguese workers enforced these rules, the Portuguese speakers explaining to those who spoke little or no English. Some women acted as mediators between disputing workers. At other times, management (the floor lady, the instructor, or the trainee supervisor) was called in to repeat the rules or to work out an equitable solution. The rules were important in socializing Portuguese workers, many of whom came from rural small-holder backgrounds and who were used to working long hours. In the factory context, the piece-rate system induced them to act on their rural values and push themselves as hard as possible to "make money." The socializing pressures of other workers, those who were more aware that the system could be used by management to lower the rates, began to bring the new worker's behavior into line with others.

A final set of workers' strategies, which I call "outguessing the conglomerate," can be identified in attempts to understand and unite against changes in management policy.

Outguessing the Conglomerate

During breaks and lunch women often talked about recent management policy in the workplace. Since the apparel industry is seasonal, layoffs were frequent after work for one season ended and before orders for the next season arrived. Thus worry over the periods between style seasons prompted intense discussion about what management might do. Our plant had been bought in 1974 by a conglomerate, which by 1977 had changed much of the top and middle management. Workers were concerned about the policies these new men would adopt.

As the end of the spring style season approached in early March, rumors flew through the plant. Several women had been laid off. Others had been sent to the warehouse to help with pinning, boxing, and filling the remaining spring orders. A woman who had worked for the company for seventeen years said, "There have never been layoffs like this before. It's this new company."

Some workers thought that there was a chance the plant would close. Angela maintained that they had been working several months without a contract, with only a temporary extension. She suspected that something funny was going on. "You know, they could just close up this place and move South." Even Christina, the instructor, thought they might close the plant and use it for offices. "They are sending all the good work down South and leaving all the junk for up here." Other older workers also speculated about a shutdown. Angela said that wages down South were very cheap, about $1.60 or $1.70 an hour. Nancy, who did quality control for several departments, thought there was trouble coming. She was not in favor of a strike and said, "We'll have to fight for things. . . . We need them more than they need us," was her comment on a possible plant closing.

Both workers and lower level management thought that the new management was handling production poorly. My floor lady blamed the sudden lack of work in early March on the engineers. "They aren't coordinated and don't seem to know what they are doing." I overheard her and the floor lady of the next department characterize a recent meeting with the "higher-ups" as "another bunch of bullshit." One older worker thought management had planned badly. "They took so many girls on. They know how many lots they need to make each season. They could plan better, instead of taking lots of people on and then laying them off."

Such gossip and rumor trading was not just a matter of "bad-mouthing" the management. It served as part of a strategy for trying to outguess the management and to figure out what was going on in the absence of information management preferred to withhold. The outguessing-the-management strategy operated to socialize new workers to a sense that things were different and that they should be critical of management policies; to prepare them for layoffs or shifts to new jobs by speculating about what was likely to happen so that individuals could better manage their work and family lives; and by spreading the word from one part of the shop to another, to make workers who experienced management policy in isolated ways understand that their situation was part of a larger pattern.

Such outguessing had the effect of raising workers' consciousness and helping to formulate work-related issues for the union. When the union did not react, such consciousness helped workers push the union to be responsive. Several warehouse women raised issues pertaining to the company's hiring and transfer policies in the warehouse at the union meeting in September 1977. The company had been hiring temporary workers through agencies (paying the agency $4.50 an hour), which reduced the possibility that sewers or those working part time on the second shift could transfer to the $4.25-an-hour "order-picking" jobs at the warehouse. At the same time, hiring temporaries kept a segment of the labor force out of the union. The business agent maintained that such a practice was against the contract, especially if there were permanent company employees who wanted work, and he promised to look into the issue.

I do not know how this issue was resolved, but two years later a wildcat strike erupted, just three days before the vote on the contract. At least ninety local issues remained unsettled including a number of grievances concerning piece rates. Workers from the knitting mill and warehouse apparently spearheaded the strike. A number of sewers who called in sick the first day participated in a picket line for the next two days and even defied a back-to-work court injunction on the last day of the wildcat. Although it was accepted on a national level, workers voted down the national contract by an overwhelming 834 to 118 votes. The vote indicated both the severity of management tactics to squeeze wages and the workers' feeling that the union was ineffective in fighting these new policies. As one worker said, "The union won't fight for us. The union's the company" (*Providence Journal*, September 5, 1979:C14).

In the years between 1979 and 1985, the union (with a new business agent and new officers) has dealt more successfully with workers' grievances, while the company has continued to attack and attempt to cripple the union. In March 1985 union members held an informational picket outside the sewing plant, protesting the company's unwillingness to pay wage increases due a number of workers and to meet with the union on several unresolved issues. Some sewers had waited months for retroactive pay that had been agreed to by the company. In the 1980s apparel corporations were feeling competition

[323]

from imports. The conglomerate was earning large profits in other sectors of its operations, and it maintained a hard line against the unionized plants in Rhode Island.

Conclusions

I have emphasized that women are active strategists at work. Their attitudes are conditioned in the workplace itself. They struggle day to day against a pay system that divides workers from one another by pushing them to make money individualistically and against management policy that over the long run operates to keep wages low. I have emphasized worker strategies that are aimed at socializing other workers, making them skeptical of management ideology concerning the benefits of the piece-rate system, and making them aware that management may work to cut pay, eliminate jobs, keep workers out of the union, or lay them off.

Women workers in Central Falls come from a variety of generational, marital, and ethnic backgrounds and include both the native born and recent immigrants from the Azores, Continental Portugal, and Colombia. In the plant in which I worked the piece-rate system exacerbated and sharpened these points of division, often playing on prejudices against recent immigrants who did not speak English. Other women we interviewed who worked in small family-run textile, jewelry, and light industrial plants experienced the same kinds of prejudice. In the apparel plant, celebrations of life-cycle events and the "familizing" of the workplace operated to bridge ethnic differences, as did the socialization of workers in an informal set of work rules. Similar mechanisms are no doubt at work in other workplaces in Central Falls.

The effectiveness of the wildcat strike in all departments of the plant in 1979 and worker protest in 1985 illustrate the themes I have developed in this chapter. Neither the piece-rate system nor ethnic divisions stifled worker protest. Production-related strategies such as the informal work rules softened the competitive effects of working on piece rates, and the nonproduction strategies, nourished by women's collective celebration of life-cycle events, blunted ethnic hostility. These strategies indicate that women, including recent Portuguese immigrants, are not passive acceptors of management tactics but engage in a day-to-day struggle to maintain and even improve their economic situation against very impressive odds.

Daily resistance strategies and informal ties among workers may be fragile and elusive. Many forces tend to push women workers apart, and some workers certainly become socialized to management's view. There are always occasions when ethnic conflict comes to the fore, breaking apart ties of solidarity between members of different ethnic groups. Whether or not informal resistance strategies can be transformed into more formal means of resistance, such as a successful union drive or a strong contract, depends on many factors beyond workers' direct control. These factors include antiunion campaigns by management, the long-term evolution of an industry, and the changing local and national economy.

Immigrant daughters, especially newly arrived Portuguese and Polish women, participated in Central Falls strikes in 1922, 1931, and 1934. They participated even though union leadership, for the most part, was male, and men were more active in strike-related action. There have been strikes in Central Falls and in Rhode Island in the recent past, but they have been less massive than those of the 1920s and 1930s. This seems less a result of the more conservative nature of women immigrant workers than of the larger political and economic context. Unions in apparel and textiles have been weakened by the movement of the industry to the southern United States and abroad, and jewelry shops have remained very difficult to organize. Companies have become more sophisticated and subtle in antiunion tactics, and the National Labor Relations Board (NLRB) has become more promanagement.

It is appropriate, therefore, to focus on the informal strategies that women use in dealing with management policy. The daily struggle between management's efforts to gain the allegiance of workers and workers' strategies of resistance suggests that such informal strategies in the past were similar to those of the present. This focus on shop-floor resistance also highlights the continuing potential of women workers to bring future change in America's workplaces.

[8]

Production, Reproduction, Ethnicity, and Strategies of Resistance: Conclusions

During the past eighty years the female paid labor force has been transformed from one of working daughters to one in which working mothers are now common. To analyze this transformation in Central Falls, I have developed a framework that focuses on production and reproduction and, within that framework, on a comparison of strategies across ethnic groups. Such an analysis helps us to make connections between work and family—spheres often treated as separate but in the lives of women workers usually interrelated. In this treatment, the creation of ethnic groups and the experiences of women within them are products of the interplay between a developing productive system and individual family strategies. Women are not passive acceptors of their situations, but they and other family members forge strategies that both cope with and resist aspects of industrial life. To illuminate this complex mix of strategies across ethnic groups and through time, I have adopted a methodology that involved a team project and that combined history and contemporary ethnography. There are continuities in the lives of working women during the last eighty years, but the changes in the productive system that have shaped the Central Falls economy have led me, in the end, to stress transformation, particularly in the organization of reproductive activities and the structure of the family.

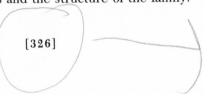

[326]

Methodology

Urban anthropology of the 1970s and 1980s is becoming more of a team effort when funds are available to finance large research projects. There are good reasons for this, especially in the urban United States. Since many topics involve studying individuals of different genders, ethnic backgrounds, or classes, it is helpful to involve researchers who match, as closely as possible, the gender, language, and cultural background of those being studied. In the case of our project, the initial aim had been to focus on Portuguese working families in contrast to an unspecified "non-Portuguese" set. As the project developed, it came to "fit" the ethnic diversity of Central Falls. I found it important to recruit researchers who could speak Portuguese and Spanish, as well as those who could work with the Polish and French-Canadian populations. The skills of Aida Redondo and Ricardo Anzaldua (who interviewed Colombian couples) and of Rebecca Matthews, Carlos Pato, Filomena Silva, and John Sousa (who interviewed Portuguese couples) were essential in providing rich interview material and a sense of how to interpret it. Ewa Hauser's command of the Polish language as well as her grasp of Polish history and the creation of an American Polonia provided insight into the Central Falls Polish community that I would have never been able to provide myself. Although Deborah Rubin was not of French-Canadian background, her reading and speaking knowledge of French, as well as her interest in the culture, were important in the success of her research in the French-Canadian population, certainly the most Americanized of those we studied. With such a diversity of ethnic backgrounds, it was impossible for one researcher to command the necessary languages, making a team effort all the more necessary.

The skills of the social historians who worked with census data, government documents, and trade journals were also essential, partially because I had very little experience in dealing with such materials in previous research. Finally, working with a team of researchers made it possible for me to take a full-time job in a factory and gain insights into the informal relations at work, which are nearly impossible to understand with other methods.

Anthropologists are much more interested in historical research in the 1980s. This interest ranges from archival studies to historical demographic research to combining history and ethnography in the way

I have done in this book. This trend has been pioneered by anthropologists conducting research in Europe (Brettell 1986; Harding 1984; Wolf 1969, 1982; Schneider and Schneider 1976; Silverman 1975) and is also represented in the research on American immigrants by Micaela di Leonardo's book in this series (di Leonardo 1984).

The new interest in history means that anthropologists have used census records, newspaper accounts, archival materials, and oral histories or interviews with historical depth to undertake an analysis that bridges both the past and the present. This is substantially different from writing an obligatory chapter on the history of a community, which provides a backdrop for what is otherwise a contemporary account.

By using census data and archival sources to examine the lives of immigrants, my research converges with that in books like *Lives of Their Own* (Bodnar, Simon, and Weber 1982), which compares the experiences of Blacks, Italians, and Poles in Pittsburgh between 1900 and 1960. Rather than taking the position that immigration and urbanization destroyed immigrant families or that preimmigration patterns persisted unchanged, these authors viewed the urbanization of working-class families "within an interactional framework in which traditional cultures and structural realities confront each other to produce distinct patterns of adjustment" (Bodnar, Simon, and Weber 1982:6). They, too, speak of strategies and family networks and examine the impact of the local economy on varying family patterns.

But anthropologists use historical material differently than do historians. Historical analysis is much more embedded in narrative, even for those social historians whose books are dotted with charts and tables. The aim seems to be to weave a complex story, leaving theory more implicit in the data and the narrative itself. Anthropologists, in contrast, are interested in taking theoretical concepts (whether they be derived from structural-functionalism, culture theory, or Marxism) that they have developed among contemporary peoples and employing them to interpret the past. Anthropological analysis is always implicitly comparative, with a problem orientation and an attempt to make a set of theoretical points that can be used by others conducting similar research, whether it is contemporary or historical. Thus historians may find my analysis of production and reproduction too disembodied from the actual tables and oral-history data I have used. Or they may be less interested in the kinds of generalizations one might derive from using an approach that emphasizes the intersection of the economy with the family developmental cycle and strategies for the allocation of productive and reproductive labor.

For me, the real strength of combining historical data with intensive interviews and participant-observation is the way that both kinds of data can illuminate each other and help us to understand better social change and transformation. Contemporary material can lay bare the importance of cultural conceptions as well as social arrangements (how labor is allocated, the ways in which kin networks are used) in a more textured way than is possible using census data and oral histories. On the other hand, historical data show us that the present cultural notions and social arrangements are not "frozen in time."

It is important, however, not to project present-day analysis into the past in some straightforward manner. In other words, the strategies of resistance that I isolated in a contemporary apparel plant may lead us to look for similar strategies during the 1920s and 1930s, but it would be inappropriate to suggest that these *particular* strategies were used—showers, retirement parties, the showing of pictures to build bonds across ethnic boundaries, or the use of informal work rules and careful accounting in notebooks to deal with piece-rate jobs. Continuity occurs at a more abstract level, whereas the particulars of work and family relationships are much more varied during any particular period and are more susceptible to change. We can see this clearly in the history of the workplace and production in Central Falls.

Production and Reproduction in the Workplace

At a very general level, women's industrial work in Central Falls has changed little. Mrs. Szymanski described her experiences as a weaver in 1916 as follows: "The noise was such that I cannot describe it for you. You couldn't imagine it, if you don't go to hear it." This could well depict work in a weave room in a modern textile plant. Conversely, the comments of Aida Rodríquez, a twister in a contemporary Central Falls spinning mill, might well describe an early twentieth-century workplace. "In that factory one works like a mule. . . . Every day when I leave work I am so dirty that not even the flies get near me. . . . One cannot stop the machine for a minute because they said one is not going to give good production."

Although the technology has changed, textile work still takes place under difficult conditions in which women are on their feet during

[329]

long days. Women are still employed in semiskilled low-paying jobs in textile firms and also in jewelry, apparel, and toy plants. There is still a hierarchical division of labor. Men command the higher paid jobs, whereas women are hired in the middle-range and lower paid positions. Management and workers remain in structurally different positions, with owners continuing to extract surplus labor from the work force. Workers still forge a number of strategies to deal with management tactics. Ethnic divisions persist in the workplace, although members of older ethnic populations blend together and constitute one block, and the Colombians and Portuguese are the newcomers. Ethnic boundaries still must be overcome if women workers are to unite against management.

These similarities gloss over the important changes in the organization of production and the reproduction of social relations in the workplace. In 1915 the Central Falls textile industry was at its peak. Large family-run firms dominated the economy, and the majority of families in Central Falls were connected with the textile industry or the related machine industry. The hierarchical division of labor within the mills divided workers by gender and ethnicity in a more complex way than at present. Men from older immigrant groups (English, Irish, and French-Canadian) dominated the better jobs, while women of all ethnic backgrounds were in middle-range semiskilled jobs. Young boys from older ethnic groups, as well as men and women from the newer groups (Poles, Italians, and Syrians), were in the lowest positions. Ethnic differentiation in the mills was mirrored in the clustering of ethnic groups in distinct neighborhoods and the establishment of ethnic institutions to help immigrants cope with industrial life.

Through the wage and skill hierarchy, owners were able to create and reproduce social relations of production that divided workers by gender and ethnicity. They were also able to keep wages low, maintain their profits, and extract surplus labor from workers. Workers, both men and women, reacted to particularly harsh policies in an attempt to gain greater control over wages and working conditions. Publicly recorded strategies of resistance included sporadic strikes and walkouts until the industry began to decline in the 1920s and 1930s. Employers met the textile depression with a number of tactics such as cutting wages and lengthening hours, organizing associations, and using scientific management to "speed up" and "stretch out" work. The massive strikes of 1922, 1931, and 1934 in Central Falls and Pawtucket were worker responses to these tactics for extracting additional labor from workers. Since the textile industry was the dominant employer in both Central Falls and Pawtucket and since the continuous decline of the industry had such a devastating impact on workers' jobs, it is not surprising that extensive strike activity should have characterized this period, especially when textile unions were active in organizing worker discontent.

Women's participation in these strikes and their public strategies of resistance (leading mass picket lines, organizing workers, or becoming involved in acts of violence against strikebreakers or firms) varied. It was shaped by the male-dominated nature of the unions, particularly the United Textile Workers of America (UTW). However, both the 1922 general textile strike and the 1931 silk strike were notable for the participation of women from new immigrant groups—Portuguese working daughters in the 1922 strike and Polish working daughters in the 1931 strike. Strikes also brought about cooperation across ethnic lines, although we do not know exactly how informal relations within the particular mills may have nurtured and built the basis for such cooperation. These public forms of resistance show, however, that employers were not always able to reproduce a divided work force and that women were able to bridge ethnic divisions in some instances.

By 1977 the Central Falls economy had been transformed. Industrial production was no longer centered in large textile companies but in small family-run firms engaged in variety of activities, from the production of narrow fabrics and synthetic cloth to jewelry, jewelry boxes, apparel, toys, and wire and cable. In an era dominated by multinational corporations and the transfer of much apparel, textile, and light manufacturing to the southern United States or abroad, these firms face an unstable future. Apparel and jewelry are inherently seasonal industries as well. Thus workers often face layoffs and plant closings; they also face an antiunion environment. Although there were layoffs and plant closings in the 1920s and 1930s and there have been strikes in the 1970s, they have taken place in a much more fragmented local economy in which unions are less visible. When unions are active, management countertactics are better organized and more effective, as, for example, in two efforts to organize jewelry firms in Providence in the 1970s (Shapiro-Perl 1983).

Using my own experiences in an apparel plant in 1977, it has been easiest to isolate informal strategies of resistance, those that take place daily on the shop floor. There the interplay of management tactics and worker counterstrategies have become apparent *within* the workplace, rather than in the more public forms of protest represented in the strikes of the 1920s and 1930s. Some shop-floor strategies are coping strategies. Keeping track of one's productivity as well as work rules that divide the work evenly help workers deal with the piece-rate system in which management error could reduce a paycheck or where worker competition could result in higher wages for only a few. Others are more clearly strategies of resistance. Letting slightly imperfect work "go through" undermines the piece-rate system as do practices that keep fellow workers from "busting the rate." Socializing new workers to a nonmanagement point of view creates a work culture, an autonomous sphere, that makes divisions between workers and owners clear. In addition, strategies that I have labeled "bringing the family to work" build ties between Portuguese and non-Portuguese workers.

In the Central Falls workplaces of the 1970s, ethnic differences between English-speaking groups (Irish, French-Canadians, Poles) remained, but they were not as great as in 1915. The major division was between new-immigrant Portuguese women and second- and third-generation women from the older immigrant groups. Thus interethnic communication may have been easier, involving only two languages (or three where Colombian women also work) rather than many. The building of interethnic ties and a unified work culture was still necessary, however, if workers were to unify against management's tactics for undercutting the union.

Although informal resistance strategies on the shop floor were undoubtedly present between 1915 and 1935, the more public forms of protest in the form of strikes and walkouts then are more muted in the present fragmented, declining economy. Nationally, unions are on the defensive, and organizing in an era of shutdowns and runaway shops is difficult. Nevertheless, data from both periods (the 1920s and 1930s and the 1970s) indicate that women workers have acted to retain an autonomous work culture and have not automatically acquiesced in reproducing the social relations of production in the model held out by management.

Production and Reproduction in the Family

Although both continuities and change are apparent in the workplace, the changes in production that have brought married women

[332]

into wage labor in increasing numbers have had a more substantial impact on the family, the unit that, under capitalism, must reproduce the labor force.

The immigrant family in Central Falls has been the site of the reproduction of the labor force in three ways. Purchased commodities are transformed into consumable items—a cooked meal, a new dress; living quarters, household items, and personal apparel must be cleaned, washed, and repaired; a new generation must be raised and cared for. Strategies for allocating labor for these tasks are intertwined with decisions about productive labor as well. Strategies concerning who will hold wage jobs, do housework, and perform child-care tasks lay at the interface between the productive system and reproduction. Family strategies that involve immigration and the incorporation of agrarian households into a capitalist economy are also decisions by various family members or even whole households to better their lives. These strategies characterized the immigration of early groups of immigrants such as the Irish, French-Canadians, Poles, and Portuguese but also are important for recent Portuguese and Colombians. Thus there are strong parallels between the experience of Central Falls immigrants in the past and in the present.

Other strategies have been drastically altered, however. Between 1900 and 1920 daughters and young female boarders universally worked in Central Falls and Pawtucket mills. The strategies that wives and mothers used to bring cash into the household varied with the stage of the household in the developmental cycle, the position of husbands and sons in the labor force, and the availability of boarders or kin who might become part of a household. Thus a few French-Canadian and English wives used their reproductive labor to support boarders, and a few Irish wives supported kin in return for cash. Most wives in these groups did housework and raised children, counting on the wages of husbands and later sons and daughters for support. Polish wives, in contrast, either continued to work for wages while they were boarding or took in boarders themselves. None of these strategies affected the gender division of labor within the household or women's primary involvement in reproductive labor.

As the capitalist economy has continued to pull in ever larger numbers of female workers, women have remained in the paid labor force for a larger proportion of their lives. Working-class daughters now remain in school past the age of fourteen, but most begin wage work at sixteen or after high school. Young married women continue to work for wages, but mothers, especially immigrant mothers, also work when their children are young. The allocation of productive labor to wives as well as to husbands has had the important effect of drawing husbands into reproductive work, even though Portuguese and Colombian wives still experience a "double day" and remain responsible for a major share of housework and child care. Although workers still maintain a family ideology that husbands are the heads of households and primary breadwinners, the behavior of husbands has changed from what it was before immigration. Some Portuguese husbands take their children to school after arriving home from a third-shift job; some Colombian husbands look after their children after school or help with the vacuuming. Couples from both groups report a range of positions on financial decisions—from Portuguese husbands who handle the money themselves to couples who jointly allocate their paychecks or jointly purchase large items.

It is perhaps unreasonable to expect that these couples, whose family ideology was shaped in a very different culture and whose marriages were already solidified by the time they immigrated to the United States, would change more than they have. The more interesting question is whether their sons and daughters and other young couples in their early twenties will go even further in sharing decision making, housework, and child care.

Ethnicity

The analysis of production and reproduction through time and the comparison of strategies used by women and their families in different ethnic groups both lead to a reconsideration of the notions of ethnicity and ethnic group. There is a trend within the study of ethnicity to see the process of ethnic group organization and identity as a historical one (Gordon 1964; Cohen 1969): the notion that "ethnic groups are made not born" (Schiller 1978). The data in this book certainly support this approach but more clearly tie the creation of ethnic neighborhoods, ethnic institutions, and variations in family strategies to the growth and change of a local economy.

The development of the textile industry with its increasing need for labor and the accompanying urban expansion of Central Falls between 1870 and 1915, pulled in successive waves of immigrants and set the stage for the creation of ethnic neighborhoods. By 1915 there were a number of distinct ethnic neighborhoods. Household patterns and family strategies contrasted between older groups who had arrived between 1840 to 1890 (the Irish, English, Scottish, and French-Canadians) and the recent immigrant groups who came between 1890 to 1915 (Portuguese and Poles). By 1935 there were still distinct neighborhoods and ethnic parishes, but household patterns and family strategies for dealing with the Depression were much more similar among both "older" and "newer" groups. Polish families now had teenage children, and boarding had declined in all neighborhoods. There were fewer ways in which wives and mothers could use their reproductive labor to bring cash into the household. The strategy of sending sons and daughters into the labor force was no longer viable and had been replaced by a more general strategy: all members of the household sought employment, including wives and mothers.

The United States immigration policy shut off immigration between 1924 and 1965 and shaped the flow of new immigrants after 1965 to encourage immigration of skilled workers and to reunite families. Hence Portuguese and Colombian families came to New England in the late 1960s and 1970s under a different set of circumstances. The older ethnic neighborhoods in Central Falls were filled with aging Poles, French-Canadians, and Irish; many of their children and grandchildren had moved to nearby working-class suburbs, and those who remained were English speaking and Americanized. Portuguese and Colombian immigrants were less concentrated in distinct neighborhoods, since they were renting the apartments and three-decker houses vacated by other ethnics throughout the city. Colombian and Portuguese household form and family strategies were similar since the timing of immigration was at the same early stage of the developmental cycle, and since men's low wages encouraged both the husband and wife to pursue the strategy of wage employment.

I am not arguing that ethnic groups are ephemeral but rather that they are created as members of a population, who share a common cultural heritage, confront industrial life, develop institutions that will help them cope with it, and work to create an ethnic identity that preserves aspects of their culture. The interview data from contemporary Portuguese and Colombian families showed how husbands and wives have reallocated their productive and reproductive labor, changing their behavior substantially from preimmigration patterns, but have maintained cultural notions about the husband's role as head of the family, the importance of a child's respect for parents, and sex-

[335]

role differences. Furthermore, there was considerable variation, even within the small samples of fifteen families, in the ways in which husbands and wives handled finances, child care, and housework and in the importance and cohesiveness of kin networks.

Kin networks, I have argued, are particularly sensitive to the process of migration. Colombian migrants, the first in their families to arrive in the United States, had very few kin and relied on employers, friends, and neighbors for jobs, housing, and child care. In contrast, Portuguese families came to New England with the help of kin and were, in the late 1970s, finding their kin networks pulled apart by a declining economy that created conflict over resources and forced some family members to take jobs in towns and cities far from relatives. This analysis helps us to see that ethnicity is not an unchanging essence but economically and socially structured. Thus ethnic or cultural values are not seen as determinative but as part of the ways in which immigrants interpret their world as they try out new behavioral strategies or retain older patterns. Far from being unimportant, ethnicity is a dynamic phenomenon.

Strategies of Resistance and Coping: Forms of Consent

The study of social movements by anthropologists and historians has focused primarily on large-scale social conflict including peasant wars (Friedrich 1970; Wolf 1969), social banditry (Hobsbawm 1959), and rituals of rebellion within African states (Gluckman 1955, 1963). Labor historians and economists have written primarily about union organizing or strike activity (Brecher 1972; Pope 1942; Brooks 1937; Zaretz 1934). The emphasis has been on the social forces that have generated conflict and the patterns of leadership that have emerged. Scholars have distinguished between reformist and revolutionary movements, on the one hand, and between rebellions and revolutions, on the other hand. As Eric Hobsbawm said, "Reformists accept the general framework of an institution or social arrangement, but consider it capable of improvement or, where abuses have crept in, reform; revolutionaries insist that it must be fundamentally transformed, or replaced" (Hobsbawm 1959:11). Likewise, conflicts of succession that arose in nineteenth-century African states sought not to overturn the system but to support one kin group's claim on political power over that of another (Gluckman 1963:35–39). Such conflicts were rebellions that were part of a political process that expresses the cleavages inherent in the political order and thus are to be distinguished from revolutionary movements that seek to overturn a system. With regard to labor movements, the effort is often to evaluate the outcome of a strike or the tactics of an organizing drive in order to understand the weakness of a particular strategy or explain why permanent trade unions were so difficult to organize in the United States.

Such distinctions are not very helpful when it comes to the study of women and work under industrial and monopoly capitalism, partially because most labor organizing and much strike activity has involved men and partially because much female resistance is not visible in overt reform movements, rebellions, or revolutions. There have been excellent recent studies of strikes and organizing efforts dominated by women such as accounts of the Lowell "turnouts" in the 1830s (Foner 1977; Eisler 1977), the Shirtwaist strike in New York in 1910 (Tax 1980), and the Farah apparel strike in the 1970s (Coyle, Hershatter, and Honig 1980). There are also general histories or collections of papers on women in the United States labor movement (Milkman 1985; Foner 1979; Wertheimer 1977). However, to explore the lives of the majority of working women and the events that have shaped their experience, many researchers in the 1970s have been led to the shop floor and to the concrete everyday lives of working women.

The twin notions of "women's work culture" and "resistance" have been key concepts in analyzing the realities observed in the workplace. Here scholars have been influenced by the work of Edward Thompson (1963) and Herbert Gutman (1976), who have analyzed the role of culture as it has mediated social class and as it has emerged from concrete work experiences. Since Thompson's and Gutman's work focused exclusively on men, feminist social historians, anthropologists, and sociologists have had to extend such analysis to a full-scale examination of gender as it operates in the workplace. This has also led to a concern with the connections between the family and the shop floor, a topic that cannot be ignored when considering women.

It is the everyday interaction with a specific labor process and with particular management policies that provides the experiences out of which an autonomous women's work culture and specific strategies of resistance emerge. It would be naive, however, to think that all women's activity on the shop floor can be described in terms of resistance strategies. I have mentioned coping strategies at work; when discuss-

[337]

ing family strategies of immigration or for the allocation of productive and reproductive labor, I have thought of these strategies as ways of coping or adjusting to local economies. In addition, some resistance strategies are individual ones that lead to isolated challenges to authority or that siphon off potential leadership. For example, "quitting," a strategy jewelry workers used when they were asked to clean their benches without additional pay, was an act of defiance but resulted in the most vocal workers leaving the workplace (Shapiro-Perl 1983).

Some activity at work and at home is best seen as consent—acquiesence to a husband's authority or to management policy either because it seems "right" or because there seems to be no alternative. Thus jewelry workers did not protest an employer's rearrangement of the work benches since it was "his" factory (Shapiro-Perl 1983). Maquiladora apparel workers in Cuidad Juarez complied with the sexual demands of male workers and supervisors because they believed to do otherwise would mean they would lose their jobs (Fernández-Kelly 1983:241). Several Colombian women we interviewed complained about their husbands' lack of help with the housework but believed they could not change a man's behavior.

Whether the particular combination of resistance, coping, or consent that takes place every day in a workplace becomes part of a larger, more public protest depends on a host of factors. Among them are the organization of a particular industry and the state of unionization efforts within that industry. Government policies in turn affect the pace of unionization, the use of force to control workers, and the adjudication of conflicting interests. A particularly harsh management tactic or the buildup of a number of tactics may bring about a union drive or trigger a walkout or strike. In the 1930s the larger political-economic climate, including significant legal changes (the Wagner Act and the National Recovery Act), meant that the labor movement could successfully organize more workers than in previous decades, despite forceful opposition from management. In the 1980s, in contrast, runaway shops and the shifting of employment to nonunionized clerical and service sectors have depleted the ranks of organized labor. Conservative government policies have eroded unions' abilities to win elections. Management has employed a whole new battery of strategies to undercut union drives, including the hiring of antiunion consulting firms and the firing of union activists (Freeman and Medoff 1984:231–36). Large nultinational corporations also have more resources than did more localized firms in the 1930s; they can more quickly move production in response to militant activity.

In this climate strikes are less likely, except as defensive efforts to keep firms from eroding union rights or closing production facilities. In the absence of large-scale labor-movement activity that might be characterized as reformist or even revolutionary, it seems all the more important to focus on shop-floor work cultures and the everyday tactics and strategies workers use to counteract management tactics. Certainly, this is where women's efforts are made. If we are to make women a visible part of labor history and contemporary politics, more attention needs to be given to resistance in its strategically important, if everyday, sense.

Implications for the Future

This book is part of an increasing effort to treat women's experience in terms of particular historical and economic contexts and to consider seriously the impact of race and ethnicity, class, and gender as they shape women's lives. In the 1980s we have come to realize and to document that the experiences of American women are not all the same. We are just beginning to conceptualize these differences and build a theory that incorporates race, class, and gender into a changing political economy. Two recent collections—*My Troubles Are Going to Have Trouble with Me*, edited by Karen Sacks and Dorothy Remy (1984), and *Women and the Politics of Empowerment: Perspectives from the Workplace and the Community*, edited by Ann Bookman and Sandra Morgen (1987)—make a good beginning. Both examine the connections between women in the family and the workplace or community. They document the varied experiences of white ethnic, Hispanic, and Black women in a variety of struggles in factories, offices, schools, clinics, and hospitals. They point to some efforts that have been effective and others that have resulted in the loss of a union drive, a cutback in services, or "burnout" on the part of activists.

In the 1980s working-class women have faced unemployment, cutbacks in federal and state funds, and a conservative political climate. We need a theory of women's work and family lives that can take account of this political and economic situation as well as those of the past. Furthermore, we need to explore more thoroughly regional differences in work and family lives. A great deal of research has been done in New England and the mid-Atlantic states, but there are now increasing numbers of studies of women, work, and family in the West, South, and Midwest. Still, we have not yet explored these differences in a comparative way, contrasting women in declining sectors in the "rustbelt" with those in the growing "sunbelt." We can see that women's lives are changing as they spend more and more years in the paid labor force. The changes in the productive system that have created this new situation have had important effects on the family as women gain new leverage on family decisions and as husbands participate more in child care and housework. In the years ahead we need to continue to document these changes and to be sensitive to the diversity they represent. The experiences of immigrant women in Central Falls represent one set of variations within a larger picture. Black, Mexican-American, Asian, Native American, and Anglo working-class women present other modes of coping and of resistance. Single parents contrast sharply with married mothers, and differences in regional political economies shape all women's work and family lives. We are beginning to see how gender intersects with class and ethnic background, but we need a better account of their interrelationships if we are to understand the changing character of working-class women's experience in all of its complexity.

Appendix A

Women's Work in the Cotton Industry

It is essential in a study of wage-earning women to understand the complexities of the work they actually did and the skills that their jobs entailed. This appendix summarizes the production process in Central Falls cotton mills; appendix B discusses the work involved in silk-cloth production. It not only draws attention to the existence of various jobs for wage-earning daughters, but demonstrates the variation in pay and conditions throughout the job hierarchy. Reconstruction of work processes and the social relations of production in 1915 is a difficult task, since it must be based on scattered and incomplete sources. However, data from the 1915 pay books of the Lorraine Company, located in Pawtucket and part of the prominent Sayles family holdings, provided material on the ethnic and gender composition of various job categories and average weekly pay. Oral-history interviews, including those collected by Ewa Hauser and those available at the University of Rhode Island, give descriptions of women's work in their own words.

Preparation of the Cotton: Picking, Carding, and Drawing

Men tended to dominate in the first steps of the process of cotton-cloth production. Many of the jobs were heavy and low paid. Young, unmarried women did tend carding machines or drawing frames as well as some of the combing machines, although men had these jobs as well. The combing and carding room at the Lorraine Mill, which employed eighty workers in 1915, provides an example of how women and men of different ethnic backgrounds were distributed among different types of jobs.[1]

Five Italian men (probably all recent immigrants) were "pickers" who broke open the cotton bales and loaded them into a "bale breaker," which broke open the cotton and separated some of the impurities. They also watched the cotton as it traveled to a "breaker lapper," which further cleaned the cotton and converted it into a "lap," or continuous sheet of fiber rolled on an iron rod. These men earned between eight and twelve dollars a week in 1915, a year when the average male wage was sixteen dollars a week in Rhode Island. In other mills this job would have been performed by Poles, Portuguese, or other recent immigrants as well as by Italians.

Next, the lap was put through a carding machine, which brushed and straightened the fibers. The carded cotton, which came out of the machine in a flimsy veil, was channeled through a hole to form it into a continuous strand called a "sliver" (pronounced "sly-ver"). In the Lorraine Mill, seven men and one woman tended the carding machines and earned between ten and seventeen dollars a week, more than pickers but less than the better male jobs of weaving and loomfixing. Carders were usually new immigrants, more often men than women. For instance in the Polish neighborhood sample described in chapter 3, twenty-three men and eleven women worked as carders, and six men and one woman worked as pickers.

An Irish woman, Katherine O'Brien, described her first job as a carder in a thread mill in 1909:

> First time I worked, I worked on carding machines; that was when the cotton comes through. . . . It rolls through and comes out like a web and you twist it around and put it . . . well, it goes in a big can. Then you move it to a drawing doubler. Every time you move it, you keep adding it; it's coming out like a stream and you keep adding it in, and next when you put it in, it comes out . . . put it in that and it comes out a little

---

1. In 1915 the Lorraine Mill employed 1,709 workers, including 704 men (41 percent) and 875 women (51 percent) (Rhode Island, Factory Inspectors, 1916). The mill produced both cotton and worsted cloth. Data on pay have not been systematically analyzed but are used only as illustrative material.

thinner, and maybe quite a few ends go in and it comes out a little stronger.[2]

Katherine was also describing the next step in the process, called "drawing," where the sliver was drawn out more uniformly and became thinner on a machine called a "drawing frame." In the Lorraine Mill, both men and women were employed to tend these machines. The four men earned between $8.00 and $10.72 a week, and the four women earned $6.50 a week.[3] This group was ethnically mixed, with several Italians as well as workers with Irish and English surnames.

Next, in many mills the cotton was put through a combing process to give it more evenness, lustre, and strength. First, sixteen to twenty-four of the slivers were "doubled" so that the fibers were combed into a narrow lap. These small laps were drawn out on a "ribbon lap machine" to become more finely prepared lap. In the Lorraine Mill, men with Polish, Italian, and Portuguese surnames tended these machines and earned between nine and eleven dollars a week. The final step was the combing itself, whereby machines combed and straightened the ribbon lap with needles and produced a finer sliver. In the Lorraine Mill the four men tending the combing machines were Italian and Portuguese and earned between ten and eleven dollars a week; the four women (with Irish and English surnames) earned nine to ten dollars a week. Three men with English and Irish surnames tended a separate set of combing machines and made between fourteen and twenty-two dollars a week.

Finally, before the cotton sliver could be spun it had to be reduced to a finer cord called "roving." A number of machines were used in this process, including slubbers, intermediate roving machines, and fine roving or "jack frames" often called "speeders." Workers who tended these jack frames are called "speeder tenders." In the Lorraine Mill, three men (one Polish, one English, and one with an unidentifiable surname) operated the slubbers and earned $10.00 to $11.00 a week; four men and seven women operated the intermediate

2. The quotation from Katherine O'Brien (a pseudonym) and from the cloth inspector were taken from interviews conducted between 1973 and 1975, which are from the University of Rhode Island Oral History Project. Other quotations, those from Polish women, are from interviews conducted by Ewa Hauser in 1977 and 1978.

3. The Rhode Island wages for female drawers in 1915 were between $7.35 and $8.60, while male combers earned between $8.79 and $15.50 and male carders between $10.86 and $11.00 a week (Rhode Island 1916:19).

roving frames and earned between $9.00 and $14.50 a week. (The range of female and male wages seemed very similar for this job, which was held by English and Portuguese men and by women with predominately English surnames.) Operating the fine speeders seemed to be entirely a woman's job, filled by English, Irish, and French-Canadian women, earning between $8.00 and $11.80 a week.

In other mills Polish and Portuguese women were speeder tenders. Mrs. Nicynski, a Polish immigrant, started work around 1910 at age twelve, making three dollars a week as a speeder tender:

> I had two machines to tend. On these machines there was roving. In a cotton factory, there are first the cards [carding machines]. From the thick thread [sliver] that comes from the carding machines we had to take it and put it on a frame. I worked on these frames. There on this machine . . . on the back there were four rows and four hundred bobbins of roving. There were one hundred bobbins in each row. They [the machines] were spinning and we were making thread for cotton fabrics. In our factory we didn't do it [make cloth]. In other factories they made fabrics. My job was called a "speeder tender."

Throughout the carding and combing department in the Lorraine Mill a number of the unskilled jobs (such as lap carriers, can boy, oiler, scrubber, and sweeper) were held by males (probably young boys) with Italian, Polish, Portuguese, and occasional Irish or English surnames. These jobs paid the least in the department, between $5.00 and $8.25. With the exception of the supervisors (the overseers and two second hands who were Irish or English males), recent immigrant men (probably both older married men and young boys) worked with young unmarried women of the more established immigrant groups (English, Irish, and French-Canadians). Young unmarried Portuguese, Italian, or Polish youths had the lowest-paying unskilled jobs, and men from the same ethnic groups were the pickers and carders and also tended some of the ribbon lap machines, the combing machines, the slubbers, and the intermediate roving frames.

Young Irish, English, and French-Canadian women were tending the intermediate roving frames, speeders, drawing frames, and combing machines. Although jobs like can boy, sweeper, picker, and carder were probably always male jobs, we could be observing an example of the use of male immigrant labor, instead of female labor, to tend roving and combing machines. The machine-tending wages are "intermediate" in the 1915 setting, indicating that recent immigrant men were willing to work for "female wages." However, in most cases men were earning more than women in the same jobs, although some women may have been earning more than individual men tending a particular kind of machine.

The Spinning Department

From roving the cotton is spun into thread that can be used for either the weft or the woof of the cloth. There are two types of spinning techniques: mule spinning and ring spinning. Mule spinning was most common in the early nineteenth century and was a male occupation. As the American-invented ring-spinning frames were perfected, they gradually came to replace mule spinning except in the woolen and worsted industries. Mule spinners were well organized and managed to keep their privileged place in the labor force long after ring spinning began gaining ground. Ring-spinning frames were less difficult to tend and the job was less demanding then mule spinning. These factors led to the almost universal employment of young women as spinners and the payment of lower wages.

The principal duties of the female ring spinner were to repair the broken ends of the yarn that had snapped while the spindles were twisting the thread, to attach the yarn from a full bobbin that had been removed to a new empty one, and to keep the machine clean. She was assisted by a "doffer" (a young man or woman) who removed the full bobbins and replaced them with empty ones. Cleaners removed the lint that gathered under the machines. The conditions in spinning rooms included excessive heat, airborne cotton dust, oily floors, and a great deal of noise from the machines, from the system of pulleys and belts that operated them, and from the rattle of doffers' trucks.

The spinning room at the Lorraine Mill, in contrast to having the gender mix of the carding and combing department, was more clearly a female province. To be sure, the overseer and section hands were male, and the sweepers and doffers were usually young boys, but the spinners were predominately women, usually of English, Irish, and French background. In spinning room no. 1, for example, there were eleven male doffers and four male sweepers but twenty-nine spinners, twenty-five of whom were women. In spinning room no. 2, there were two teams of spinners, one with seventeen women and another with

[345]

seven women and ten men. Women earned $4.00 to $10.00 a week and men from $8.00 to $16.00 a week. Of the first group of all-female spinners, two had English surnames, with eight Italian, five Portuguese, and two French-Canadian surnames among the rest. In the mixed-sex group, five males had English surnames, and three had French-Canadian and two had Italian surnames. Among the women, three had an English, three a French-Canadian, and one an Italian surname. Another section of spinning room no. 2 contained the twisting machines that twisted two or three threads of spun yarn together. Several spools of thread were loaded onto a creel and twisted together as they passed through the machine. In 1915 there were six twister tenders, five female and one male, earning between $5.00 and $8.50 a week. During the year there was a good deal of labor turnover; for example, among the mixed-sex group of seventeen spinners in spinning room no. 2, by July 1915 five men and three women had left, and three men and five women had been hired. Furthermore, this second group of spinners entirely disappeared from the pay books in September and October, perhaps indicating that they had been laid off. A new group of spinners were hired in January. They included four Irish or English males, two English females, four French-Canadian women, three Italian women, two Portuguese men, and one male whose ethnicity could not be determined from his surname. These records indicate that although women dominated the spinning room, there were men hired as spinners, and that there could be considerable ethnic heterogeneity within a work group as well as labor turnover and job instability even in a period of relative good times for the textile industry as a whole.

Oral-history interviews from Central Falls indicate that young girls of English, French, and Polish background left school at fourteen and entered the mill. These interviews suggest that young daughters were able to move up from the lowest paid jobs of sweepers to increasing responsibility as spinners or "second girls" (i.e., machine helpers) over several years of mill work. For example, Mrs. Mankovich, who immigrated from Poland, started working in 1909 and earned as little as three dollars a week sweeping floors. Then she became a spinner and earned four to five dollars a week. Mrs. Fortier, a French-Canadian, also started out as a sweeper but worked in a thread mill. She progressed to a job as a "second girl" or machine helper and then tended twenty-five machines under the direction of a male overseer.

Preparing the Warp for the Loom

The "filling," or the threads that run across the cloth, had to be transferred from the large bobbins that came off the spinning machines to those that fit on to the shuttle of the loom. This process is called "quilling" and was also a job done by working daughters. In the Lorraine Mill, both men and women were hired to do quilling, a job divided into piece workers and hourly workers. The seven males on hourly rates (possibly young boys) made only between $4.50 and $7.50 a week, while the three males working on piece rates made between $9.00 and $15.00 a week. The eight women on piece rates earned between $10.00 and $14.78 a week. Here women made wages comparable to men, but without data on age and experience, it is impossible to tell whether the pay differentials meant that young unmarried daughters were consistently earning more than young men their age and less than older married men or whether experience, speed, and skill really determined how individuals fared in the mill structure.

After quilling the weft thread was ready for weaving. In contrast, there were several stages in preparing the warp, or lengthwise threads in a piece of cloth. The first step was winding, or placing the thread from the relatively small bobbins that came from the spinning and twisting machines onto much larger spools. Again, this job was assigned primarily to women who earned wages comparable to the quillers and spinners. In the Lorraine Mill, the twelve winders, all women, earned between six and thirteen dollars a week. Spooler tenders in the Lorraine Mill did a similar job, worked in a room with the warper tenders, and earned between three and ten dollars a week. This group of twenty-five women included nine English women, eight French-Canadians, four Italians, one Portuguese, and four women whose ethnicity could not be determined from their surnames.

Next, the large spools of warp thread were placed on a creel or frame, which usually held between five hundred and six hundred spools. The threads from the spools were taken separately and passed through a machine so that they were wound on a "warper's beam." The beam was a long, revolving cylinder; the threads lay side by side, and as the beam revolved, they were wound on the beam making a warp about twenty-five thousand yards long. The "warper-tender" or "beamer" was in charge of watching the process, repairing any breaks in the thread and assisting the "creel girl" in replenishing the thread supply. The heavy beams were usually loaded on and off the machine by men, but both men and women worked as beamers. In the Lorraine Mill in 1915, there were four male beamers earning between nine and twenty-one dollars a week on day rates and between fifteen and seventeen dollars a week on piece rates. There were also five women beamers on piece rate earning between nine and fourteen dollars. Seven women were listed in pay books as warper tenders earning between seven and eleven dollars a week, while four women worked as creelers and earned between three and eleven dollars a week. Here we see clear pay differentials between male and female, although women who were beamers may have been able to earn more than creelers and warper tenders whose wages approximated those of spinners, quillers, and winders.

Mrs. Wendoloski, a Polish woman described her job as a beamer: "And before I went weaving, I also worked in Jenckes, that was a cotton mill and we made warps and during the war—1916, 1917. . . . There were . . . these things that I was doing . . . putting cotton thread on a beam. . . . You know, it's a big beam like a spool. . . . I used to run four of them, and they used to use those threads to make tires see? And I worked there for a few years."

From the beamer, the warp-yarn was then taken to the "slashing" department where it was unwound, rolled through a hot-starch mixture, and rewound on another beam. Slashers were primarily men since the work was heavy, hot, and difficult. However, the final process in the preparation of the warp—drawing-in—is one in which female labor was almost exclusively employed.

Drawing-in, which may be done in the warping room or at one end of the weave room, involved separating the ends of the warp and drawing them through the "harness": a long narrow frame with many wires, each having a loop or needle's eye in the middle. All threads to be raised are threaded through the needles on one frame, while the threads to be lowered are passed through another set of loops on a second frame. The lowering and raising of the frames forms the necessary "shed" through which the shuttle is passed. The threads were drawn through the loops by inserting a hook through the eye, catching the thread and pulling it through. Drawing-in was one of the most highly skilled jobs that women held in the mills. Women at the Lorraine Mill made between five and thirteen dollars a week. Often young women worked in pairs, one separating out five or six of the next loops and the other drawing the thread through. Mrs. Wendoloski, who described her work as a beamer above, held her first job in 1916 drawing in in a weave shop when she was fourteen years old. "Have you any idea what a weave shop is like? You know the harness that goes up and down? So I was putting the headles on. And I made the sets for the girl that was drawing in. That was my first job."

Weaving

Technological innovations in the weave room, including the addition of stop mechanisms and automatic bobbin changers, deskilled weaving and at the same time made it possible for looms to be run at a faster pace and for workers to tend more looms. Thus the weave room was one area where men had replaced women to a substantial degree. By 1915 both men and women worked in weave sheds, often in equal numbers. For immigrant men (French-Canadians, Poles, Italians, and Syrians), weaving was one of the highest-paid jobs in the mill since it paid better than work on the picking, carding, or roving machines for which men earned ten to eleven dollars a week. In Central Falls in 1915, the silk industry was beginning to expand. Since silk weaving entailed many more warp threads per inch, the number of looms that a weaver could tend was very small (two to four looms). The weave-room labor force was relatively large and provided work for many Polish men and women and Syrian men. Wages in the silk industry were probably lower than in cotton in 1915, but they rose considerably during World War I as did wages in cotton.

For a woman, once she was trained and had enough experience to do well on the piece-rate system, a job as a weaver was clearly better paid than one in twisting, spooling, winding, or even spinning, the other common jobs women held in the mills. In the Lorraine Mill in 1915, there were approximately seventy men and seventy-nine women in the weave room. Women earned an average of $9.00 to $10.00 a week but might earn as much as $17.50. Men earned $9.00 a week on the average and as much as $18.00 to $20.00 a week.

Conditions in a weave room, however, were far from ideal. As in other parts of the mill, there the humidity and temperature had to be kept high to keep the cotton threads from breaking. In addition, the noise of the machines was deafening and created loss of hearing among long-term employees. In large mills weave rooms were immense, with several hundred machines and more than one hundred fifty weavers. Besides the weavers, other workers in the room included the more highly paid male loomfixers, the lesser paid "smash hands," who repaired breaks in the thread; and the "battery hands," who kept the automatic looms filled with bobbins of thread for the weft.

Women often commented on the work conditions in the weave room. For example, Mrs. Szymanski, a Polish immigrant, said of her first job in a cotton mill:

> The noise was such that I cannot describe it for you. You couldn't imagine it if you don't go to hear it. It was such a crash that nobody can communicate with others, perhaps only to look and read lips or use sign language. . . . Those people who worked as weavers now often are deaf. This noise at the beginning, I heard all the time, day and night, even when I wasn't in the factory; it was always in my head. It took me a long time to get used to it. It was very unpleasant. I'll tell you what it meant to me personally. Perhaps a million times I wished this ship on which I came here had sunk before I got there. But to go back. . . . There wasn't any money. No one could save anything from four dollars a week.

Another Polish woman, born in the United States, began work in a textile mill in the 1930s. She expressed the same feelings: "I didn't work there long. You know, a weave shift is deafening for your ears, and it's really a hot place, and if you have ever been in one, you know clang, clank, and it's really hot. So I stayed there a short while."

Women also stated that it took at least a year to be able to learn weaving well enough to make good money. For example, Mrs. Sadowski commented, "I was on training for two weeks without any pay. And then I got two looms to tend. But to really learn cotton it takes . . . to be able to make some money, it takes at least a year, to get money like the others, it took me a year." Mrs. Okolowicz, another Polish woman, born in this country, learned silk weaving from her mother by working next to her for a year until she was good enough to tend a loom of her own. The fineness of the silk thread and the increased number of breaks in the thread along with the difficulty of tying them up made the training period for silk weavers longer.

Finishing

After the cloth was woven it was finished, often in a separate mill that specialized in bleaching, dyeing, or printing. In these mills, a male labor force predominated, partially because operating the bleaching and dyeing machines entailed heavy work in difficult conditions, and the process of engraving and printing cloth involved skilled labor accessible only to men. Women were employed as less-skilled, auxiliary workers in the printing process. For example, they were employed as pantograph operators working on a machine that transferred an image in reduced size to a copper printing plate. Also women were hired as cloth inspectors: "They had hooking machines and they put the cloth in on rolls and then they came over a rod and a woman looked at it, or a man sometimes, . . . and they put a piece of paper or an old strip of cloth or something in [marking an irregularity]. So the next man who picked it up was a folder, and he looked [at] wherever these markers were, and then he cut out the bad parts and then he folded it and yarded it."

Afterward the cloth was labeled with the correct yardage and wrapped in paper. Sometimes women, as well as men, did the folding, wrapping, and labeling. Most workers in the cloth room (inspectors, trimmers, and folders, both male and female) earned between seven and nine dollars a week in 1915 (Rhode Island 1916:19).

Appendix B

Women's Work in the Silk Industry

Whereas in the nineteenth and early twentieth centuries Central Falls daughters were predominantly employed in the cotton industry, by the 1920s and 1930s many were working in the silk mills that had moved into Central Falls and Pawtucket as the cotton industry declined.

Large numbers of women were employed in four processes: skein winding, quilling, warping, and weaving. In the first process, skeins of silk that had already been "thrown," or spun silk, were placed on a light skeleton reel called a "swift" and wound off onto bobbins. For example, Rose Noel, a French-Canadian resident of Central Falls, left school at fourteen and worked in Hamlet Textiles between 1920 and 1922 as a skein winder. She worked with eight or nine young women, all between the ages of sixteen and eighteen. "But skein winding them days, was to me . . . I always liked it. We used to have what they called raw silk, and it'd be like strawy, you know and you'd have to wind that, put it on a big skein: 'swifts' we used to call them. And you'd put the skein on it and from there of course it would wind onto spools. Then it would go to either the . . . as I said . . . the beamers, and so forth."[1]

---

1. This and the next quotation were taken from interviews conducted in 1973 and 1975, which are from the University of Rhode Island Oral History Project.

Some women wound the filling or tram onto quills to be used for weft, and others worked at winding the warp threads on large reels or warpers and then in a reverse operation onto the loom beam. The warp was wound onto the huge reel in sections to prevent the many threads from tangling or breaking. To keep the threads separate, the silk filaments passed through a comblike contrivance (U.S. International Trade Commission 1926:74). As former weaver Lucille Paquin explained the process:

> Well, then the warper tenders had great big stands [creels] with all these spools on them and they all came together in a small reed which is metal with holes in it you know, to pull the silk through. And then it would go on a great big wheel to make the warp, see. Well, in the weaving, you got your warp and it came through the harnesses and you'd have as much as twenty-five harnesses on some of them—satins, satin-backed cotton— and they'd be about twenty-five harnesses. All that yarn would come through and then through another reed and then that weaves back and forth and just shuttles the other way and makes the cloth. You'd have stripes and everything else.

Mrs. Okolowicz, who worked at the large Royal Weaving Mill, which employed many Polish women, described how she learned weaving:

> Ya, I liked it. You've got to learn . . . how to weave. . . . It took a year before you got a loom. . . . I had to stand with my mother, like an apprentice for a long, long time. . . . My mother had four [looms] and when you begin, like when you're starting, they give you two, one— sometimes two. . . . They see how you're doing. . . . When I started to work there was a lot of strikes. There was a depression and they were going on strikes every once in a while and. . . . So that was say 1930 right? I got married in 1937—well I was working there . . . so I must have worked there like five years.[2]

Mrs. Wendoloski described a similar experience in which she was trained by another woman worker:

> It took a long time, it takes a long time to be able to make any money when you are weaving—a learner. They take you on. The girl had four looms and she has to stop the loom if something happens. You've got to

2. The remaining quotes in this appendix are taken from interviews with Polish women conducted by Ewa Hauser in 1977 and 1978.

stop it, if you do it wrong. She has to do it over and by the time you know what's going on, it's been a long time. And I had little problem because I understood the drawing-in and could handle the headles and the hook. So I didn't have so much trouble and . . . there was about a month with the lady that's teaching you, and then they gave you two looms. Somebody gets through something, and they have a couple of learners to split two and two—two for this learner and two for that. So you're weaving yourself—already on your own and for one month you'd work with someone and then you'd get two looms. You're not making any money, you know, very little because when you get a cut down, when you get to stop it, and get the thread through, you've got to weave its knots so it doesn't slip you know.

Silk weaving was difficult because there are hundreds of very fine threads in an inch of fabric. Mrs. Szymanski explained: "Then you had to loosen the warp and get all the threads straight, and I had to do it. A weaver had to do it and such that there wouldn't be any mark. That was the most difficult part of the work. And you had to watch so that there would be as few of these accidents as possible. When it happened, one had to go to the inspector, if we couldn't repair it. Oh, that was the worst part. When it happened to me, that's when I wished my ship had drowned on the way to this place."

Appendix C

Networks of Support
for New Immigrants

Table 20. Role of kin and friends in instrumental activities, Azorean and Continental families

Family	Source of visa	Initial housing	Husband's first job	Wife's first job	Child-care arrangements
Azorean families					
1. Almeida	Husband's parents	Friend of husband's mother	Foreman from hometown	Foreman from hometown	Older children
2. Carvalho	Husband arranged his own papers	Friends who lived 50 miles from Central Falls, then friends in Central Falls	Friends	Friends	Azorean neighbors downstairs
3. Estrella	Husband's parent	Husband's parents	No information	No information	Husband's mother
4. Ferreira	Husband's brother; wife and children came four years later	Husband's brother and wife's sister	Husband's sister	Friend	Not needed
5. Gomes	Wife's mother	Wife's mother	Wife's sister	Wife's sister-in-law (her brother's wife)	Wife's sister
6. Costa	Wife's brother	Wife's mother, in house owned by wife's brother	Through a friend	Wife's sister-in-law	Wife's mother
7. Dias	Husband's mother and older brother	Husband's brother and, later, husband's sister	Saw shop on Smith Street (sick and out of work three months)	Saw shop on Smith Street	Husband's sister; husband, older daughter

8. Pacheco	Wife's sister	Wife's second sister	Relative of wife's sister	Landlord (Portuguese)	Wife's cousin (also a *comadre*)
9. Lopes	Husband's brother	Husband's brother, 25 miles away	Husband's brother	Portuguese friend	Husband; later, day-care center
10. Nunes	Wife's father came on work contract; husband came through her resident status after they married	Wife's parents	Labor contract	Labor contract; second job through husband's sister	Wife's mother
11. Mello	Husband's parents	Husband's parents	No information	Husband's cousin	Husband's mother
Continental families					
12. Paiva	Wife's work contract	No information	Work contract	Through husband's sister	Different shifts: she worked third; he worked first
13. Mendes	Wife's sister	With wife's sister	Through friend	Went with sister's daughter to apply; later heard through sister that same factory was hiring	Different shifts: she worked second; he worked third; he cared for son after school
14. Santos	Work contract through husband's sister	Through son's baby-sitter	Work contract	Through Portuguese friend whose daughter worked at factory	Baby-sitter
15. Machado	Labor contract	Through husband's employer	Labor contract (in another town in Rhode Island)	Through husband; same factory	Baby-sitter

Table 21. Role of kin and friends in instrumental activities, Colombian families

Family	Source of visa	Initial housing	Husband's first job	Wife's first job	Child-care arrangements
1. Fernández	Friend from Colombia got him a job in New York; both came on tourist visas; another Colombian friend suggested that he come to Central Falls	Lived with friend who subsequently returned to Colombia	Through Colombian friend in New York City; job in Central Falls through friend who encouraged move to Rhode Island	Through husband's cousins in New York City; then in Central Falls through other Colombian friend	No children until they moved to Rhode Island; then he worked third; wife's friend baby-sat
2. Rodríguez	Work contract with Phoenix Textiles arranged through friend with whom he worked in Barranquilla; he came alone. She arrived seven months later	Lived with José Cruz, who was one of the first workers recruited; he met Cruz through the friend who arranged his visa	Work contract	Through husband	Baby born two years after their arrival; he worked first shift; she worked second; then used sister
3. Escobár	His sister's husband and Rodríguez helped with work contract; she arrived six months later	Husband lived with his sister	Heard about job through his sister	Through friend from Barranquilla (friend of his sister's husband)	Her sister (living in same house)
4. Balboa	Work contract with Phoenix Textiles; she came several years later; then older children came	Lived with José Cruz; then found house with friend	Work contract	Through friend	All older children

5. Cardoso	Husband arranged his own visa; wife came five years later	Immigrated to Connecticut	Job through Colombian friend	No information	Wife's aunt
6. Pino	Work contract with Carter Textiles arranged through owner and Mr. Vicente; wife came three years later	Apartment; arranged by owner and Colombian worker	Work contract	No information	Colombian friend; later the older children looked after the younger children (five–six years old); Different shifts: he worked second; she worked first
7. Valencia	No information; she came one year later	No information	No information	Through friends	Different shifts: he worked second; she worked first; later he worked first; she worked second; Colombian neighbor was baby-sitter
8. Penza	Brother in Central Falls	No information	No information	No information	Different shifts: she worked first; he worked second; then he worked third. Baby born in 1976; with second baby, she worked part time

Table 21.—cont.

Family	Source of visa	Initial housing	Husband's first job	Wife's first job	Child-care arrangements
9. García	Work contract with Liberty Silk arranged through Mr. Torres, who had worked for owner of Liberty Silk in Barranquilla; she came two months later	No information	Work contract	Through helping friend look for job	Her sister baby-sat while both worked first; after sister left, he worked second shift
10. Sánchez	Work contract with Liberty Silk arranged by younger brother	Apartment in house owned by younger brother	Work contract; then another job through younger brother	No information	Different shifts: he worked first; she worked second; baby-sitter hired for hours between; then sent three children to his mother in Colombia
11. Ramírez	Work contract with Carter Textiles; she immigrated one year later with work contract for same company; Mr. Vicente helped arrange contract	No information	Work contract	Work contract	Different shifts: he worked third; she worked second
12. Valdéz	Visit to friends in New York; came to Central	Through friend	Through friend's sister-in-law, who	Through husband	After older children arrived he worked

	Falls two years later to visit friends; wife came one and one half years later; older children came five years later		owned the firm		second or third shift; older children looked after baby born in 1973
13. Lucero	Work contract with Waldorf Mills; wife came one and one-half years later	Apartment with friends; then apartment through seeing sign in window	Work contract	Through friend	Different shifts: he worked second; she worked first; used day-care center for brief period
14. Olivera	Work contract with textile company in New Bedford; came to Central Falls after New Bedford mill closed	Through employer	Work contract; aided by friend who also helped him find job in Central Falls	No information	Different shifts: he worked third; she worked first
15. Martínez	Husband came to New York City on tourist visa; *compadre* signed affidavit of support; residents' visa two years later, after returning to Colombia; she came eight months later; moved to Rhode Island in 1974	Through friend in New York City; stayed with friends; found apartment through "for rent" sign after coming to Central Falls	Through friends; no information about job in Rhode Island	No information	Mother, who visits periodically on tourist visa

Appendix D

Child-Care Arrangements in New Immigrant Families

Table 22. Shift work and child-care arrangements, Azorean and Continental families

Family	Number of children	Age of youngest child	Father's shift	Mother's shift	Child-care arrangements
Azorean families					
1. Almeida	7	2	Third	Second	Different shifts: mother during day; father during evening
2. Carvalho	1	16	First	Second	Not needed
3. Estrella	3	2	Laid off	First	Husband's sister
4. Ferreira	5*	9	First	First	Twelve-year-old baby-sat nine-year-old sibling
5. Gomes	5**	7	First	First	Older children
6. Costa	5***	7	First and third (10:30 P.M. to 7:00 A.M.)	First	Older children
7. Dias	4	5	Third	First	Different shifts: father during day
8. Pacheco	3	7	Disability	First	Father disabled; father during day
9. Lopes	7****	7	Third (7:00 P.M. to 7:00 A.M.)	First	Different shifts: father during day

10. Nunes	1	First	7	Third	Different shifts: mother after school
11. Mello	2	Third (1:00 A.M. to 12:00 P.M.)	10	First	Different shifts: father after school
Continental families					
12. Paiva	3	First	4	First	Baby-sitter next door
13. Mendes	2	Third	9	Second	Different shifts: father after school
14. Santos	1	First (plus three–five hours of overtime)	7	First	Baby-sitter in same house; sister, when laid off
15. Machado	2	Second	6	First	Different shifts

Summary: n = 11: six parents work different shifts; four families depended on older children for child care and one on a relative.

*Both the twenty-three-year-old son and the eighteen-year-old daughter work.

**The twenty-seven-year-old daughter works; the twenty-three-year-old daughter also works but has moved out of the household; the mother quit her job between the first and second interview to have an eye operation.

***The sixteen-year-old son quit school to look for a job; the father is holding down two jobs to make ends meet—one on first shift and the other at night.

****Two married sons are still in the Azores; one married son is in the United States but no longer lives with the family; a fourth son, who is seventeen, is working and helping to support the household.

Table 23. Shift work and child-care arrangements, Colombian families

Family	Number of children	Age of youngest child	Father's shift	Mother's shift	Child-care arrangements
1. Fernández	1*	<2	Unemployed, then first	Second	Baby-sitter (wife's friend); at times, husband
2. Rodríguez	1	7	First	First	Wife's sister downstairs (before and after school)
3. Escobár	2	7	First	First	After school, neighbor looks after seven-year-old
4. Balboa	7	8	Second	Second	Older children (thirteen-year-old girl, sixteen- and nineteen-year-old boys)
5. Cardoso	5	<1	First	First	Wife's mother's sister
6. Pino	3	9	Second	Second	Colombian friend
7. Valencia	1	7	First	First	Neighbor of friend
8. Penza	1*	>1	Second, then third	First (8:00 A.M. to 2:00 P.M.; then 8:00 A.M. to 3:00 P.M.)	Different shifts: husband during day; wife during evening

9. García	2	5	Second	First	Different shifts: husband takes children to and picks them up from school; wife during evening; wife's sister baby-sat when both were on first shift
10. Sánchez	3	3	First (7:00 A.M. to 4:00 P.M. plus two hours overtime)	Third	Different shifts: wife during day
11. Ramírez	3	2	Third	First	Different shifts: husband during morning; older children during afternoon
12. Valdéz	6	3	Second	Second	Older children during afternoon and evening
13. Lucero	5	<1	Second	First	Different shifts: (wife laid off before baby born)
14. Olivera	3	4	Third	Second	Different shifts
15. Martínez	3	9	Second	First	Different shifts

Summary: n = 15; seven parents work different shifts; two depended on relatives for child care, two on older children, and four on a baby-sitter or a neighbor.

*Another child expected.

Bibliography

Abramson, Adolph G. 1936. "Forces Affecting the Geographical Distribution of the Cotton Textile Industry in the United States." M.A. thesis, Department of Economics, Brown University.

Aldous, Joan. 1982. *Two Paychecks: Life in Dual-Earner Families*. Beverly Hills, Calif.: Sage Publications.

Aronowitz, Stanley. 1974. *False Promises: The Shaping of American Working-Class Consciousness*. New York: McGraw-Hill.

Ashley, Jo Ann. 1976. *Hospitals, Paternalism, and the Role of the Nurse*. New York: Teachers College Press.

Barrett, Michele. 1980. *Women's Oppression Today: Problems in Marxist Feminist Analysis*. London: Verso Editions. New York: Schocken Books.

Barth, Fredrik. 1959. *Political Leadership among the Swat Pathans*. London: Athlone Press.

Baxandall, Rosalyn, Linda Gordon, and Susan Reverby. 1976. *America's Working Women*. New York: Random House; Vintage Books.

Benson, Susan Porter. 1986. *Counter Cultures: Saleswomen, Customers, and Managers in American Department Stores, 1890–1940*. Urbana: University of Illinois Press.

Berthoff, Rowland. 1953. *British Immigrants in Industrial America, 1790–1950*. Cambridge: Harvard University Press.

Bledsoe, Caroline. 1980. *Kpelle Women*. Stanford, Calif.: Stanford University Press.

Bodnar, John, Roger Simon, and Michael P. Weber. 1982. *Lives of Their Own: Blacks, Italians, and Poles in Pittsburgh, 1900–1960*. Urbana: University of Illinois Press.

Bonier, Marie Louise. 1920. *Debut de la colonie franco-americaine de Woonsocket, Rhode Island*. Framingham, Mass.: Lakeview Press.

[371]

Bookman, Ann. 1977. "The Process of Political Socialization among Women and Immigrant Workers: A Case Study of Unionization in the Electronics Industry." Ph.D. diss., Harvard University.

Bookman, Ann, and Sandra Morgen, eds. 1987. *Women and the Politics of Empowerment: Perspectives from the Workplace and the Community.* Philadelphia: Temple University Press.

Borker, Ruth. 1976. "Strategies of Activity and Passivity: Women in Evangelical Churches." Paper presented in symposium "Social Structure, Ideology, and Women's Choices." American Anthropological Association, Washington, D.C., November 20.

Braverman, Harry. 1974. *Labor and Monopoly Capital: The Degradation of Work in the Twentieth Century.* New York: Monthly Review Press.

Brecher, Jeremy. 1972. *Strike!* San Francisco: Straight Arrow Books.

Brettell, Caroline. 1982. *We Have Cried Many Tears.* Boston: Schenkman.

———. 1986. *Men Who Migrate, Women Who Wait: The Demographic History of a Portuguese Parish.* Princeton, N.J.: Princeton University Press.

Brooks, Robert R. R. 1937. *When Labor Organizes.* New Haven: Yale University Press.

Buhle, Paul. 1977. "The Knights of Labor in Rhode Island." *Radical History Review* 17:39–73.

Buhle, Paul, Scott Molloy, and Gail Sansbury. 1983. *A History of Rhode Island Working People.* Providence: Regine.

Burlak, Ann. 1976. Address to the Rhode Island Labor History Association. University of Rhode Island Special Collections.

Cantor, Milton, and Bruce Laurie. 1977. *Class, Sex, and the Woman Worker.* Westport, Conn.: Greenwood Press.

Chaney, Elsa. 1976a. "Colombian Migration to the United States (Part 2)." In *The Dynamics of International Migration.* Occasional Monograph no. 5. Vol. 2, pp. 87–141. Washington, D.C.: Smithsonian Institution, Interdisciplinary Communications Program.

———. 1976b. Unpublished article on Colombians.

Cohen, Abner. 1969. *Custom and Politics in Urban Africa: A Study of Hausa Migrants in Yoruba Towns.* Berkeley: University of California Press.

Collier, Jane. 1974. "Women in Politics." In *Woman, Culture, and Society,* edited by Michelle Z. Rosaldo and Louise Lamphere, pp. 89–96. Stanford, Calif.: Stanford University Press.

Community Focus. 1976. *Central Falls, Community Focus Report.* Providence: Committee for the Humanities.

Conley, Patrick T., and Matthew J. Smith, eds. 1976. *Catholicism in Rhode Island: The Formative Era.* Providence: The Diocese of Providence.

Cooper, Patricia. 1986. *Fire and Smoke: Men, Women, and Work Culture in American Cigar Factories.* Urbana: University of Illinois Press.

Copeland, Melvin Thomas. 1917. *The Cotton Manufacturing Industry of the U.S.* Reprint. Cambridge: Harvard University Press, 1923, 1966.

———. 1935. "Background and Future." In *Production and Distribution of Silk and Rayon Broadgoods,* prepared by Melvin T. Copeland and W. Homer Turner for the Textile Foundation and the National Federation of Textiles, Inc. New York: National Foundation of Textiles.

Cott, Nancy, and Elizabeth Pleck. 1979. *A Heritage of Her Own.* New York: Simon and Schuster.

Coyle, Laurie, Gail Hershatter, and Emily Honig. 1980. "Women at Farah: An Unfinished Story." In *Mexican Women in the United States: Struggles Past and Present,* edited by Magdalena Mora and Adelaida R. Del Castillo, pp. 117–44. Los Angeles: Chicano Studies Research Center Publications, University of California, Los Angeles.

Cruz, C. I., and J. Castaño. 1976. "Colombian Migration to the United States, (Part 1)." In *The Dynamics of International Migration.* Occasional Monograph no. 5. Vol. 2, pp. 41–86. Washington, D.C.: Smithsonian Institution, Interdisciplinary Communications Program.

di Leonardo, Micaela. 1984. *The Varieties of Ethnic Experience: Kinship, Class, and Gender among California Italian-Americans.* Ithaca, N.Y.: Cornell University Press.

Dublin, Thomas. 1979. *Women at Work: The Transformation of Work and Community in Lowell, Massachusetts, 1826–1860.* New York: Columbia University Press.

———. 1982. *Farm to Factory: Women's Letters, 1830–1860.* New York: Columbia University Press.

Ducharme, Jacques. 1943. *The Shadows of the Trees.* New York: Harper and Brothers.

Dufresne, Marcel. 1977. *Central Falls Oral History Project on French-Canadians.* Tapes available at the Central Falls Library, Central Falls, R.I.

Dunn, Robert W., and Jack Hardy. 1931. *Labor and Textiles.* New York: International Publishers.

Dunwell, Steve. 1978. *The Run of the Mill.* Boston: David R. Godine.

Edholm, Felicity, Olivia Harris, and Kate Young. 1977. "Conceptualising Women." *Critique of Anthropology* 9/10:101–31.

Eisler, Benitta. 1977. *The Lowell Offering: Writings by New England Mill Women (1840–1845).* Philadelphia: Lippincott.

Epstein, Cynthia. 1970. *Women's Place: Options and Limits in Professional Careers.* Berkeley: University of California Press.

Erickson, Charlotte. 1972. *Invisible Immigrants: The Adaptation of English and Scottish Immigrants in Nineteenth Century America.* Coral Gables, Fla.: University of Miami Press.

Ferguson, Robert H. 1940. "Textile Unions in Rhode Island." M.A. thesis, Department of Economics, Brown University.

Fernández-Kelly, María Patricia. 1983. *For We Are Sold, I and My People.* Albany: SUNY Press.

Ferst, Susan Terry. 1971. "The Immigration and the Settlement of the Portuguese in Providence, 1890–1924." M.A. thesis, Brown University.

Fogarty, Michael, A. J. Allen, Isobel Allen, and Patricia Walters. 1971. *Women in Top Jobs.* London: George Allen and Unwin.

Fogarty, Michael, Rhoda Rapoport, and Robert N. Rapoport. 1971. *Sex, Career, and Family.* London: George Allen and Unwin.

Foner, Phillip S. 1977. *The Factory Girls.* Urbana: University of Illinois Press.

———. 1979. *Women and the American Labor Movement.* New York: The Free Press.

Fortes, Meyer, ed. 1958. *The Developmental Cycle of Domestic Groups.* Cambridge Papers in Social Anthropology, no. 1. Cambridge: Cambridge University Press.

Fox, Paul. 1922. *The Poles in America*. New York: George H. Doran.

Freeman, Richard B., and James L. Medoff. 1984. *What Do Unions Do?* New York: Basic Books.

Friedrich, Paul. 1970. *Agrarian Revolt in a Mexican Village*. Englewood Cliffs, N.J.: Prentice-Hall.

Gans, Herbert. 1962. *The Urban Villagers*. New York: The Free Press.

Garraty, John Arthur. 1978. *Unemployment in History: Economic Thought and Public Policy*. New York: Harper and Row.

Garson, Barbara. 1972. *All the Livelong Day: The Meaning and Demeaning of Routine Work*. New York: Penguin Books.

Gerstle, Gary. 1978. "The Mobilization of the Working-Class Community: The Independent Textile Union in Woonsocket, 1931–1946." *Radical History Review* 17:161–73.

Glazer, Nathan, and Patrick Moynihan. 1963. *Beyond the Melting Pot: The Negroes, Puerto Ricans, Jews, Italians, and Irish of New York City*. Cambridge, Mass.: MIT Press.

Glenn, Evelyn Nakano, and Roslyn L. Feldberg. 1979. "Proletarianizing Clerical Work." In *Case Studies in the Labor Process*, edited by Andrew Zimbalist, pp. 51–72. New York: Monthly Review Press.

Gluckman, Max. 1955. *Custom and Conflict in Africa*. Oxford: Blackwell.

––––––. 1963. *Order and Rebellion in Tribal Africa*. London: Cohen and West.

Gordon, Milton. 1964. *Assimilation in American Life: The Role of Race, Religion, and National Origins*. New York: Oxford University Press.

Grieve, Robert. 1897. *An Illustrated History of Pawtucket, Central Falls, and Vicinity*. Pawtucket, R.I.: Pawtucket Gazette and Chronicle.

Groneman, Carol. 1978. "Working-Class Immigrant Women in Mid-Nineteenth-Century New York: The Irish Woman's Experience." *Journal of Urban History* 4, no. 3:255–73.

Gutman, Herbert G. 1976. *Work, Culture, and Society in Industrializing America: Essays in American Working-Class and Social History*. New York: Knopf.

Harding, Susan. 1984. *Remaking Ibieca: Rural Life in Aragon under Franco*. Chapel Hill: University of North Carolina Press.

Hareven, Tamara, and Randolph Langenbach. 1978. *Amoskeag*. New York: Pantheon Books.

Hartmann, Heidi. 1976. "Capitalism, Patriarchy, and Job Segregation by Sex." *Signs* 3, pt. 2:137–70.

Hauser, Ewa Krystyna. 1981. "Ethnicity and Class Consciousness in a Polish American Community." Ph.D. diss., The Johns Hopkins University.

Hedges, James Blaine. 1968. *The Browns of Providence Plantations*. Vol. 2. Providence: Brown University Press.

Hobsbawm, Eric J. 1959. *Primitive Rebels: Studies in Archaic Forms of Social Movement in the Nineteenth and Twentieth Centuries*. New York: W. W. Norton.

Hodgins, Lois A. 1958. "Labor Mobility and Adjustment in a Wire Cable Company." Honors thesis, Sociology, Brown University.

Hoffman, Charles, and Tess Hoffman. 1983. "Black Bridget Strikes." In *A History of Rhode Island Working People*, edited by Paul Buhle, Scott Molloy, and Gail Sansbury. Providence: Regine.

Holy Trinity Parish. 1972. *Golden Jubilee Book, Holy Trinity Parish*. Central Falls, R.I.

Hutchins, Grace. 1919. *Labor and Silk*. New York: International Publishers.

Jaffee, Susan. 1974. "Ethnic Working Class Protest: The Textile Strike of 1922 in Rhode Island." Honors thesis, Brown University.

Kanter, Rosabeth Moss. 1977. *Men and Women of the Corporation*. New York: Basic Books.

Kayal, Philip M., and Joseph M. Kayal. 1975. *The Syrian-Lebanese in America: A Study in Religion and Assimilation*. Boston: Twayne.

Kennedy, Pamela. 1978. *Central Falls, Rhode Island*. Providence: Rhode Island Historical Preservation Commission.

Kennedy, Stephen Jay. 1936. *Profits and Losses in Textiles: Cotton Textile Financing since the War*. New York: Harper and Brothers.

Kertzer, David. 1977. "Historical Demography and Household Structure: Toward a Better Analytical Framework." Paper presented to the American Anthropological Association, Houston, December 1.

Kessler-Harris, Alice. 1980. *Women Have Always Worked*. Old Westbury, N.Y.: The Feminist Press.

———. 1982. *Out to Work: A History of Wage-Earning Women in the United States*. New York: Oxford University Press.

Kieniewicz, Stefan. 1969. *The Emancipation of the Polish Peasantry*. Chicago: University of Chicago Press.

Kim, Sookon, Roger D. Roderick, and John R. Shea. 1972. *Dual Careers: A Longitudinal Study of Labor Market Experience of Women*. Columbus: Ohio State University, Center for Human Resource Research.

Komarovsky, Mirra. 1964. *Blue-Collar Marriage*. New York: Random House; Vintage Books.

Kubat, Daniel, ed., with Ursula Merlander and Ernst Gehmacher. 1979. *The Politics of Migration Policies: The First World in the 1970s*. New York: Center for Migration Studies.

Kubiak, Hieronim. 1970. *Polski Narodowy Katolicki w Stancach Ziednoczonych Ameryki w latach, 1897–1965. Jego spolecsne uwarunkowanie i spoleczne funckcje*. Wroclow: Zaklad Narodowy im. Ossolinskich.

Kulik, Gary. 1978. "Pawtucket Village and the Strike of 1824: The Origins of Class Conflict in Rhode Island." *Radical History Review* 17 (Spring 1978): 5–37.

———. 1980. "The Beginnings of the Industrial Revolution in America: Pawtucket, Rhode Island, 1672–1829." Ph.D. diss., Brown University.

———. 1983. "Rhode Island's First Strike: The Pawtucket Turnout of 1824." In *A History of Rhode Island Working People*, edited by Paul Buhle, Scott Molloy, and Gail Sansbury. Providence: Regine.

Kulik, Gary, and Julia C. Bonham. 1979. *Rhode Island: An Inventory of Historic Engineering and Industrial Sites*. Washington, D.C.: Smithsonian Institution.

Lahne, Phillip. 1944. *The Cotton Mill Worker*. New York: Farrar and Rinehart.

Lamphere, Louise. 1977. *To Run after Them: The Cultural and Social Bases of Cooperation in a Navajo Community*. Tucson: University of Arizona Press.

———. 1979. "Fighting the Piece-Rate System: New Dimensions of an Old

Struggle in the Apparel Industry." In *Case Studies in the Labor Process*, edited by Andrew Zimbalist, pp. 257–76. New York: Monthly Review Press.

———. 1984. "On the Shop Floor: Multi-Ethnic Unity against the Conglomerate." In *My Troubles Are Going to Have Trouble with Me: Everyday Trials and Triumphs of Women Workers*, edited by Karen Brodkin Sacks and Dorothy Remy, pp. 247–63. Brunswick, N.J.: Rutgers University Press.

———. 1985. "Bringing the Family to Work: Women's Culture on the Shop Floor." *Feminist Studies* 11, no. 3:519–40.

———. 1986a. "From Working Daughters to Working Mothers: Production and Reproduction in an Industrial Community." *American Ethnologist* 13, no. 1:118–30.

———. 1986b. "Working Mothers and Family Strategies: Portuguese and Colombian Immigrant Women in a New England Community." In *International Migration: The Female Experience*, edited by Rita J. Simon and Caroline Brettel, pp. 266–83. Totowa, N.J.: Rowman and Allanheld.

Lamphere, Louise, with Filomena M. Silva and John P. Sousa. 1980a. "Kin Networks and Strategies of Working-Class Portuguese Families in a New England Town." In *The Versatility of Kinship*, edited by Linda Cordell and Stephen Beckerman, pp. 219–49. New York: Academic Press.

Lamphere, Louise, with Ewa Hauser, Dee Rubin, Sonya Michel, and Christina Simmons. 1980b. "The Economic Struggle of Female Factory Workers: A Comparison of French, Polish, and Portuguese Immigrants." In *Conference on the Educational and Occupational Needs of White Ethnic Women*, pp. 129–52. National Institute of Education. Washington, D.C.: U.S. Government Printing Office.

Langer, Elinor. 1972. "Inside the New York Telephone Company." In *Women at Work*, edited by William O'Neill, pp. 307–60. Chicago: Quadrangle Paperbacks.

Lawrence, Henry W. 1931. "Historical Sketch of Woonsocket, R.I." In *An Ethnic Survey of Woonsocket, R.I.*, edited by Bessie Wessel. Chicago: University of Chicago Press.

Leach, Edmund. 1954. *Political Systems of Highland Burma*. Reprint. Boston: Beacon Press, 1964.

Lees, Lynn H., and John Modell. 1977. "The Irish Countryman Urbanized: A Comparative Perspective on the Famine Migration." *Urban History* 3, no. 4:391–409.

Lewin, Ellen, and Carol Browner. 1982. "Female Masochism Reconsidered: The Virgin Mary as Economic Woman." *American Ethnologist* 9, no. 1:61–75.

Lopata, Helena Znaniecki. 1976. *Polish Americans: Status Competition in an Ethnic Community*. Englewood Cliffs, N.J.: Prentice-Hall.

Lopate, Carole. 1968. *Women in Medicine*. Baltimore: Johns Hopkins University Press.

McLaughlin, William. 1978. *Rhode Island: A Bicentennial History*. New York: W. W. Norton.

Mattfeld, Jacquelyn A., and Carol G. Van Aken, eds. 1965. *Women and the Scientific Professions*. Cambridge, Mass.: MIT Press.

Meintel, Deirdre. 1984. *Race, Culture, and Portuguese Colonialism in Cabo*

Verde. Foreign and Comparative Studies/African Series, no. 41. Syracuse, N.Y.: Syracuse University.

Melosh, Barbara. 1982. *The Physician's Hand: Work Culture and Conflict in American Nursing*. Philadelphia: Temple University Press.

Milkman, Ruth, ed. 1985. *Women, Work, and Protest: A Century of U.S. Women's Labor History*. Boston: Routledge, Kegan and Paul.

Miner, Horace. 1939. *St. Denis: A French Canadian Parish*. Chicago: University of Chicago Press.

Murchison, Claudius T. 1930a. *King Cotton Is Sick*. Chapel Hill: University of North Carolina Press.

———. 1930b. "Management Problems in the Cotton-Textile Industry." In *Management Problems with Special Reference to the Textile Industry*, edited by (?) Swenning. Chapel Hill: University of North Carolina Press.

Nardella, Luigi. 1978. Interview. *Radical History Review* 17:153–60.

Nash, June, and María Patricia Fernández-Kelly. 1983. *Women, Men, and the International Division of Labor*. Albany: SUNY Press.

Nord, Elizabeth. 1976. Interview by Ruth Milkman and Christina Simmons. University of Rhode Island Special Collections.

Notre Dame Church. 1974. *Centennial Yearbook, Notre Dame Parish*, Central Falls, R.I. Hackensack, N.J.: Custombook, Inc.

O'Laughlin, Bridget. 1974. "Mediation of a Contradiction: Why Mbum Women Don't Eat Chicken." In *Woman, Culture, and Society*, edited by Michelle Z. Rosaldo and Louise Lamphere, pp. 301–20. Stanford, Calif.: Stanford University Press.

———. 1975. "Marxist Approaches in Anthropology." In *Annual Review of Anthropology* 4:341–70. Palo Alto, Calif.: Annual Reviews.

Peiss, Kathy Lee. 1985. *Cheap Amusements: Working Women and Leisure in Turn-of-the Century New York*. Philadelphia: Temple University.Press.

Phillips, Ann. 1977. "The Immigrant Woman." Oral Histories of Rhode Island Immigrant Women. *Mirror* 3, no. 1. Providence: University of Rhode Island Extension Division.

Pope, Liston. 1942. *Millhands and Preachers: A Study of Gastonia*. New Haven: Yale University Press.

Pulaski Society. 1954. *Jubiliee Book*. Central Falls, R.I.

Radical History Review. 1978. *Labor and Community Militance in Rhode Island*, no. 17. Special issue.

Rainwater, Lee, Richard P. Coleman, and Gerald Handel. 1959. *Working Man's Wife*. New York: Oceana Publications.

Rake, Julie. 1976. "Active and Passive Female Strategies in a Catholic Prayer Group." Paper presented at symposium "Social Structure, Ideology, and Women's Choices." American Anthropological Association, Washington, D.C., November 20.

Rapoport, Robert, and Rhona Rapoport. 1971. *Dual-Career Families*. London: Penguin.

Rapoport, Robert, and Rhona Rapoport, with Janice M. Bumstead. 1978. *Working Couples*. New York: Harper and Row; London: Routledge and Kegan Paul.

Remy, Dorothy, and Larry Sawers. 1984. "Economic Stagnation and Discrimination." In *My Troubles Are Going to Have Trouble with Me: Everyday Trials and Triumphs of Women Workers*, edited by Karen Brodkin

Sacks and Dorothy Remy, pp. 95–112. New Brunswick, N.J.: Rutgers University Press.

Rhode Island. 1902. *Fifteenth Annual Report of the Commissioner of Industrial Statistics: Strikes, Lockouts, and Shutdowns in 1901*. Providence: E. L. Freeman, State Printers.

———. 1907. *Twentieth Annual Report of the Commissioner of Industrial Statistics: Strikes among Wage Earners, 1906*. Providence: E. L. Freeman, State Printers.

———. 1908. *Twenty-First Annual Report of the Commissioner of Industrial Statistics: Strikes and Lockouts among the Wage Earners of Rhode Island in 1907*. Providence: E. L. Freeman, State Printers.

———. 1916. *Twenty-Ninth Annual Report of the Commissioner of Industrial Statistics*. Providence: E. L. Freeman, State Printers.

———. 1921. *Report of the Commissioner of Labor, 1916–1919*. Made to the General Assembly. Providence: E. L. Freeman, State Printers.

Rhode Island, Factory Inspectors. 1916. *Annual Report*. Providence: E. L. Freeman, State Printers.

Rhode Island, State Bureau of Information. 1930. *The Book of Rhode Island*. Providence: Remington Press.

Rossi, Alice, and Ann Calderwood. 1973. *Academic Women on the Move*. New York: Russell Sage Foundation.

Rubin, Deborah. 1977. "Draft Report on French Canadians." Manuscript in possession of author. Prepared for NIMH Grant.

———. 1978. "French-Canadian Working Families: Labor Participation in a New England Textile Center." Paper prepared for Seminar in Atlantic History and Culture, The Johns Hopkins University.

Sacks, Karen. 1984. "Kinship and Class Consciousness: Family Values and Work Experience among Hospital Workers in an American Southern Town." In *Interest and Emotion: Essays on the Study of Family and Kinship*, edited by Hans Medick and David Sabear. Cambridge: Cambridge University Press.

Sacks, Karen Brodkin, and Dorothy Remy, eds. 1984. *My Troubles Are Going to Have Trouble with Me: Everyday Trials and Triumphs of Women Workers*. New Brunswick, N.J.: Rutgers University Press.

Safa, Helen. 1983. "Women, Production, and Reproduction in Industrial Capitalism: A Comparison of Brazilian and U.S. Factory Workers." In *Women, Men, and the International Division of Labor*, edited by June Nash and María Patricia Fernández-Kelly, pp. 95–116. Albany: SUNY Press.

Safilios-Rothschild, Constantina. 1976. "Dual Linkages between the Occupational and Family Systems: A Macrosociological Analysis." *Signs: Journal of Women in Culture and Society* 1, no. 3, pt. 2:51–60.

Schiller, Nina Glick. 1977. "Ethnic Groups Are Made, Not Born. The Haitian Immigrant and American Politics." In *Ethnic Encounters: Identities and Contexts*, edited by George L. Hicks and Philip E. Leis, pp. 23–36. North Scituate, Mass.: Duxbury Press.

Schneider, Naomi. 1981. "An Analysis of the Characteristics of Two Immigrant Communities in Pawtucket, R.I., in 1915." Paper in possession of Louise Lamphere, prepared for a Brown University history course.

Schneider, Peter, and Jane Schneider. 1976. *Culture and Political Economy in Western Sicily*. New York: Academic Press.

Shapiro-Perl, Nina. 1977. "The Piece Rate: Class Struggle on the Shop Floor: Evidence from the Costume Jewelry Industry in Providence, Rhode Island." In *Case Studies in the Labor Process*, edited by Andrew Zimbalist, pp. 277–98. New York: Monthly Review Press.

————. 1983. *Labor Process and Class Relations in the Costume Jewelry Industry: A Study of Women's Work.* Ph.D. diss., University of Connecticut.

Silverman, Sydel. 1975. *Three Bells of Civilization.* New York: Columbia University Press.

————. 1976. "The Model of Economic Woman: Strategy, Adaptation, and Choice." Unpublished comments on symposium "Social Structure, Ideology, and Women's Choices." American Anthropological Association, Washington, D.C., November 20.

Smith, Judith. 1985. *Family Connections: A History of Italian and Jewish Immigrant Lives in Providence Rhode Island, 1900–1940.* Albany: SUNY Press.

Stromberg, Ann, and Shirley Harkess. 1978. *Women Working: Theories and Facts in Perspective.* Palo Alto, Calif.: Mayfield.

Swartz, Marc J., Victor W. Turner, and Arthur Tuden, eds. 1966. *Political Anthropology.* Chicago: Aldine Press.

Taft, Donald Reed. 1923. *Two Portuguese Communities in New England.* New York: Columbia University Press.

Tax, Meredith. 1980. *The Rising of Women: Feminist Solidarity and Class Conflict, 1880–1917.* New York: Monthly Review Press.

Tentler, Leslie Woodcock. 1979. *Wage-Earning Women: Industrial Work and Family Life in the United States, 1900–1930.* Oxford: Oxford University Press.

Tepperman, Jean. 1976. *Not Servants, Not Machines.* Boston: Beacon Press.

Theodore, Athena. 1971. *The Professional Woman.* Cambridge, Mass.: Schenkman.

Thomas, Brinley. 1973. *Migration and Economic Growth: A Study of Great Britain and the Atlantic Economy.* 2d ed. Cambridge: Cambridge University Press.

Thompson, Edward P. 1963. *The Making of the English Working Class.* New York: Pantheon Books.

Tilly, Louise A., and Joan W. Scott. 1978. *Women, Work, and Family.* New York: Holt, Rhinehart & Winston.

U.S. Bureau of the Census. *Historical Statistics of the United States: Colonial Times to 1975.* Bicentennial Edition. Washington, D.C.: U.S. Government Printing Office.

U.S. International Trade Commission. 1926. *Broad-silk Manufacture and Tariff.* Washington, D.C.: U.S. Government Printing Office (TC/2: 513).

U.S. Senate. Committee on Interstate and Foreign Commerce. 1958. *Problems of the Domestic Textile Industry: A Study of the Textile Industry in the United States.* Hearing, July 8, 9, 10. Washington, D.C.: U.S. Government Printing Office (Y4Im 8/3:T31/2/part 1).

Vogel, Lise. 1983. *Marxism and the Oppression of Women: Toward a Unitary Theory.* New Brunswick, N.J.: Rutgers University Press.

Wallace, Anthony F. C. 1978. *Rockdale: The Growth of an American Village in the Early Industrial Revolution.* New York: Alfred Knopf.

Ware, Caroline. 1966. *The Early New England Cotton Manufacture: A Study in Industrial Beginnings*. 1931. Reprint. New York: Russell and Russell.

Wertheimer, Barbara. 1977. *We Were There: The Story of Working Women in America*. New York: Pantheon Books.

Westwood, Sallie. 1984. *All Day, Every Day: Factory and Family in the Making of Women's Lives*. London: Pluto Press.

Witos, Vicenty. 1964. *Moje Wsponmienia*. Paris. Instytut Literacki.

Wolf, Eric. 1969. *Peasant Wars of the Twentieth Century*. New York: Harper and Row.

_____. 1982. *Europe and the People without History*. Berkeley: University of California Press.

Yans-McLaughlin, Virginia. 1979. *Family and Community: Italian Immigrants in Buffalo*. Ithaca, N.Y.: Cornell University Press.

Young, Michael, and Peter Willmott. 1957. *Family and Kinship in East London*. Baltimore: Penguin Books.

Zaretz, Elbert. 1934. *The Amalgamated Clothing Workers of America: A Study of Progressive Trade Unionism*. New York: Ancon.

Zavella, Patricia. 1987. *Women's Work and Chicano Families: Cannery Workers of the Santa Clara Valley*. Ithaca, N.Y.: Cornell University Press.

Zubrzycki, J. 1953. "Emigration from Poland in the Nineteenth and Twentieth Centuries." *Population Studies* 5–6:248–72.

Index

[381]

Picking: as a job for women, 342
Piece rate, 291, 347; cuts in, 190; explanation of, 293–94; minimum wage
and, 291, 296, 301, 303, 306, 307;
resistance strategies and, 294, 296,
299–301, 303–11, 313–14, 319–21,
323, 324, 332
Pinning: as a job for women, 302
Pino family, 244, 286, 361, 368; Hector,
254–55, 265, 268; María, 268–69,
274–75, 281–82
PNCC (Polish National Catholic
Church), 115–16
Polacek, Mrs., 162
Polish families: boarding and, 35, 36,
125, 127, 130, 157–59, 163–64, 165,
170, 212, 333; Central Falls Aerie of
the Eagles, 194; Central Falls Polish-
American Citizens' Club, 194; child
care/rearing and, 48, 157, 162–65;
Depression of the 1930s and, 207–13,
214, 215, 216–17; family/social networks and, 80–82, 90, 93–94, 108,
112–14, 116, 187, 194, 222, 238, 239,
255; French-Canadian conflicts with,
187; immigration of, 33, 38, 47, 64,
77–82, 84, 87, 90, 92, 111–12, 117,
124, 222, 234, 238, 333, 335;
Kosciuszko Polish-American Citizens'
Club, 194; male-female division of labor and, 48, 85–86, 87, 163–65;
neighborhood description of, 94, 108–
16, 117, 124, 203–4; pay scales and,
85–86, 88, 89, 155–57, 161, 162, 163,
166–67, 291, 342, 343, 344; Polish
Falcons, 112–13; Polish National Alliance, 113, 194; Polish National
Home, 93, 113; Portuguese conflicts
with, 313; production strategies of,
30–31, 33, 34–35, 37, 48–49, 64, 77,
81, 82, 85–86, 87, 88, 89, 90, 109–
10, 112, 113, 117, 125, 127, 130,
155–57, 159, 161–65, 166–67, 168,
176–77, 187, 190, 194–96, 207–13,
214, 216–17, 256, 258, 291, 292, 299,
311–12, 313, 317, 320, 325, 330, 331,
332, 342, 344, 350; Pulaski Mutual
Aid Society, 112; religion and, 77, 94,
112, 114–16; reproduction strategies
of, 35, 36, 48–49, 82, 87, 112, 125,
127, 130, 155–59, 162–65, 170, 207–
13, 333; reistance strategies of, 311–

12, 313, 317, 320, 332; St. Joseph's
Brotherly Aid Society, 112, 113, 114;
St. Joseph's Church, 114; Society of
Polish Knights, 113; strikes and, 35,
113, 187, 190, 194–96, 325, 331;
Union of Polish Young, 113; West-
Side Polish-American Citizens' Club,
194
Polish National Alliance, 113, 194
Polish National Catholic Church
(PNCC), 115–16
Polish National Home, 93, 113
Polofsky, Mrs., 80
Pope, Liston, 173, 336
Portuguese families: boarding and, 127,
130, 165, 167–68, 272; child care/
rearing and, 38, 41, 48, 167–68, 251,
260–61, 262–64, 266–67, 272, 278–
83, 287, 334, 358–59, 366–67; fami-
ly/social networks and, 38, 39, 85, 90,
93, 168, 170, 188, 238–39, 245–51,
252–55, 336, 358–59; French-Canadian conflicts with, 187–88, 313; Holy
Ghost Brotherhood, 255; immigration
of, 33, 38, 39–40, 47, 64, 77, 82–86,
87, 90, 124, 221–22, 229–30, 232–34,
238, 245–51, 256, 333, 335; male-
female division of labor and, 41, 48,
85–86, 87, 167–68, 189, 257–58,
260–88, 334; pay scales and, 85–86,
88, 89, 166–67, 189, 239, 249, 259–
60, 274, 278, 287, 291, 294, 335, 342,
343, 344, 346; Polish conflicts with,
313; Portuguese Club, 255; production strategies of, 33, 37, 39–40, 48–
49, 64, 77, 85–86, 87, 88, 89, 90,
155–68, 170, 184–88, 189, 194,
196, 229–30, 233–34, 239, 246, 247–
49, 251, 256, 259–60, 261, 262–63,
270–80, 283, 284–85, 287, 291, 292,
293–94, 298, 311–18, 320–21, 324,
325, 330, 331, 332, 334, 335, 342,
344, 346, 358–59, 366–67; religion
and, 39, 85, 253, 255; reproduction
strategies of, 38, 40–41, 48–49, 87,
127, 130, 165–68, 247, 248, 249, 251,
260–73, 278–88, 333, 334, 358–59,
366–67; resistance strategies of, 311–
18, 320–21, 332; strikes and, 35, 168,
184–88, 189, 194, 196, 325, 331
Power loom tending: as a job for wom-
en, 56, 57

Library of Congress Cataloging-in-Publication Data

Lamphere, Louise.
   From working daughters to working mothers.

   (Anthropology of contemporary issues)
   Bibliography.
   Includes index.
   1. Women—Employment—Rhode Island—Central Falls—
History.   2. Alien labor—Rhode Island—Central Falls—
History.   3. Women immigrants—Rhode Island—Central
Falls—History. I. Title. II. Series.
HD6096.R4L36   1987   331.4′09745′1   86-32952
ISBN 0-8014-1945-X (alk. paper)